STUDY GUIDE

to accompany

MARK RUSH
University of Florida

Boston   San Francisco   New York
London   Toronto   Sydney   Tokyo   Singapore   Madrid
Mexico City   Munich   Paris   Cape Town   Hong Kong   Montreal

Reproduced by Pearson Addison Wesley from electronic files supplied by author.

Copyright © 2009 Pearson Education, Inc.
Publishing as Pearson Addison Wesley, 75 Arlington Street, Boston, MA 02116

All rights reserved. No part of this publication may be reproduced, stored in a retrieval system, or transmitted, in any form or by any means, electronic, mechanical, photocopying, recording, or otherwise, without the prior written permission of the publisher. Printed in the United States of America. For information on obtaining permission for use of material in this work, please submit a written request to Pearson Education, Inc., Rights and Contracts Department, 75 Arlington Street, Suite 300, Boston, MA 02116, fax your request to 617-848-7047, or e-mail at http://www.pearsoned.com/legal/permissions.htm.

ISBN-13   978-0-321-56024-7
ISBN-10   0-321-56024-8

1 2 3 4 5 6 BB 11 10 09 08

Table of Contents

Preface	Your Complete Learning Package	v
Preface	Your Course and Your Study Guide	vii

■ Part 1 Introduction

Chapter 1	Getting Started	1
	Appendix: Making and Using Graphs	9
Chapter 2	The U.S. and Global Economies	19
Chapter 3	The Economic Problem	31
Chapter 4	Demand and Supply	45

■ Part 2 A Closer Look at Markets

Chapter 5	Elasticities of Demand and Supply	63
Chapter 6	Efficiency and Fairness of Markets	77

■ Part 3 How Governments Influence the Economy

Chapter 7	Markets in Action	95
Chapter 8	Taxes	111
Chapter 9	Global Markets in Action	127
Chapter 10	Externalities	143
Chapter 11	Public Goods and Common Resources	157

■ Part 4 A Closer Look at Decision Makers

Chapter 12	Consumer Choice and Demand	171
	Appendix: Indifference Curves	185
Chapter 13	Production and Cost	193

■ Part 5 Prices, Profits, and Industry Performance

Chapter 14	Perfect Competition	209
Chapter 15	Monopoly	225
Chapter 16	Monopolistic Competition	241
Chapter 17	Oligopoly	253

■ Part 6 Incomes, Uncertainty, and Inequality

Chapter 18	Markets for Factors of Production	269

Chapter 19	Uncertainty and Information	283
Chapter 20	Inequality and Poverty	297

Your Complete Learning Package

YOUR FOUNDATIONS LEARNING TOOLS

■ The Complete Package

Your *Foundations of Microeconomics* package consists of:

- Textbook
- Study Guide
- MyEconLab Access Kit

MyEconLab is a powerful and tightly integrated homework and tutorial system that puts you in control of your own learning. MyEconLab includes

- Practice Tests that let you test your understanding and identify where you need to concentrate your studying
- A personalized Study Plan that evaluates your test results and provides further practice
- Tutorial instruction that will guide you through the areas you have difficulty with
- eText—the entire textbook in Flash format with animated figures accompanied by audio explanations prepared by us and with hyperlinks to all the other components of the Web site
- Economics in the News updated daily during the school year
- Online "Office Hours"—ask a question via e-mail, and one of us will respond within 24 hours!
- Economic links—links to sites that keep you up to date with what's going on in the economy and that enable you to work end-of-chapter Web Exercises

Each new textbook arrives with a MyEconLab Student Access Card that unlocks protected areas of the Web site.

■ Checklist and Checkpoints: The Glue That Holds Your Tools Together

Each chapter of your textbook opens with a Chapter Checklist that tells you what you'll be able to do when you've completed the chapter. The number of tasks varies from two to five and most often is three or four. Begin by reviewing this list thoughtfully and get a good sense of what you are about to learn.

Each part of a chapter in the textbook, Study Guide, and MyEconLab Web site is linked directly to a Checklist item to enable you to know exactly what you're studying and how it will enable you to accomplish your learning objective.

Each part of a chapter in the textbook ends with a Checkpoint—a page that offers you a Practice Problem to test your understanding of the key ideas of the part, a worked and illustrated solution to the Practice Problem, and a further (parallel) exercise. The Checkpoints enable you to review material when it's fresh in your mind—the most effective and productive time to do so. The Checkpoints guide you through the material in a step-by-step approach that takes the guesswork out of learning. The Study Guide reinforces each Checkpoint by providing Additional Practice Problems. Use these if you're still not sure you understand the material or if you want to review before an exam.

The self-test questions in the Study Guide, the Study Plan Exercises on the MyEconLab Web site, and the chapter resources on the MyEconLab Web site are organized by Checkpoint so that you can maintain your focus as you work through the material.

■ Practice Makes Perfect

As you study, distinguish between *practice* and *self-test*. Practice is part of the learning process, learning by doing. Self-test is a check. It shows you where you need to go back and reinforce your understanding, and it helps you build confidence in your knowledge of the material.

The Checkpoint Practice Problems and Exercises, the end-of-chapter Exercises, and the Checkpoint Exercises in MyEconLab are designed for practice. The self-test questions in the Study Guide, the pre- and post-tests, and Study Plan Exercises in MyEconLab are designed to reveal your gaps in understanding and to target your final examination of the material.

■ Learn Your Learning Style

It is unlikely that you'll need to use all the tools that we've created all of the time. Try to discover how you learn best. Then exploit what you discover.

If you learn best by reading with a marker or pencil in your hand, you'll use the textbook and Study Guide more often than the other items. If you learn best by seeing the action, you'll often use the eText and MyEconLab tutorials. If you learn best by hearing, you'll use the eText audio explanations of the action in key figures. If you learn best by participating and acting, you'll often use the Study Plan Exercises.

■ Tell Us What Works for *You*

Please tell us the tools that you find most helpful. And tell us what you think we can improve. You can email us at robin@econ100.com or michael.parkin@uwo.ca, or use the Office Hours in your MyEconLab Web site.

Robin Bade
Michael Parkin
Ontario, Canada
December, 2007

Your Course and Your Study Guide

SUGGESTIONS FOR CLASS

■ Introduction

My experience has taught me that what students want most from a study guide is help in mastering course material in order to do well on examinations. This Study Guide has been created to respond specifically to that demand. Using this Study Guide alone, however, is not enough to guarantee that you will earn an A or do well in your course. In order to help you overcome the problems and difficulties that most students encounter, I have some general advice on how to study, as well as some specific advice on how best to use this Study Guide.

Economics requires a different style of thinking than what you may encounter in other courses. Economists make extensive use of assumptions to break down complex problems into simple, analytically manageable parts. This analytical style, while ultimately not more demanding than the styles of thinking in other disciplines, feels unfamiliar to most students and requires practice. As a result, it is not as easy to do well in economics on the basis of your raw intelligence and high school knowledge as it is in many other courses. Many students who come to my office are frustrated and puzzled by the fact that they are getting A's and B's in their other courses but only a C or worse in economics. They have not recognized that economics is different and requires practice. In order to avoid a frustrating visit to your instructor after your first test, I suggest you do the following.

■ Don't rely solely on your high school economics.

If you took high school economics, you have seen the material on supply and demand which your instructor will lecture on in the first few weeks. Don't be lulled into feeling that the course will be easy. Your high school knowledge of economic concepts will be very useful, but it will not be enough to guarantee high scores on exams. Your college or university instructors will demand much more detailed knowledge of concepts and ask you to apply them in new circumstances.

■ Keep up with the course material on a weekly basis.

Skim or read the appropriate chapter in the textbook before your instructor lectures on it. In this initial reading, don't worry about details or arguments you can't quite follow — try to get a general understanding of the basic concepts and issues. You may be amazed at how your instructor's ability to teach improves when you come to class prepared. After the lecture, return to the book and read the material more thoroughly and completely. As soon as your instructor has finished covering a chapter, complete the corresponding Study Guide chapter. Avoid cramming the day before or even just the week before an exam. Because economics requires practice, cramming is an almost certain recipe for failure.

■ Keep a good set of lecture notes.

Good lecture notes are vital for focusing your studying. Your instructor will only lecture on a subset of topics from the textbook. The topics your instructor covers in a lecture should usually be given priority when studying. Also give priority to studying the figures and graphs covered in the lecture.

Instructors differ in their emphasis on lecture notes and the textbook, so ask early on in the course which is more important in reviewing for exams — lecture notes or the textbook. If your instructor answers that both are important, then ask the following, typical economic question: which will be more beneficial — spending an extra hour re-reading your lecture notes or an extra hour re-reading the textbook? This question assumes that you have read each textbook chapter twice (once before lecture for a general understanding, and then later for a thorough understanding); that you have prepared a good set of lecture notes; and that you have worked through all of the problems in the appropriate Study Guide chapters. By applying this style of analysis to the problem of efficiently allocating your study time, you are already beginning to think like an economist!

■ Use your instructor and/or teaching assistants for help.

When you have questions or problems with course material, come to the office to ask questions. Remember, you are paying for your education and instructors are there to help you learn. Don't be shy. The personal contact that comes from one-on-one tutoring is professionally gratifying for instructors as well as (hopefully) beneficial for you.

■ Form a study group.

A very useful way to motivate your studying and to learn economics is to discuss the course material and problems with other students. Explaining the answer to a question out loud is a very effective way of discovering how well you understand the question. When you answer a question only in your head, you often skip steps in the chain of reasoning without realizing it. When you are forced to explain your reasoning aloud, gaps and mistakes quickly appear, and you (with your fellow group members) can quickly correct your reasoning. The Exercises at the end of each textbook chapter are extremely good study group material. You might also get together after having worked the Study Guide problems, but before looking at the answers, and help each other solve unsolved problems.

■ Work old exams.

One of the most effective ways of studying is to work through exams your instructor has given in previous years. Old exams give you a feel for the style of question your instructor might ask, and give you the opportunity to get used to time pressure if you force yourself to do the exam in the allotted time. Studying from old exams is not cheating, as long as you have obtained a copy of the exam legally. Some institutions keep old exams in the library, others in the department. If there is a class web page, check there—many instructors now post old exams on their class web pages. Students who have previously taken the course are usually a good source as well. Remember, though, that old exams are a useful study aid only if you use them to understand the reasoning behind each question. If you simply memorize answers in the hopes that your instructor will repeat the identical question, you are likely to fail. From year to year, instructors routinely change the questions or change the numerical values for similar questions.

■ Use All Your Tools

The authors of your book, Robin Bade and Michael Parkin, have created a rich array of learning tools that they describe in the preceding section, "Your Complete Learning Package." Make sure that you read this section because it makes sense to use *all* your tools!

Preface 2 Your Course and Your Study Guide   ix

USING THE STUDY GUIDE

You should only attempt to complete a chapter in the Study Guide after you have read the corresponding textbook chapter and listened to your instructor lecture on the material. Each Study Guide chapter contains the following sections.

Chapter Checklist

This first section is a short summary of the key material. It is designed to focus you quickly and precisely on the core material that you must master. It is an excellent study aid for the night before an exam. Think of it as crib notes that will serve as a final check of the key concepts you have studied.

Additional Practice Problems

In each checkpoint in the textbook is at least one and generally more than one practice problem. These problems are extremely valuable because they help you grasp what you have just studied. In the Study Guide are additional Practice Problems. These Practice Problems either extend the Practice Problem in the text or cover another important topic from the Checkpoint. Although the answer is given to the additional Practice Problem, try to solve it on your own before reading the answer.

Following the additional Practice Problem is the Self Test section of the Study Guide. This section has fill in the blank, true or false, multiple choice, complete the graph, and short answer and numeric questions. The questions are designed to give you practice and to test skills and techniques you must master to do well on exams. Before I describe the parts of the Self Test section, here are some general tips that apply to all parts.

First, use a pencil to write your answers in the Study Guide so you have neat, complete pages from which to study and recall how you answered a question when the test approaches. Draw graphs wherever they are applicable. Some questions will ask explicitly for graphs; many others will not but will require a chain of reasoning that involves shifts of curves on a graph. Always draw the graph. Don't try to work through the reasoning in your head — you are much more likely to make mistakes that way. Whenever you draw a graph, even in the margins of the Study Guide, label the axes. You might think that you can keep the labels in your head, but you will be confronting many different graphs with many different variables on the axes. Also, be sure to understand what the axes are measuring. After finishing Chapter 4, some students think that the vertical axis always shows the price. That belief is simply not so. Hence you must be careful with the axes. In other words, avoid confusion and label. As an added incentive, remember that on exams where graphs are required, instructors often will deduct points for unlabelled axes.

Do the Self Test questions as if they were real exam questions, which means do them without looking at the answers. This is the single most important tip I can give you about effectively using the Study Guide to improve your exam performance. Struggling for the answers to questions that you find difficult is one of the most effective ways to learn. The adage — no pain, no gain — applies well to studying. You will learn the most from right answers you had to struggle for and from your wrong answers and mistakes. Only after you have attempted all the questions should you look at the answers. When you finally do check the answers, be sure to understand where you went wrong and why the right answer is correct.

Fill in the Blanks

This section covers the material in the checkpoint and has blanks for you to complete. Often suggested phrases are given but sometimes there are no hints—in that case you are on your own! Well, not really, because the answers are given at the end of each Study Guide chapter. This section also can help you review for a test because, once completed, they serve as a *very* brief statement of the important points within the important points within the checkpoint.

True or False

Next are true or false questions. Some instructors use true or false questions on exams or quizzes, so these questions might prove very valuable. The answers to the questions are given at the end of the chapter. The answer has a page reference to the textbook. If you missed the question or did not completely understand the answer, definitely turn to the textbook and study the topic so that you will not miss similar questions on your exams.

Multiple Choice

Many instructors use multiple choice questions on exams, so pay particular attention to these questions. Similar to the true or false questions, the answers are given at the end of the Study Guide chapter and each answer references the relevant page in the text. If you had any difficulty with a question, use this page reference to look up the topic and then study it to remove this potential weakness.

Complete the Graph

The complete the graph questions allow you to practice using one of economists' major tools, graphs. If you will have essay questions on your exams, it is an extremely safe bet that you will be expected to use graphs on at least some of the questions. This section is designed to ensure that you are well prepared to handle these questions. Use the graph in the Study Guide to answer the questions. Although the answer is given at the end of the Study Guide chapter, do *not* look at the answer before you attempt to solve the problem. It is much too easy to deceive yourself into thinking you understand the answer when you simply look at the question and then read the answer. Involve yourself in the material by answering the question and then looking at the answer. If you cannot answer the question or if you got the answer wrong, the Study Guide again has a reference to the relevant page number in the text. Use the text and study the material!

Short Answer and Numeric Questions

The last set of questions are short answer and numeric questions. Short answer and numeric questions are classic exam questions, so pay attention to these questions. Approach them similarly to how you approach all the other questions: Answer them before you look at the answers in the back of the Study Guide. These questions are also excellent for use in a study group. If you and several friends are studying for an exam, you can use these questions to quiz your understanding. If you have disagreements about the correct answers, once again there are page references to the text so that you can settle these disagreements and be sure that everyone has a solid grasp of the point!

FINAL COMMENTS

This Study Guide combines the efforts of many talented individuals. The author of the Chapter in Perspective and many of the additional Practice Problem and answer is Tom Meyer, from Rochester Community and Technical College. It was a pleasure to work with Tom; I always looked forward to his emails and the resulting conversations.

For the multiple choice questions, we assembled a team of truly outstanding teachers:

- Seemi Ahmad, Dutchess Community College
- Susan Bartlett, University of South Florida
- Jack Chambless, Valencia Community College
- Paul Harris, Camden County Community College
- William Mosher, Assumption College
- Terry Sutton, Southeast Missouri State University

I added a few multiple choice questions and wrote the fill in the blank, true or false, complete the graph, and short answer and numeric questions. I also served as an editor to assemble the material into the book before you.

The Study Guide and other supplements were checked for accuracy by a team of instructors. For a previous edition, the team included:

- Carol Conrad, Cerro Coso Community College
- Marie Duggan, Keene State University
- Steven Hickerson, Mankato State University
- Douglas Kinnear, Colorado State University
- Tony Lima, California State University, at Eastbay (Tony, I believe you were one of my instructors when I was an undergraduate—thanks for helping excite me about economics!)
- Michael Milligan, Front Range Community College
- Barbara Ross-Pfeiffer, Kapiolani Community College

Jeannie Shearer-Gillmore, University of Western Ontario, checked every word, every sentence, every paragraph, and every page of the first edition of this book and many of the words, sentences, paragraphs, and pages of the third edition. She made a huge number of corrections and comments. The easiest way to distinguish her work and mine is to determine if there is an error in a passage. If there is, it's my work; if there is not, it's her work.

Students who have used this book in earlier editions also have found errors that I did not catch. I think we owe these students a special thanks for their conscientious work and generous initiative to report the errors:

- Lisa Salazar-Rich, at Cal Poly Pomona
- Professor Tom McCaleb's class at Florida State University

Robin Bade and Michael Parkin, the authors of your book, also need thanks. Not only have they written such a superior book that it was easy to be enthusiastic about writing the Study Guide to accompany it, both Robin and Michael played a very hands-on role in creating this Study Guide. They corrected errors and made suggestions that vastly improved the Study Guide.

I want to thank my family: Susan, Tommy, Bobby, and Katie, who, respectively: allowed me to work all hours on this book; helped me master the intricacies of FTPing computer files; let me postpone working on our trains with him until after the book was concluded; and would run into my typing room to share her new discoveries. Thanks a lot!

Finally, I want to thank Butterscotch, Mik, Lucky, (and the late, beloved Snowball) and Pearl, who sometimes sat on my lap and sometimes sat next to the computer in a box peering out the window (and occasionally meowed) while I typed.

We (well, all of us except the cats) have tried to make the Study Guide as helpful and useful as possible. Undoubtedly I have made some mistakes; mistakes that you may see. If you find any, I, and following generations of students, would be grateful if you could point them out to me. At the end of my class at the University of Florida, when I ask my students for their advice, I point out to them that this advice won't help them at all because they have just completed the class. But comments they make will influence how future students are taught. Thus just as they owe a debt of gratitude for the comments and suggestions that I received from students before them, so too will students after them owe them an (unpaid and unpayable) debt. If you have questions, suggestions, or simply comments, let me know. You can reach me via e-mail at MARK.RUSH@CBA.UFL.EDU. Your input probably won't benefit you directly, but it will benefit following generations. And if you give me permission, I will note your name and school in following editions so that any younger siblings (or, years down the road, maybe even your children!) will see your name and offer up thanks.

Mark Rush
Economics Department
University of Florida
Gainesville, Florida 32611
December, 2007.

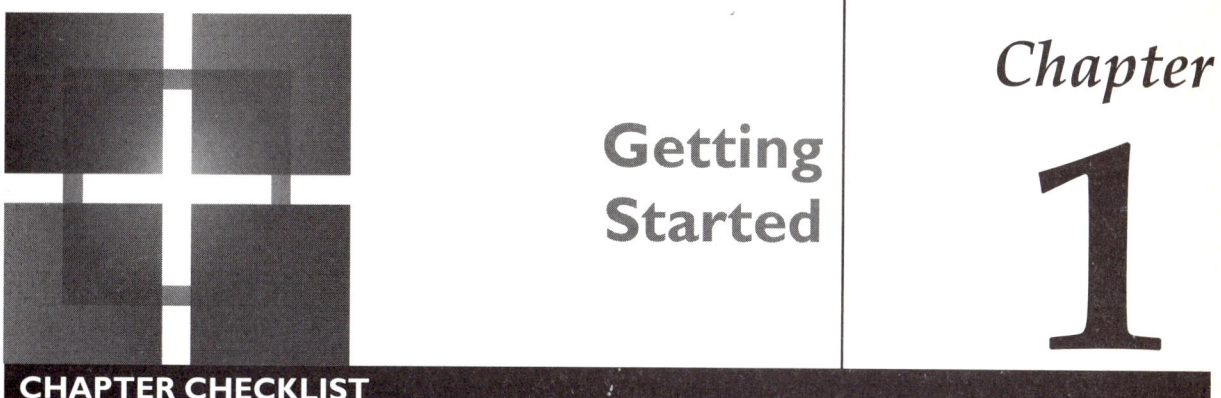

Chapter 1
Getting Started

CHAPTER CHECKLIST

Chapter 1 defines economics, discusses the three major questions of *what, how,* and *for whom,* covers the five core economic ideas that shape how economists think about issues, defines the differences between microeconomics and macroeconomics, and examines methods used by economists to study the economic world.

1 Define economics and explain the kinds of questions that economist try to answer.

Economic questions exist because of scarcity, the point that wants exceed the ability of resources to satisfy them. Economics is the social science that studies the choices that individuals, businesses, government, and entire societies make as they cope with scarcity and the incentives that influence these choices. Economics studies how choices wind up determining: *what* goods and services get produced?; *how* are goods and services produced?; and *for whom* are goods and services produced? Economics also studies when choices made in someone's self-interest also serve the social interest. For instance, are the self-interested choices made about globalization and international outsourcing, use of tropical rain forests, and social security also promote the social interest about these issues?

2 Explain the core ideas that define the economic way of thinking.

The five ideas that are the core of the economic approach: people make rational choices by comparing benefits and costs; cost is what you must give up to get something; benefit is what you gain when you get something and is measured by what you are willing to give up to get it; a rational choice is made on the margin; and choices respond to incentives. A rational choice uses the available resources to most effectively satisfy the wants of the person making the choice. The opportunity cost of an activity is the highest-valued alternative forgone. The benefit of a good or service is the gain or pleasure it brings and is measured by what someone is willing to give up to get the good or service. Making choices on the margin means comparing all the relevant alternatives systematically and incrementally to determine which is the best choice. A choice on the margin is one that adjusts a plan. The marginal cost is the cost of a one-unit increase in an activity; the marginal benefit is the gain from a one-unit increase in an activity. Rational choices compare the marginal benefit of an activity to its marginal cost. Microeconomics studies choices made by individuals and businesses. Macroeconomics studies the national economy and global economy. Statements about "what is" are positive statements; statements about "what should be" are normative statements. Economists are interested in positive statements about cause and effect but determining causality can be difficult because usually many things change simultaneously. So economists often use the idea of *ceteris paribus,* a Latin term that means "other things equal" and is used to sort out the effect of individual influence. Correlation is the tendency for the values of two variables to move together in a predictable way. Economics can be used by individuals, business, and governments as a policy tool to help them make better decisions.

CHECKPOINT 1.1

■ **Define economics and explain the kinds of questions that economist try to answer.**

Quick Review
- *Self-interest* The choices that people make that they think are the best for them.
- *Social interest* The choices that are best for society as a whole.

Additional Practice Problems 1.1
1. Which of the following headlines deals with *what, how,* and *for whom* questions?:
   a. A new government program is designed to provide high-quality school lunches for children from poorer families.
   b. Intel researchers discover a new chip-making technology.
   c. Regis Hairstyling sets a record for hairstylings in month of July

2. Which of the following headlines concern social interest and self interest?
   a. A new government program is designed to provide high-quality school lunches for children from poorer families.
   b. Intel researchers discover a new chip-making technology.
   c. Regis Hairstyling sets a record for hairstylings in month of July.

Solutions to Additional Practice Problems 1.1
1a. "More lunches" is a *what* question and "for children from poorer families" is a *for whom* question.
1b. "New chip-making technology" is a *how* question because it deals with how computer chips will be manufactured.
1c. "Record for hairstylings" is a *what* question because it notes that a record number of hairstylings have taken place in July.
2a. The decision to implement a new government program is a decision that is most likely made in the social interest. The self-interest of the government bureaucrat who made the decision might also be involved, particularly if the bureaucrat also will help manage the program.
2b. Intel's decision to research new chip-making technology is made in Intel's self-interest.
2c. Regis's decision to offer hairstylings is made in its self-interest as are the decisions of the people who had their hair styled by Regis.

■ **Self Test 1.1**

Fill in the blanks
Economic questions arise because ____ (human wants; resources) exceed the ____ (human wants; resources) available to satisfy them. Faced with ____, people must make choices. Choices that are the best for the person who makes them are choices made in ____ (self-interest; social interest). Choices that are best for everyone as a whole are choices made in ____ (self-interest; social interest).

True or false
1. Faced with scarcity, we must make choices.
2. The question of *what* refers to what production method should a firm use?
3. The answers to the *what, how* and *for whom* questions depend on the interactions of the choices people, businesses, and governments make.
4. If Sam buys a pizza because she is hungry, her choice is made in the social interest.
5. Because everyone is a member of society, all choices made in self-interest are also in the social interest.

Multiple choice
1. The characteristic from which all economic problems arise is
   a. political decisions.
   b. providing a minimal standard of living for every person.
   c. how to make a profit.
   d. hunger.
   (e.) scarcity.

2. Scarcity results from the fact that
   a. people's wants exceed the resources available to satisfy them.
   b. not all goals are desirable.
   c. we cannot answer the major economic questions.
   d. choices made in self-interest are not always in the social interest.
   e. the population keeps growing.

3. To economists, scarcity means that
   a. limited wants cannot be satisfied by the unlimited resources.
   b. a person looking for work is not able to find work.
   c. the number of people without jobs rises when economic times are bad.
   d. there can never be answers to the *what, how* or *for whom* questions.
   e. unlimited wants cannot be satisfied by the limited resources.

4. The question "Should we produce video tapes or DVD discs?" is an example of a ____ question.
   a. what
   b. how
   c. for whom
   d. where
   e. why

5. The question "Should we produce houses using bricks or wood?" is an example of a ____ question.
   a. what
   b. how
   c. for whom
   d. where
   e. why

6. The question "Should economics majors or sociology majors earn more after they graduate?" is an example of a ____ question.
   a. what
   b. how
   c. for whom
   d. where
   e. why

7. If a decision is made and it is the best choice for society, the decision is said to be
   a. a valid economic choice.
   b. made in self-interest.
   c. made in social interest.
   d. consistent with scarcity.
   e. a want-maximizing choice.

Short answer and numeric questions

1. Will there ever come a time without scarcity?
2. If there was no scarcity, would there be a need for economics?
3. What are the three major questions answered by people's economic choices?
4. Why is the distinction between choices made in self-interest and choices made in social interest important?

CHECKPOINT 1.2

■ **Explain the core ideas that define the economic way of thinking.**

Quick Review

- *Opportunity cost* The opportunity cost of something is the best thing you must give up to get it.
- *Marginal cost* The opportunity cost that arises from a one-unit increase in an activity.
- *Marginal benefit* The benefit that arises from a one-unit increase in an activity.
- *Rational choice* A choice that uses the available resources to most effectively satisfy the wants of the person making the choice.
- *Positive statement* A positive statement tells what is currently understood about the way the world operates. We can test a positive statement.
- *Normative statement* A normative statement tells what ought to be. It depends on values. We cannot test a normative statement.

Practice Problems 1.2

1. What are the opportunity costs of using this *Study Guide*?

2. Kate usually plays tennis for two hours a week and her grade on each math test is usually 70 percent. Last week, after playing two hours of tennis, Kate thought long and hard about playing for another hour. She decided to play another hour of tennis and cut her study time by one additional hour. But the grade on last week's math test was 60 percent.
    a. What was Kate's opportunity cost of the third hour of tennis?
    b. Given that Kate made the decision to play the third hour of tennis, what can you conclude about the comparison of her marginal benefit and marginal cost of the second hour of tennis?
    c. Was Kate's decision to play the third hour of tennis rational?

3. Classify each of the following statements as positive or normative:
    a. There is too much poverty in the United States.
    b. An increase in the gas tax will cut pollution.
    c. Cuts to social security in the United States have been too deep.

Solutions to Additional Practice Problems 1.2

1. The opportunity cost is mainly the time spent using the *Study Guide* because that time could be devoted to other activities. The highest-valued activity forgone, be it studying for another class, or sleeping, or some other activity, which is forgone because of the time spent using the *Study Guide* is the opportunity cost. Once you have purchased this *Study Guide*, its price is *not* an opportunity cost of using the *Study Guide* because you have already paid the price. The price is, instead, a sunk cost.

2a. The opportunity cost of the third hour of tennis was the 10 percentage point drop on her math test grade because she cut her studying time by one hour to play an additional hour of tennis. If Kate had not played tennis for the third hour, she would have studied and her grade would not have dropped.

2b. Kate chose to play the third hour of tennis, so the marginal benefit of the third hour of tennis was greater than the marginal cost of the third hour. If the marginal benefit of the third hour of tennis was less than the marginal cost of the third hour, Kate would have chosen to study rather than play tennis.

2c. Even though her grade fell, Kate's choice used the available time to most effectively satisfy her wants because the marginal benefit of the third hour of playing tennis exceeded the marginal cost of the third hour. This was a choice made in her self-interest.

3a. A normative statement because it depends on the speaker's values and cannot be tested.

3b. A positive statement because it can be tested by increasing the gas tax and then measuring the change in pollution.

3c. A normative statement because it depends on the speaker's values (someone else might propose still deeper cuts) and cannot be tested.

■ Self Test 1.2

Fill in the blanks

A ____ choice uses the available resources to most effectively satisfy the wants of the person making the choice. The opportunity cost of an activity is ____ (all of the activities forgone; the highest-valued alternative forgone). The benefit of an activity is measured by what you ____ (are willing to; must) give up. We make a rational choice to do an activity if the marginal benefit of the activity ____ the marginal cost. (Macroeconomics; Microeconomics) ____ is the study of the choices of individuals and businesses, the interaction of these choices, and the influences that governments exert on these classes. A statement that tells "what is" is a ____ (positive; normative) statement. A statement that tells "what ought to be" is a ____ (positive; normative) statement. The term meaning "other things being equal" is ____ (ceteris paribus; sunk cost).

True or false
1. Instead of attending his microeconomics class for two hours, Jim can play a game of tennis or watch a movie. For Jim the opportunity cost of attending class is forgoing the game of tennis *and* watching the movie.
2. Marginal cost is what you gain when you get one more unit of something.
3. A rational choice involves comparing the marginal benefit of an action to its marginal cost.
4. A change in marginal benefit or a change in marginal cost brings a change in the incentives that we face and leads us to change our actions.
5. The subject of economics divides into two main parts, which are macroeconomics and microeconomics.
6. The statement, "When more people volunteer in their communities, crime rates decrease" is a positive statement.

Multiple choice
1. Jamie has enough money to buy either a Mountain Dew, or a Pepsi, or a bag of chips. He chooses to buy the Mountain Dew. The opportunity cost of the Mountain Dew is
   a. the Pepsi and the bag of chips.
   b. the Pepsi or the bag of chips, whichever the highest-valued alternative forgone.
   c. the Mountain Dew.
   d. the Pepsi because it is a drink, as is the Mountain Dew.
   e. zero because he enjoys the Mountain Dew.

2. The benefit of an activity is
   a. purely objective and measured in dollars.
   b. the gain or pleasure that it brings.
   c. the value of its sunk cost.
   d. measured by what must be given up to get one more unit of the activity.
   e. not measurable on the margin.

3. The cost of a one-unit increase in an activity
   a. is the total one-unit cost.
   b. is called the marginal cost.
   c. decreases as you do more of the activity.
   d. is called the marginal benefit/cost.
   e. is called the sunk cost.

4. The marginal benefit of an activity is
   i. the benefit from a one-unit increase in the activity.
   ii. the benefit of a small, unimportant activity.
   iii. measured by what the person is willing to give up to get one additional unit of the activity.
   a. i only.
   b. ii only.
   c. iii only.
   d. i and iii.
   e. ii and iii.

5. If the marginal benefit of the next slice of pizza exceeds the marginal cost, you will
   a. eat the slice of pizza.
   b. not eat the slice of pizza.
   c. be unable to choose between eating or not eating.
   d. eat half the slice.
   e. More information is needed about how much the marginal benefit exceeds the marginal cost to determine if you will or will not eat the slice.

6. When people make rational choices, they
   a. behave selfishly.
   b. do not consider their emotions.
   c. weigh the costs and benefits of their options and act to satisfy their wants.
   d. necessarily make a decision in the social interest.
   e. are necessarily making the best decision.

7. Which of the following is a microeconomic issue?
   a. Why has unemployment risen nationwide?
   b. Why has economic growth been rapid in China?
   c. What is the impact on the quantity of Pepsi purchased if consumers' tastes change in favor of non-carbonated drinks?
   d. Why is the average income lower in Africa than in Latin America?
   e. Why did overall production within the United States increase last year?

8. A positive statement
   a. must always be right.
   b. cannot be tested.
   c. can be tested against the facts.
   d. depends on someone's value judgment.
   e. cannot be negative.

9. Which of the following is an example of a normative statement?
   a. If cars become more expensive, fewer people will buy them.
   b. Car prices should be affordable.
   c. If wages increase, firms will fire some workers.
   d. Fewer people die in larger cars than in smaller cars.
   e. Cars emit pollution.

10. The Latin term *ceteris paribus* means
    a. after this, therefore because of this.
    b. other things being equal.
    c. what is correct for the part is not correct for the whole.
    d. on the margin.
    e. when one variable increases, the other variable decreases.

Short answer and numeric questions

1. What is an opportunity cost?
2. You have $12 and can buy a pizza, a movie on a DVD, or a package of CD-Rs. You decide to buy the pizza and think that if you hadn't been so hungry, you would have purchased the DVD. What is the opportunity cost of your pizza?
3. What is a sunk cost?
4. What is benefit and how is it measured?
5. What is a marginal cost? A marginal benefit? How do they relate to rational choice?
6. Explain the difference between microeconomics and macroeconomics.
7. Becky is writing an essay about the law that requires all passengers in a car to use a seat belt and its effectiveness. What might be a positive statement and a normative statement that she will include in her essay?

SELF TEST ANSWERS

■ CHECKPOINT 1.1

Fill in the blanks

Economic questions arise because <u>human wants</u> exceed the <u>resources</u> available to satisfy them. Faced with <u>scarcity</u>, people must make choices. Choices that are the best for the person who makes them are choices made in <u>self-interest</u>. Choices that are best for everyone as a whole are choices made in <u>social interest</u>.

True or false

1. True; page 2
2. False; page 3
3. True; page 4
4. False; page 4
5. False; page 5

Multiple choice

1. e; page 2
2. a; page 2
3. e; page 2
4. a; page 3
5. b; page 3
6. c; page 4
7. c; page 4

Short answer and numeric questions

1. There will never be a time without scarcity because human wants are unlimited; page 2.

2. If there was no scarcity, then there likely would be no need for economics. Economics studies the choices that people make to cope with scarcity, so if there was no scarcity, then people's choices would not be limited by scarcity; page 3.

3. The questions are "*What* goods and services get produced and in what quantities?", "*How* are goods and services produced?", and "*For whom* are the goods and services produced?" page 3.

4. In general economists believe that people make choices according to their self-interest. These choices might or might not be in the social interest. Part of what economists study is when choices made in people's self-interest also further the social interest; page 5.

■ CHECKPOINT 1.2

Fill in the blanks

A <u>rational</u> choice uses the available resources to most effectively satisfy the wants of the person making the choice. The opportunity cost of an activity is <u>the highest-valued alternative forgone</u>. The benefit of an activity is measured by what you <u>are willing to</u> give up. We make a rational choice to do an activity if the marginal benefit of the activity <u>exceeds</u> the marginal cost. <u>Microeconomics</u> is the study of the choices of individuals and businesses, the interaction of these choices, and the influences that governments exert on these classes. A statement that tells "what is" is a <u>positive</u> statement. A statement that tells "what ought to be" is a <u>normative</u> statement. The term meaning "other things being equal" is <u>ceteris paribus</u>.

True or false

1. False; page 11
2. False; page 12
3. True; page 13
4. True; page 13
5. True; page 14
6. True; page 15

Multiple choice

1. b; page 11
2. b; page 11
3. b; page 12
4. d; page 12
5. a; page 13
6. c; page 13
7. c; page 14
8. c; page 15
9. b; page 15
10. b; page 15

Short answer and numeric questions

1. The opportunity cost of something is the highest-valued other thing that must be given up. The opportunity cost is only the single highest-valued alternative forgone, *not* all alternatives forgone; page 11.

2. The opportunity cost of the pizza is the highest-valued alternative forgone, which in this case is the DVD. The opportunity cost is *not* the DVD and the CD-Rs because you would not have been able to purchase both of them with your $12; page 11.

3. A sunk cost is a previously occurred and irreversible cost; page 11.

4. The benefit of something is the gain or pleasure that it brings. Economists measure the benefit of something by what a person is willing to give up to get it; pages 11, 12.

5. Marginal cost is the cost of a one-unit increase in an activity. Marginal benefit is the benefit of a one-unit increase in an activity. A rational choice is made by comparing the marginal cost and marginal benefit, so that if the marginal benefit of an activity exceeds or equals the marginal cost, the activity is undertaken; pages 12-13.

6. Microeconomics studies individual units within the economy, such as a consumer, a firm, a market, and so forth. Macroeconomics studies the overall, or aggregate, economy, such as the overall unemployment rate, or overall economic growth rate; page 14.

7. A positive statement is "People who wear seat belts are involved in fewer road deaths." This statement can be tested. A normative statement is "People should be free to choose whether to wear a seat belt or not." This statement cannot be tested; page 15.

Chapter 1

Appendix: Making and Using Graphs

APPENDIX CHECKLIST

After you have completed the appendix, you will have thoroughly reviewed the graphs used in your economics course.

1 Making and using graphs.

Graphs represent quantities as distances. The vertical axis is the y-axis and the horizontal axis is the x-axis. A scatter diagram plots a graph of one variable against the value of another variable. A time-series graph measures time along the x-axis and the variable (or variables) of interest along the y-axis. A cross-section graph shows the values of an economic variable for different groups in the population at a point in time. Graphs can show the relationship between two variables in an economic model. Variables that move in the same direction have a positive, or direct, relationship. Variables that move in the opposite direction have a negative, or inverse, relationship. Some relationships have minimum or maximum points. The slope of a relationship is the change in the value of the variable measured on the y-axis divided by the change in the value of the variable measured on the x-axis. To graph a relationship among more than two variables, we use the *ceteris paribus* assumption and graph the relationship between two of the variables, holding the other variables constant.

CHECKPOINT 1

■ Making and using graphs.

Additional Practice Problems

1. You have data on the average monthly rainfall and the monthly expenditure on umbrellas in Seattle, Washington. What sort of graph would be the best to reveal if any relationship exists between these variables?

2. In Figure A1.1, draw a straight line showing a positive relationship and another straight line showing a negative relationship.

■ **FIGURE A1.1**

Year	Price (dollars per gallon)
1997	1.29
1998	1.12
1999	1.22
2000	1.56
2001	1.53
2002	1.44
2003	1.64
2004	1.92
2005	2.34
2006	2.64

3. The table has the average price of a gallon of gasoline, including taxes, for ten years. In Figure A1.2, label the axes and then plot these data. What type of graph are you creating? What is the general trend of gas prices during this decade?

■ **FIGURE A1.2**

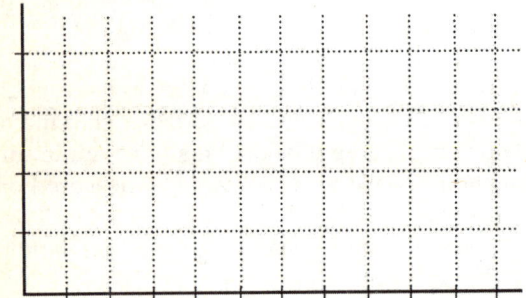

4. Figure A1.3 shows the relationship between the price of a paperback book and the quantity of paperback books a publisher is willing to sell. What is the slope of the line in Figure A1.3?

■ **FIGURE A1.3**

Price (dollars per paperback book)

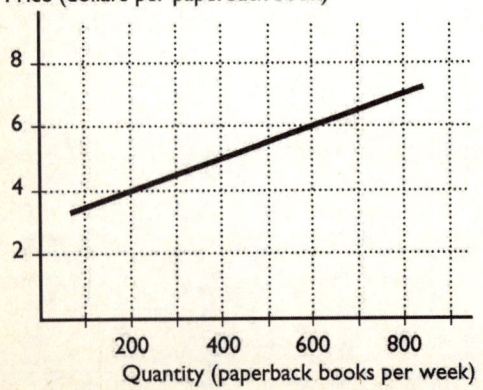

Quantity (paperback books per week)

Solution to Additional Practice Problems 1

1. A scatter diagram would be the best graph to use. A scatter diagram would plot the monthly value of, say, rainfall along the vertical axis (the y-axis) and the monthly value of umbrella expenditure along the horizontal axis (the x-axis).

■ **FIGURE A1.4**

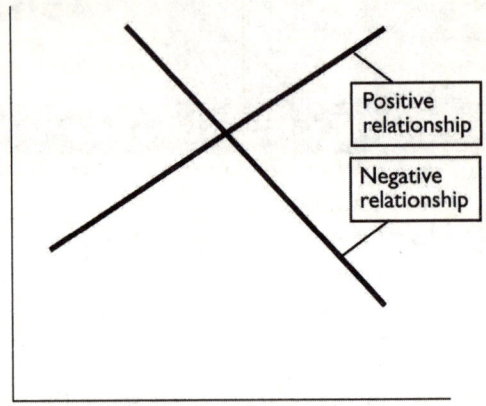

2. Figure A1.4 has two lines, one showing a positive relationship and the other showing a negative relationship. Your figure does not need to have identical lines. The key point your figure needs is that the line for the positive relationship slopes up as you move rightward along it and the line for the negative relationship slopes down as you move rightward along it.

■ **FIGURE A1.5**

Price (dollars per gallon)

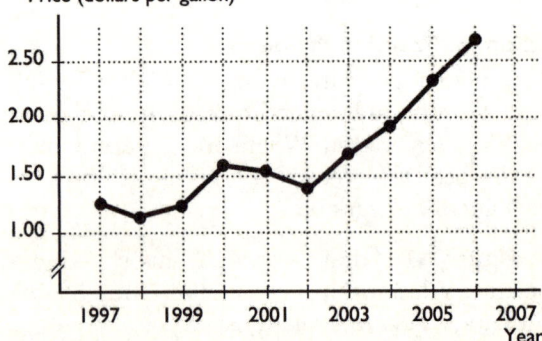

3. Figure A1.5 labels the axes and plots the data in the table. The graph is a time-series graph. The trend is positive because gas prices generally increased during these years.

■ FIGURE A1.6

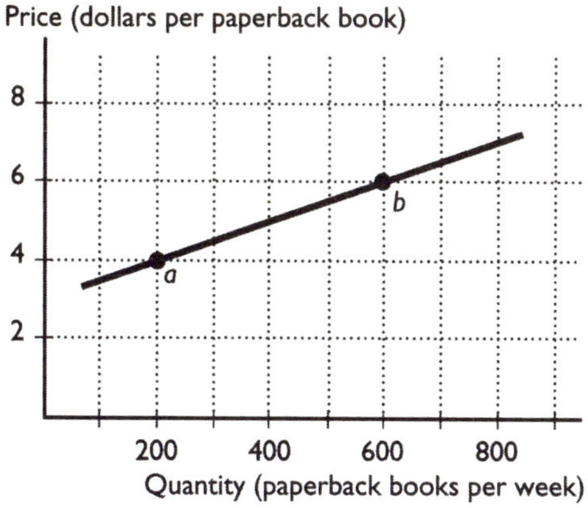

Price (dollars per paperback book)

4. The slope of a line is the change the variable measured on the y-axis divided by the change in the variable measured on the x-axis. To calculate the slope of the line in the figure, use points a and b in Figure A1.6. Between a and b, y rises by 2, from 4 to 6. And x increases by 400, from 200 to 600. The slope equals 2/400 = 0.005.

■ Self Test 1

Fill in the blanks

In a graph, the vertical line is called the ____ (x-axis; y-axis) and the horizontal line is called the ____ (x-axis; y-axis). A ____ (scatter diagram; time-series graph; cross-section graph) is a graph of the value of one variable against the value of another variable. A ____ (scatter diagram; time-series graph; cross-section graph) measures time along the x-axis and the variable along the y-axis. A ____ (scatter diagram; time-series graph; cross-section graph) shows the values of an economic variable for different groups in the population at a point in time. If the graph of a relationship between two variables slopes up to the right, the two variables have a ____ (positive; negative) relationship. If the graph between two variables is a vertical line, the two variables ____ (are; are not) related. The slope of a relationship is the change in the value of the variable measured along the ____ (x-axis; y-axis) divided by the change in the value of the variable measured along the ____ (x-axis; y-axis). By using the *ceteris paribus* assumption, it ____ (is; is not) possible to graph a relationship that involves more than two variables.

True or false

1. A point that is above and to the right of another point will have a larger value of the x-axis variable and a larger value of the y-axis variable.
2. A scatter diagram shows the values of an economic variable for different groups in a population at a point in time.
3. A time-series graph compares values of a variable for different groups at a single point in time.
4. A trend is a measure of the closeness of the points on a graph.
5. A positive relationship is always a linear relationship.
6. A relationship that starts out sloping upward and then slopes downward has a maximum.
7. A graph that shows a horizontal line indicates variables that are unrelated.
8. The slope at a point on a curve can be found by calculating the slope of the line that touches the point and no other point on the curve.

Multiple choice

1. Demonstrating how an economic variable changes from one year to the next is best illustrated by a
   a. scatter diagram.
   b. time-series graph.
   c. linear graph.
   d. cross-section graph.
   e. trend-line
2. To show the values of an economic variable for different groups in a population at a point in time, it is best to use a
   a. scatter diagram.
   b. time-series graph.
   c. linear graph.
   d. cross-section graph.
   e. trend diagram.

3. If whenever one variable increases, another variable also increases, these variables are
   a. positively related.
   b. negatively related.
   c. inversely related.
   d. cross-sectionally related.
   e. not related.

4. A graph of the relationship between two variables is a line that slopes down to the right. These two variables are ____ related.
   a. positively
   b. directly
   c. negatively
   d. not
   e. trend-line

5. Two variables are unrelated if their graph is
   i. a vertical line.
   ii. a 45 degree line.
   iii. a horizontal line.
   a. i only.
   b. ii only
   c. iii only
   d. i and iii.
   e. i, ii, and iii.

■ FIGURE A1.7

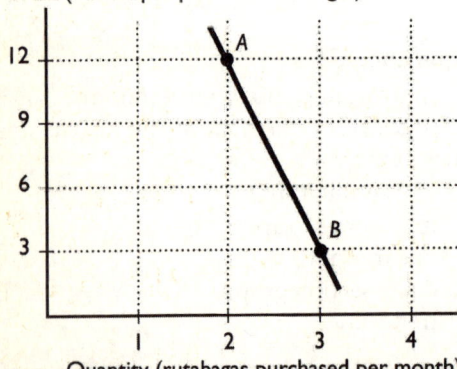

6. In figure A1.7, between points A and B, what is the slope of the line?
   a. 12
   b. 3
   c. 9
   d. -9
   e. 0

■ FIGURE A1.8

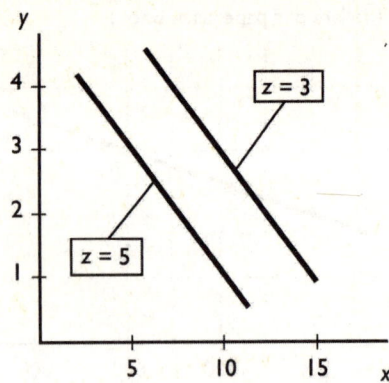

7. In Figure A1.8, an increase in z leads to a
   a. movement up along one of the lines showing the relationship between x and y.
   b. movement down along one of the lines showing the relationship between x and y.
   c. rightward shift of the line showing the relationship between x and y.
   d. leftward shift of the line showing the relationship between x and y.
   e. trend change in both x and y.

8. In Figure A1.8, *ceteris paribus*, an increase in x is associated with
   a. an increase in y.
   b. a decrease in y.
   c. an increase in z.
   d. a random change in z.
   e. no change in either y or z.

Complete the graph

Year	Workers (millions)
1990	6.5
1991	6.5
1992	6.6
1993	6.8
1994	7.1
1995	7.4
1996	7.5
1997	7.6
1998	7.8
1999	7.9

1. The table above gives the number of people working in restaurants and bars in the United States during the decade of the 1990s.

■ FIGURE A1.9

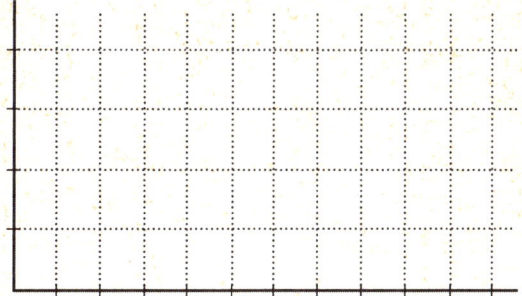

■ FIGURE A1.10

In Figure A1.9, measure time on the horizontal axis and the number of workers on the vertical axis, and then plot these data.
a. What type of graph are you creating?
b. Using your figure, what was the trend in the number of people working in restaurants and bars during the 1990s?

Year	Revenue (billions of dollars)	Workers (millions)
1990	190	6.5
1991	194	6.5
1992	200	6.6
1993	213	6.8
1994	222	7.1
1995	230	7.4
1996	239	7.5
1997	254	7.6
1998	267	7.8
1999	285	7.9

2. The table above gives the annual revenue for restaurants and bars and the number of people employed in restaurants and bars in the United States during the decade of the 1990s. In Figure A1.10, measure the revenue along the horizontal axis and the number of workers along the vertical axis and plot the data.
a. What type of graph are you creating?
b. What relationship do you see in your figure between the revenue and the number of workers?

Price (dollars per sack of cat food)	Quantity (sacks of cat food per month)
1	10,000
2	8,000
3	7,000
4	4,000

3. The number of sacks of premium cat food that cat lovers will buy depends on the price of a sack of cat food. The relationship is given in the table above. In Figure A1.11, plot this relationship, putting the price on the vertical axis and the quantity on the horizontal axis.

■ FIGURE A1.11

a. If the price of a sack of cat food is $2, how many sacks will be purchased?
b. If the price of a sack of cat food is $3, how many sacks will be purchased?
c. Is the relationship between the price and the quantity positive or negative?

4. In Figure A1.12, label the maximum and minimum points.

■ **FIGURE A1.12**

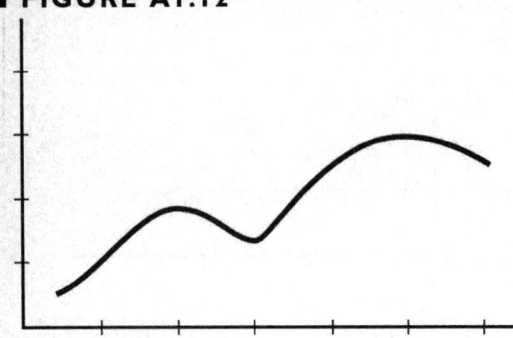

5. In Figure A1.13, draw a line through point A with a slope of 2. Label the line "1." Draw another line through point A with a slope of –2. Label this line "2."

■ **FIGURE A1.13**

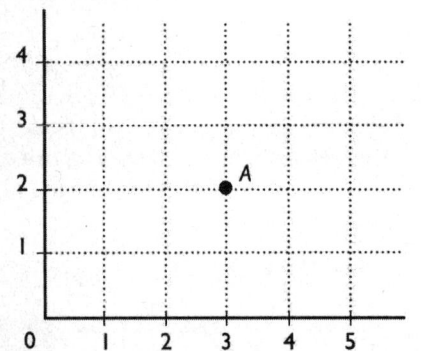

Price (dollars per DVD)	Quantity of DVDs purchased, low income	Quantity of DVDs purchased, high income
11	4	5
12	3	4
13	1	3
14	0	2

6. Bobby says that he buys fewer DVDs when the price of a DVD is higher. Bobby also says that he will buy more DVDs after he graduates and his income is higher. The table above shows the number of DVDs Bobby buys in a month at different prices when his income is low and when his income is high.

■ **FIGURE A1.14**

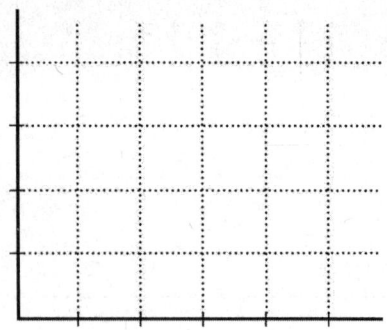

a. In Figure A1.14, put the price on the vertical axis and the quantity purchased on the horizontal axis. Show the relationship between the number of DVDs purchased and the price when Bobby's income is low.
b. On the same figure, draw the relationship between the number of DVDs purchased and the price when his income is high.
c. Does an increase in Bobby's income shift the relationship between the price of a DVD and the number of DVDs purchased rightward or leftward?

Short answer and numeric questions

1. What are the three types of graphs?
2. If two variables are positively related, will the slope of a graph of the two variables be positive or negative? If two variables are negatively related, will the slope of a graph of the two variables be positive or negative?
3. If a line slopes upward to the right, is its slope positive or negative? If a line slopes downward to the right, is its slope positive or negative?

■ **FIGURE A1.15**

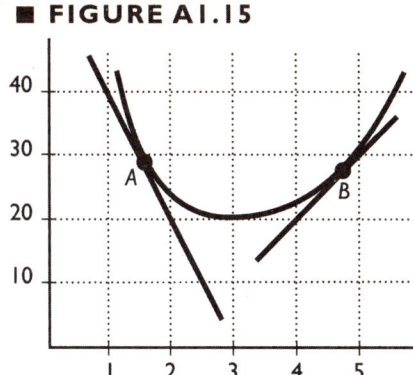

4. In Figure A1.15, what is the slope of the curved line at point *A*? At point *B*?

SELF TEST ANSWERS

■ CHECKPOINT 1

Fill in the blanks

In a graph, the vertical line is called the _y-axis_ and the horizontal line is called the _x-axis_. A _scatter diagram_ is a graph of the value of one variable against the value of another variable. A _time-series graph_ measures time along the x-axis and the variable along the y-axis. _A cross-section graph_ shows the values of an economic variable for different groups in the population at a point in time. If the graph of a relationship between two variables slopes up to the right, the two variables have a _positive_ relationship. If the graph between two variables is a vertical line, the two variables _are not_ related. The slope of a relationship is the change in the value of the variable measured along the _y-axis_ divided by the change in the value of the variable measured along the _x-axis_. By using the *ceteris paribus* assumption, it _is_ possible to graph a relationship that involves more than two variables.

True or false

1. True; page 23
2. False; page 24
3. False; page 24
4. False; page 24
5. False; page 26
6. True; page 28
7. True; page 28
8. True; page 29

Multiple choice

1. b; page 24
2. d; page 24
3. a; page 26
4. c; page 27
5. d; page 28
6. d; page 29
7. d; page 30
8. b; page 30

Complete the graph

■ FIGURE A1.16

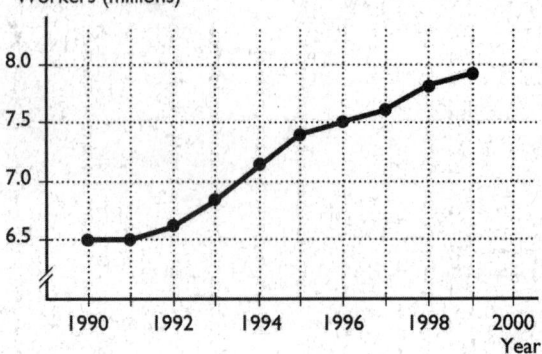

1. Figure A1.16 plots the data.
    a. This is a time-series graph; page 24.
    b. The trend is positive. During the 1990s there is an increase in the number of people working in restaurants and bars; page 24.

■ FIGURE A1.17

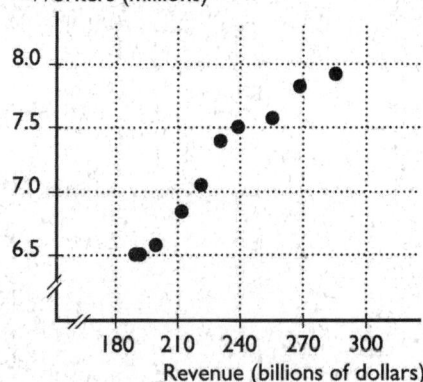

2. Figure A1.17 plots the data.
    a. The figure is a scatter diagram; page 24.
    b. The relationship between the revenue and the number of workers is positive; page 26.

Appendix 1 · Making and Using Graphs   17

■ **FIGURE A1.18**

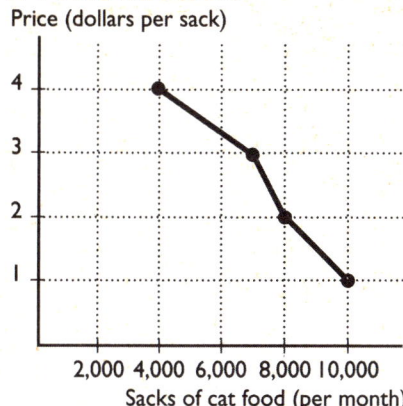

3. Figure A1.18 plots the relationship.
   a. If the price is $2 per sack, 8,000 sacks are purchased; page 23.
   b. If the price is $3 per sack, 7,000 sacks are purchased; page 23.
   c. The relationship between the price and quantity of sacks is negative; page 27.

■ **FIGURE A1.19**

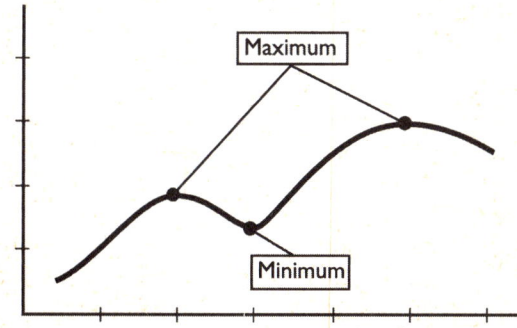

4. Figure A1.19 labels the two maximum points and one minimum point; page 28.

■ **FIGURE A1.20**

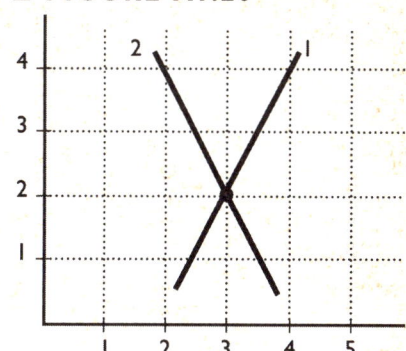

5. Figure A1.20 shows the two lines; page 29.

■ **FIGURE A1.21**

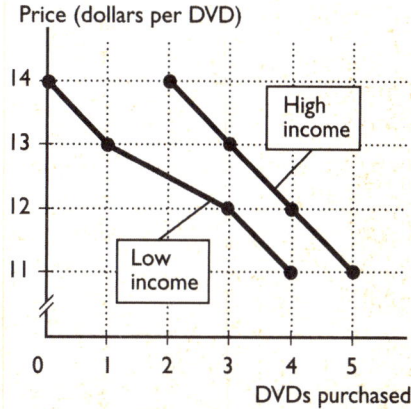

6. a. Figure A1.21 plots the relationship; page 30.
   b. Figure A1.21 plots the relationship; page 30.
   c. An increase in Bobby's income shifts the relationship rightward; page 30.

Short answer and numeric questions

1. The three types of graphs are scatter diagram, time-series graph, and cross-section graph; page 24.
2. If two variables are positively related, a graph of the relationship will have a positive slope. If two variables are negatively related, a graph of the relationship will have a negative slope; pages 26, 27, 29.
3. If a line slopes upward to the right, its slope is positive. If a line slopes downward to the right, its slope is negative; page 29.
4. The slope of a curved line at a point equals the slope of a straight line that touches that point and no other point on the curve. The slope of the curved line at point A is -20 and the slope of the curved line at point B is 10; page 29.

Chapter 2

The U.S. and Global Economies

CHAPTER CHECKLIST

Chapter 2 introduces fundamental concepts about how households, firms, markets, and government are linked together. A circular flow model is presented to show how goods and services and expenditures flow from and to households, firms, and the government.

1 Describe what, how, and for whom goods and services are produced in the United States.

The production of goods and services, the "what" question, is divided into four broad categories defined in terms of the ultimate buyer: individuals (consumption goods and services), businesses (capital goods), governments (government goods and services), and other countries (export goods and services). The "how" of production involves the factors of production: land, labor, capital, and entrepreneurship. Goods and services are sold to those who have income, so the personal distribution of income is one way of showing who ends up with our national output. The functional distribution of income shows how much is paid to the owners of each type of productive resource. The largest share of national income goes to labor, so workers get the largest share of our nation's goods and services.

2 Use the circular flow model to provide a picture of how households, firms, and government interact.

The circular flow model shows that households provide the services from the factors of production, and firms hire these services in factor markets. The circular flow also shows that households purchase goods and services, and firms sell goods and services in goods markets. The decisions made by households and firms (and the government) in these markets determine the answers to the "what," "how," and "for whom" questions. The federal government provides public goods and services, and makes social security and other benefit payments. In the circular flow, the government purchases goods and services in goods markets. It makes transfers to firms and households and also taxes them. The federal government's largest expenditure is Social Security benefits and its largest source of tax revenue is personal income taxes.

3 Describe what, how, and for whom goods and services are produced in the global economy.

Countries are divided into advanced economies, the richest 29 countries, and emerging market and developing economies. The advanced economies produce 51 percent of the world's total output, with 20 percent produced in the United States. Two third's of the world's oil reserves and two fifths of the natural gas reserves are in the Middle East. The share of agriculture in the advanced economies is much smaller than in the other countries but the advanced economies still produce one third of the world's food. The advanced economies have much more human capital and physical capital than the developing countries. Inequality of incomes across the entire world has decreased during the past twenty years, primarily because incomes in China and India have grown rapidly.

CHECKPOINT 2.1

■ **Describe what, how, and for whom goods and services are produced in the United States.**

Quick Review
- *Consumption goods and services* Goods and services that are bought by individuals and used to provide personal enjoyment and contribute to a person's standard of living.
- *Capital goods* Goods that are bought by businesses to increase their productive resources.
- *Government goods and services* Goods and services that are bought by governments.
- *Exports* Goods and services produced in the United States and sold in other countries.

Additional Practice Problems 2.1
1. Tell whether the following goods and services are consumption goods and services, capital goods, government goods and services, or exports.
   a. A taco at Taco Bell purchased for lunch by Shaniq.
   b. An HP printer manufactured in Idaho purchased by Maria in Peru.
   c. A new grill purchased by Taco Bell.
   d. A tour down the Colorado river from Rimrock Adventures purchased by the Miller family.
   e. CamelBak drinking packs purchased by the U.S. Marine Corp.
   f. CamelBak drinking packs purchased by Rimrock Adventures for use by their customers during tours.
   g. A CamelBak drinking pack purchased by Anne for use while mountain biking.
   h. A CamelBak drinking pack purchased by Sebastian, a German racing in the Tour de France.

2. How much labor is there in the United States? What determines the quantity of labor?

Solutions to Additional Practice Problems 2.1
1a. Shaniq's taco is a consumption good.
1b. Maria's printer is an export good.
1c. The new grill is a capital good.
1d. The tour is a consumption service.
1e. The drinking pack purchased by the Marines is a government good because it is purchased by the government.
1f. The drinking pack purchased by Rimrock Adventures is a capital good because it is purchased by a business.
1g. The drinking pack purchased by Anne is a consumption good.
1h. The drinking pack purchased by Sebastian is an export good.

2. In the United States, in 2007 about 152 million people had jobs or were available for work and they provided about 270 billion hours of labor a year. The quantity of labor depends on the size of the population, the percentage of the population that takes jobs, and on social relationships that influence things such as how many women take paid work. An increase in the proportion of women who have taken paid work has increased the quantity of labor in the United States over the past 50 years.

■ **Self Test 2.1**

Fill in the blanks
Goods and services that are bought by individuals and used to provide personal enjoyment and to contribute to a person's standard of living are ____ (consumption; capital; export) goods. Goods that are bought by businesses to increase their productive resources are ____ (consumption; capital; export) goods. Goods that are produced in the United States and sold in other countries are ____ (consumption; capital; export) goods. Of the four large groups of goods and services in the United States, ____ (consumption goods and services; capital goods; government goods and services; export goods and services) have the largest share of total production. Productive resources are called ____ and are grouped into four categories: ____,

___, ___, and ___. In 2006, ___ (labor; capital) received 64 percent of total income. The distribution of income among households is called the ___ (functional; personal) distribution of income.

True or false

1. Consumption goods and services include a slice of pizza purchased to eat at home.
2. A gold mine is included in the "land" category of productive resources.
3. Michael Dell, the person who founded and manages Dell computers, is an example of an entrepreneur.
4. In the United States, the factor of production that earns the most income is labor.
5. In the United States, the richest 20 percent of individuals earn approximately 30 percent of total income.

Multiple choice

1. When the total U.S. production of goods and services is divided into consumption goods and services, capital goods, government goods and services, and export goods and services, the largest component is
   a. consumption goods and services.
   b. capital goods.
   c. government goods and services.
   d. export goods and services.
   e. capital goods and government goods and services tie for the largest component.

2. An example of a capital good is
   a. a fiber optic cable TV system.
   b. an insurance policy.
   c. a hair cut.
   d. an iPod.
   e. a slice of pizza.

3. Goods and services produced in the United States and sold in other countries are called
   a. consumption goods and services.
   b. capital goods.
   c. government goods and services.
   d. export goods and services.
   e. import goods and services.

4. Which of the following correctly lists the categories of factors of production?
   a. machines, buildings, land, and money
   b. hardware, software, land, and money
   c. capital, money, and labor
   d. owners, workers, and consumers.
   e. land, labor, capital, and entrepreneurship

5. Human capital is
   a. solely the innate ability we are born with.
   b. the money humans have saved.
   c. the knowledge humans accumulate through education and experience.
   d. machinery that needs human supervision.
   e. any type of machinery.

6. Wages are paid to ___ and interest is paid to ___.
   a. entrepreneurs; capital
   b. labor; capital
   c. labor; land
   d. entrepreneurs; land
   e. labor; entrepreneurs

7. Dividing the nation's income among the factors of production, the largest percentage is paid to
   a. labor.
   b. land.
   c. capital.
   d. entrepreneurship.
   e. labor and capital, with each receiving about 41 percent of the total income.

8. The personal distribution of income shows
   a. that labor receives the largest percentage of total income.
   b. how profit accounts for the largest fraction of total income.
   c. that the richest 20 percent of people earn 23 percent of total income.
   d. that interest accounts for most of the income of the richest 20 percent of people.
   e. that the poorest 20 percent of people earn less than 4 percent of total income.

Short answer and numeric questions

1. Is an automobile a consumption good or a capital good?
2. Compare the incomes earned by the poorest and richest 20 percent of individuals.

CHECKPOINT 2.2

■ **Use the circular flow model to provide a picture of how households, firms, and governments interact.**

Quick Review
- *Circular flow model* A model of the economy, illustrated in Figure 2.1, that shows the circular flow of expenditures and incomes that result from firms', households', and governments' choices.

■ **FIGURE 2.1**

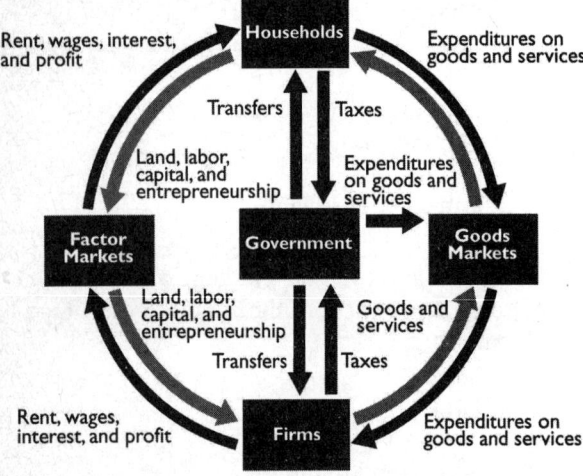

Additional Practice Problem 2.2
1. Describe where the following money flows fit in the circular flow.
   a. Shaniq pays for a taco at Taco Bell.
   b. Sam receives his monthly Social Security payment.
   c. Jennifer gets a $10,000 end of the year bonus from Bank of America, where she works.
   d. Exxon pays landowners in Texas $20,000 for the oil under their land.
   e. Bill pays property tax of $6,000.
2. In the circular flow, what is the relationship between the flow of expenditures into the goods markets (from households and the government) and the flow of revenues out of the goods markets to firms?

Solutions to Additional Practice Problems 2.2
1a. Shaniq's payment is an expenditure on a good that flows from households through the goods market to Taco Bell, a firm.
1b. Sam's check is a transfer payment from the government to households.
1c. Jennifer's payment is wages flowing from a firm, Bank of America, through the factor market to households.
1d. Exxon's payment is rent flowing from a firm, Exxon, through the factor market to households.
1e. Bill's payment is a tax flowing from households to government.

2. The flow of expenditures into the goods markets–the funds that households and the government spend on the goods and services they purchase–equals the flow of revenue out of the goods markets.

■ **Self Test 2.2**

Fill in the blanks
The ____ model shows the flows of expenditure and incomes. An arrangement that brings buyers and sellers together is a ____ (firm; household; market). A market in which goods and services are bought and sold is a ____ (goods; factor) market and a market in which the services of the factors of production are bought and sold is a ____ (goods; factor) market. In 2006, as a percentage of the total value of the goods and services produced in the United States, the federal government spent about ____ (20; 13) percent while state and local governments spent about ____ (20; 13) percent. A large part of what the federal government spends is ____ (social security payments; personal income taxes). The two components that account for most of the federal government's tax revenue are ____. The largest part of the expenditures of state and local governments is spending on ____ (education; highways).

True or false
1. Firms own the factors of production.
2. A market is any arrangement where buyers and sellers meet face-to-face.
3. Factors of production flow from households to firms through goods markets.
4. Rent, wages, interest, and profit are the payments made by firms to households through factor markets.
5. Social security payments are made by state and local governments.
6. The largest part of the expenditures of state and local government is on education.

Multiple choice
1. Within the circular flow model, economists define households as
   a. families with at least 2 children.
   b. families living in their own houses.
   c. individuals or groups living together.
   d. married or engaged couples.
   e. individuals or groups within the same legally defined family.
2. A market is defined as
   a. the physical place where goods are sold.
   b. the physical place where goods and services are sold.
   c. any arrangement that brings buyers and sellers together.
   d. a place where money is exchanged for goods.
   e. another name for a store such as a grocery store.
3. In the circular flow model,
   a. only firms sell in markets.
   b. only households buy from markets.
   c. some firms only sell and some firms only buy.
   d. the money used to buy goods and the goods themselves travel in the same direction.
   e. both firms and households buy or sell in different markets.
4. ____ choose the quantities of goods and services to produce, while ____ choose the quantities of goods and services to buy.
   a. Households; firms
   b. Firms; households and the government
   c. The government; firms
   d. Firms; only households
   e. Households; the government
5. A circular flow model shows the interrelationship between the ____ market and the ____ markets.
   a. household; goods
   b. household; factor
   c. business; household
   d. expenditure; income
   e. goods; factor
6. In the circular flow model, the expenditures on goods and services flow in the
   a. same direction as goods and services in all cases.
   b. same direction as goods and services *only if* they both flow through the goods market.
   c. same direction as goods and services *only if* they both flow through the factor market.
   d. opposite direction as goods and services.
   e. same direction as factor markets.
7. Of the following, the smallest expenditure category of the federal government is
   a. national defense and homeland security.
   b. Social Security.
   c. Social Security benefits.
   d. Medicare and Medicaid.
   e. interest on the national debt.
8. Of the following, the largest source of revenue for the federal government is
   a. personal income taxes.
   b. sales taxes.
   c. corporate income taxes.
   d. property taxes.
   e. lottery revenue.

Complete the graph

■ FIGURE 2.2

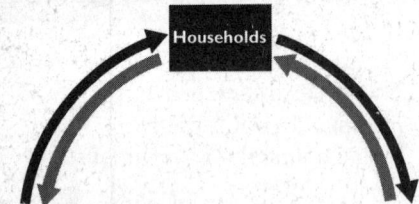

1. Figure 2.2 ignores the government and shows the flows into and out of households. Label the flows and identify who they come from and who they go to.

■ FIGURE 2.3

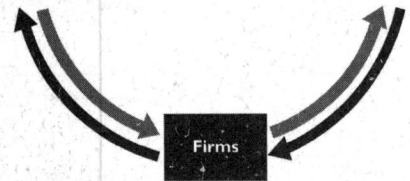

2. Figure 2.3 ignores the government and shows the flows into and out of firms. Label the flows and identify who they come from and who they go to.

■ FIGURE 2.4

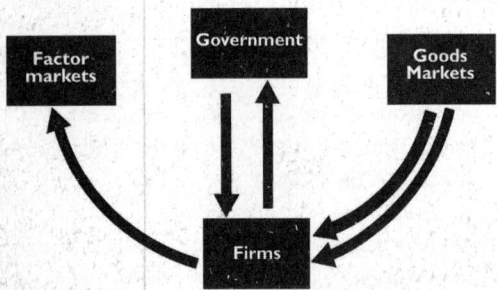

3. Figure 2.4 now includes the government and shows the money flows into and out of firms. Label the money flows.

Short answer and numeric questions

1. Ignoring taxes and transfer payments, what funds flow into firms and what funds flow out of them?

2. In the circular flow model, what are the sources of expenditures on goods and services?

3. Is it possible for something to affect households and not firms? To affect firms and not households? Explain your answers.

4. The circular flow reveals that which two groups interact to determine what will be the payments to the factors of production?

5. In 2006, which spent more, the federal government or state and local governments?

CHECKPOINT 2.3

■ **Describe what, how, and for whom goods and services are produced in the global economy.**

Quick Review

- *Advanced economies* The 29 countries (or areas) that have the highest living standards.
- *Emerging markets and Developing economies* Emerging markets are the 28 countries in Europe and Asia that were until the early 1990s part of the Soviet Union or its satellites and are changing the way they organize their economies. Developing economies are the 118 countries in Africa, the Middle East, Europe, and Central and South America that have not yet achieved a high standard of living for their people.

Additional Practice Problems 2.3

1. What percentage of the world's population live in developing economies? In places such as China, India, and Africa, what was the average income per day?

2. What percentage of the world's population live in advanced economies? In countries such as the United States, Canada, and Japan, what was the average income per day?

3. How does production within the advanced economies, the emerging market economies, and the developing economies compare?

4. How is it possible that income inequality within most countries has increased in recent years yet income inequality across the whole world has decreased in recent years?

Solutions to Additional Practice Problems 2.3

1. The world's population is about 6.6 billion. More than 5 billion of the people live in developing economies. So, approximately 80 percent of the world's population lives in developing economies. Average daily income in China is $24, in India is $10, and in Africa is $8. Because these are the average, many people live on less than these amounts.

2. About 1 billion people, or 15 percent of the world's population live in the 28 advanced economies. The average income per day in the United States was $124, in Canada was $102, and in Japan was $90.

3. Of the world's total production, the advanced economies produce 51 percent (20 percent is produced in the United States). The emerging market economies produce 7 percent of the world's production and the developing economies produce the remainder, 42 percent.

4. While income inequality within nations has been increasing, the difference in incomes among different nations has been decreasing. In particular, both China and India have seen rapid growth in income. The growth in income for these two poor but populous nations has decreased income inequality in the world as a whole.

■ Self Test 2.3

Fill in the blanks

Most of the world's population lives in the ____ (advanced economies; emerging market economies; developing economies). The lowest average income is in the ____ (advanced economies; emerging market economies; developing economies). Advanced economies produce about ____ (24; 51; 72) percent of the world's total production and the United States, alone, produces about ____ (6; 20; 33) percent of the world's total production. About ____ (33; 50; 67) percent of the world's proven oil reserves are located in ____ (North America; the Middle East). As a fraction of total output, agricultural is a ____ (larger; smaller) part of the economy in developing economies than in advanced economies. Factories in advanced economies are much ____ (less; more) capital intensive than in developing economies. During the past 20 years, the distribution of income in the world economy has become ____ (more; less) equal.

True or false

1. About 50 percent of the world's population lives in the advanced economies.

2. Mexico is an emerging market economy.

3. Taken as a group, the 118 developing economy nations produce a larger percentage of total world production than do the 29 advanced economy nations.

4. Most of the world's energy reserves are in North America.

5. Workers in the advanced economies have much more human capital than workers in the developing economies.

6. Income inequality within most nations has increased over the past years.

Multiple choice

1. The world population is approximately ____ people.
    a. 6.6 million
    b. 2 trillion
    c. 6.6 billion
    d. 1.4 trillion
    e. 660 million

2. The percentage of the world's population that lives in the advanced economies is
    a. more than 51 percent.
    b. between 41 percent and 50 percent.
    c. between 31 percent and 40 percent.
    d. between 20 percent and 30 percent.
    e. less than 20 percent.

3. Which of following groups of countries are *all* advanced economies?
   a. Australia, Brazil, and the United States
   b. Hong Kong, Japan, France, and the United Kingdom
   c. Italy, the United States, China, and Russia
   d. Singapore, Russia, France, and Chad
   e. Mexico, Canada, Germany, and Egypt

4. The emerging market economies are
   a. the largest grouping including the nations of China and India.
   b. in transition from state-owned production to free markets.
   c. most of the nations of Western Europe.
   d. the nations that are currently agricultural in nature.
   e. the nations with the highest standards of living.

5. As a percentage of total world production, production in the 29 advanced economies is about ____ percent of total world production and in the 118 developing economies is about ____ percent of total world production.
   a. 51; 42
   b. 23; 62
   c. 59; 12
   d. 30; 46
   e. 19; 73

6. Agricultural is about ____ percent of total production within advanced economies and the advanced economies produce about ____ percent of the world's food.
   a. 2; 33
   b. 12; 12
   c. 28; 63
   d. 4; 12
   e. 8; 20

7. Compared to the developing economies, the advanced economies have ____ human capital and ____ physical capital.
   a. more; more
   b. more; less
   c. the same; the same
   d. less; more
   e. less; less

8. Among the United States, Canada, Russia, India, and the United Kingdom, the country with the highest average income per person and the highest living standard is
   a. the United States.
   b. Russia.
   c. India.
   d. Canada.
   e. the United Kingdom.

Short answer and numeric questions
1. What are the groups the International Monetary Fund uses to classify countries? Describe each group. Which group has the largest number of countries? The largest number of people?
2. As a fraction of total production, how does agricultural production within the advanced economies compare to agricultural production within the developing economies? Why are the advanced economies able to produce about one third of the world's food?
3. How does the amount of human capital in the advanced economies compare to that in the developing economies?
4. How does the distribution of income within the United States compare to the distribution of income in the world economy?

SELF TEST ANSWERS

■ CHECKPOINT 2.1

Fill in the blanks

Goods and services that are bought by individuals and used to provide personal enjoyment and to contribute to a person's standard of living are <u>consumption</u> goods. Goods that are bought by businesses to increase their productive resources are <u>capital</u> goods. Goods that are produced in the United States and sold in other countries are <u>export</u> goods. Of the four large groups of goods and services in the United States, <u>consumption goods and services</u> have the largest share of total production. Productive resources are called <u>factors of production</u> and are grouped into four categories: <u>labor</u>, <u>land</u>, <u>capital</u>, and <u>entrepreneurship</u>. In 2006, <u>labor</u> received 64 percent of total income. The distribution of income among households is called the <u>personal</u> distribution of income.

True or false
1. True; page 34
2. True; page 36
3. True; page 39
4. True; page 40
5. False; page 40

Multiple choice
1. a; page 34
2. a; page 34
3. d; page 34
4. e; page 36
5. c; page 37
6. b; page 39
7. a; page 40
8. e; page 40

Short answer and numeric questions
1. An automobile might be either a consumption or a capital good. It is a consumption good if it is purchased by a household. It is a capital good if it is purchased by a business for use within the business; page 34.

2. The richest 20 percent of households earn about 50 percent of the total U.S. income. The poorest 20 percent of individuals have an average income of about $11,000 and earn about 3 percent of the total U.S. income; page 40.

■ CHECKPOINT 2.2

Fill in the blanks

The <u>circular flow</u> model shows the flows of expenditures and incomes. An arrangement that brings buyers and sellers together is a <u>market</u>. A market in which goods and services are bought and sold is a <u>goods</u> market and a market in which the services of the factors of production are bought and sold is a <u>factor</u> market. In 2006, as a percentage of the total value of the goods and services produced in the United States, the federal government spent about <u>20</u> percent while state and local governments spent about <u>13</u> percent. A large part of what the federal government spends is <u>social security payments</u>. The two components that account for most of the federal government's tax revenue are <u>personal income taxes and Social Security taxes</u>. The largest part of the expenditures of state and local governments is spending on <u>education</u>.

True or false
1. False; page 42
2. False; pages 42-43
3. False; pages 42-43
4. True; pages 42-43
5. False; page 44
6. True; page 47

Multiple choice
1. c; page 42
2. c; page 42
3. e; pages 42-43
4. b; pages 42-43
5. e; pages 42-43
6. d; page 43
7. e; page 46
8. a; page 46

Complete the graph
■ FIGURE 2.5

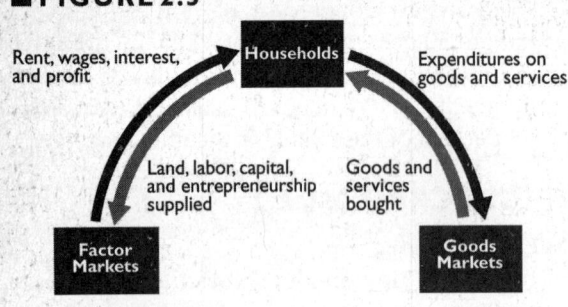

1. Figure 2.5 labels the flows. Rent, wages, interest, and profits (or losses) flow from the factor markets while the services from land, labor, capital, and entrepreneurship flow to the factor markets. In addition, expenditures on goods and services flow to the goods market, and goods and services flow from the goods market; page 43.

■ FIGURE 2.6

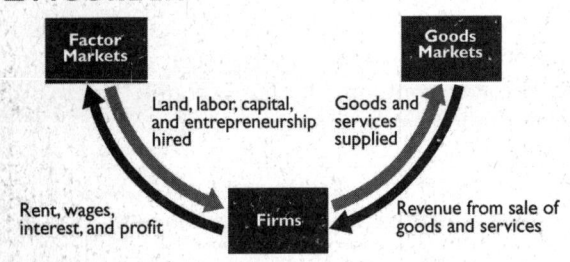

2. Figure 2.6 labels the flows. Revenue from the sale of goods and services, which are the expenditures on goods and services, flow to firms from the goods market and payments of rent, wages, interest, and profit (or loss) flow from firms into the factor market. The services from land, labor, capital, and entrepreneurship flow to firms from the factor markets, and goods and services flow from firms into the goods markets; page 43.

3. Figure 2.7 labels the money flows into and out of firms. The difference between this figure and Figure 2.6 is the addition of transfers and taxes; page 45.

■ FIGURE 2.7

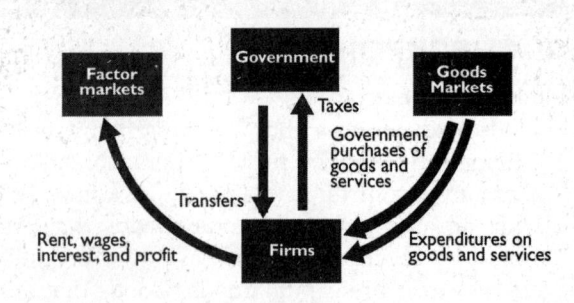

Short answer and numeric questions

1. Funds that flow into firms are households' expenditures and government purchases of goods and services. Funds that flow out of firms are payments for rent, wages, interest, and profit (or loss) to households in exchange for the factors of production; pages 43, 45.

2. The circular flow identifies two sources of expenditures on goods and services, expenditures by households and expenditures by the government; page 45.

3. The circular flow shows that at the macroeconomic level it is impossible for something to influence only firms or only households. An influence that changes households' buying behavior in goods markets affects firms because they sell to households in goods markets; page 43.

4. Payments to the factors of production are determined by the interaction of households, who own and provide the services from the factors of production, and firms, who employ the services from these factors; page 43.

5. In 2006, the federal government spent $2.9 trillion and state and local governments spent $1.6 trillion. The federal government spent significantly more than state and local governments; page 46.

■ CHECKPOINT 2.3

Fill in the blanks

Most of the world's population lives in the <u>developing economies</u>. The lowest average income is in the <u>developing economies</u>. Advanced economies produce about 51 percent of the world's total production and the United States, alone, produces about 20 percent of the world's total production. About 67 percent of the world's proven oil reserves are located in the Middle East. As a fraction of total output, agricultural is a larger part of the economy in developing economies than in advanced economies. Factories in advanced economies are much more capital intensive than in developing economies. During the past 20 years, the distribution of income in the world economy has become more equal.

True or false
1. False; page 49
2. False; page 49
3. False; page 50
4. False; page 51
5. True; page 53
6. True; page 55

Multiple choice
1. c; page 49
2. e; page 49
3. b; page 49
4. b; page 49
5. a; page 50
6. a; page 52
7. a; page 53
8. a; page 55

Short answer and numeric questions
1. The groups are the advanced economies and the emerging market and developing economies. Advanced economies have the highest standard of living. Emerging market and developing economies have yet to achieve a high standard of living. The emerging market economies are changing their economies from government management and state-ownership of capital to market-based economies similar to that in the United States. There are more nations, 118, and more people, almost 5 billion, in developing economies; page 49.

2. Agriculture accounts for about 1.8 percent of total production in advanced economies and about 14 percent of total production within developing economies. Even though advanced economies have a much smaller fraction of their total production devoted to food, because the farms within these nations are large, efficient, and well-equipped with capital and because farmers within these nations are paid by their governments to produce food, the advanced economies produce about one third of world's food; page 52.

3. The human capital possessed by workers in the advanced economies is *much* larger than that in the developing economies. People in the advanced economies have vastly more education, more on-the-job training and, in general, better health than in the developing economies; page 53.

4. The distribution of income within the United States is more equal than the distribution of income in the world economy. In the United States, the poorest 20 percent of households receive about 3 percent of the total income and the richest 20 percent of households receive about 50 percent of total income. In the world economy, the poorest 20 percent of households receive about 2 percent of total income and the richest 20 percent receive about 70 percent of total income; page 54.

Chapter 3
The Economic Problem

CHAPTER CHECKLIST

Chapter 3 develops an economic model, the production possibilities frontier, or *PPF*, model. The *PPF* shows how the opportunity cost of a good or service increases as more of the good or service is produced. It can be used to illustrate economic growth and to demonstrate societies and individuals gain by specializing according to comparative advantage.

1 Explain and illustrate the concepts of scarcity, production efficiency, and tradeoff using the production possibilities frontier.

The production possibilities frontier, *PPF*, is the boundary between the combinations of goods and services that can be produced and those that cannot be produced, given the available factors of production and technology. Production points outside the *PPF* are unattainable. Points on and inside the *PPF* are attainable. Production points on the *PPF* are production efficient while production points within the *PPF* are inefficient. Moving along the *PPF* producing more of one good, less of another good is produced—a tradeoff. Moving from inside the *PPF* to a point on the *PPF*, more of some goods and services can be produced without producing less of others—a free lunch.

2 Calculate opportunity cost.

Along the *PPF* all choices involve a tradeoff. Along the *PPF*, the opportunity cost of the good on the *x*-axis is the loss of the good measured along the *y*-axis and is equal to the decrease in the good on the *y*-axis divided by the increase in the good on the *x*-axis. As more of a good is produced, its opportunity cost increases, so the *PPF* is bowed outward. The opportunity cost increases because resources are not equally productive in all activities. In the real world, most activities have increasing opportunity cost.

3 Explain what makes production possibilities expand.

Economic growth is the sustained expansion of production possibilities. If more capital is accumulated production possibilities increase and the *PPF* shifts outward. The (opportunity) cost of economic growth is that resources used to increase capital cannot be used to produce current consumption goods and services.

4 Explain how people gain from specialization and trade.

A person has a comparative advantage in an activity if he or she can perform the activity at lower opportunity cost than someone else. People can gain from specializing in production according to comparative advantage and then trading with others. In this situation people (and nations) can consume combinations of goods and services that lie beyond their production possibilities frontiers. An absolute advantage occurs when one person is more productive than another person in several or even all activities. A person can have an absolute advantage in all activities but cannot have a comparative advantage in all activities.

CHECKPOINT 3.1

■ **Explain and illustrate the concepts of scarcity, production efficiency, and tradeoff using the production possibilities frontier.**

Quick Review
- *Production possibilities frontier* The boundary between combinations of goods and services that can be produced and combinations that cannot be produced, given the available factors of production and the state of technology.
- *Unattainable points* Production points outside the *PPF* are unattainable.
- *Tradeoff* A constraint or limit to what is possible that forces an exchange or a substitution of one thing for something else.

Additional Practice Problem 3.1

Possibility	Fish (pounds)		Fruit (pounds)
A	0.0	and	36.0
B	4.0	and	35.0
C	7.5	and	33.0
D	10.5	and	30.0
E	13.0	and	26.0
F	15.0	and	21.0
G	16.5	and	15.0
H	17.5	and	8.0
I	18.0	and	0.0

1. The table above shows Crusoe's *PPF*. Can Crusoe gather 21 pounds of fruit and catch 30 pounds of fish? Explain your answer. Suppose that Crusoe discovers another fishing pond with more fish, so that he can catch twice as many fish as before. Now can Crusoe gather 21 pounds of fruit and catch 30 pounds of fish? Explain your answer.

Solution to Additional Practice Problem 3.1

1. Initially, Crusoe cannot gather 21 pounds of fruit and catch 30 pounds of fish. This production point lies outside his *PPF* and so is unattainable. Once Crusoe discovers the new pond, however, he can gather 21 pounds of fruit and catch 30 pounds of fish. (In Row F, double the amount of Crusoe's fish.) The *PPF* depends on the available factors of production and when the factors of production increase, Crusoe's production possibilities change.

■ **Self Test 3.1**

Fill in the blanks

The ____ is the boundary between the combinations of goods and services that can and that cannot be produced given the available ____ (goods; factors of production) and ____ (number of services; state of technology). Production points outside the *PPF* ____ (are unattainable; are attainable; represent a free lunch). Production points ____ (on; beyond; within) the *PPF* are production efficient. Society has the possibility of a free lunch if production occurs ____ (inside; on; outside) the *PPF*. When resources are fully employed we face a ____ (free lunch; tradeoff).

True or false

1. A point outside the production possibilities frontier is unattainable.
2. If all the factors of production are fully employed, the economy will produce at a point on the production possibilities frontier.
3. Moving from one point on the *PPF* to another point on the *PPF* illustrates a free lunch.
4. All production points on the *PPF* are production efficient.

Multiple choice

1. The production possibilities frontier is a graph showing the
   a. exact point of greatest efficiency for producing goods and services.
   b. tradeoff between free lunches.
   c. maximum combinations of goods and services that can be produced.
   d. minimum combinations of goods and services that can be produced.
   e. resources available for the economy's use.

2. The production possibilities frontier is a boundary that separates
   a. the combinations of goods that can be produced from the combinations of services.
   b. attainable combinations of goods and services that can be produced from unattainable combinations.
   c. equitable combinations of goods that can be produced from inequitable combinations.
   d. reasonable combinations of goods that can be consumed from unreasonable combinations.
   e. affordable production points from unaffordable points.

3. Points inside the *PPF* are all
   a. unattainable and have fully employed resources.
   b. attainable and have fully employed resources.
   c. unattainable and have some unemployed resources.
   d. attainable and have some unemployed resources.
   e. unaffordable.

4. Points on the *PPF* are all
   a. unattainable and have fully employed resources.
   b. free lunches.
   c. inefficient.
   d. attainable and have some unemployed resources.
   e. production efficient.

5. During a time with high unemployment, a country can increase the production of one good or service
   a. without decreasing the production of something else.
   b. but must decrease the production of something else.
   c. and must increase the production of something else.
   d. by using resources in the production process twice.
   e. but the opportunity cost is infinite.

6. Moving along the production possibilities frontier itself illustrates
   a. the existence of tradeoffs.
   b. the existence of unemployment of productive resources.
   c. the benefits of free lunches.
   d. how free lunches can be exploited through trade.
   e. how tradeoffs need not occur if the economy is efficient.

Complete the graph

■ **FIGURE 3.1**
Computers (millions per year)

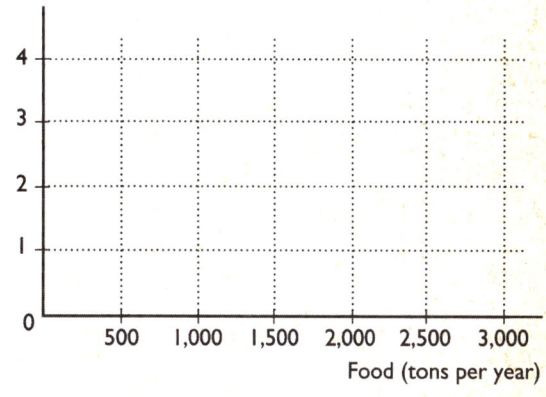

1. In Figure 3.1, draw a production possibilities frontier showing combinations of computers and food. Label the points that are attainable and unattainable. Label the points that have full employment and the points that have unemployment.

Short answer and numeric questions

1. What factors limit the amount of our production?
2. What points are production efficient? Moving between these points, is there a tradeoff or a free lunch?
3. What is the relationship between unemployment and a free lunch? Between full employment and a tradeoff?

CHECKPOINT 3.2

■ Calculate opportunity cost.

Quick Review
- *Opportunity cost is a ratio* Along a *PPF*, the opportunity cost of one good equals the quantity of the other good forgone divided by the increase in the good.

Additional Practice Problem 3.2

Possibility	Fish (pounds)		Fruit (pounds)
A	0.0	and	36.0
B	4.0	and	35.0
C	7.5	and	33.0
D	10.5	and	30.0
E	13.0	and	26.0
F	15.0	and	21.0
G	16.5	and	15.0
H	17.5	and	8.0
I	18.0	and	0.0

1. The table above shows Robinson Crusoe's production possibilities. How does Crusoe's opportunity cost of a pound of fish change as he catches more fish?

Solution to Additional Practice Problem 3.2

Move from	Increase in fish (pounds)	Decrease in fruit (pounds)	Opportunity cost of fish (pounds of fruit)
A to B	4.0	1.0	0.25
B to C	3.5	2.0	0.57
C to D	3.0	3.0	1.00
D to E	2.5	4.0	1.60
E to F	2.0	5.0	2.50
F to G	1.5	6.0	4.00
G to H	1.0	7.0	7.00
H to I	0.5	8.0	16.00

1. The table above shows Crusoe's opportunity cost of a pound of fish. His opportunity cost of a pound of fish increases as he catches more fish. As he moves from point A to point B and catches his first fish, the opportunity cost is only 0.25 pounds of fruit per pound of fish. But as he moves from point H to point I and catches only fish, the opportunity cost has increased to 16.0 pounds of fruit per pound of fish.

■ Self Test 3.2

Fill in the blanks
Along a production possibilities frontier, the opportunity cost of obtaining one more unit of a good is the amount of another good that is ____ (gained; forgone). The opportunity cost is equal to the quantity of the good forgone ____ (plus; divided by) the increase in the quantity of the other good. As more of a good is produced, its opportunity cost ____.

True or false
1. Moving from one point on the *PPF* to another point on the *PPF* has no opportunity cost.
2. When moving along the *PPF*, the quantity of CDs increases by 2 and the quantity of DVDs decreases by 1, so the opportunity cost is 2 CDs minus 1 DVD.
3. Increasing opportunity costs are common.

Multiple choice
1. The opportunity cost of one more slice of pizza in terms of sodas is the
   a. number of pizza slices we have to give up to get one extra soda.
   b. number of sodas we have to give up to get one extra slice of pizza.
   c. total number of sodas that we have divided by the total number of pizza slices that we have.
   d. total number of pizza slices that we have divided by the total number of sodas that we have.
   e. price of pizza minus the price of the soda.
2. Moving between two points on a *PPF*, a country gains 6 automobiles and forgoes 3 trucks. The opportunity cost of 1 automobile is
   a. 3 trucks.
   b. 6 automobiles – 3 trucks.
   c. 2 trucks.
   d. 1/2 of a truck.
   e. 1 automobile.

3. Moving between two points on a *PPF*, a country gains 8 desktop computers and forgoes 4 laptop computers. The opportunity cost of 1 desktop computer is
   a. 4 laptops.
   b. 8 desktops.
   c. 1 desktop.
   d. 2 laptops.
   e. 1/2 of a laptop.

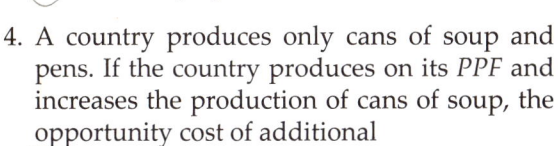

4. A country produces only cans of soup and pens. If the country produces on its *PPF* and increases the production of cans of soup, the opportunity cost of additional
   a. cans of soup is increasing.
   b. cans of soup is decreasing.
   c. cans of soup remain unchanged.
   d. ink pens is increasing.
   e. More information is needed to determine what happens to the opportunity cost.

5. Moving along a country's *PPF*, a reason opportunity costs increase is that
   a. unemployment decreases as a country produces more and more of one good.
   b. unemployment increases as a country produces more and more of one good.
   c. technology declines as a country produces more and more of one good.
   d. some resources are better suited for producing one good rather than the other.
   e. technology must advance in order to produce more and more of one good.

6. Increasing opportunity costs exist
   a. in the real world.
   b. as long as there is high unemployment.
   c. only in theory but not in real life.
   d. for a country but not for an individual.
   e. inside the *PPF* but not on the *PPF*.

Complete the graph

1. The table at the top of the next column shows the production possibilities for a nation.
   a. Placing MP3 players on the vertical axis, label the axes in Figure 3.2 and graph the production possibilities frontier.

Production point	MP3 players (millions per year)		DVD players (millions per year)
A	4.0	and	0.0
B	3.0	and	3.0
C	2.0	and	4.0
D	1.0	and	4.7
E	0.0	and	5.0

■ **FIGURE 3.2**

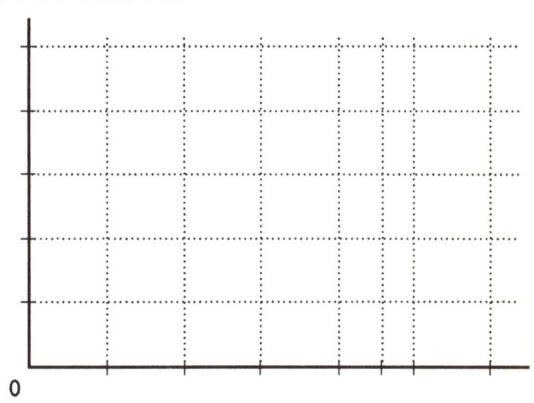

   b. What is the opportunity cost per DVD player of moving from point *A* to point *B*? *B* to *C*? *C* to *D*? *D* to *E*? How does the opportunity cost change as more DVD players are produced?

Short answer and numeric questions

Production point	Cans of soda (millions per year)		Candy bars (millions per year)
A	8.0	and	0.0
B	6.0	and	4.0
C	4.0	and	6.0
D	2.0	and	7.0
E	0.0	and	7.5

1. The table above shows the production possibilities for Sweetland.
   a. What is the opportunity cost per candy bar player of moving from point *A* to point *B*? *B* to *C*? *C* to *D*? *D* to *E*?
   b. What is the opportunity cost per can of soda of moving from point *E* to point *D*? *D* to *C*? *C* to *B*? *B* to *A*?
   c. How does the opportunity cost of a candy bar change as more candy bars are produced? How does the opportunity cost of

a soda change as more sodas are produced?
2. What is the opportunity cost of increasing the production of a good while moving along a *PPF*? Why does this opportunity cost increase?
3. What does it mean for the opportunity cost to be a ratio?

CHECKPOINT 3.3

■ **Explain what makes production possibilities expand.**

Quick Review
- *Opportunity cost of growth* The opportunity cost of economic growth is the current consumption goods and services forgone.

Additional Practice Problem 3.3
1. Does economic growth eliminate scarcity?

Solution to Additional Practice Problem 3.3
1. Economic growth does not eliminate scarcity. Scarcity exists as long as people's wants exceed what can be produced. Economic growth increases the goods and services that can be produced but people's wants will continue to outstrip the ability to produce. While economic growth means that additional wants can be satisfied, people's wants are infinite and so scarcity will continue to be present even with economic growth.

■ **Self Test 3.3**

Fill in the blanks
A sustained expansion of production possibilities is called ____. Economic growth shifts the *PPF* ____ (inward; outward). The *PPF* shows that economic growth requires ____ (a decrease; an increase) in the current production of consumption goods. The opportunity cost of increasing economic growth is the loss of the ____ (current; future) goods that can be consumed.

True or false
1. Economic growth abolishes scarcity.
2. The opportunity cost of economic growth is less consumption goods in the future.
3. Production possibilities per person in the United States have remained constant during the last 30 years.

Multiple choice
1. To increase its economic growth, a nation should
   a. limit the number of people in college because they produce nothing.
   b. encourage spending on goods and services.
   c. encourage education because that increases the quality of labor.
   d. increase current consumption.
   e. eliminate expenditure on capital goods.

2. If Mexico devotes more resources to train its population than Spain,
   a. Mexico will be able to eliminate opportunity cost faster than Spain.
   b. Mexico will be able to eliminate scarcity faster than Spain.
   c. Spain will grow faster than Mexico.
   d. Mexico will grow faster than Spain.
   e. Mexico will have more current consumption than Spain.

3. If a nation devotes a larger share of its current production to consumption goods, then
   a. its economic growth will slow down.
   b. the *PPF* will shift outward.
   c. the *PPF* will shift inward.
   d. some productive factors will become unemployed.
   e. it must produce at a point within its PPF.

4. Which of the following is correct?
   i. As an economy grows, the opportunity costs of economic growth decrease.
   ii. Economic growth has no opportunity cost.
   iii. The opportunity cost of economic growth is current consumption forgone.
   a. i only.
   b. ii only.
   c. iii only.
   d. i and iii.
   e. i and ii.

5. When a country's production possibilities frontier shifts outward over time, the country is experiencing
   a. no opportunity cost.
   b. economic growth.
   c. higher unemployment of resources.
   d. a decrease in unemployment of resources.
   e. an end to opportunity cost.

6. The opportunity cost of economic growth is ____ and the benefit of economic growth is ____.
   a. increased current consumption; increased future consumption
   b. increased current consumption; decreased future consumption
   c. decreased current consumption; increased future consumption
   d. decreased current consumption; decreased future consumption.
   e. nothing; increased future consumption.

Complete the graph

■ FIGURE 3.3

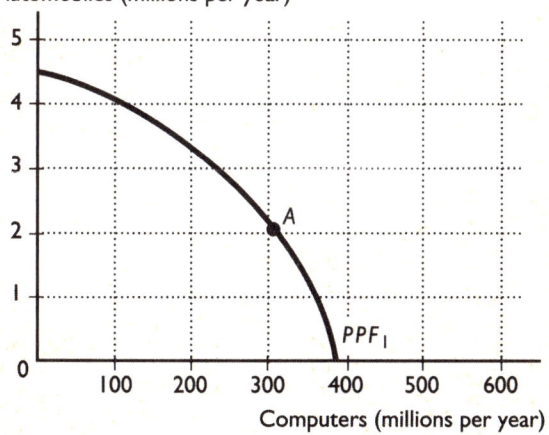

1. In the above figure, illustrate what happens if there is a technological breakthrough in the production of computers but not in the production of automobiles.
   a. Suppose the economy was initially producing at point A. After the breakthrough, is it possible for the economy to produce more computers *and* more automobiles?

Short answer and numeric questions

1. What is the opportunity cost of economic growth?
2. What is the benefit of economic growth?

CHECKPOINT 3.4

■ **Explain how people gain from specialization and trade.**

Quick Review
- *Comparative advantage* The ability of a person to perform an activity or produce a good or service at a lower opportunity cost than someone else.

Additional Practice Problem 3.4

1. Tony and Patty produce scooters and snowboards. The figure shows their production possibilities per day. With these production possibilities, the opportunity cost of a snowboard for Patty is 1/2 a scooter and for Tony is 2 scooters. Patty has a lower opportunity cost and therefore she has the comparative advantage in snowboards. The opportunity cost of a scooter for Patty is 2 snowboards and for Tony is 1/2 of a snowboard. Tony has a lower opportunity cost and so he has the comparative advantage in scooters.

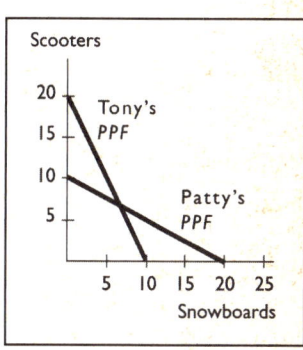

Suppose Patty acquires new equipment for scooter production that lets her produce a maximum of 60 rather than 10 scooters a day, should Patty and Tony specialize and trade?

Solution to Additional Practice Problem 3.4

1. Once Patty can produce 60 scooters a day, her opportunity costs change. Her opportunity cost of a scooter falls to 1/3 of a snowboard per scooter and her opportunity cost of a snowboard rises to 3 scooters per snowboard. With these opportunity costs, the comparative ad-

vantages have switched: Patty now has a comparative advantage in scooters and Tony in snowboards. Patty and Tony should still specialize and trade, only now Patty will specialize in scooters and Tony will specialize in snowboards. Comparative advantage can switch as the production possibilities frontier shifts outward.

■ Self Test 3.4

Fill in the blanks

A person has ____ (a comparative; an absolute) advantage in an activity if that person can perform the activity at a lower opportunity cost than someone else. If people specialize according to ____ (comparative; absolute) advantage and then trade, they can get ____ (outside; inside) their production possibilities frontiers. A person has ____ (a comparative; an absolute) advantage if they are more productive than someone else in all activities. It ____ (is; is not) possible for someone to have a comparative advantage in all activities. It ____ (is; is not) possible for someone to have an absolute advantage in all activities.

True or false

1. A person has an absolute advantage in an activity if the person can perform the activity at lower opportunity cost than someone else.
2. To achieve the gains from trade, a producer specializes in the product in which he or she has a comparative advantage and then trades with others.
3. Specialization and trade can make both producers better off even if one of them has an absolute advantage in producing all goods.

Multiple choice

1. "Comparative advantage" is defined as a situation in which one person can produce
   a. more of all goods than another person.
   b. more of a good than another person.
   c. a good for a lower dollar cost than another person.
   d. a good for a lower opportunity cost than another person.
   e. all goods for lower opportunity costs than another person.

For the next three questions, use the following information: Scott and Cindy both produce only pizza and tacos. In one hour, Scott can produce 20 pizzas or 40 tacos. In one hour, Cindy can produce 30 pizzas or 40 tacos.

2. Scott's opportunity cost of producing 1 taco is
   a. 1/2 of a pizza.
   b. 1 pizza.
   c. 2 pizzas.
   d. 20 pizzas.
   e. 2 tacos

3. Cindy's opportunity cost of producing 1 taco is
   a. 3/4 of a pizza.
   b. 1 pizza.
   c. 30 pizzas.
   d. 40 pizzas.
   e. 1 taco.

4. Based on the data given,
   a. Cindy has a comparative advantage in producing tacos.
   b. Scott has a comparative advantage in producing tacos.
   c. Cindy and Scott have the same comparative advantage when producing tacos.
   d. neither Cindy nor Scott has a comparative advantage when producing tacos.
   e. Cindy and Scott have the same comparative advantage when producing pizzas.

5. In one hour John can produce 20 loaves of bread or 8 cakes. In one hour Phyllis can produce 30 loaves of bread or 15 cakes. Which of the following statements is true?
   a. Phyllis has a comparative advantage when producing bread.
   b. John has a comparative advantage when producing cakes.
   c. Phyllis has an absolute advantage in both goods.
   d. John has an absolute advantage in both goods.
   e. Phyllis has a comparative advantage in producing both cakes and bread.

6. In one hour John can produce 20 loaves of bread or 16 cakes. In one hour Phyllis can produce 30 loaves of bread or 15 cakes. Which of the following statements is true?
   a. Phyllis has a comparative advantage when producing cakes.
   b. John has a comparative advantage when producing cakes.
   c. Phyllis has an absolute advantage in both goods.
   d. John has an absolute advantage in both goods.
   e. Phyllis has a comparative advantage in producing both cakes and bread.

Complete the graph

■ **FIGURE 3.4**

Shirts (per day)

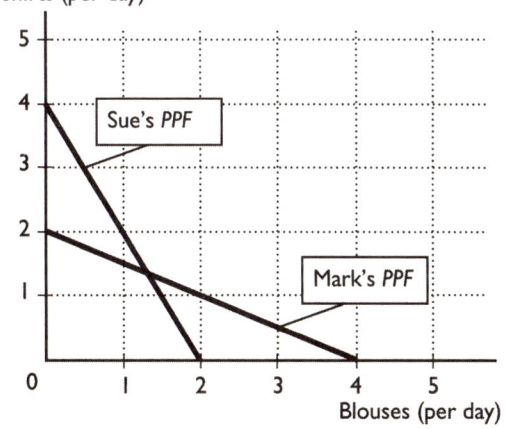

Sue's *PPF*

Mark's *PPF*

Blouses (per day)

1. Figure 3.4 shows Mark and Sue's *PPF*s.
   a. What is Sue's opportunity cost of producing a shirt? What is Mark's opportunity cost of producing a shirt?
   b. Who has the comparative advantage in producing shirts?
   c. What is Sue's opportunity cost of producing a blouse? What is Mark's opportunity cost of producing a blouse?
   d. Who has the comparative advantage in producing blouses?
   e. Who should specialize in producing blouses and who should specialize in producing shirts?
   f. If Mark and Sue specialize according to their comparative advantage, indicate the total production of shirts and blouses by putting a point in Figure 3.4 showing the total production. Label the point *A*.
   g. How does point *A* show the gains from trade?

Short answer and numeric questions

1. Why should people specialize according to their comparative advantage?
2. To achieve gains from trade, the opportunity costs of the trading partners must diverge. Why?
3. When it comes to trading one good for another, why is comparative advantage crucial and absolute advantage unimportant?

SELF TEST ANSWERS

■ CHECKPOINT 3.1

Fill in the blanks

The <u>production possibilities frontier or PPF</u> is the boundary between the combinations of goods and services that can and that cannot be produced given the available <u>factors of production</u> and <u>state of technology</u>. Production points outside the PPF <u>are unattainable</u>. Production points <u>on</u> the PPF are production efficient. Society has the possibility of a free lunch if production occurs <u>inside</u> the PPF. When resources are fully employed we face a <u>tradeoff</u>.

True or false
1. True; page 64
2. True; page 64
3. False; page 65
4. True; pages 64-65

Multiple choice
1. c; page 62
2. b; page 64
3. d; page 64
4. e; pages 64-65
5. a; page 65
6. a; page 65

Complete the graph

■ **FIGURE 3.5**

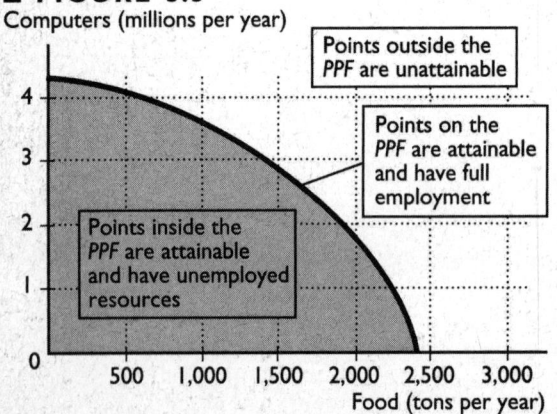

1. Figure 3.5 shows a PPF between computers and food; pages 63-64.

Short answer and numeric questions
1. The factors that limit the amount of our production are the available resources and the state of technology; page 62.
2. All points *on* the production possibilities frontier are production efficient. Moving from one point to another incurs an opportunity cost so there is tradeoff; pages 64-66
3. When the nation is producing at a point with unemployment, there are free lunches available because the production of some goods and services can be increased without decreasing the production of anything else. When the nation is producing at full employment, it is on the PPF and so only tradeoffs are available: If the production of one good or service is increased, the production of something else must be decreased; pages 65-66.

■ CHECKPOINT 3.2

Fill in the blanks

Along a production possibilities frontier, the opportunity cost of obtaining one more unit of a good is the amount of another good that is <u>forgone</u>. The opportunity cost is equal to the quantity of the good forgone <u>divided by</u> the increase in the quantity of the other good. As more of a good is produced, its opportunity cost <u>increases</u>.

True or false
1. False; page 68
2. False; page 69
3. True; page 70

Multiple choice
1. b; page 68
2. d; page 68
3. e; page 68
4. a; page 69
5. d; page 70
6. a; page 70

Complete the graph
■ FIGURE 3.6

MP3 players (millions per year)

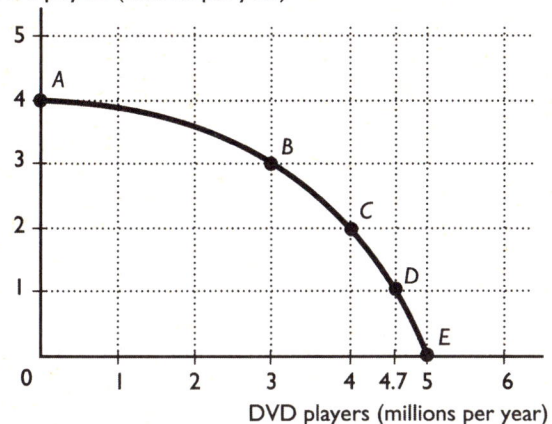

[Graph showing PPF curve with points A(0,4), B(3,3), C(4,2), D(4.7,1), E(5,0); x-axis: DVD players (millions per year)]

1. a. Figure 3.6 illustrates the production possibilities frontier; page 68.
   b. The opportunity cost of moving from point A to point B to is 0.33 MP3 players per DVD player; from B to C is 1.00 MP3 player per DVD player; from C to D is 1.43 MP3 players per DVD player; and, from D to E is 3.33 MP3 players per DVD player. The opportunity cost increases; page 68

Short answer and numeric questions
1. a. The opportunity cost of moving from point A to point B to is 0.5 cans of soda per candy bar; from B to C is 1.0 can of soda per candy bar; from C to D is 2.0 cans of soda per candy bar; and, from D to E is 4.0 cans of soda per candy bar; page 68.
   b. The opportunity cost of moving from point E to point D to is 0.25 candy bars per can of soda; from D to C is 0.50 candy bars per can of soda; from C to B is 1.00 candy bar per can of soda; and, from B to A is 2.00 candy bars per can of soda; page 68.
   c. As more candy bars are produced, the opportunity cost increases. As more cans of soda are produced, the opportunity cost increases; page 69.
2. The opportunity cost of increasing production of one good is the production of some other good forgone. The opportunity cost increases, so that increasingly large amounts of the other good are forgone, because resources are not equally productive in all activities. When initially increasing the production of one good, resources that are well suited for its production are used. When still more of the good is produced, resources that are less well suited must be used. Because the resources are ill suited, more are necessary to increase the production of the first good, and the forgone amount of the other good increases; page 70.
3. The opportunity cost is the amount of a good forgone to gain an additional unit another good. We divide the quantity of the good forgone by the increase in the other good. So opportunity cost is a ratio—the change in the quantity of one good divided by the change in the quantity of another good; page 70.

■ CHECKPOINT 3.3
Fill in the blanks
A sustained expansion of production possibilities is called <u>economic growth</u>. Economic growth shifts the *PPF* <u>outward</u>. The *PPF* shows that economic growth requires <u>a decrease</u> in the current production of consumption goods. The opportunity cost of increasing economic growth is the loss of the <u>current</u> goods that can be consumed.

True or false
1. False; page 73
2. False; pages 73-74
3. False; page 74

Multiple choice
1. c; page 73
2. d; pages 73-74
3. a; page 73
4. d; page 73
5. b; page 73
6. c; pages 73-79

Complete the graph
■ FIGURE 3.7

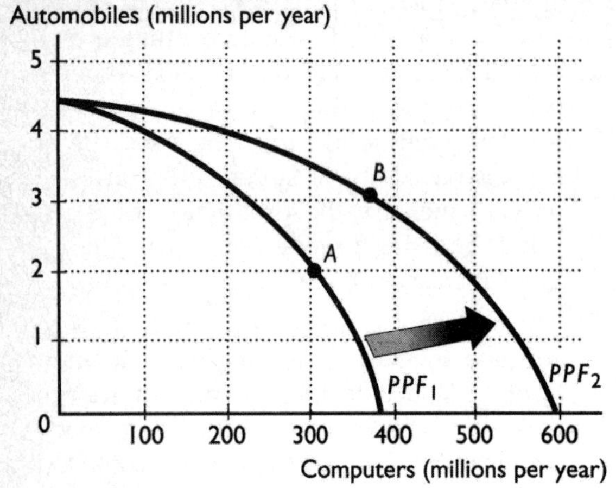

1. Figure 3.7 illustrates the new production possibilities frontier. Because the technological breakthrough did not affect automobile production, the maximum amount of automobiles that can be produced on the vertical axis does not change; pages 73-74.
1. a. Figure 3.7 shows that it is possible for the production of *both* automobiles and computers to increase, as a movement from the initial point A to a possible new point B illustrates; page 73.

Short answer and numeric questions
1. Economic growth requires either developing new technologies, accumulating more human capital, or accumulating more capital. All of these avenues require resources, so the opportunity cost of economic growth is the decrease in the current production of goods and services; page 73.
2. The benefit from economic growth is increased consumption per person in the future after the production possibilities frontier has expanded; page 73.

■ CHECKPOINT 3.4
Fill in the blanks
A person has <u>a comparative</u> advantage in an activity if that person can perform the activity at a lower opportunity cost than someone else. If people specialize according to <u>comparative</u> advantage and then trade, they can get <u>outside</u> their production possibilities frontiers. A person has <u>an absolute</u> advantage if they are more productive than someone else in all activities. It <u>is not</u> possible for someone to have a comparative advantage in all activities. It <u>is</u> possible for someone to have an absolute advantage in all activities.

True or false
1. False; pages 75-76
2. True; page 76
3. True; pages 76-77

Multiple choice
1. d; page 75
2. a; page 75
3. a; page 75
4. b; pages 75-76
5. c; page 76
6. b; page 76

Complete the graph
1. a. Sue's opportunity cost of a shirt is 1/2 of a blouse because, when moving along her PPF to produce 1 more shirt she forgoes 1/2 of a blouse. Mark's opportunity cost of a shirt is 2 blouses; page 75
   b. Sue has the comparative advantage in producing shirts because her opportunity cost is lower; page 75.
   c. Sue's opportunity cost of a blouse is 2 shirts because, when moving along her PPF, to produce 1 more blouse she forgoes 2 shirts. Mark's opportunity cost of a blouse is 1/2 of a shirt; page 75.
   d. Mark has the comparative advantage in producing blouses because his opportunity cost is lower; page 76.
   e. Mark should specialize in producing blouses and Sue should specialize in producing shirts; page 76.

■ FIGURE 3.8

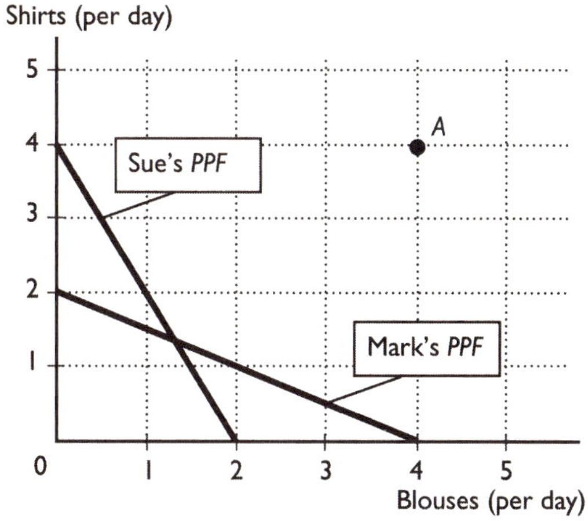

Shirts (per day) vs Blouses (per day). Sue's PPF and Mark's PPF shown, with point A at (4, 4).

f. Mark produces 4 blouses and Sue produces 4 shirts, so a total of 4 shirts and 4 blouses are produced. Figure 3.8 shows this production as point A; pages 76-77.

g. If the total production at point A is divided evenly, both Mark and Sue will receive 2 shirts and 2 blouses. When both were producing only for themselves, they could not produce 2 shirts and 2 blouses because this point is beyond both their PPFs. By specializing and trading, Mark and Sue get outside their PPFs; page 77.

Short answer and numeric questions

1. A person's comparative advantage is the good that the person can produce at a lower opportunity cost than other people. When this person specializes in the production of the good, it is produced at the lowest cost; page 76.

2. If the trading partners' opportunity costs are the same, there is no incentive for them to trade. For instance, if two people produce either gum or soda and both have the same opportunity cost of 5 gums for 1 soda, neither is willing to buy or sell to the other. Only when opportunity costs diverge will one person be willing to buy (the person with the higher opportunity cost) and the other willing to sell (the person with the lower opportunity cost); page 75-76.

3. People are willing to trade if they can obtain a good at lower opportunity cost than what it costs them to produce the good. Comparative advantage tells which person has a lower opportunity cost. Even if a person has an absolute advantage in all goods, he or she does not have a comparative advantage in all goods. So comparative advantage determines who produces a product and who buys it; page 76.

Chapter 4

Demand and Supply

CHAPTER CHECKLIST

The tools of demand and supply explain how competitive markets work. We use the demand and supply tools to determine the quantities and prices of the goods and services produced and consumed.

1 Distinguish between quantity demanded and demand, and explain what determines demand.

The quantity demanded is the amount of any good, service, or resource that people are willing and able to buy during a specified period at a specified price. Demand is the relationship between the quantity demanded and the price of a good when all other influences on buying plans remain the same. The law of demand states that other things remaining the same, if the price of a good rises, the quantity demanded of that good decreases; and if the price of a good falls, the quantity demanded of that good increases. A demand curve is a graph of the relationship between the quantity demanded of a good and its price when all other influences on buying plans remain the same. The market demand is the sum of the demands of all the buyers in a market. A change in price leads to a *change in the quantity demanded* and a movement along the demand curve. Factors that *change demand* and shift the demand curve are: prices of related goods; income; expectations; number of buyers; and preferences.

2 Distinguish between quantity supplied and supply, and explain what determines supply.

The quantity supplied is the amount of any good, service, or resource that people are willing and able to sell during a specified period at a specified price. Supply is the relationship between the quantity supplied and the price of a good when all other influences on selling plans remain the same. The law of supply states that other things remaining the same, if the price of a good rises, the quantity supplied of that good increases; and if the price of a good falls, the quantity supplied of that good decreases. A supply curve is a graph of the relationship between the quantity supplied of a good and its price when all other influences on selling plans remain the same. A change in price leads to a *change in the quantity supplied* and a movement along the supply curve. Factors that *change supply* and shift the supply curve are: prices of related goods; prices of resources and other inputs; expectations; number of sellers; and productivity. If supply increases (decreases), the supply curve shifts rightward (leftward).

3 Explain how demand and supply determine price and quantity in a market and explain the effects of changes in demand and supply.

The equilibrium price and equilibrium quantity occur when the quantity demanded equals the quantity supplied. An increase in demand raises the price and increases the quantity. An increase in supply lowers the price and increases the quantity. An increase in both demand and supply increases the quantity and the price might rise, fall, or not change. An increase in demand and a decrease in supply raises the price and the quantity might increase, decrease, or not change. Changes in demand and supply in the opposite direction to those given above lead to reverse changes in price and quantity.

CHECKPOINT 4.1

■ **Distinguish between quantity demanded and demand, and explain what determines demand.**

Quick Review

- *Change in the quantity demanded* A change in the quantity of a good that people plan to buy that results from a change in the price of the good.
- *Law of demand* If the price of a good rises, the quantity demanded of that good decreases; and if the price of a good falls, the quantity demanded of that good decreases.
- *Change in demand* A change in the quantity that people plan to buy when any influence on buying plans, other than the price of the good, changes. These other influences include: prices of related goods, income, expectations, number of buyers, and preferences.

Additional Practice Problems 4.1

1. In the market for motor scooters, several events occur, one at a time. Explain the influence of each event on the quantity demanded of scooters and on the demand for scooters. Illustrate the effects of each event either by a movement along the demand curve or a shift in the demand curve for scooters and say which event (or events) illustrates the law of demand in action. These events are:
    a. The price of a scooter falls.
    b. The price of a car falls.
    c. Citing rising injury rates, cities and towns ban scooters from busy streets.
    d. Scooters are a normal good and income increases.
    e. Scooters become unfashionable and the number of buyers decreases.

2. Suppose that each year Anna, Ben, Carol, and Dana are willing and able to buy scooters as shown in the table.

Price (dollars per scooter)	Anna	Ben	Carol	Dana
100	0	0	0	0
75	1	0	0	0
50	2	1	1	0
25	2	1	2	1

■ **FIGURE 4.1**

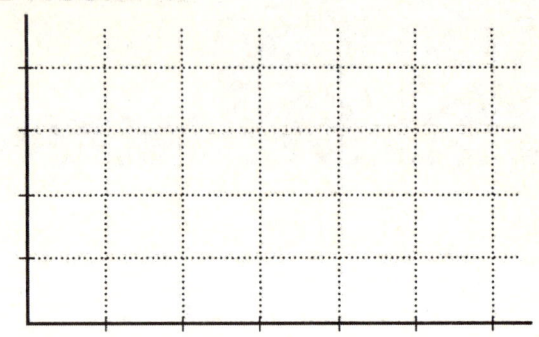

Using the information in the table:
a. Label the axes in Figure 4.1 above.
b. Graph the market demand curve.

Solutions to Additional Practice Problems 4.1

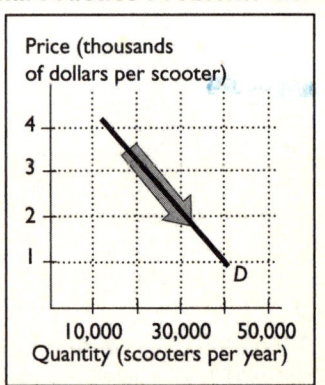

1a. This problem emphasizes the distinction between a change in the quantity demanded and a change in demand. A fall in the price of a scooter brings an increase in the quantity demanded of scooters, which is illustrated by a movement down along the demand curve for scooters as shown in the figure. This event illustrates the law of demand in action.

1b. A car is a substitute for a scooter. With the lower price of a car, some people who previously would have bought a scooter will now buy a car instead. So a fall in the price of cars decreases the demand for scooters. The demand curve for scooters shifts leftward as shown in the figure below.

1c. Rising injury rates and banning scooters from streets changes preferences and makes scooters less desirable. The demand for scooters decreases and the demand curve for the scooters shifts leftward as shown in the figure leftward as shown in the figure by the shift from demand curve D_0 to demand curve D_1.

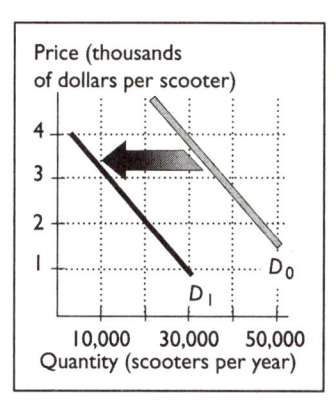

1d. A scooter is a normal good, so people will buy more scooters when their income increases. The demand for scooters increases and the demand curve shifts rightward as illustrated in the figure.

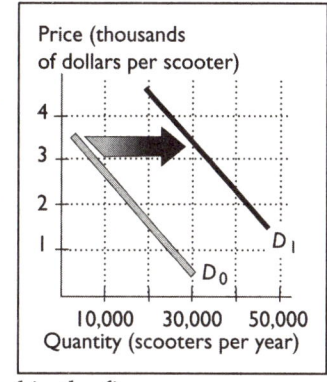

1e. A decrease in the number of buyers decreases the demand for scooters. The demand curve shifts leftward.

■ **FIGURE 4.2**

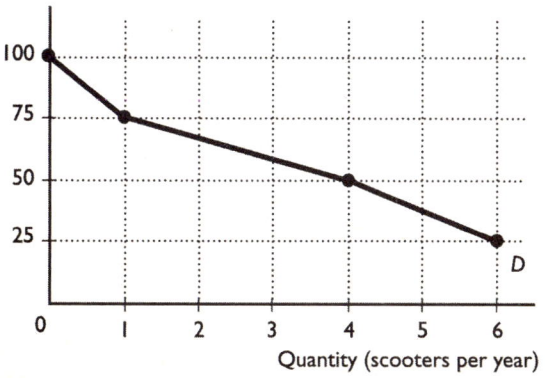

2a. Figure 4.2 labels the axes.

2b. The market demand curve is derived by adding the quantities demanded by Anna, Ben, Carol, and Dana at each price. The market demand curve is illustrated in Figure 4.2.

■ **Self Test 4.1**

Fill in the blanks

The ____ (demand schedule; law of demand) states that other things remaining the same, if the price of a good rises, the ____ (quantity demanded of; demand for) that good decreases. A ____ is a graph of the relationship between the quantity demanded of a good and its price. Demand curves are ____ (downward; upward) sloping. An increase in demand shifts the demand curve ____. Factors that change demand lead to a ____ (shift of; movement along) the demand curve. Factors that change demand are ____, ____, ____, ____, and ____.

True or false

1. The law of demand states that other things remaining the same, if the price of a good rises, the quantity demanded of that good increases.

2. If the quantity of ice cream demanded at each price increases, there is a movement along the demand curve for ice cream.

3. When Sue's income increases, her demand for movies increases. For Sue, movies are a normal good.

4. A rise in the price of a computer increases the demand for computers because a computer is a normal good.

5. If people's incomes fall and all other influences on buying plans remain the same, the demand for computers will decrease and there will be a movement along the demand curve.

Multiple choice

1. The "law of demand" indicates that if the University of Maine increases the tuition, all other things remaining the same,
   a. the demand for classes will decrease at the University of Maine.
   b. the demand for classes will increase at the University of Maine.
   c. the quantity of classes demanded will increase at the University of Maine.
   d. the quantity of classes demanded will decrease at the University of Maine.
   e. both the demand for and the quantity of classes demanded will decrease at the University of Maine.

2. Other things remaining the same, the quantity of a good or service demanded will increase if the price of the good or service
   a. rises.
   b. falls.
   c. does not change.
   d. rises or does not change.
   e. rises or falls.

3. Teenagers demand more soda than other age groups. If the number of teenagers increases, everything else remaining the same,
   a. market demand for soda increases.
   b. market demand for soda decreases.
   c. market demand for soda does not change.
   d. there is a movement along the market demand curve for soda.
   e. None of the above answers is correct because the effect on the demand depends whether the supply curve shifts.

4. One reason the demand for laptop computers might increase is a
   a. fall in the price of a laptop computers.
   b. fall in the price of a desktop computer.
   c. a change in preferences as laptops have become more portable, with faster processors and larger hard drives.
   d. poor quality performance record for laptop computers.
   e. a decrease in income if laptops are a normal good.

5. The number of buyers of sport utility vehicles, SUVs, decreases sharply. So
   a. the demand curve for SUVs shifts leftward.
   b. the demand curve for SUVs shifts rightward.
   c. there is neither a shift nor a movement along the demand curve for SUVs.
   d. there is a movement down along the demand curve for SUVs.
   e. the supply curve for SUVs shifts rightward.

■ FIGURE 4.3

Price (dollars per pizza)

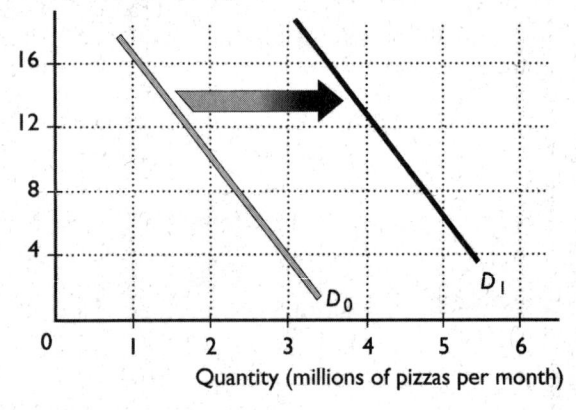

6. The shift of the demand curve for pizza illustrated in Figure 4.3 could be the result of
   a. a rise in income if pizza is a normal good.
   b. a fall in the price of fried chicken, a substitute for pizza.
   c. consumers coming to believe that pizza is unhealthy.
   d. the belief that pizza will fall in price next month.
   e. a fall in the price of a pizza.

7. The shift of the demand curve for pizza illustrated in Figure 4.3 could be the result of
   a. a rise in income if pizza is an inferior good.
   b. a fall in the price of soda, a complement for pizza.
   c. a decrease in the number of college students if college students eat more pizza than other age groups.
   d. a rise in the price of a pizza.
   e. a fall in the price of a pizza.

8. When moving along a demand curve, which of the following changes?
   a. the consumers' incomes
   b. the prices of other goods
   c. the number of buyers
   d. the price of the good
   e. the consumers' preferences

9. If the price of a CD falls,
   i. the demand curve for CDs shifts rightward.
   ii. the demand curve for CDs will not shift.
   iii. there is a movement along the demand curve for CDs.
   a. i only.
   b. ii only.
   c. iii only.
   d. ii and iii.
   e. i and iii.

10. Pizza and tacos are substitutes and the price of a pizza increases. Which of the following correctly indicates what happens?
    a. The demand for pizzas decreases and the demand for tacos increases.
    b. The demand for both goods decreases.
    c. The quantity of tacos demanded increases and the quantity of pizza demanded decreases.
    d. The quantity of pizza demanded decreases and the demand for tacos increases.
    e. The demand for each decreases because both are normal goods.

Complete the graph

Price (dollars per bundle of cotton candy)	Quantity (bundles of cotton candy per month)
1	10,000
2	8,000
3	7,000
4	4,000

1. The demand schedule for cotton candy is given in the following table. In Figure 4.4, draw the demand curve. Label the axes.
   a. If the price of cotton candy is $2 a bundle, what is the quantity demanded?

■ FIGURE 4.4

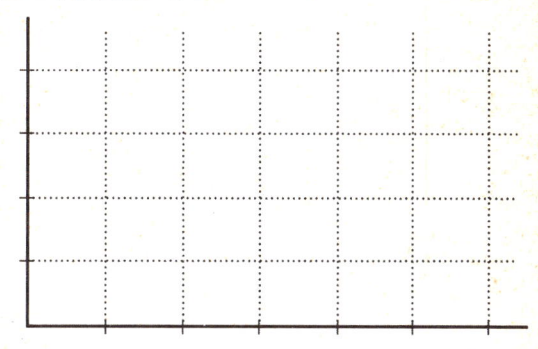

   b. If the price of cotton candy is $3 a bundle, what is the quantity demanded?
   c. Does the demand curve you drew slope upward or downward?

■ FIGURE 4.5
Price (dollars per pound of butter)

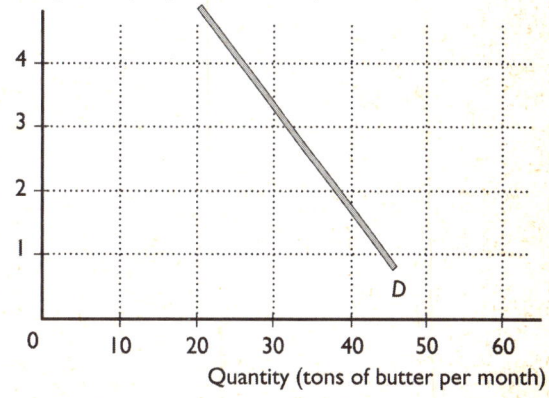

2. Butter is a normal good and margarine is substitute for butter. Figure 4.5 shows the demand curve for butter.
   a. In Figure 4.5, show how the demand curve shifts if incomes rise. Label this demand curve D_1.
   b. In Figure 4.5, show how the demand curve shifts if margarine falls in price. Label this demand curve D_2.
   c. If the price of butter falls from $4 a pound to $3 a pound, does the demand curve shift toward demand curve D_1, D_2, or neither? Explain your answer.

Short answer and numeric questions

Price (dollars per gallon)	Quantity demanded (gallons per week)
3.10	320
3.20	316
3.30	310
3.40	300
3.50	205

1. The table above gives the demand schedule for gasoline for a group of students. If the price of gasoline falls from $3.30 to $3.20 per gallon, how much gas will the students buy?
2. Explain the difference between a change in quantity demanded and a change in demand.
3. What is the difference between a movement along a demand curve and a shift in a demand curve?

CHECKPOINT 4.2

■ **Distinguish between quantity supplied and supply and explain what determines supply.**

Quick Review

- *Change in quantity supplied* A change in the quantity of a good that suppliers plan to sell that results from a change in the price of the good.
- *Change in supply* A change in the quantity that suppliers plan to sell when any influence on selling plans, other than the price of the good, changes. These other influences include: prices of related goods, prices of inputs, expectations, number of sellers, and productivity.

Additional Practice Problems 4.2

1. In the market for motor scooters, several events occur, one at a time. Explain the influence of each event on the quantity supplied of scooters and on the supply of scooters. Illustrate the effects of each event either by a movement along the supply curve or a shift in the supply curve and say which event (or events) illustrates the law of supply in action. These events are:
    a. The price of a scooter rises.
    b. The price of the steel used to make scooters rises.
    c. The number of firms making scooters decreases.
    d. Technological change increases the productivity of the factories making scooters.

Price (dollars per ton of plywood)	Quantity supplied (tons of plywood per month)			
	Eddy	Franco	George	Helen
100	2	2	1	1
75	2	1	1	1
50	1	1	1	0
25	0	0	1	0

■ **FIGURE 4.6**

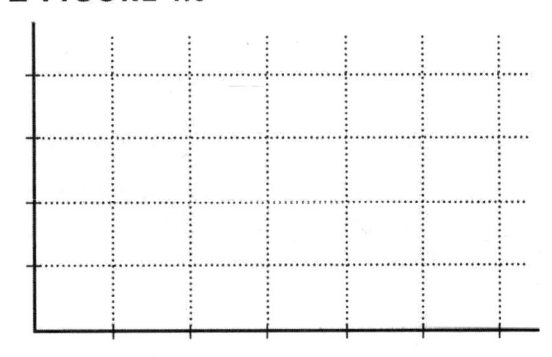

2. Each month Eddy, Franco, George, and Helen are willing and able to sell plywood as shown in the table above.
    a. Label the axes in Figure 4.6.
    b. Graph the market supply curve.

Solutions to Additional Practice Problems 4.2

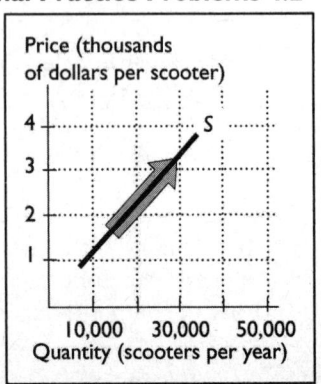

1a. This problem emphasizes the distinction between a change in the quantity supplied and a change in supply. A rise in the price of a motor scooter brings an increase in the quantity supplied of scooters, which is illustrated by a movement up along the supply curve for scooters as shown in the figure. There is no change in the supply and the supply curve does not shift. This event illustrates the law of supply in action.

1b. When the price of the steel used to make scooters rises, the cost to produce scooters increases. As a result, the supply of scooters decreases. The supply curve shifts leftward as illustrated.

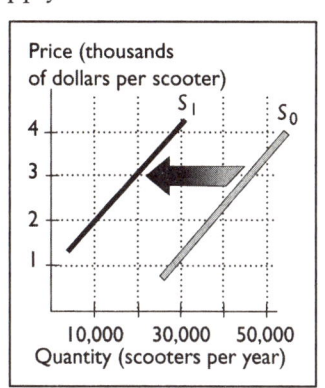

1c. A decrease in the number of firms producing scooters decreases the supply of scooters. The supply curve shifts leftward, as illustrated in the figure above.

1d. An increase in the productivity of the factories making scooters lowers the costs of producing scooters. The supply of scooters increases and the supply curve shifts rightward, as illustrated in the figure.

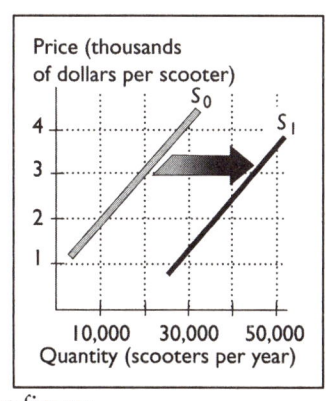

2a. The axes are labeled in Figure 4.7.

Price (dollars per ton of plywood)	Quantity supplied (tons per month)
100	6
75	5
50	3
25	1

2b. The market supply curve is derived by adding the quantities supplied by Eddy, Franco, George, and Helen at each price. The table above gives the resulting sum and the market supply curve is illustrated in Figure 4.7.

■ FIGURE 4.7
Price (dollars per ton of plywood)

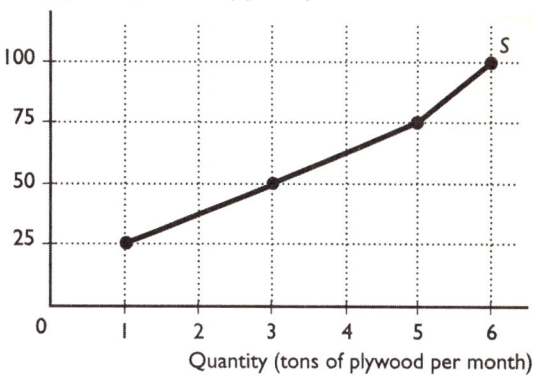

■ Self Test 4.2
Fill in the blanks

The ____ (quantity supplied; supply) of a good is the amount people are willing and able to sell during a specified period at a specified price. The law of supply states that other things remaining the same, if the price of a good rises, the quantity supplied ____. A supply curve is ____ (upward; downward) sloping. A change in the price of a good changes ____ (supply; the quantity supplied) and is illustrated by a ____ the supply curve. Factors that change supply are ____, ____, ____, ____, and ____.

True or false

1. The law of supply states that other things remaining the same, if the price of a good rises, the supply of the good increases.

2. When new technology for producing computers is used by manufacturers, the supply of computers increases.

3. If the wage rate paid to chefs rises and all other influences on selling plans remain the same, the supply of restaurant meals will increase.

4. If the price of coffee is expected to rise next month, the supply of coffee this month will decrease.

5. The supply of a good will increase and there will be a movement up along the supply curve of the good if the price of one of its substitutes in production falls.

Multiple choice

1. The quantity supplied of a good, service, or resource is ____ during a specified period and at a specified price.
   a. the amount that people are able to sell
   b. the amount that people are willing to sell
   c. the amount that people are able and willing to sell
   d. the amount that people are willing and able to buy
   e. the amount sold

2. One reason supply curves have an upward slope is because
   a. increased supply will require increased technology.
   b. people will pay a higher price when less is supplied.
   c. a higher price brings a greater profit, so firms want to sell more of that good.
   d. to have more of the good supplied requires more firms to open.
   e. None of the above answers is correct because supply curves have a downward slope.

3. Which of the following indicates that the law of supply applies to makers of soda?
   a. An increase in the price of a soda leads to an increase in the demand for soda.
   b. An increase in the price of a soda leads to an increase in the supply of soda.
   c. An increase in the price of a soda leads to an increase in the quantity of soda supplied.
   d. A decrease in the price of a soda leads to an increase in the quantity of soda demanded.
   e. A decrease in the price of a soda leads to an increase in the supply of soda.

4. The market supply curve is the ____ of the ____.
   a. horizontal sum; individual supply curves
   b. vertical sum; individual supply curves
   c. horizontal sum; individual supply curves minus the market demand
   d. vertical sum; individual supply curves minus the market demand
   e. vertical average; individual supply curves

5. If the costs to produce pizza increase, which will occur?
   a. The supply of pizza will decrease.
   b. The quantity of pizzas supplied will increase as sellers try to cover their costs.
   c. Pizza will cease to be produced and sold.
   d. The demand curve for pizza will shift leftward when the price of a pizza increases.
   e. The demand curve for pizza will shift rightward when the price of a pizza increases.

6. A rise in the price of a substitute in production for a good leads to
   a. an increase in the supply of that good.
   b. a decrease in the supply of that good.
   c. no change in the supply of that good.
   d. a decrease in the quantity of that good supplied.
   e. no change in either the supply or the quantity supplied of the good.

7. An increase in the productivity of producing jeans results in
   a. the quantity of jeans supplied increasing.
   b. the supply of jeans increasing.
   c. buyers demanding more jeans because they are now more efficiently produced.
   d. buyers demanding fewer jeans because their price will fall, which signals lower quality.
   e. some change but the impact on the supply of jeans is impossible to predict.

■ FIGURE 4.8
Price (dollars per pizza)

Complete the graph

Price (dollars per bundle of cotton candy)	Quantity (bundles of cotton candy per month)
1	4,000
2	8,000
3	10,000
4	12,000

1. The supply schedule for cotton candy is given in the table above. In Figure 4.4, you previously drew a demand curve for cotton candy. Now use the supply schedule to draw the supply curve in Figure 4.4.
   a. If the price of cotton candy is $2 a bundle, what is the quantity supplied?
   b. If the price of cotton candy is $3 a bundle, what is the quantity supplied?
   c. Does the supply curve you drew slope upward or downward?

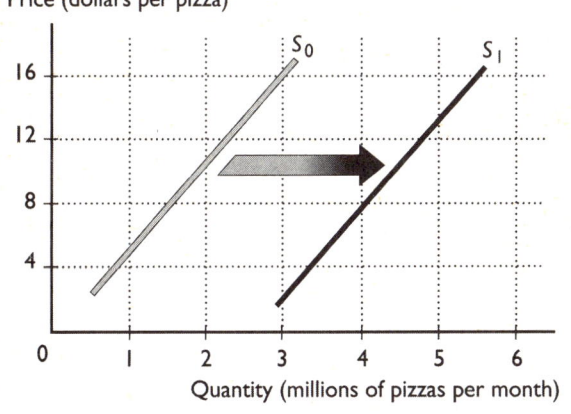

8. The shift of the supply curve of pizza illustrated in Figure 4.8 could be the result of
   a. a rise in the price of cheese used to produce pizza.
   b. a decrease in the number of firms producing pizza.
   c. an increase in the productivity of the firms producing pizza.
   d. a rise in the price of a substitute in production.
   e. a rise in the price of a pizza.

■ FIGURE 4.9
Price (dollars per ton of rubber bands)

9. The shift of the supply curve of pizza illustrated in Figure 4.8 could be the result of
   a. a rise in income if pizza is a normal good.
   b. a fall in the price of soda, a consumer complement for pizza.
   c. an increase in the number of firms producing pizza.
   d. a rise in the price of a pizza.
   e. a rise in the wage paid the workers who make pizza.

10. Suppose the price of leather used to produce shoes increases. As a result, there is ____ in the supply of shoes and the supply curve of shoes ____.
    a. an increase; shifts rightward
    b. an increase; shifts leftward
    c. a decrease; shifts rightward
    d. a decrease; shifts leftward
    e. no change; does not shift

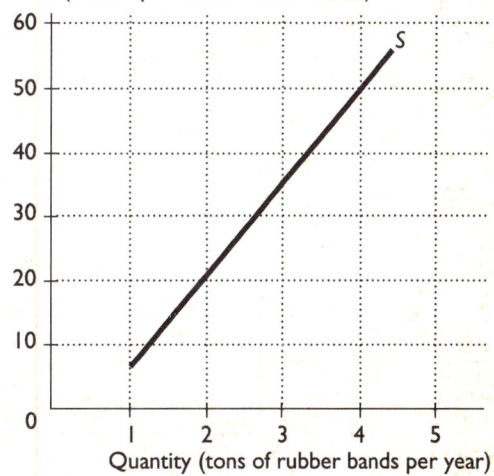

2. Figure 4.9 shows a supply curve for rubber bands. Suppose the productivity of producing rubber bands increases. In Figure 4.9, illustrate the effect of this event.

FIGURE 4.10
Price (dollars per ton of copper)

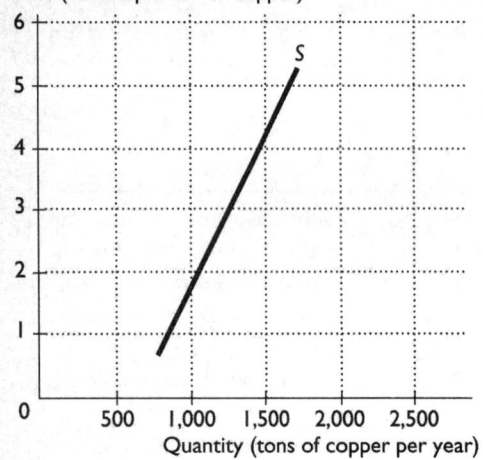

3. Figure 4.10 shows the supply curve for copper. The cost of the natural gas used to refine copper ore into copper rises. In Figure 4.10, show the effect of this event.

Short answer and numeric questions
1. What is the law of supply?

Price	Quantity supplied (pizza per day)			
(dollars per pizza)	Tom	Bob	Kate	Market supply
14	20	12	15	___
12	16	10	10	___
10	12	8	5	___
8	8	6	0	___

2. The table gives the supply schedules for the three pizza producers in a small town. Calculate the market supply schedule.
3. What influence(s) lead to a change in the quantity supplied?
4. What influences lead to a change in supply?

CHECKPOINT 4.3

■ **Explain how demand and supply determine the price and quantity in a market and explain the effects of changes in demand and supply.**

Quick Review
- *Market equilibrium* When the quantity demanded equals the quantity supplied.

Additional Practice Problems 4.3
1. Hot dogs are an inferior good and people's incomes rise. What happens to the equilibrium price and quantity of hot dogs?
2. Hot dog producers develop new technology that increases their productivity. What happens to the price and quantity of hot dogs?
3. The price of a hot dog bun falls and, simultaneously, the number of hot dog producers increases. The effect of the fall in the price of a hot dog bun is less than the effect of the increase in the number of producers. What happens to the equilibrium price and quantity of hot dogs?

Solutions to Additional Practice Problems 4.3
1. When income increases, the demand for an inferior good decreases and the demand curve shifts leftward. The supply does not change and the supply curve does not shift. The equilibrium price of a hot dog falls and the equilibrium quantity decreases, as illustrated in the figure.

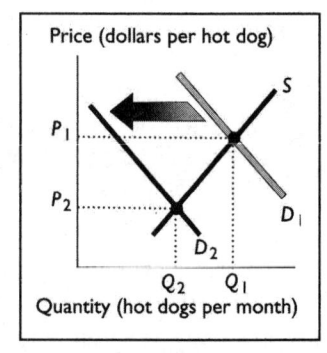

2. When the productivity of producing a good increases, the supply of the good increases and the supply curve shifts rightward. So the supply curve of hot dogs shifts rightward. The demand does not change and so the demand curve does not shift. As illustrated, the price of a hot dog falls and the quantity increases.

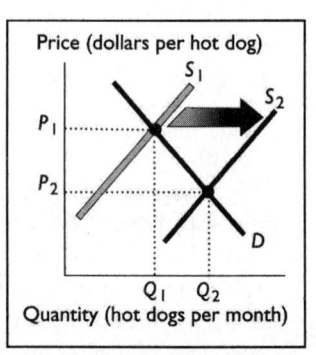

3. The fall in the price of a complement, hot dog buns, increases the demand for hot dogs and the demand curve for hot dogs shifts rightward. The increase in the number of producers increases the supply of hot dogs and the supply curve shifts rightward. Because the increase in supply exceeds the increase in demand, the price of a hot dog falls and the quantity increases, as shown in the figure.

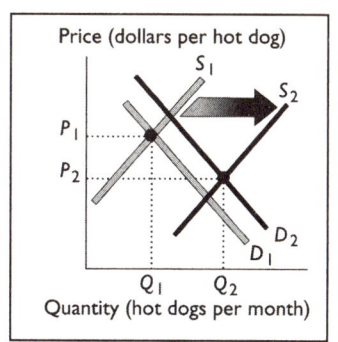

■ Self Test 4.3

Fill in the blanks

The price at which the quantity demanded equals the quantity supplied is the ____. In a diagram, the ____ is determined where the supply and demand curves intersect. If the price exceeds the equilibrium price, the price ____ (rises; falls). An increase in demand ____ (raises; lowers) the equilibrium price and ____ (increases; decreases) the equilibrium quantity. An increase in supply ____ (raises; lowers) the equilibrium price and ____ (increases; decreases) the equilibrium quantity. If both the demand and supply increase, definitely the equilibrium ____ increases but the effect on the equilibrium ____ is ambiguous.

True or false

1. If the price of asparagus is below the equilibrium price, there is a shortage of asparagus and the price of asparagus will rise until the shortage disappears.
2. When the demand for skateboards decreases and the supply of skateboards remains unchanged, the quantity supplied of skateboards decreases as the price rises.
3. Gasoline refiners expect the price of oil will fall next month. If the supply of oil does not change, the equilibrium price of oil today falls and the equilibrium quantity today decreases.
4. As summer comes to an end and winter sets in, the demand for and supply of hamburger buns decrease. The price of a hamburger bun definitely remains the same.
5. The number of buyers of grapefruit juice increases and at the same time severe frost decreases the supply of grapefruit juice. The price of grapefruit juice will rise.

Multiple choice

1. The equilibrium price of a good occurs if the
   a. quantity of the good demanded equals the quantity of the good supplied.
   b. quantity of the good demanded is greater than the quantity of the good supplied.
   c. quantity of the good demanded is less than the quantity of the good supplied.
   d. demand for the good is equal to the supply of the good.
   e. price of the good seems reasonable to most buyers.

2. Which of the following is correct?
   i. A surplus puts downward pressure on the price of a good.
   ii. A shortage puts upward pressure on the price of a good
   iii. There is no surplus or shortage at equilibrium.
   a. i and ii..
   b. i and iii.
   c. ii and iii.
   d. i, ii, and iii.
   e. only iii.

3. The number of buyers of ceiling fans increases, so there is an increase in the
   a. quantity of ceiling fans demanded and a surplus of ceiling fans.
   b. demand for ceiling fans and a rise in the price of a ceiling fan.
   c. demand for ceiling fans and a surplus of ceiling fans.
   d. supply of ceiling fans and no change in the price of a ceiling fan.
   e. demand for ceiling fans and in the supply of ceiling fans.

4. Which of the following is the best explanation for why the price of gasoline increases during the summer months?
   a. Oil producers have higher costs of production in the summer.
   b. Sellers have to earn profits during the summer to cover losses in the winter.
   c. There is increased driving by families going on vacation.
   d. There is less competition among oil refineries in the summer.
   e. The number of gas stations open 24 hours a day rises in the summer months and so the price must rise to cover the higher costs.

5. Suppose that the price of lettuce used to produce tacos increases. As a result, the equilibrium price of a taco ____ and the equilibrium quantity ____.
   a. rises; increases
   b. rises; decreases
   c. falls; increases
   d. falls; decreases
   e. does not change; decreases

6. The technology associated with manufacturing computers has advanced enormously. This change has led to the price of a computer ____ and the quantity ____.
   a. rising; increasing
   b. rising; decreasing
   c. falling; increasing
   d. falling; decreasing
   e. falling; not changing

7. Candy makers accurately anticipate the increase in demand for candy for Halloween so that the supply of candy and the demand for candy increase the same amount. As a result, the price of candy ____ and the quantity of candy ____.
   a. rises; does not change
   b. falls; increases
   c. does not change; increases
   d. does not change; does not change
   e. rises; rises

8. During 2007 the supply of petroleum decreased while at the same time the demand for petroleum increased. If the magnitude of the increase in demand was greater than the magnitude of the decrease in supply, then the equilibrium price of gasoline ____ and the equilibrium quantity ____.
   a. increased; increased
   b. increased; decreased
   c. increased; did not change
   d. decreased; did not change
   e. did not change; increased

Complete the graph

1. In Checkpoint 4.1 you drew a demand curve in Figure 4.4; in Checkpoint 4.2, you drew a supply curve in that figure. Return to Figure 4.4 and answer the following questions.
   a. If the price of cotton candy is $1, what is the situation in the market?
   b. If the price of cotton candy is $3, what is the situation in the market?
   c. What is the equilibrium price and equilibrium quantity of cotton candy?

Price (dollars per sweatshirt)	Quantity demanded (sweatshirts per season) Hockey team	Quantity demanded (sweatshirts per season) Soccer team	Quantity supplied (sweatshirts per season)
35	5	8	32
30	6	9	25
25	8	11	19
20	12	15	12
15	17	20	8

2. The table gives the demand and supply schedules for sweatshirts. What is the market demand schedule? At what price will the quantity demanded be equal to the quantity supplied? What is the equilibrium quantity?

■ FIGURE 4.11
Price (dollars per piece of gold jewelry)

[Graph showing supply and demand curves for gold jewelry, with equilibrium at approximately 600 thousand pieces and $1,000]

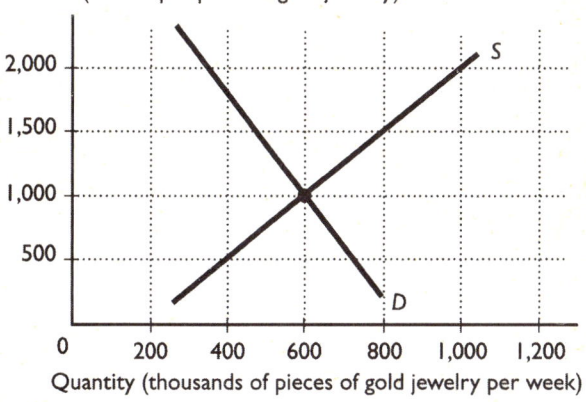

3. Figure 4.11 shows the supply and demand for gold jewelry. In the figure, show what happens to the price and quantity if gold jewelry is a normal good and people's incomes rise.

■ FIGURE 4.12
Price (dollars per piece of gold jewelry)

[Graph showing supply and demand curves for gold jewelry, with equilibrium at approximately 600 thousand pieces and $1,000]

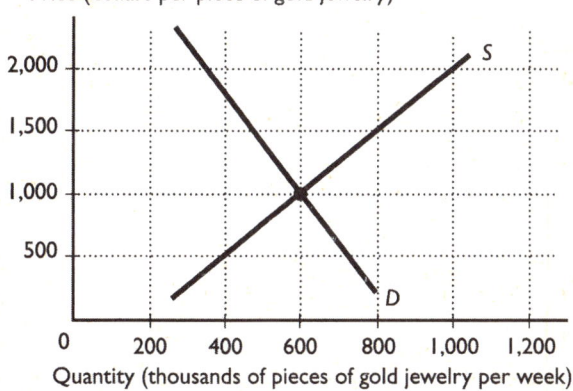

4. Figure 4.12 shows the supply and demand for gold jewelry. Suppose that consumers think that silver jewelry is a substitute for gold jewelry. In Figure 4.12, show what happens to the price and quantity if the price of silver jewelry falls.

■ FIGURE 4.13
Price (dollars per piece of gold jewelry)

[Graph showing supply and demand curves for gold jewelry, with equilibrium at approximately 600 thousand pieces and $1,000]

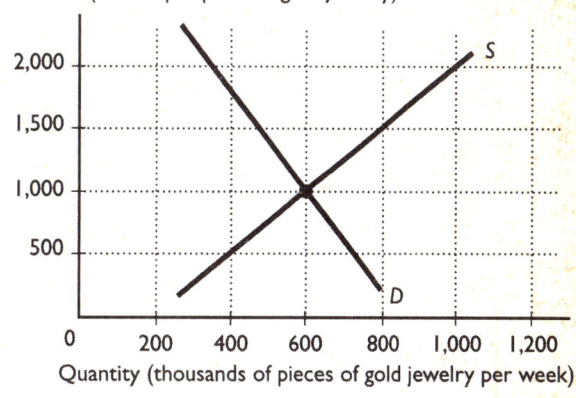

5. Figure 4.13 shows the supply and demand for gold jewelry. Suppose the price of the gold that is used to produce gold jewelry rises. In the figure, show what happens to the price and quantity of gold jewelry.

Short answer and numeric questions

1. How is a shortage different from a surplus?
2. People read that drinking orange juice helps prevent heart disease. What is the effect on the equilibrium price and quantity of orange juice?
3. The cost of memory chips used in computers falls. What is the effect on the equilibrium price and quantity of computers?
4. New cars are a normal good and people's incomes increase. Simultaneously, auto manufacturers must pay more for their workers' health insurance. What is the effect on the price and quantity of new cars?
5. The Eye on Your Life on page 105 points out that supply and demand will be a big part of your life. How can you use the model to make day-to-day decisions, such as when to buy gasoline?

SELF TEST ANSWERS

■ CHECKPOINT 4.1

Fill in the blanks

The <u>law of demand</u> states that other things remaining the same, if the price of a good rises, the <u>quantity demanded of</u> that good decreases. A <u>demand curve</u> is a graph of the relationship between the quantity demanded of a good and its price. Demand curves are <u>downward</u> sloping. An increase in demand shifts the demand curve <u>rightward</u>. Factors that change demand lead to a <u>shift of</u> the demand curve. Factors that change demand are <u>prices of related goods</u>, <u>income</u>, <u>expectations</u>, <u>number of buyers</u>, and <u>preferences</u>.

True or false
1. False; page 85
2. False; page 84
3. True; page 89
4. False; page 89
5. False; page 90

Multiple choice
1. d; page 85
2. b; page 85
3. a; page 89
4. c; page 89
5. a; page 89
6. a; page 89
7. b; page 89
8. d; page 90
9. d; page 90
10. d; page 89-90

Complete the graph
1. a. Figure 4.14 illustrates the demand curve, labeled D in the diagram. (The supply curve is from the first "Complete the Graph" question in Checkpoint 4.2.)
   a. 8,000 bundles per month
   b. 7,000 bundles per month
   c. The demand curve slopes downward; pages 90.

■ **FIGURE 4.14**
Price (dollars per bundle of cotton candy)

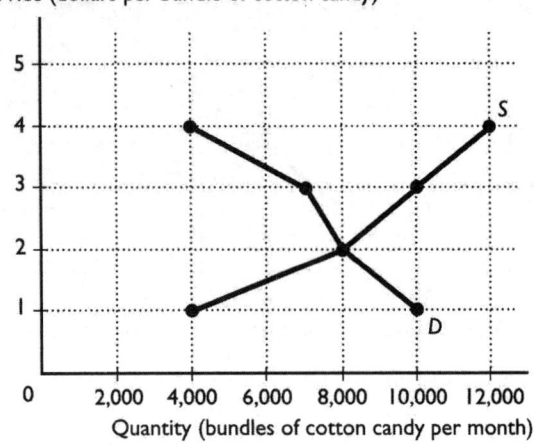

■ **FIGURE 4.15**
Price (dollars per pound of butter)

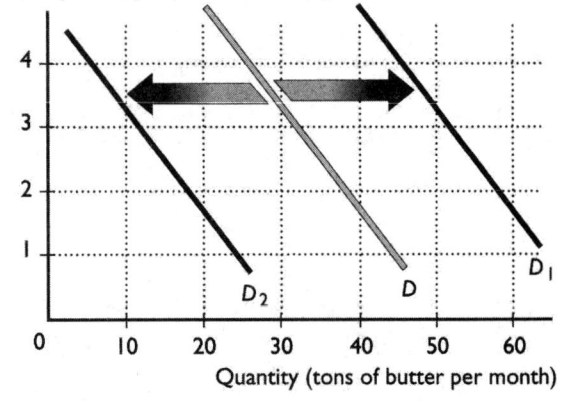

2. a. The demand increases and the demand curve shifts rightward, as shown in Figure 4.15 by the shift to D_1; page 90
   b. The demand decreases and the demand curve shifts leftward, as shown in Figure 4.15 by the shift to D_2; page 90
   c. The demand curve does not shift. The fall in the price of butter leads to an increase in the quantity demanded and a movement along the demand curve, not a shift of the demand curve; page 90.

Short answer and numeric questions
1. When the price falls from $3.30 a gallon to $3.20 a gallon, the quantity of gasoline de-

manded increases from 310 gallons to 316 gallons; page 86.

2. A change in the quantity demanded occurs when the price of the good changes. A change in demand occurs when any other influence on buying plans other than the price of the good changes; page 88.

3. A movement along a demand curve reflects a change in the quantity demanded and is the result of a change in the price of the product. A shift in a demand curve reflects a change in demand and is the result of a change in any factor, other than the price, that affects demand; page 90.

■ CHECKPOINT 4.2

Fill in the blanks

The <u>quantity supplied</u> of a good is the amount people are willing and able to sell during a specified period at a specified price. The law of supply states that other things remaining the same, if the price of a good rises, the quantity supplied <u>increases</u>. A supply curve is <u>upward</u> sloping. A change in the price of a good changes <u>the quantity supplied</u> and is illustrated by a <u>movement along</u> the supply curve. Factors that change supply are <u>prices of related goods</u>, <u>prices of resources and other inputs</u>, <u>expectations</u>, <u>number of sellers</u>, and <u>productivity</u>.

True or false

1. False; page 92
2. True; page 96
3. False; page 96
4. True; page 96
5. False; page 96

Multiple choice

1. c; page 92
2. c; page 92
3. c; page 92
4. a; page 94
5. a; page 96
6. b; page 96
7. b; page 96
8. c; page 96
9. c; page 96
10. d; page 97

Complete the graph

1. The supply curve is illustrated in Figure 4.14, labeled S in the diagram.
   a. 8,000 bundles per month.
   b. 10,000 bundles per month.
   c. The supply curve slopes upward; page 93.

■ **FIGURE 4.16**

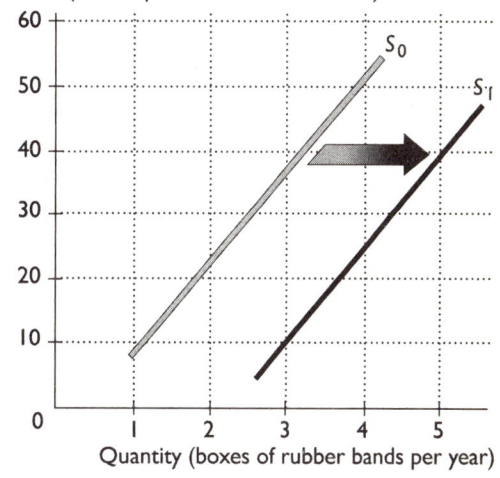

2. Figure 4.16 illustrates the shift; pages 96-97.

■ **FIGURE 4.17**

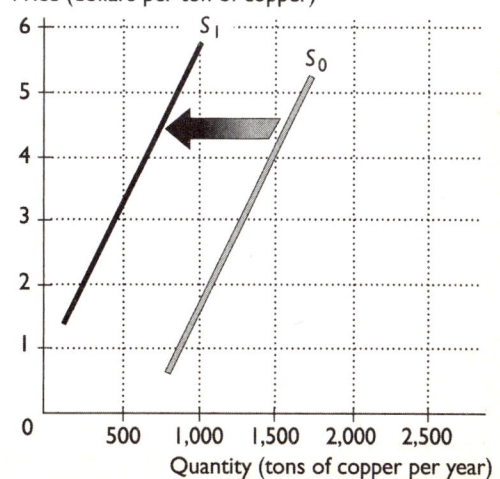

3. Figure 4.17 illustrates the shift; pages 96-97.

Short answer and numeric questions

1. If other things remain the same, when the price of a good or service falls (rises), sellers decrease (increase) the quantity they supply. page 92.

Price (dollars per pizza)	Market supply (pizzas per day)
14	47
12	36
10	25
8	14

2. The market supply schedule is in the last column in the table above; page 94.
3. Change in the price of the product; page 97.
4. Changes in: prices of related goods; prices of resources and other inputs; expectations; number of sellers; and productivity; page 97.

■ CHECKPOINT 4.3

Fill in the blanks

The price at which the quantity demanded equals the quantity supplied is the <u>equilibrium price</u>. In a diagram, the <u>equilibrium</u> <u>price</u> is determined where the supply and demand curves intersect. If the price exceeds the equilibrium price, the price <u>falls</u>. An increase in demand <u>raises</u> the equilibrium price and <u>increases</u> the equilibrium quantity. An increase in supply <u>lowers</u> the equilibrium price and <u>increases</u> the equilibrium quantity. If both the demand and supply increase, definitely the equilibrium <u>quantity</u> increases but the effect on the equilibrium <u>price</u> is ambiguous.

True or false

1. True; page 99
2. False; page 101
3. True; page 102
4. False; page 104
5. True; page 104

Multiple choice

1. a; page 99
2. d; page 100
3. b; page 101
4. c; page 101
5. b; page 102
6. c; page 102
7. c; page 104
8. a; page 104

Complete the graph

1. a. A shortage of 6,000 bundles a month; page 100.
    b. A surplus of 3,000 bundles a month; page 100.
    c. The equilibrium price is $2 a bundle of cotton candy and the equilibrium quantity is 8,000 bundles a month; page 100.

Price (dollars per sweatshirt)	Quantity demanded (sweatshirts per season)
35	13
30	15
25	19
20	27
15	37

2. The market demand schedule is obtained by summing the Hockey team's demand and the Soccer team's demand and is in the table above. The price that equates the quantity demanded to the quantity supplied is $25 and the equilibrium quantity is 19 sweatshirts; page 100.

■ FIGURE 4.18
Price (dollars per piece of gold jewelry)

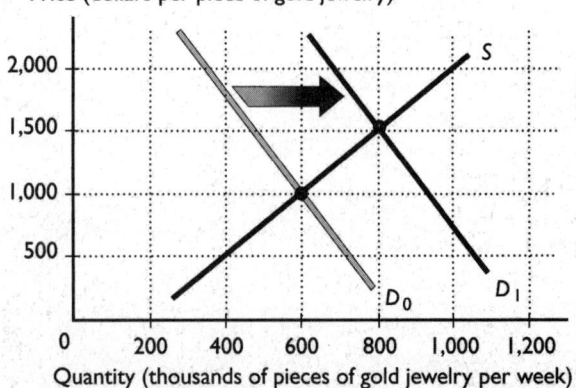

3. Figure 4.18 shows the effect of the increase in income. The increase in income increases the demand for normal goods, such as gold jew-

elry. The demand curve shifts rightward and the supply curve does not shift. The price of gold jewelry rises, to $1,500 in the figure, and the quantity increases, to 800 pieces per week in the figure; page 101.

■ **FIGURE 4.19**
Price (dollars per piece of gold jewelry)

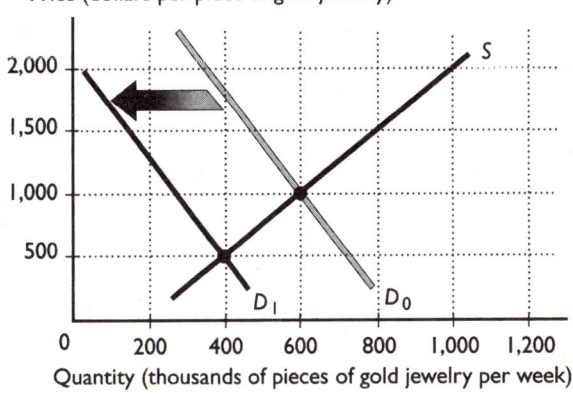

4. Figure 4.19 shows the effect of the fall in price of silver jewelry. A fall in the price of a substitute decreases the demand gold jewelry. The demand curve shifts leftward and the supply curve does not shift. The price of gold jewelry falls, to $500 in the figure, and the quantity decreases, to 400 pieces per week in the figure; page 101.

■ **FIGURE 4.20**
Price (dollars per piece of gold jewelry)

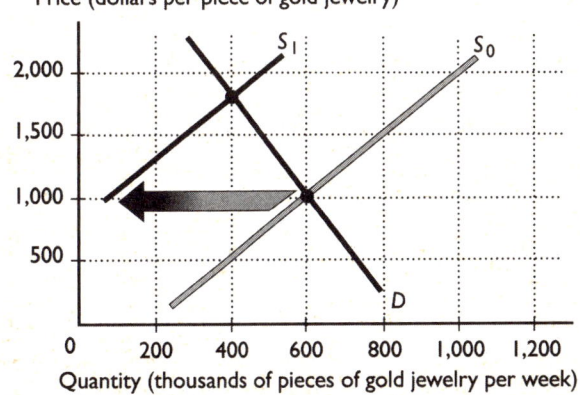

5. Figure 4.20 shows the effect of the fall in the price of gold. The price of gold is a cost to the producers of gold jewelry. A rise in the cost decreases the supply of the good. The supply curve shifts leftward and the demand curve does not shift. The price of gold jewelry rises, to $1,750 in the figure, and the quantity decreases, to 400 pieces per week in the figure; page 102.

Short answer and numeric questions

1. When a shortage exists, the price of the good is below the equilibrium price. The quantity demanded is greater than the quantity supplied. When a surplus exists, the price of the good is above the equilibrium price. The quantity demanded is less than the quantity supplied; page 100.

2. The increase in preferences increases the demand for orange juice and the demand curve shifts rightward. The price of orange juice rises and the quantity increases; page 101.

3. The fall in cost increases the supply of computers. The supply curve of computers shifts rightward. The price falls and the quantity increases; page 102.

4. The increase in income increases the demand for normal goods and shifts the demand curve for new cars rightward. The increase in health insurance premiums decreases the supply of new cars and shifts the supply curve of new cars leftward. The price of a new car definitely rises. The effect on the quantity is ambiguous: it rises if the demand effect is larger, falls if the supply effect is larger, and does not change if the two effects are the same size; page 104.

5. You can use supply and demand to determine if you want to buy gasoline immediately or perhaps hold off for a few days. For instance, if you read that a hurricane threatens oil derricks in the Gulf of Mexico, you can reason that if the hurricane actually strikes, the supply of oil will decrease and price of oil will soar. In this case, you ought to fill up your car today to beat the potential of paying a higher price next week.

Chapter 5

Elasticities of Demand and Supply

CHAPTER CHECKLIST

In Chapter 5 we study the price elasticity of demand, the price elasticity of supply, the cross elasticity of demand, and the income elasticity of demand.

1. Define, explain the factors that influence, and calculate the price elasticity of demand.

The price elasticity of demand is a measure of the extent to which the quantity demanded of a good changes when the price of the good changes and all other influences on buyers' plans remain the same. The price elasticity of demand equals the percentage change in the quantity demanded divided by the percentage change in price, with the negative sign ignored. Demand is elastic if the percentage change in the quantity demanded exceeds the percentage change in price. Demand is unit elastic if the percentage change in the quantity demanded equals the percentage change in price. Demand is inelastic if the percentage change in the quantity demanded is less than the percentage change in price. Elasticity is a *units-free* measure. Along a linear demand curve demand is unit elastic at the midpoint of the curve, demand is elastic at all points above the midpoint of the curve, and demand is inelastic at all points below the midpoint of the curve. The total revenue from the sale of a good equals the price of the good multiplied by the quantity sold. If a price change changes total revenue in the opposite direction, demand is elastic. If a price change leaves total revenue unchanged, demand is unit elastic. If a price change changes total revenue in the same direction, demand is inelastic.

2. Define, explain the factors that influence, and calculate the price elasticity of supply.

The price elasticity of supply is a measure of the extent to which the quantity supplied of a good changes when the price of the good changes and all other influences on sellers' plans remain the same. The two main influences on the price elasticity of supply are production possibilities and storage possibilities. If the good can be stored, supply is more elastic. The price elasticity of supply equals the percentage change in the quantity supplied divided by the percentage change in the price. If the price elasticity of supply is greater than 1, supply is elastic. If the price elasticity of supply equals 1, supply is unit elastic. If the price elasticity of supply is less than 1, supply is inelastic.

3. Define and explain the factors that influence the cross elasticity of demand and the income elasticity of demand.

The cross elasticity of demand is a measure of the responsiveness of the demand for a good to a change in the price of a substitute or complement, other things remaining the same. The cross elasticity of demand is positive for substitutes and negative for complements. The income elasticity of demand is a measure of the responsiveness of the demand for a good to a change in income changes, other things remaining the same. The income elasticity of demand is positive for a normal good and negative for an inferior good.

CHECKPOINT 5.1

■ **Define, explain the factors that influence, and calculate the price elasticity of demand.**

Quick Review

- *Price elasticity of demand* The price elasticity of demand equals the magnitude of the percentage change in the quantity demanded divided by the percentage change in the price.
- *Elastic demand* When the percentage change in the quantity demanded exceeds the percentage change in price. The elasticity of demand is greater than 1 in value.
- *Inelastic demand* When the percentage change in the quantity demanded is less than the percentage change in price. The elasticity of demand is less than 1 in value.
- *Factors affecting elasticity* The demand for a good is more elastic if a substitute is easy to find. The factors that influence the ability to find a substitute for a good are whether the good is a luxury or a necessity, how narrowly it is defined, and the amount of time available to find a substitute for it.

Additional Practice Problems 5.1

1. For each of the following price changes, calculate the price elasticity of demand. Is the demand elastic, unit elastic, or inelastic?
   a. A 10 percent increase in price results in a 5 percent decrease in the quantity demanded.
   b. A 6 percent increase in price results in a 12 percent decrease in the quantity demanded.
   c. A 4 percent increase in price results in a 4 percent decrease in the quantity demanded.

Price (dollars per bag of cat food)	Quantity (bags of cat food per year)	Total revenue (dollars)
5	4	___
4	8	___
3	12	___
2	16	___
1	20	___

2. The table above gives the demand schedule for bags of cat food. A graph of this demand schedule gives a linear demand curve.
   a. Finish the table by calculating the total revenue for each row.
   b. When is the demand elastic? inelastic? unit elastic?
   c. Explain your answers to part (b).

Solutions to Additional Practice Problems 5.1

1a. The price elasticity of demand equals the magnitude of the percentage change in the quantity demanded divided by the percentage change in the price. So the elasticity of demand equals (5 percent) ÷ (10 percent) = 0.5. Because the elasticity of demand is less than 1, demand is inelastic.

1b. The price elasticity of demand equals (12 percent) ÷ (6 percent) = 2.0. Because the elasticity of demand is greater than 1, demand is elastic.

1c. The price elasticity of demand equals (4 percent) ÷ (4 percent) = 1.0. Because the elasticity of demand equals 1, demand is unit elastic.

Price (dollars per bag of cat food)	Quantity (bags of cat food per year)	Total revenue (dollars)
5	4	20
4	8	32
3	12	36
2	16	32
1	20	20

2a. The completed table is above. Total revenue equals the price times the quantity sold.

2b. The demand is elastic at prices greater than $3 a bag. The demand is inelastic at prices less than $3 a bag. The demand is unit elastic at a price of $3 a bag.

2c. Demand is unit elastic at the midpoint of the demand curve. When demand is unit elastic, a price change leaves total revenue unchanged. The midpoint of the curve occurs when the price is $3 a bag, so demand is unit elastic at a price of $3 a bag.

Demand is elastic at all points above the midpoint of the demand curve. So when the price is greater than $3 a bag, demand is elastic. When demand is elastic, price and total revenue change in opposite directions. For example, when the price *rises* from $4 to $5, total revenue *decreases* from $32 to $20.

Demand is inelastic at all points below the midpoint of the demand curve. So when the price is less than $3 a bag, demand is inelastic. When demand is inelastic, price and total revenue change in the same direction. For example, when the price *rises* from $1 to $2, total revenue *increases* from $20 to $32.

■ Self Test 5.1

Fill in the blanks

To calculate the percentage change in price, the midpoint formula divides the change in price by the ____ (initial price; new price; average of the initial and the new price) and then multiplies by 100. If the percentage change in the quantity demanded exceeds the percentage change in the price, demand is ____ (elastic; inelastic). The demand for a product is more elastic if there are ____ (more; fewer) substitutes for it. The demand for a necessity is generally ____ (elastic; inelastic). The price elasticity of demand equals the percentage change in the ____ (price; quantity demanded) divided by the percentage change in the ____ (price; quantity demanded). Moving along a straight-line demand curve, the slope ____ (is constant; varies) and the elasticity ____ (is constant; varies). If demand is elastic, an increase in price ____ (increases; decreases) total revenue.

True or false

1. The price elasticity of demand equals the magnitude of the slope of the demand curve.

2. If the price increases by 10 percent and the quantity demanded decreases by 8 percent, the price elasticity of demand equals 1.25.

3. As the price of a good increases, if the quantity demanded of it remains the same, then demand for the good is perfectly inelastic.

4. Above the midpoint of a straight-line demand curve, demand is elastic.

5. When the price of a service increases by 5 percent and the quantity demanded decreases by 5 percent, total revenue remains unchanged.

6. If the price of tuna increases by 5 percent and the total revenue of tuna producers increases, then the demand for tuna is inelastic.

Multiple choice

1. The price elasticity of demand is a measure of the extent to which the quantity demanded of a good changes when ____ changes and all other influences on buyers' plans remain the same.
    a. income
    b. the price of a related good
    c. the price of the good
    d. the demand alone
    e. both the demand and supply simultaneously

2. Suppose the price of a movie falls from $9 to $7. Using the midpoint method, what is the percentage change in price?
    a. 33 percent
    b. –33 percent
    c. 25 percent
    d. –25 percent
    e. –97 percent

3. Suppose the price of a tie rises from $45 to $55. Using the midpoint method, what is the percentage change in price?
    a. 10 percent
    b. –10 percent
    c. 20 percent
    d. –20 percent
    e. 100 percent

4. Demand is elastic if
   a. consumers respond strongly to changes in the product's price.
   b. a large percentage change in price brings about a small percentage change in quantity demanded.
   c. a small percentage change in price brings about a small percentage change in quantity demanded.
   d. the quantity demanded is not responsive to price changes.
   e. the demand curve is vertical.

5. During the winter of 2000–2001, the price of electric power increased enormously in California but the quantity demanded decreased only a little. This response indicates that the demand for electric power in California was
   a. inelastic.
   b. elastic.
   c. unit elastic.
   d. perfectly elastic.
   e. perfectly inelastic.

6. If substitutes for a good are readily available, the demand for that good
   a. does not change substantially if the price rises.
   b. does not change substantially if the price falls.
   c. is inelastic.
   d. is elastic.
   e. Both answers (a) and (b) are correct.

7. If the price of a product increases by 5 percent and the quantity demanded decreases by 5 percent, then the elasticity of demand is
   a. 0.
   b. 1.
   c. indeterminate.
   d. 5.
   e. 25.

8. The price of a bag of pretzels rises from $2 to $3 and the quantity demanded decreases from 100 to 60. What is the price elasticity of demand?
   a. 1.0
   b. 1.25
   c. 40.0
   d. 20.0
   e. 0.80

9. When a firm raises the price of its product, what happens to total revenue?
   a. If demand is elastic, total revenue decreases.
   b. If demand is unit elastic, total revenue increases.
   c. If demand is inelastic, total revenue decreases.
   d. If demand is elastic, total revenue increases.
   e. If demand is unit elastic, total revenue decreases.

Complete the graph

■ **FIGURE 5.1**

1. In Figure 5.1, label the axes and then draw a demand curve for a good that has a perfectly elastic demand.

■ **FIGURE 5.2**

2. In Figure 5.2, label the axes and then draw a demand curve for a good that has a perfectly inelastic demand.

■ **FIGURE 5.3**

Price (dollars per unit)

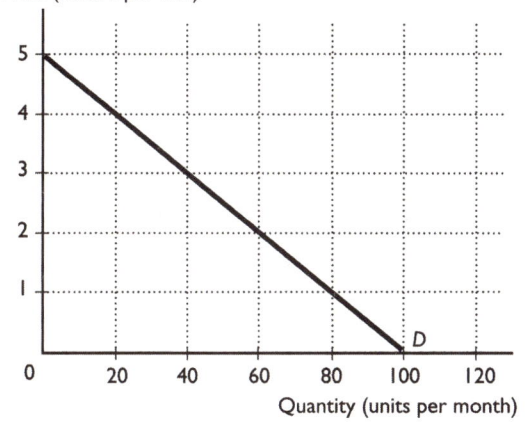

3. In Figure 5.3, darken the part of the demand curve along which demand is elastic. Label the point on the demand curve at which demand is unit elastic.

Short answer and numeric questions

	Percentage change in price	Percentage change in quantity demanded	Price elasticity of demand
A	5	10	____
B	8	4	____
C	3	0	____
D	6	6	____
E	1	8	____

1. Complete the table above by calculating the price elasticity of demand.
   a. Which row has the most elastic demand?
   b. Which row has the least elastic demand?

2. Suppose the price elasticity of demand for oil is 0.3. If the quantity of oil decreases by 6 percent, what is the effect on the price of oil?

3. What does it mean when the demand for a good is inelastic?

4. What is the relationship between how narrowly a good is defined and the number of substitutes it has?

5. The Eye on Your Life explains how you can use elasticity in your personal life. You can also use it in your business life. Suppose you are a brand manager for Crest toothpaste and you are thinking about raising its price. How will this price hike affect the total revenue from sales of Crest?

CHECKPOINT 5.2

■ **Define, explain the factors that influence, and calculate the price elasticity of supply.**

Quick Review
- *Price elasticity of supply* A measure of the extent to which the quantity supplied of a good changes when the price of the good changes and all other influences on sellers' plans remain the same.

Additional Practice Problems 5.2

1. For each of the following price changes, calculate the price elasticity of supply.
   a. A 10 percent increase in price results in a 15 percent increase in the quantity supplied.
   b. A 6 percent increase in price results in a 3 percent increase in the quantity supplied.
   c. A 7 percent increase in price results in a 7 percent increase in the quantity supplied.

2. Over one month the elasticity of supply of avocados is 0.1 and over 5 years the elasticity of supply of avocados is 2.0. If the price of avocados rises 10 percent, what is the increase in the quantity supplied in one month and in 5 years? Why is there a difference in the quantities?

Solutions to Additional Practice Problems 5.2

1a. The elasticity of supply equals the percentage change in the quantity supplied divided by the percentage change in price, which is (15 percent) ÷ (10 percent) = 1.5.

1b. The elasticity of supply equals (3 percent) ÷ (6 percent) = 0.5.

1c. The elasticity of supply equals (7 percent) ÷ (7 percent) = 1.0.

2. The increase in the quantity supplied equals the percentage change in the price times the elasticity of supply. In one month the quantity supplied increases by (10 percent) × (0.1), which is 1 percent. In 5 years the quantity supplied increases by (10 percent) × (2.0), which is 20 percent. The increase in the quantity supplied is much greater after 5 years because more changes can be made as more time passes. Existing avocado trees can be more carefully cultivated and additional fertilizer used. Eventually additional avocado trees can be planted, mature, and then be harvested. The supply of avocados increases as time passes, making the supply more elastic.

■ Self Test 5.2

Fill in the blanks

When supply has a vertical supply curve, then the supply of the good is perfectly ____ (elastic; inelastic). Goods that can be produced at an almost constant opportunity cost have an ____ (elastic; inelastic) supply. As time passes, the elasticity of supply ____ (increases; decreases). The price elasticity of supply equals the percentage change in the ____ (price; quantity supplied) divided by the percentage change in the ____ (price; quantity supplied). If the elasticity of supply is greater than 1, supply is ____ (elastic; inelastic).

True or false

1. If the percentage change in the quantity supplied is zero when the price changes, supply is perfectly elastic.

2. Goods that can be produced at a constant (or very gently rising) opportunity cost have an elastic supply.

3. The supply of apples is perfectly elastic on the day of a price change.

4. The supply of a storable good is perfectly inelastic.

5. When the price of a pizza is $20, 10 pizzas are supplied and when the price rises to $30 a pizza, 14 pizzas are supplied. The price elasticity of supply of pizzas is 0.83.

6. If a 5 percent increase in price increases the quantity supplied by 10 percent, the elasticity of supply equals 2.0.

Multiple choice

1. The price elasticity of supply is a measure of the extent to which the quantity supplied of a good changes when only the
   a. cost of producing the product increases.
   b. quantity of the good demanded increases.
   c. supply increases.
   d. price of the good changes.
   e. number of firms changes.

2. When the percentage change in the quantity supplied exceeds the percentage change in price, then supply is
   a. elastic.
   b. inelastic.
   c. unit elastic.
   d. perfectly inelastic.
   e. perfectly elastic.

3. The supply of beachfront property on St. Simon's Island is
   a. elastic.
   b. unit elastic.
   c. negative.
   d. inelastic.
   e. perfectly elastic.

4. For a product with a rapidly increasing opportunity cost of producing additional units,
   a. demand is price elastic.
   b. supply is price elastic.
   c. demand is price inelastic.
   d. supply is price inelastic.
   e. the demand curve is vertical.

Chapter 5 • Elasticities of Demand and Supply

5. The greater the amount of time that passes after a price change, the
   a. less elastic supply becomes.
   b. more elastic supply becomes.
   c. more negative supply becomes.
   d. steeper the supply curve becomes.
   e. more vertical the supply curve becomes.

6. The price elasticity of supply equals the percentage change in the
   a. quantity demanded divided by the percentage change in the price of a substitute or complement.
   b. quantity supplied divided by the percentage change in price.
   c. quantity demanded divided by the percentage change in price.
   d. supply divided by the percentage change in the demand.
   e. quantity supplied divided by the percentage change in income.

7. If a firm supplies 200 units at a price of $50 and 100 units at a price of $40, using the midpoint formula what is the price elasticity of supply?
   a. 0.33
   b. 1.00
   c. 3.00
   d. 5.00
   e. 8.50

8. If the quantity supplied increases by 8 percent when the price rises by 2 percent, the price elasticity of supply is ____ percent.
   a. 10.0
   b. 6.0
   c. 0.25
   d. 16.0
   e. 4.0

9. If the price of a good increases by 10 percent and the quantity supplied increases by 5 percent, then the elasticity of supply is
   a. greater than one and supply is elastic.
   b. negative and supply is inelastic.
   c. less than one and supply is elastic.
   d. less than one and supply is inelastic.
   e. greater than one and supply is inelastic.

Complete the graph

■ **FIGURE 5.4**

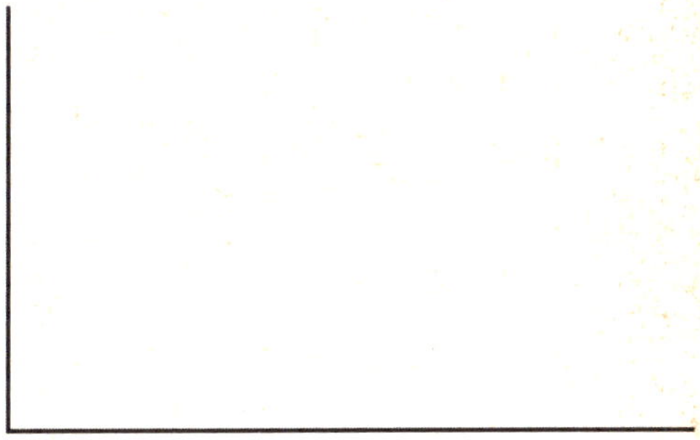

1. In Figure 5.4, label the axes and then draw a supply curve for a good that has a perfectly inelastic supply.

Short answer and numeric questions

1. Suppose the elasticity of supply of wheat is 0.3 and the elasticity of supply of magazines is 1.3. If the price of wheat rises 10 percent, what is the increase in the quantity of wheat supplied? If the price of a magazine rises 10 percent, what is the increase in the quantity of magazines supplied?

	Price (dollars)	Quantity supplied (units per week)
A	5	10
B	15	30
C	25	50
D	35	90

2. The table above gives a supply schedule. Calculate the price elasticity of supply between points A and B; between points B and C; and between points C and D.

	Percentage change in price	Percentage change in quantity supplied	Price elasticity of supply
A	6	8	____
B	8	4	____
C	4	8	____

3. Complete the table above by calculating the price elasticity of supply.

4. Describe the elasticity of supply of a good that can be stored.

5. Why does the elasticity of supply increase as time passes after a price change?

CHECKPOINT 5.3

■ **Define and explain the factors that influence the cross elasticity of demand and the income elasticity of demand.**

Quick Review
- *Cross elasticity of demand* A measure of the extent to which the demand for a good changes when the price of a substitute or complement changes, other things remaining the same.
- *Income elasticity of demand* A measure of the extent to which the demand for a good changes when income changes, other things remaining the same.

Additional Practice Problems 5.3

1. For each of the following, calculate the cross elasticity of demand. Are the goods substitutes or complements?
   a. A 10 percent increase in the price of lettuce results in a 15 percent increase in the quantity of spinach demanded.
   b. A 5 percent increase in the price of beef results in a 10 percent increase in the quantity of pork demanded.
   c. A 4 percent increase in the price of a golf club results in a 2 percent decrease in the quantity of golf balls demanded.

2. For each of the following, calculate the income elasticity of demand. Are the goods normal or inferior goods?
   a. A 3 percent increase in income results in a 1 percent increase in the quantity demanded.
   b. A 6 percent increase in income results in a 3 percent decrease in the quantity demanded.
   c. A 2 percent increase in income results in a 4 percent increase in the quantity demanded.

3. Pepsi and Coke are substitutes. Pepsi and Tropicana orange juice also are substitutes. But quite likely the two cross elasticities of demand differ in size. Which cross elasticity do you think is larger and why?

Solutions to Additional Practice Problems 5.3

1a. The cross elasticity of demand equals the percentage change in the quantity demanded of one good divided by the percentage change in the price of the other good, which is (15 percent) ÷ (10 percent) = 1.5. The cross elasticity of supply is positive for substitute and negative for complements, so lettuce and spinach are substitutes.

1b. The cross elasticity of demand equals (10 percent) ÷ (5 percent) = 2.0. Beef and pork are substitutes.

1c. The cross elasticity of demand equals (–2 percent) ÷ (4 percent) = –0.5. Golf clubs and golf balls are complements.

2a. The income elasticity of demand equals the percentage change in the quantity demanded divided by the percentage change in income, which is (1 percent) ÷ (3 percent) = 0.33. The income elasticity is positive for a normal good and negative for an inferior good, so this good is a normal good.

2b. The income elasticity of demand equals (–3 percent) ÷ (6 percent) = –0.5. The good is an inferior good.

2c. The income elasticity of demand equals (4 percent) ÷ (2 percent) = 2.0. The good is a normal good.

3. The cross elasticity between Pepsi and Coke is likely much larger than the cross elasticity between Pepsi and Tropicana orange juice. For many people, Pepsi and Coke are close to indistinguishable. Even a slight rise in the price of a Coke will increase the quantity of Pepsi demanded significantly, so their cross elasticity is large. Pepsi and Tropicana orange juice are less close substitutes. So, although an increase in the price of Tropicana orange juice will increase the demand for Pepsi, the increase will be relatively slight and the cross elasticity will be small.

Self Test 5.3

Fill in the blanks

The ____ (price; cross; income) elasticity of demand is a measure of the extent to which the demand for a good changes when the price of a substitute or complement changes, other things remaining the same. The cross elasticity of demand is ____ (positive; negative) for a substitute and ____ (positive; negative) for a complement. The income elasticity of demand equals the percentage change in ____ (the quantity demanded; income) divided by the percentage change in ____ (quantity demanded; income). The income elasticity of demand is ____ (positive; negative) for a normal good and ____ (positive; negative) for an inferior good.

True or false

1. If the cross elasticity of demand is negative, the two goods are substitutes.
2. If the cross elasticity between hamburgers and hot dogs is positive, then hamburgers and hot dogs are substitutes.
3. An inferior good has a negative income elasticity of demand.
4. When the income elasticity of demand is positive, the good is a normal good.
5. A normal good is a good that has a positive cross elasticity of demand.

Multiple choice

1. The measure used to determine whether two goods are complements or substitutes is called the
   a. price elasticity of supply.
   b. cross elasticity of demand.
   c. price elasticity of demand.
   d. income elasticity.
   e. substitute elasticity of demand.

2. If beef and pork are substitutes, the cross elasticity of demand between the two goods is
   a. negative.
   b. positive.
   c. indeterminate.
   d. elastic.
   e. greater than one.

3. When the price of a pizza is $10, the quantity of soda demanded is 300 drinks. When the price of pizza is $15, the quantity of soda demanded is 100 drinks. The cross elasticity of demand equals
   a. –0.25.
   b. –0.40.
   c. –2.50.
   d. –25.00.
   e. 4.0.

4. When the price of going to a movie rises 5 percent, the quantity of DVDs demanded increases 10 percent. The cross elasticity of demand equals
   a. 10.0.
   b. 0.50.
   c. –0.50.
   d. –2.0.
   e. 2.0.

5. If two goods have a cross elasticity of demand of –2, then when the price of the one increases, the demand curve of the other good
   a. shifts rightward.
   b. shifts leftward.
   c. remains unchanged.
   d. may shift rightward, leftward, or remain unchanged.
   e. remains unchanged but the supply curve shifts leftward.

6. The income elasticity of demand is the percentage change in the ____ divided by the percentage change in ____.
   a. quantity demanded; the price of a substitute or complement
   b. quantity supplied; price
   c. quantity demanded; price
   d. quantity demanded; income
   e. quantity demanded when income changes; the quantity supplied

7. When income increases from $20,000 to $30,000 the number of home-delivered pizzas per year increases from 22 to 40. The income elasticity of demand for home-delivered pizza equals
   a. 1.45.
   b. 0.69.
   c. 0.58.
   d. 0.40.
   e. 2.86.

8. When income increases by 6 percent, the demand for potatoes decreases by 2 percent. The income elasticity of demand for potatoes equals
   a. −2.00.
   b. 3.00.
   c. −3.00.
   d. 0.33.
   e. −0.33.

9. If a product is a normal good, then its income elasticity of demand is
   a. zero.
   b. positive.
   c. negative.
   d. indeterminate.
   e. greater than one.

10. The income elasticity of demand for used cars is less than zero. So, used cars are
    a. an inferior good.
    b. a normal good.
    c. an inelastic good.
    d. a perfectly inelastic good.
    e. substitute goods.

Complete the graph
■ **FIGURE 5.5**
Price (dollars per large screen television)

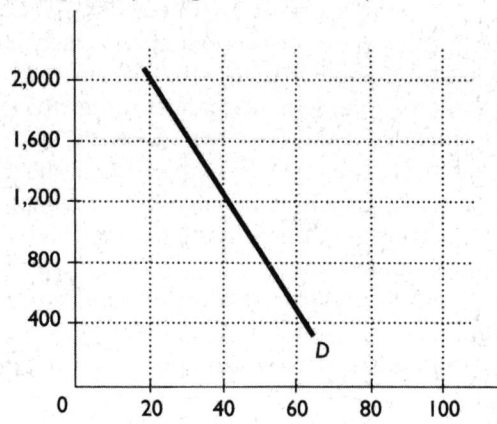

[Graph showing demand curve D with price on y-axis (0 to 2,000) and Quantity (millions of large screen televisions per year) on x-axis (0 to 100)]

1. The income elasticity of demand for large screen televisions is positive. In Figure 5.5, show the change when income increases.

Short answer and numeric questions

1. Do you think the cross elasticity of demand between Pepsi and Coke is positive or negative, large or small? Why?

	Percentage change in price of good A	Percentage change in quantity demanded of good B	Cross elasticity of demand
A	3	6	___
B	5	−10	___
C	−4	−8	___
D	8	4	___

2. Complete the table above. Which row has substitutes and which row has complements?

3. The income elasticity of demand for inter-city bus trips is negative. What does this fact tell you about inter-city bus trips?

	Percentage change in income	Percentage change in quantity demanded	Income elasticity of demand
A	5	10	___
B	5	−10	___
C	5	2	___
D	6	6	___

4. Complete the table above. Which row indicates an inferior good and which row indicates a good that is income elastic?

Chapter 5 · Elasticities of Demand and Supply

SELF TEST ANSWERS

■ CHECKPOINT 5.1

Fill in the blanks

To calculate the percentage change in price, the midpoint formula divides the change in price by the <u>average of the initial and the new price</u> and then multiplies by 100. If the percentage change in the quantity demanded exceeds the percentage change in the price, demand is <u>elastic</u>. The demand for a product is more elastic if there are <u>more</u> substitutes for it. The demand for a necessity is generally <u>inelastic</u>. The price elasticity of demand equals the percentage change in the <u>quantity demanded</u> divided by the percentage change in the <u>price</u>. Moving along a straight-line demand curve, the slope <u>is constant</u> and the elasticity <u>varies</u>. If demand is elastic, an increase in price <u>decreases</u> total revenue.

True or false

1. False; page 116
2. False; page 116
3. True; page 114
4. True; page 118
5. True; page 120
6. True; page 120

Multiple choice

1. c; page 112
2. d; page 112
3. c; page 113
4. a; page 114
5. a; page 114
6. d; page 114
7. b; page 116
8. b; page 116
9. a; page 120

Complete the graph

1. Figure 5.6 labels the axes and illustrates a demand curve for a good with a perfectly elastic demand; page 115.
2. Figure 5.7 labels the axes and illustrates a demand curve for a good with a perfectly inelastic demand; page 115.

■ **FIGURE 5.6**
Price (dollars)

■ **FIGURE 5.7**
Price (dollars)

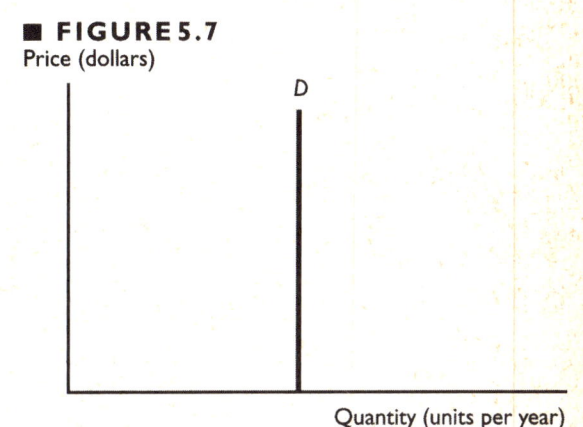

■ **FIGURE 5.8**
Price (dollars per unit)

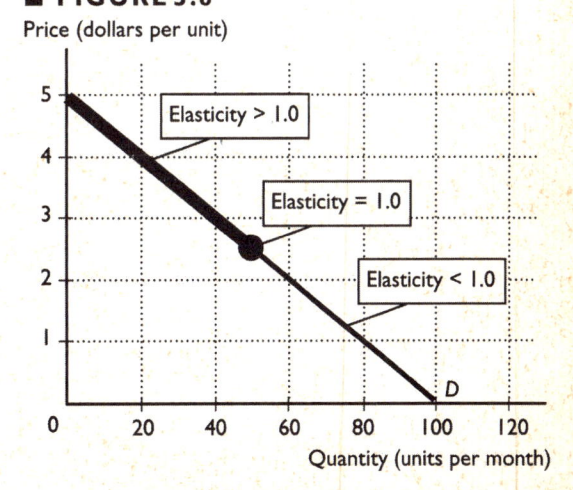

2. In Figure 5.8, demand is elastic along the dark portion of the demand curve. Demand

is unit elastic at the midpoint of curve. Demand is inelastic along the demand curve below the midpoint; page 118.

Short answer and numeric questions

	Percentage change in price	Percentage change in quantity demanded	Price elasticity of demand
A	5	10	2.0
B	8	4	0.5
C	3	0	0.0
D	6	6	1.0
E	1	8	8.0

1. The complete table is above; page 116.
   a. The most elastic demand is in row E; page 116.
   b. The least elastic demand is in row C (the demand is perfectly inelastic); page 116.
2. The price rises by 20 percent; page 116.
3. Demand is inelastic if the percentage change in the quantity demanded is less than the percentage change in the price; page 114.
4. The more narrow the definition of the good, the more substitutes exist. For example, there are more substitutes for a slice of Pizza Hut pizza than for pizza in general; page 116.
5. When the price of a good rises, total revenue increases if demand is inelastic, does not change if demand is unit elastic, and decreases if demand is elastic. As brand manager, you can use this relationship to predict whether the total revenue from Crest will rise, fall, or stay the same if you boost its price; page 120.

■ CHECKPOINT 5.2

Fill in the blanks

When supply has a vertical supply curve, then the supply of the good is perfectly <u>inelastic</u>. Goods that can be produced at an almost constant opportunity cost have an <u>elastic</u> supply. As time passes, the elasticity of supply <u>increases</u>. The price elasticity of supply equals the percentage change in the <u>quantity supplied</u> divided by the percentage change in the <u>price</u>. If the elasticity of supply is greater than 1, supply is <u>elastic</u>.

True or false
1. False; page 124
2. True; page 124
3. False; page 126
4. False; page 126
5. True; page 126
6. True; page 126

Multiple choice
1. d; page 126
2. a; page 126
3. d; page 126
4. d; page 126
5. b; page 126
6. b; page 126
7. c; page 126
8. e; page 126
9. d; page 126

Complete the graph

■ **FIGURE 5.9**

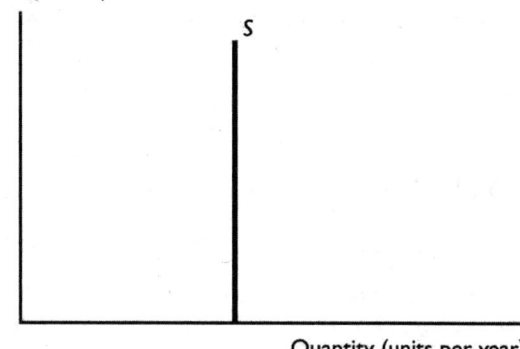

1. Figure 5.9 labels the axes and illustrates a supply curve for a good with a perfectly inelastic supply; page 125.

Short answer and numeric questions
1. If the price of wheat rises 10 percent, the increase in the quantity supplied equals (10 percent) × (0.3), which is 3 percent. If the price of a magazine rises 10 percent, the increase in the quantity supplied equals (10 percent) × (1.3), which is 13 percent; pages 124 and 126.

2. The price elasticity of supply between points A and B is 1.00; between points B and C is 1.00; and between points C and D is 1.71; page 126.

	Percentage change in price	Percentage change in quantity supplied	Price elasticity of supply
A	6	8	1.33
B	8	4	0.50
C	4	8	2.00

3. The completed table is above; page 126.

4. The elasticity of supply of a good that can be stored depends on the decision to keep the good in storage or offer it for sale. A small price change can make a big difference to this decision, so the supply of a storable good is highly elastic; page 126.

5. As time passes after a price change, it becomes easier to change production plans and supply becomes more elastic. For example, many manufactured goods have an inelastic supply if production plans have had only a short period in which to change. But after all the technologically possible ways of adjusting production have been exploited, supply is extremely elastic for most manufactured items; page 126.

■ CHECKPOINT 5.3

Fill in the blanks

The <u>cross</u> elasticity of demand is a measure of the extent to which the demand for a good changes when the price of a substitute or complement changes, other things remaining the same. The cross elasticity of demand is <u>positive</u> for a substitute and <u>negative</u> for a complement. The income elasticity of demand equals the percentage change in <u>quantity demanded</u> divided by the percentage change in <u>income</u>. The income elasticity of demand is <u>positive</u> for a normal good and <u>negative</u> for an inferior good.

True or false

1. False; page 129
2. True; page 129
3. True; page 130
4. True; page 130
5. False; page 130

Multiple choice

1. b; page 129
2. b; page 129
3. c; page 129
4. e; page 129
5. b; page 130
6. d; page 130
7. a; page 130
8. e; page 130
9. b; page 130

Complete the graph

■ FIGURE 5.10

1. Because the income elasticity of demand is positive, we know that large screen televisions are a normal good. In Figure 5.10 an increase in income shifts the demand curve rightward from D_0 to D_1; page 130.

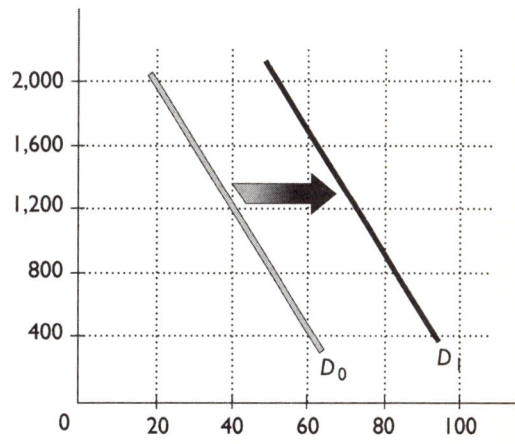

Short answer and numeric questions

1. The cross elasticity of demand between Pepsi and Coke is most likely positive and large. Pepsi and Coke are substitutes for most people, so their cross elasticity of demand is positive. They are close substitutes for many people, so their cross elasticity of demand is large; page 129.

	Percentage change in price of good A	Percentage change in quantity demanded of good B	Cross elasticity of demand
A	3	6	2.0
B	5	−10	−2.0
C	−4	−8	2.0
D	8	4	0.5

2. The completed table is above. The goods in row B are complements; the goods in rows A, C, and D are substitutes; page 129.

3. The fact that the income elasticity of demand for inter-city bus trips is negative indicates that an inter-city bus trip is an inferior good. When people's incomes increase, they take fewer inter-city bus trips and instead fly, drive, or take the train; page 130.

	Percentage change in income	Percentage change in quantity demanded	Income elasticity of demand
A	5	10	2.0
B	5	−10	−2.0
C	5	2	0.4
D	6	6	1.0

4. The completed table is above. The good in Row B is an inferior good. The good in row A is income elastic; page 130.

Chapter 6
Efficiency and Fairness of Markets

CHAPTER CHECKLIST

1 Describe the alternative methods of allocating scarce resources and define and explain the features of an efficient allocation.

Ways of allocating resources include: market price; command; majority rule; contest; first-come, first-served; sharing equally; lottery; personal characteristics; and force. Allocative efficiency occurs when we produce the quantities of goods and services on the *PPF* that people value most highly. Marginal benefit is the benefit that people receive from consuming one more unit of the product; marginal cost is the opportunity cost of producing one more unit of the product. The marginal benefit curve is downward sloping and the marginal cost curve is upward sloping. Allocative efficiency requires producing where the curves intersect, at the quantity that makes the marginal benefit equal the marginal cost.

2 Distinguish between value and price and define consumer surplus.

Value is what buyers get and price is what buyers pay. The value is the *marginal benefit*, which is the maximum price that buyers are willing to pay for another unit of the good. The demand curve is the marginal benefit curve. Consumer surplus is the marginal benefit from a good minus the price paid for it, summed over the quantity consumed.

3 Distinguish between cost and price and define producer surplus.

Cost is what a seller gives up to produce a good and price is what a seller receives when the good is sold. The cost of producing one more unit of a good or service is its *marginal cost*. The supply curve is the marginal cost curve. Producer surplus is the price of a good minus the marginal cost of producing it, summed over the quantity produced.

4 Evaluate the efficiency of the alternative methods of allocating scarce resources.

When marginal benefit equals the marginal cost, the efficient quantity is produced. The sum of consumer surplus and producer surplus is maximized at a competitive equilibrium. According to Adam Smith, each participant in a competitive market is "led by an invisible hand" to promote the efficient use of resources. Underproduction and overproduction create a deadweight loss. Government imposed price and quantity regulations, taxes and subsidies, externalities, public goods, common resources, monopoly, and high transactions costs are obstacles to efficiency. Other means of allocation are sometimes but not necessarily efficient.

5 Explain the main ideas about fairness and evaluate the fairness of the alternative methods of allocating scarce resources.

Two views of fairness are: it's not fair if the *rules* aren't fair and it's not fair if the *result* isn't fair. When private property and property rights are protected and exchanges are voluntary, competitive markets are fair according to the rules view of fairness. The fair results idea of income equality ignores the cost of making income transfers, which leads to the big tradeoff between efficiency and fairness.

CHECKPOINT 6.1

■ **Describe the alternative methods of allocating scarce resources and define and explain the features of an efficient allocation.**

Quick Review
- *Allocation methods* Resources can be allocated by: using the market price; command; majority rule; a contest, first-come, first served; sharing equally; lottery; personal characteristics; and force.
- *Allocation methods* Resources can be allocated by: using the market price; command; majority rule; a contest, first-come, first served; sharing equally; lottery; personal characteristics; and force.
- *Marginal benefit* The benefit that a person receives from consuming one more unit of a good or service.
- *Marginal cost* The opportunity cost of producing one more unit of a good or service.

Additional Practice Problems 6.1
1. Why is it necessary to allocate resources?
2. What is the command method of allocating resources?
3. Explain the relationship between production efficiency and allocative efficiency.

Solutions to Additional Practice Problems 6.1
1. Resources are scarce, so not everyone's wants can be fulfilled. As a result, some method must be used to determine whether or not resources are to be allocated to fulfilling each specific want.
2. The command method of allocating resources relies upon someone in authority to order how resources shall be allocated. The former Soviet Union and currently North Korea and Cuba are examples of entire economies in which command was (and is for North Korea and Cuba) the major allocation method.
3. Production efficiency is a situation in it is impossible to produce more of one good or service without producing less of some other good or service—production is at a point on the *PPF*. Allocative efficiency is the most highly valued combination of goods and services on the *PPF*.

■ **Self Test 6.1**

Fill in the blanks
Because only one person can become chair of General Electric and collect a salary of tens of millions of dollars, this position is allocated in a type of ____ (first-come, first-served; contest; command) allocation scheme. ____ (Production; Allocative) efficiency occurs at each combination of goods and services on the *PPF*. ____ (Production; Allocative) efficiency occurs when the economy produces the most highly valued combination of goods and services on the *PPF*. As more of a good is consumed, its marginal benefit ____ (increases; decreases), and as more of a good is produced, its marginal cost ____ (increases; decreases). Allocative efficiency occurs when the marginal benefit of a good is ____ (greater than; equal to; less than) the marginal cost of the good.

True or false
1. When market prices are used to allocate resources, only the people who are able and willing to pay get the resources.
2. All combinations of goods and services on the production possibilities frontier are combinations of allocative efficiency.
3. The marginal benefit of a good increases as more of the good is consumed.
4. A production point can be allocative efficient but not production efficient.

Multiple choice
1. If a person will rent an apartment only to married couples over 30 years old, that person is allocating resources using a ____ allocation method.
   a. first-come, first-served
   b. market price
   c. contest
   d. personal characteristics
   e. command

2. Allocative efficiency occurs when
   a. the most highly valued goods and services are produced.
   b. all citizens have equal access to goods and services.
   c. the environment is protected at all cost.
   d. goods and services are free.
   e. production takes place at any point on the PPF.

3. Marginal benefit equals the
   a. benefit that a person receives from consuming another unit of a good.
   b. additional efficiency from producing another unit of a good.
   c. increase in profit from producing another unit of a good.
   d. cost of producing another unit of a good.
   e. total benefit from consuming all the units of the good or service.

4. In general, the marginal cost curve
   a. has a positive slope.
   b. has a negative slope.
   c. is horizontal.
   d. is vertical.
   e. is U-shaped.

5. Allocative efficiency is achieved when the marginal benefit of a good
   a. exceeds marginal cost by as much as possible.
   b. exceeds marginal cost but not by as much as possible.
   c. is less than its marginal cost.
   d. equals the marginal cost.
   e. equals zero.

Complete the graph
■ **FIGURE 6.1**
Marginal benefit and marginal cost (trucks per tractor)

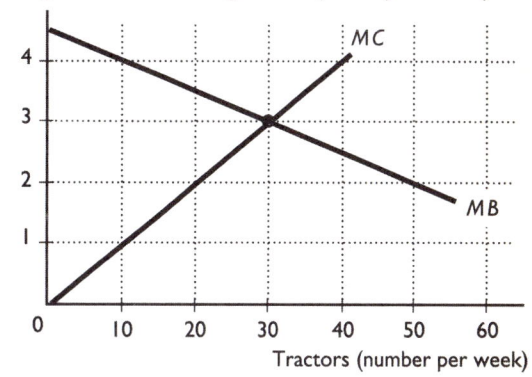

1. An economy produces only trucks and tractors and Figure 6.1 shows the marginal benefit and marginal cost of tractors. How many tractors are produced at the point of allocative efficiency?

Short answer and numeric questions
1. Suppose the price of a new BMW is $50,000. Which two kinds of people decide not to buy these BMWs? Is it true that when resources are allocated by market price, the rich always consume everything?

2. Only one person can become President of Sony, yet many of Sony's top executives would like that job. What allocation method is typically used to determine who becomes President? How does this allocation method benefit Sony?

3. Along a production possibilities frontier, to produce the first skateboard, 1 pair of roller blades must be forgone. To produce the second skateboard, 2 more pairs of roller blades must be forgone. Is the marginal cost of the second skate board 2 or 3 pairs of roller blades?

4. Why does allocative efficiency require producing where marginal benefit equals marginal cost rather than where marginal benefit exceeds marginal cost?

CHECKPOINT 6.2

■ **Distinguish between value and price and define consumer surplus.**

Quick Review

- *Value* In economics the idea of value is called marginal benefit, which we measure as the maximum price that people are willing to pay for another unit of a good or service.
- *Consumer surplus* Consumer surplus is the marginal benefit from a good or service minus the price paid for it, summed over the quantity consumed.

Additional Practice Problem 6.2

1. The figure shows the demand curve for magazines and the market price of a magazine. Use the figure to answer the following questions. 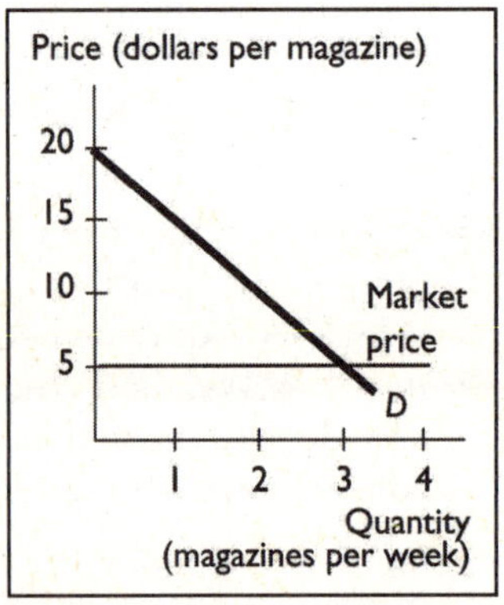
   a. What is the value of the 1st magazine? What is the marginal benefit of the 1st magazine? What is the consumer surplus of the 1st magazine?
   b. What is the marginal benefit of the 2nd magazine? What is the consumer surplus of the 2nd magazine?
   c. What is the total quantity of magazines bought and the consumer surplus?
   d. If the price of a magazine rises to $10, what is the quantity bought and what is the consumer surplus?

2. Your friend paid a lawyer $50 for the hour it took the lawyer to write a letter to settle a rent dispute. Your friend wonders if the concepts of value, marginal benefit, and consumer surplus apply not only to goods but also to services, such as the lawyer's letter. What do you tell your friend?

Solutions to Additional Practice Problems 6.2

1a. The value of the 1st magazine equals the maximum price a consumer is willing to pay for the magazine. The figure shows that the maximum price for the 1st magazine is $15, so the value of the magazine equals $15. The marginal benefit of the magazine is equal to the maximum price the consumer will pay, which is $15. The consumer surplus is equal to the marginal benefit of the 1st magazine ($15) minus the price of the magazine ($5) so the consumer surplus is $10.

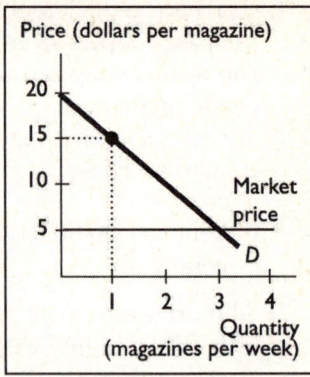

1b. The marginal benefit of the magazine is equal to the maximum price the consumer will pay. The figure shows that the maximum price for the 2nd magazine is $10, so the marginal benefit of the magazine equals $5. The consumer surplus is equal to $5.

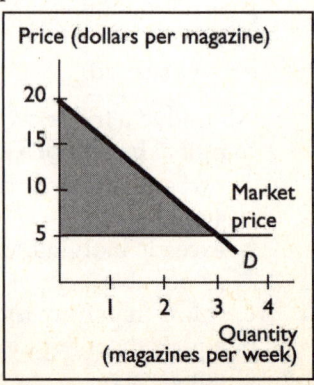

1c. The quantity bought is 3 magazines because the demand curve shows that the quantity demanded at the price of $5 is 3 magazines. The consumer surplus equals the area of the darkened triangle in the figure. Calculating the area of the consumer surplus triangle, which is equal to one half the base of the triangle multiplied by the height or 1/2 × (3 − 0) × ($20 − $5), which is $22.50.

1d. If the price of a magazine rises to $10, the quantity bought is 2 magazines. The consumer surplus now equals 1/2 × (2 − 0) × ($20 − $10), which is $10.00.

2. All the concepts of value, marginal benefit, and consumer surplus apply to services as well as to goods. In your friend's case, there was some maximum amount your friend was willing to pay the attorney to write the letter. This maximum amount was the value to your friend of the letter. It is also the marginal benefit of the letter. Presumably your friend got the letter for some amount less than the maximum your friend was willing to pay. The difference between the marginal benefit of the letter and the price paid it is the consumer surplus your friend enjoyed from the letter.

■ Self Test 6.2

Fill in the blanks

The benefit a person receives from consuming one more unit of a good is its ____. The opportunity cost of producing one more unit of a good is its ____. Allocative efficiency is at the quantity where the marginal benefit is ____ (greater than; equal to; less than) marginal cost. The demand curve ____ (is; is not) the marginal benefit curve. The consumer surplus equals the marginal benefit of a good ____ (plus; multiplied by; minus) the price paid for it.

True or false

1. In economics, value and price refer to the same thing.
2. A demand curve is a marginal benefit curve.
3. The consumer surplus from one unit of a good is the marginal benefit from the good minus the price paid for it.
4. Consumer surplus always equals zero because consumers always pay for the goods and services they consume.

Multiple choice

1. Value is
   a. the price we pay for a good.
   b. the cost of resources used to produce a good.
   c. objective so that it is determined by market forces, not preferences.
   d. the marginal benefit we get from consuming another unit of a good or service.
   e. the difference between the price paid for a good and the marginal cost of producing that unit of the good.

2. A marginal benefit curve
   a. is the same as a demand curve.
   b. is the same as a supply curve.
   c. slopes upwards.
   d. is a vertical line at the efficient quantity.
   e. is U-shaped.

3. In general, as the consumption of a good or service increases, the marginal benefit from consuming that good or service
   a. increases.
   b. decreases.
   c. stays the same.
   d. at first increases and then decreases.
   e. at first decreases and then increases.

4. The difference between the marginal benefit from a new pair of shoes and the price of the new pair of shoes is
   a. the consumer surplus from that pair of shoes.
   b. what we get.
   c. what we have to pay.
   d. the price when the marginal benefit is maximized.
   e. the consumer's expenditure on the shoes.

5. Suppose the price of a scooter is $200 and Cora Lee is willing to pay $250. Cora Lee's
   a. consumer surplus from that scooter is $200.
   b. consumer surplus from that scooter is $50.
   c. marginal benefit from that scooter is $200.
   d. consumer surplus from that scooter is $200.
   e. consumer surplus from that scooter is $250.

6. If the price of a pizza is $10 per pizza, the consumer surplus from the first pizza consumed ____ the consumer surplus from the second pizza consumed.
   a. is greater than
   b. equals
   c. is less than
   d. cannot be compared to
   e. None of the above answers is correct because more information is needed about the marginal cost of producing the pizzas to answer the question.

Complete the graph

■ **FIGURE 6.2**

Price (dollars per pair of roller blades)

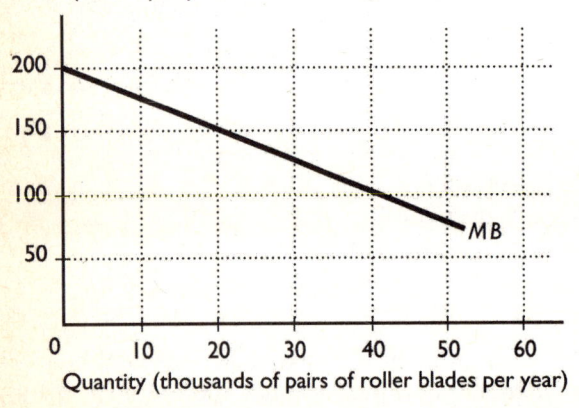

Quantity (thousands of pairs of roller blades per year)

1. Figure 6.2 shows the demand curve for roller blades.
   a. What is the marginal benefit of the 20,000th pair of roller blades?
   b. What is the marginal benefit of the 40,000th pair of roller blades?
   c. If the price of a pair of roller blades is $100, what is the consumer surplus on the 20,000th pair of roller blades?
   d. If the price of a pair of roller blades is $100, what is the consumer surplus on the 40,000th pair of roller blades?
   e. If the price of a pair of roller blades is $100, what is the quantity of roller blades purchased? What is the amount of the consumer surplus?

■ **FIGURE 6.3**

Price (dollars per bag of potato chips)

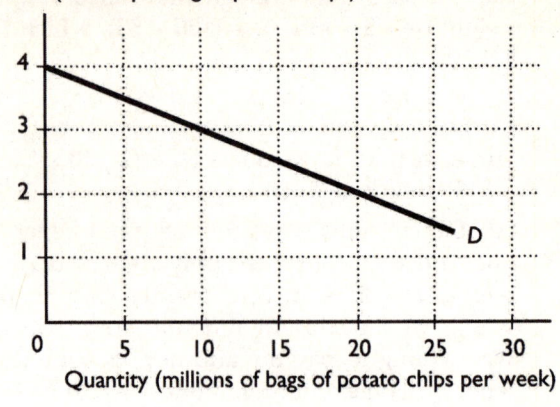

Quantity (millions of bags of potato chips per week)

2. Figure 6.3 shows the demand curve for bags of potato chips.
   a. What is the maximum price a consumer is willing to pay for the 10 millionth bag of chips?
   b. What is the marginal benefit from the 10 millionth bag of chips? What is the relationship between your answer to part (a) and your answer to this part?
   c. If the price of a bag of chips equals $2, in Figure 6.3 shade the area that equals the amount of the consumer surplus.
   d. If the price of a bag of chips equals $2, what is the amount of consumer surplus?

Short answer and numeric questions

Price (dollars per MP3 player)	Quantity (millions of MP3 players per year)	Consumer surplus (dollars)
500	4	____
400	8	____
300	12	____
200	16	____
100	20	____

1. The table above gives the demand schedule for MP3 players. Suppose the price of an MP3 player is $200.
   a. Complete the table by calculating the consumer surplus. In the first row, calculate the consumer surplus for the 4 millionth MP3 player; in the second row, calculate the consumer surplus for the 8 millionth MP3 player; and so on.

b. As more MP3 players are purchased, what happens to the consumer surplus of the last unit purchased? Why?

2. What is the relationship between the value of a good, the maximum price a consumer is willing to pay for the good, and the marginal benefit from the good?

3. What is the relationship between the marginal benefit of a slice of pizza, the price paid for the slice, and its consumer surplus?

CHECKPOINT 6.3

■ **Distinguish between cost and price and define producer surplus.**

Quick Review
- *Cost* Cost is what the seller must give up to produce a good.
- *Producer surplus* The producer surplus of a good equals the price of a good minus the marginal cost of producing it.

Additional Practice Problems 6.3
1. The figure shows the supply curve of magazines and the market price of a magazine. Use the figure to answer the following questions. 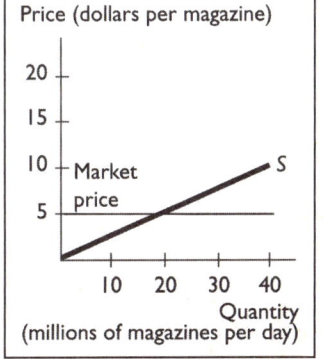
   a. What is the marginal cost of the 10 millionth magazine?
   b. What is the minimum supply price of the 10 millionth magazine?
   c. What is the producer surplus on the 10 millionth magazine?
   d. What are the quantity of magazines sold and the total producer surplus?
2. Why is the minimum price for which a seller will produce a product equal to the product's marginal cost?

Solutions to Additional Practice Problems 6.3
1a. The marginal cost of the 10 millionth magazine is equal to the minimum supply price of the 10 millionth magazine. The supply curve, which is also the marginal cost curve, shows this price. In the figure, the supply curve shows that the marginal cost of 10 millionth magazine is $2.50.

1b. The minimum supply price of the 10 millionth magazine equals its marginal cost, $2.50.

1c. The producer surplus on the 10 millionth magazine is equal to its market price minus its marginal cost, which is $5 − $2.50 = $2.50.

1d. At the market price of $5, 20 million magazines are sold. The producer surplus equals the area of the grey triangle in the figure. Calculating the area of the triangle as one half the base multiplied by the height, or 1/2 × (20 million − 0) × ($5 − 0), the producer surplus equals $50 million.

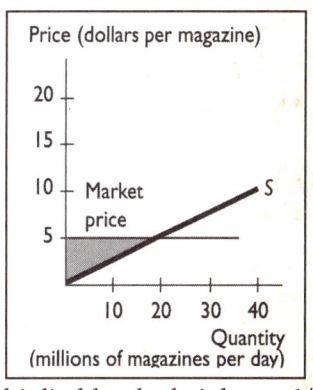

2. A seller is willing to produce a good as long as the price the seller receives covers all the costs of producing the good. So the minimum price for which a seller is willing to produce a unit of the good must be the amount that just equals the cost of the producing that unit. But the cost of producing any unit of a good is its marginal cost, so the minimum supply price equals the good's marginal cost.

Self Test 6.3

Fill in the blanks

____ (Price; Cost) is what a seller must give up to produce a good and ____ (price; cost) is what a seller receives when the good is sold. A ____ (demand; supply) curve is a marginal cost curve. A firm receives a producer surplus when price is ____ (greater; less) than marginal cost.

True or false

1. In economics, cost and price are the same thing.
2. The minimum price for which Bobby will grow another pound of rice is 20¢, so the marginal cost of an additional pound of rice is 20¢.
3. A supply curve is a marginal benefit curve.
4. Producer surplus equals the marginal benefit of a good minus the cost of producing it.

Multiple choice

1. Cost
    a. is what the buyer pays to get the good.
    b. is always equal to the marginal benefit for every unit of a good produced.
    c. is what the seller must give up to produce the good.
    d. is greater than market price, which results in a profit for firms.
    e. means the same thing as price.

2. If a firm is willing to supply the 1,000th unit of a good at a price of $23 or more, we know that $23 is the
    a. highest price the seller hopes to realize for this output.
    b. minimum price the seller must receive to produce this unit.
    c. average price of all the prices the seller could charge.
    d. price that sets the marginal benefit equal to the marginal cost.
    e. only price for which the seller is willing to sell this unit of the good.

3. A supply curve shows the ____ of producing one more unit of a good or service.
    a. producer surplus
    b. consumer surplus
    c. total benefit
    d. marginal cost
    e. marginal benefit to the producer

4. Producer surplus is
    a. equal to the marginal benefit from a good minus its price.
    b. equal to the price of a good minus the marginal cost of producing it.
    c. always equal to consumer surplus.
    d. Both answers (a) and (c) are correct.
    e. Both answers (b) and (c) are correct.

5. Suppose you're willing to tutor a student for $10 an hour. The student pays you $15 an hour. What is your producer surplus?
    a. $5 an hour
    b. $10 an hour
    c. $15 an hour
    d. $25 an hour
    e. more than $25 an hour

6. In a figure that shows a supply curve and a demand curve, producer surplus is the area
    a. below the demand curve and above the market price.
    b. below the supply curve and above the market price.
    c. above the demand curve and below the market price.
    d. above the supply curve and below the market price.
    e. between the demand curve and the supply curve.

Complete the graph

1. Figure 6.4 (on the next page) shows the supply curve for bags of potato chips.
    a. What is the minimum price for which a supplier is willing to produce the 10 millionth bag of chips?
    b. What is the marginal cost of the 10 millionth bag of chips? What is the relationship between your answer to part (a) and your answer to this part?

■ FIGURE 6.4
Price (dollars per bag of potato chips)

[Graph showing supply curve S, with Price axis 0-4 and Quantity axis 0-30 (millions of bags of potato chips per week)]

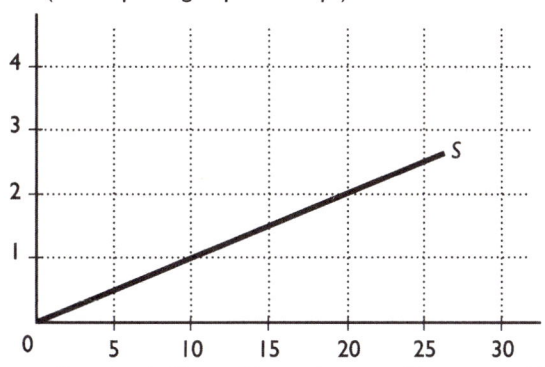

c. If the price of a bag of chips equals $2, in Figure 6.4 shade the area that equals the amount of the producer surplus.

d. If the price of a bag of chips equals $2, calculate the producer surplus.

Short answer and numeric questions

1. What is the relationship between the minimum price a supplier must receive to produce a slice of pizza and the marginal cost of the slice of pizza? What is the relationship between the marginal cost curve and the supply curve?

2. What is producer surplus? As the price of a good or service rises and the supply curve does not shift, what happens to the amount of the producer surplus?

CHECKPOINT 6.4

■ Evaluate the efficiency of the alternative methods of allocating scarce resources.

Quick Review

- *Efficiency of competitive equilibrium* The condition that marginal benefit equals marginal cost delivers an efficient use of resources. It allocates resources to the activities that create the greatest possible value. Marginal benefit equals marginal cost at a competitive equilibrium, so a competitive equilibrium is efficient.

- *Deadweight loss* The decrease in consumer surplus and producer surplus that results from an inefficient level of production.

Additional Practice Problems 6.4

1. The figure shows the market for paper. Use the figure to answer the following questions.

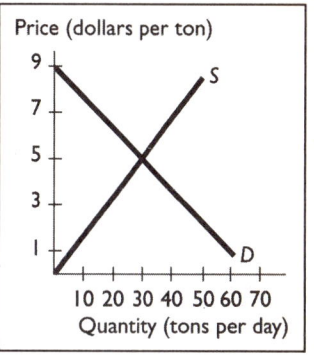

   [Graph showing supply S and demand D curves for paper, Price axis 1-9 dollars per ton, Quantity axis 10-70 tons per day]

   a. What are the equilibrium price and the equilibrium quantity of paper? What is the efficient quantity of paper?

   b. In the market equilibrium, use the figure above to shade the consumer surplus and the producer surplus.

   c. What does the consumer surplus equal? What does the producer surplus equal? What does the total surplus equal?

   d. Is the market for paper efficient? Why or why not? Can the total surplus be any larger at any other level of production?

2. Who benefits from a deadweight loss?

Solutions to Additional Practice Problems 6.4

1a. The equilibrium is shown in the figure and is where the supply and demand curves intersect. The equilibrium price is $5 a ton and the equilibrium quantity is 30 tons a day. The efficient quantity is where the marginal benefit and marginal cost curves intersect. Because the demand curve is the marginal benefit curve and the supply curve is the marginal cost curve, the efficient quantity is 30 tons a day.

1b. The consumer surplus is illustrated in the figure on the next page as the area of the top, dark triangle. The producer surplus equals the area of the lower, lighter triangle.

1c. The consumer surplus equals the area of the darker triangle, or 1/2 × (30 tons) × ($4 per ton) = $60, where $4 a ton is the height of the triangle, $9 a ton − $5 a ton. The producer surplus equals the area of the lighter triangle, or 1/2 × (30 tons) × ($5 per ton) = $75, where $5 a ton is the height of the triangle, $5 a ton − $0 a ton. The total surplus equals the sum of the consumer surplus plus the producer surplus, which is $135.

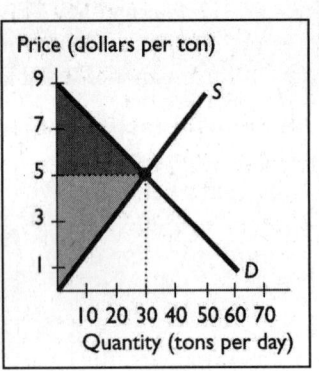

1d. The efficient use of resources occurs when marginal benefit equals marginal cost. The market equilibrium is efficient because the marginal benefit of a ton of paper equals its marginal cost. The sum of the consumer surplus and producer surplus, which equals the total surplus, is at its maximum at the efficient level of production so the total surplus cannot be larger at any other amount of production.

2. No one gains from a deadweight loss. Deadweight loss is a decrease in consumer surplus and producer surplus that results from an inefficient level of production. The deadweight loss is borne by the entire society. It is not a loss for the consumers and a gain for the producer. It is a social loss.

■ Self Test 6.4

Fill in the blanks

Equilibrium in a competitive market ____ (is; is not) efficient. Adam Smith believed that each participant in a competitive market is "led by ____ (an invisible hand; government actions)." A price ____ (ceiling; floor) is a regulation that makes it illegal to charge a price higher than a specified level. ____ (An externality; A public good) is a good or service that is consumed simultaneously by everyone, even if they don't pay for it. Deadweight loss is the decrease in ____ (only consumer surplus; consumer surplus and producer surplus; only producer surplus) that results from an inefficient level of production.

True or false

1. When the demand curve is the marginal benefit curve and the supply curve is the marginal cost curve, the competitive equilibrium is efficient.
2. When the efficient quantity of a good is produced, the consumer surplus is always zero.
3. According to Adam Smith, the invisible hand suggests that competitive markets require government action to ensure that resources are allocated efficiently.
4. Producing less than the efficient quantity of a good results in a deadweight loss but producing more than the efficient quantity does not result in a deadweight loss.

Multiple choice

■ FIGURE 6.5

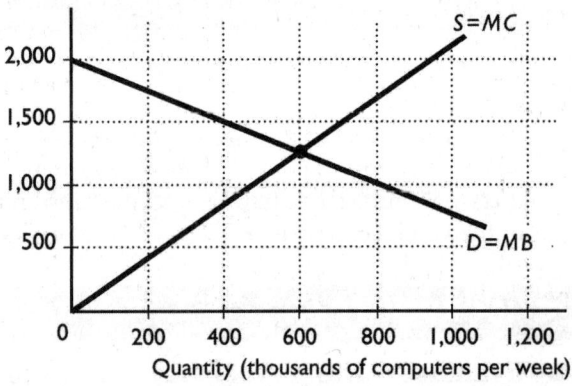

1. Figure 6.5 shows the market for computers. What is the equilibrium quantity of computers?
   a. 0 computers per week
   b. 200,000 computers per week
   c. 400,000 computers per week
   d. 600,000 computers per week
   e. more than 600,000 computers per week

2. Figure 6.5 shows the market for computers. What is the efficient quantity of computers?
   a. 0 computers per week
   b. 200,000 computers per week
   c. 400,000 computers per week
   d. 600,000 computers per week
   e. more than 600,000 computers per week

3. When a market is efficient the
   a. sum of consumer surplus and producer surplus is maximized.
   b. deadweight gain is maximized.
   c. quantity produced is maximized.
   d. marginal benefit of the last unit produced exceeds the marginal cost by as much as possible.
   e. total benefit equals the total cost.

4. Which of the following occurs when a market is efficient?
   a. producers earn the highest income possible
   b. production costs equal total benefit
   c. consumer surplus equals producer surplus
   d. scarce resources are used to produce the goods and services that people value most highly
   e. every consumer has all of the good or service he or she wants.

5. The concept of "the invisible hand" suggests that markets
   a. do not produce the efficient quantity.
   b. are always fair.
   c. produce the efficient quantity.
   d. are unfair though they might be efficient.
   e. allocate resources unfairly and inefficiently.

6. When underproduction occurs,
   a. producers gain more surplus at the expense of consumers.
   b. marginal cost is greater than marginal benefit.
   c. consumer surplus increases to a harmful amount.
   d. there is a deadweight loss that is borne by the entire society.
   e. the deadweight loss harms only consumers.

7. When production moves from the efficient quantity to a point of overproduction,
   a. consumer surplus definitely increases.
   b. the sum of producer surplus and consumer surplus increases.
   c. there is a deadweight loss.
   d. consumers definitely lose and producers definitely gain.
   e. consumers definitely gain and producers definitely lose.

8. Which of the following can result in a market producing an inefficient quantity of a good?
   i.   competition
   ii. an external cost or an external benefit
   iii. a tax
       a. i only.
       b. ii only.
       c. iii only.
       d. ii and iii.
       e. i and iii.

Complete the graph

■ **FIGURE 6.6**
Price (thousands of dollars per automobile)

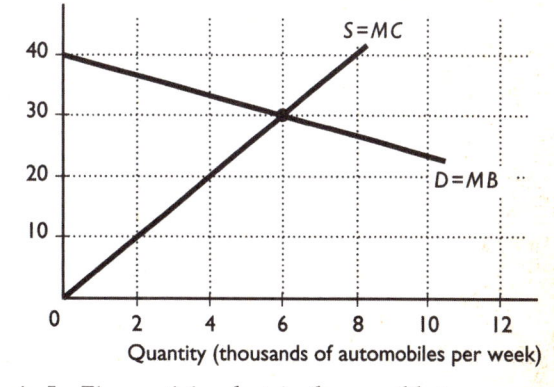

1. In Figure 6.6, what is the equilibrium quantity of automobiles? What is the efficient quantity of automobiles? Shade the consumer surplus and the producer surplus and calculate their amounts.

2. Figure 6.7 (on the next page) is identical to Figure 6.6.
   a. Suppose that 8,000 automobiles are produced. Shade the deadweight loss light grey and calculate its amount.

FIGURE 6.7
Price (thousands of dollars per automobile)

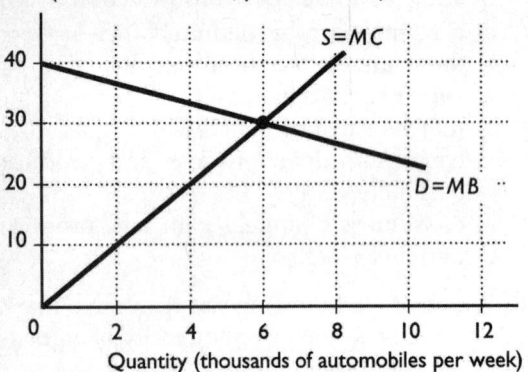

[Graph showing S=MC upward sloping line and D=MB downward sloping line, intersecting around quantity 6 and price 30. Y-axis: 0 to 40 in increments of 10. X-axis: 0 to 12 in increments of 2, labeled "Quantity (thousands of automobiles per week)"]

b. Suppose that 4,000 automobiles are produced. Shade the deadweight loss dark grey and calculate its amount.

Short answer and numeric questions
1. What is the relationship between a competitive market, efficiency, and the invisible hand?
2. Suppose the demand for cotton clothing increases. What effect does the increase in demand have on the equilibrium quantity and on the efficient quantity?
3. What factors might lead a market to produce an inefficient amount of a product?

CHECKPOINT 6.5

■ **Explain the main ideas about fairness and evaluate the fairness of alternative methods of allocating scarce resources.**

Quick Review
- *Big tradeoff* The big tradeoff is the tradeoff between efficiency and fairness that results when income transfers are made.

Additional Practice Problem 6.5
1. If Bill Gates gives $1,000 to a homeless person, would the transaction be fair? If Mr. Gates is taxed $1,000 by the government and the government gives the $1,000 to the same homeless person, would the transaction be fair? Comment on your answers.

Solution to Additional Practice Problem 6.5
1. If Mr. Gates gives $1,000 to a homeless person, the action is considered fair. The exchange is fair according to the fair rules principle because the exchange is voluntary. And the outcome is fair according to the fair results principle because there is more equality of income. If Mr. Gates is taxed by the government, the outcome is fair according to the fair results principle because there is more equality of income. But the transaction is not fair according to the fair rules principle because the exchange does not occur voluntarily.

■ Self Test 6.5

Fill in the blanks
Two views of fairness are that "it's not fair if the ____ (result; income distribution) isn't fair;" and "it's not fair if the ____ (rules; tradeoffs) aren't fair." According to Robert Nozick, fair-rules ideas require ____ (government intervention; property rights and voluntary exchange).

True or false
1. The principle that "it's not fair if the result isn't fair" can conflict with the principle that "it's not fair if the rules aren't fair."
2. The big tradeoff is the tradeoff between efficiency and happiness.
3. According to the "fair-rules" view of fairness, in times of natural disasters it is fair to force people to make available necessary goods and services at lower than usual prices.

Multiple choice
1. The "fair-rules" view of fairness is based on
   a. income transfers from the rich to the poor.
   b. property rights and voluntary exchange.
   c. efficiency.
   d. the big tradeoff.
   e. allocating resources using majority rule.

2. The idea that unequal incomes is unfair generally uses the ____ principle of fairness.
   a. big tradeoff
   b. involuntary exchange
   c. voluntary exchange
   d. it's not fair if the result isn't fair
   e. it's not fair if the rules aren't fair

3. Which of the following is an example in which "the big tradeoff" can occur?
   a. the government redistributes income from the rich to the poor
   b. Ford increases the price of a pickup truck
   c. a basketball player signs a $5 million contract
   d. a college lowers tuition
   e. the price of personal computers falls year after year

4. Suppose a hurricane is poised to strike Miami and the price of plywood jumps from $15 a board to $28. If the government buys all the plywood at $28 and offers it to consumers for $15, which of the following is true?
   a. There will be enough plywood for everyone at the $15 government price.
   b. There will be a surplus of plywood at the $15 government price.
   c. Some people who buy plywood at the $15 government price will resell the plywood to consumers who are willing to pay $28, earning a producer surplus of $13.
   d. Because the government is both buying and selling the plywood, there is no need to impose a tax to pay for the government intervention.
   e. The big tradeoff means that more plywood will be purchased with the government intervention than would be the case without the government intervention.

Short answer and numeric questions

1. In the United States, richer people generally pay a larger fraction of their income as taxes than do poorer people. Is this arrangement fair? Answer from a fair-results view and from a fair-rules view.

2. Suppose that during their working lifetimes, Matt and Pat have earned identical incomes as computer programmers. The only difference between the two is that Matt spent all of his income while Pat saved a large portion of hers. Now that they are retired, Pat's income is substantially higher than Matt's because of Pat's saving. Is it fair for Pat's income to be higher than Matt's? Answer from a fair results and from a fair rules perspective.

3. What is the effect of the big tradeoff in transferring income from people with high incomes to people with low incomes?

4. Is it fair for the government to limit the prices sellers charge for bottled water after a flood destroys a town's water supply? Why or why not?

SELF TEST ANSWERS

■ CHECKPOINT 6.1

Fill in the blanks

Because only one person can become chair of General Electric and collect a salary of tens of millions of dollars, this position is allocated in a type of <u>contest</u> allocation scheme. <u>Production</u> efficiency occurs at each combination of goods and services on the *PPF*. <u>Allocative</u> efficiency occurs when the economy produces the most highly valued combination of goods and services on the *PPF*. As more of a good is consumed, its marginal benefit <u>decreases</u>, and as more of a good is produced, its marginal cost <u>increases</u>. Allocative efficiency occurs when the marginal benefit of a good is <u>equal to</u> the marginal cost of the good.

True or false

1. True; page 138
2. False; page 141
3. False; page 142
4. False; page 138

Multiple choice

1. d; page 140
2. a; page 141
3. a; page 142
4. a; page 143
5. d; pages 143-144

Complete the graph

1. Allocative efficiency is the most highly valued combination of goods and services on the *PPF*. It is the combination where marginal cost equals marginal benefit. In Figure 6.1, allocative efficiency is achieved when 30 tractors a week are produced; page 144.

Short answer and numeric questions

1. The people who do not buy these BMWs are the people cannot afford to pay $50,000 for the new BMW and the people who can afford to pay but choose not to pay it. The fact that people can decide not to buy a particular good or service shows that the rich do not necessary consume everything; they buy and consume only the goods and services for which they choose to pay the market price; page 138.
2. Sony is using a contest allocation method. Sony benefits from this allocation scheme because all the top executives who want to be President will work extremely hard for Sony in an effort to win the contest; page 139.
3. The marginal cost of the second skate board is 2 pairs roller blades. Marginal cost is the opportunity cost of producing one more unit of a good or service. It is not the cost of all the units produced; pages 142-143.
4. As long as the marginal benefit from an additional good or service exceeds the marginal cost, the unit should be produced because its production benefits society more than it costs society to produce. Producing where marginal benefit equals marginal cost insures that *all* units that have a net benefit for society are produced, so this level of production is the point of allocative efficiency; page 144.

■ CHECKPOINT 6.2

Fill in the blanks

The benefit a person receives from consuming one more unit of a good is its <u>marginal benefit</u>. The opportunity cost of producing one more unit of a good is its <u>marginal cost</u>. Allocative efficiency is at the quantity where the marginal benefit is <u>equal to</u> marginal cost. The demand curve <u>is</u> the marginal benefit curve. The consumer surplus equals the marginal benefit of a good <u>minus</u> the price paid for it.

True or false

1. False; page 146
2. True; page 146
3. True; page 147
4. False; page 147

Multiple choice

1. d; page 146
2. a; page 146
3. b; page 146

4. a; page 147
5. b; page 147
6. a; page 147

Complete the graph
1. a. The marginal benefit of the 20,000th pair of roller blades is the maximum price a consumer is willing to pay for that pair, which is $150; page 146.
   b. The marginal benefit of the 40,000th pair of roller blades is the maximum price a consumer is willing to pay for that pair, which is $100; page 146.
   c. The consumer surplus is the difference between the marginal benefit, $150, minus the price paid, $100, or $50; page 147.
   d. The consumer surplus is the difference between the marginal benefit, $100, minus the price paid, $100, or $0; page 147.
   e. If the price is $100, then 40,000 pairs of roller blades will be purchased. The consumer surplus equals 1/2 × ($200 − $100) × (40,000 − 0), or $40,000,000; page 147.
2. a. The maximum price is $3; page 146.
   b. The marginal benefit is $3. The marginal benefit is the maximum price a consumer is willing to pay for another bag of potato chips; page 146.

■ **FIGURE 6.8**
Price (dollars per bag of potato chips)

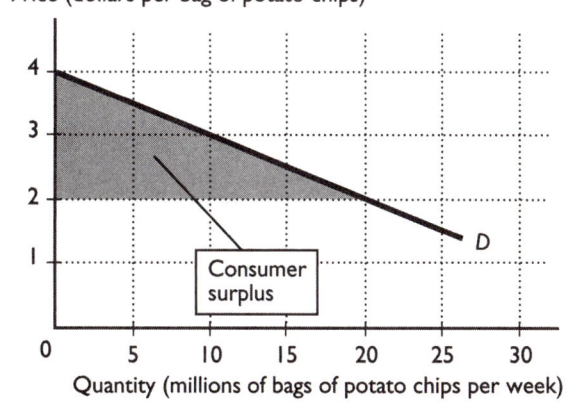

[Graph showing demand curve D from $4 at quantity 0 sloping down, with shaded triangular area labeled "Consumer surplus"; x-axis: Quantity (millions of bags of potato chips per week) from 0 to 30]

   c. Figure 6.8 shades the area of the consumer surplus; page 147.
   d. The consumer surplus equals the area of the shaded triangle in Figure 6.8, which is 1/2 × ($4 − $2) × 20 million = $20 million; page 147.

Short answer and numeric questions

Price (dollars per MP3 player)	Quantity (millions of MP3 players per year)	Consumer surplus (dollars)
500	4	300
400	8	200
300	12	100
200	16	0
100	20	0

1. a. The table above has the consumer surpluses. The consumer surplus is zero for the 20 millionth MP3 player because when the price is $200, the 20 millionth MP3 player is not purchased. For the remaining quantities, the consumer surplus is the marginal benefit, which equals the maximum price consumers are willing to pay minus the price; page 147.
   b. The consumer surplus decreases as more MP3 players are purchased because the value of an additional MP3 player decreases as more are purchased; page 147.
2. The value of a good is equal to the maximum price a buyer is willing to pay, which also equals the marginal benefit; page 146.
3. The marginal benefit of the slice of pizza equals the price paid plus the consumer surplus on that slice; page 147.

■ **CHECKPOINT 6.3**

Fill in the blanks

<u>Cost</u> is what a seller must give up to produce a good and <u>price</u> is what a seller receives when the good is sold. A <u>supply</u> curve is a marginal cost curve. A firm receives a producer surplus when price is <u>greater</u> than marginal cost.

True or false
1. False; page 149
2. True; page 149
3. False; page 149
4. False; page 150

Multiple choice
1. c; page 149

2. b; page 149
3. d; page 149
4. b; page 150
5. a; page 150
6. d; page 150

Complete the graph
1. a. The minimum price is $1; page 149.
   b. The marginal cost is $1. The marginal cost of the 10 millionth bag is the minimum price for which a supplier is willing to produce that bag of chips; page 149.

■ **FIGURE 6.9**
Price (dollars per bag of potato chips)

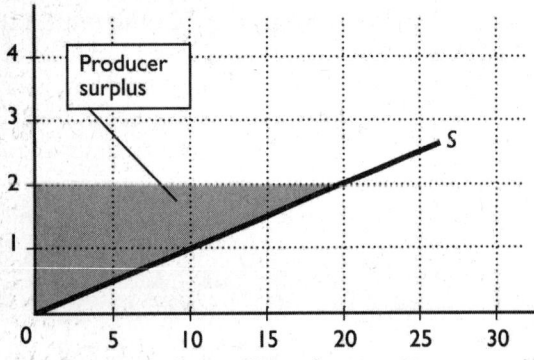

[Graph showing supply curve S with Producer surplus shaded region; x-axis: Quantity (millions of bags of potato chips per week) 0 to 30; y-axis: 0 to 4]

   c. Figure 6.9 shades the area of the producer surplus; page 150.
   d. The producer surplus equals the area of the shaded triangle in Figure 6.9, so producer surplus is 1/2 × ($2 − $0) × 20 million, which equals $20 million; page 150.

Short answer and numeric questions
1. The minimum price for which a firm will produce a slice of pizza equals the marginal cost of producing that slice. It is just worth producing one more slice of pizza if the price for which it can be sold equals its marginal cost. The supply curve tells us this price. So the supply curve is the same as the marginal cost curve; page 149.
2. Producer surplus equals the price of a good or service minus the marginal cost of producing it. As the price of a good or service rises and the supply curve does not shift, the producer surplus increases; page 150.

■ **CHECKPOINT 6.4**

Fill in the blanks
Equilibrium in a competitive market <u>is</u> efficient. Adam Smith believed that each participant in a competitive market is "led by <u>an invisible hand</u>." A price <u>ceiling</u> is a regulation that makes it illegal to charge a price higher than a specified level. <u>A public good</u> is a good or service that is consumed simultaneously by everyone, even if they don't pay for it. Deadweight loss is the decrease in <u>consumer surplus and producer surplus</u> that results from an inefficient level of production.

True or false
1. True; page 152
2. False; page 152
3. False; page 153
4. False; page 155

Multiple choice
1. d; page 152
2. d; page 152
3. a; page 153
4. d; page 152
5. c; page 153
6. d; page 155
7. c; page 155
8. d; page 156

Complete the graph
■ **FIGURE 6.10**
Price (thousands of dollars per automobile)

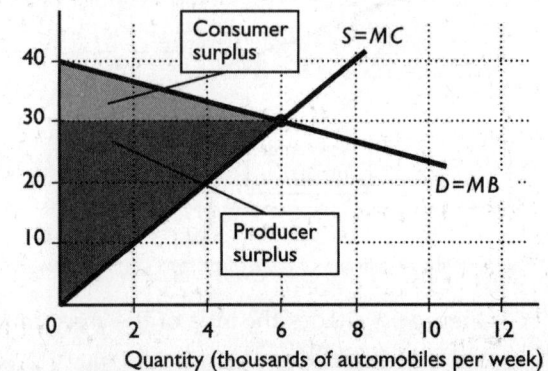

[Graph showing S=MC supply curve, D=MB demand curve, Consumer surplus and Producer surplus regions; x-axis: Quantity (thousands of automobiles per week) 0 to 12; y-axis: 0 to 40]

1. In Figure 6.10 the equilibrium quantity of

automobiles is 6,000 a week. The efficient quantity of automobiles is also 6,000 a week because that is the quantity at which the marginal benefit equals the marginal cost. The consumer surplus and producer surplus are the shown in the figure. The consumer surplus is the area of the light grey triangle, which is 1/2 × ($40.00 − $30.00) × (6,000) = $60,000. The producer surplus is the area of the dark grey triangle, which is 1/2 × ($30.00 − $0.00) × (60,000) = $90,000; page 152.

■ **FIGURE 6.11**
Price (thousands of dollars per automobile)

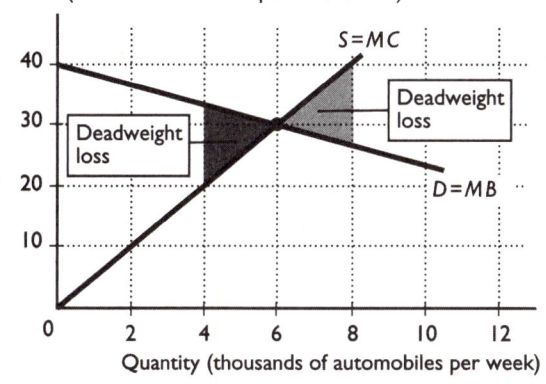

2. a. When 8,000 automobiles are produced, there is a deadweight loss from overproduction because for the last 2,000 automobiles, the marginal cost exceeds the marginal benefit. The deadweight loss is the area of the light grey triangle in Figure 6.11, which is 1/2 × ($40.00 − $26.67) × (8,000 − 6,000) = $1,330; page 155.

   b. If 4,000 automobiles are produced, there again is a deadweight loss, this time from underproduction, because automobiles for which the marginal benefit exceeds the marginal cost are not produced. The amount of the deadweight loss is the area of dark grey triangle in Figure 6.11, which is 1/2 × ($33.33 − $20.00) × (6,000 − 4,000) = $1,330; page 155.

Short answer and numeric questions
1. Adam Smith was the first to suggest that competitive markets send resources to the uses in which they have the highest value so that competitive markets are efficient. Smith said that each participant in a competitive market is "led by an invisible hand to promote an end [the efficient use of resources] which is no part of his intention;" page 153.

2. If the demand for cotton clothing increases, the demand curve for cotton clothing shifts rightward and the equilibrium quantity increases. The demand curve is the marginal benefit curve, so when the demand curve shifts rightward, the marginal benefit curve also shifts rightward. The efficient quantity also increases; page 152.

3. Governments influence markets by setting price and quantity regulations as well as taxes and subsidies, all of which can create inefficiency. Other obstacles to achieving an efficient allocation of resources are externalities, public goods, common resources, monopoly, and high transactions costs; pages 156-157.

■ **CHECKPOINT 6.5**

Fill in the blanks
Two views of fairness are that "it's not fair if the result isn't fair;" and "it's not fair if the rules aren't fair." According to Robert Nozick, fair-rules ideas require property rights and voluntary exchange.

True or false
  1. True; page 159
  2. False; page 160
  3. False; page 161

Multiple choice
  1. b; page 159
  2. b; page 160
  3. a; page 160
  4. c; page 161

Short answer and numeric questions
1. The tax arrangement is fair from a fair-results view because it leads to a greater equality of income. The tax arrangement is not fair from a fair-results view because the tax is not a voluntary exchange; pages 159-160.

2. From a fair-results view, it is not fair for Pat's income to be substantially higher than Matt's. From a fair-rules view, it is fair because Pat and Matt had the same opportunities; pages 159-160.
3. Income can be transferred from people with high incomes to people with low incomes only by taxing incomes, which discourages work. This tax results in the quantity of labor being less than the efficient quantity. Similarly, taxing income from capital discourages saving, which results in the quantity of capital being less than the efficient quantity. With less labor and less capital than the efficient amounts, the total amount of production is less than the efficient amount. So the greater the amount of income redistribution through income taxes, the greater is the inefficiency and the smaller is the economic pie; page 160.
4. Limiting the price that can be charged is unfair because it compels the seller to help and such compulsion is unfair; page 161.

Chapter 7

Markets in Action

CHAPTER CHECKLIST

In Chapter 7 we look at the inefficiency that is created when the government imposes a rent ceiling in the housing market, a minimum wage in the labor market, and a price support in an agricultural market.

1 **Explain how a price ceiling works and show how a rent ceiling creates a housing shortage, inefficiency, and unfairness.**

A price ceiling is an *upper* limit on the price at which it is legal to trade a particular good, service, or factor of production. A rent ceiling is an example of a price ceiling. A rent ceiling set above the equilibrium rent is ineffective. A housing shortage occurs when a rent ceiling is set below the equilibrium rent because the quantity of housing demanded exceeds the quantity of housing supplied. A black market is an illegal market that operates alongside a government regulated market. When a rent ceiling creates a shortage of housing, search activity, which is the time spent looking for someone with whom to do business, increases. A rent ceiling creates a deadweight loss and decreases consumer surplus and producer surplus. Rent ceilings violate the fair-rules view of fairness because they block voluntary exchange. Rent ceilings exist because of political support from current renters.

2 **Explain how a price floor works and show how the minimum wage creates unemployment, inefficiency, and unfairness.**

A minimum wage law is a government regulation that makes hiring labor services for less than a specified wage illegal. A minimum wage law is an example of a price floor. A minimum wage set below the equilibrium wage rate is ineffective. Unemployment occurs when the minimum wage is set above the equilibrium wage rate because the quantity of labor supplied exceeds the quantity of labor demanded. A minimum wage increases job search activity and illegal hiring when some firms and workers agree to do business at an illegal wage rate below the minimum wage. The minimum wage creates a deadweight loss. The minimum wage is unfair because it delivers an unfair result and imposes unfair rules.

3 **Explain how a price support in the market for an agricultural product creates a surplus, inefficiency, and unfairness.**

When governments intervene in agricultural markets, they isolate the domestic market from global competition by limiting imports. The government introduces a price floor, which in an agricultural market is called a price support. The price support leads to a surplus, so the government pays the farmers a subsidy by purchasing the surplus to keep the price at the support level. Consumers are worse off because the price rises and the quantity they purchase decreases. Consumer surplus shrinks. Farmers are better off because the price is higher and the government purchases the surplus to keep the price higher. A deadweight loss is created. Farmers in developing economies are harmed two ways: First, their exports to the domestic nation are limited and, second, the government sells the surplus it has purchased in the rest of the world, thereby lowering the price these farmers receive.

CHECKPOINT 7.1

■ **Explain how a price ceiling works and show how a rent ceiling creates a housing shortage, inefficiency, and unfairness.**

Quick Review

- *Price ceiling* A government regulation that places an *upper* limit on the price at which a particular good, service, or factor of production may be traded.
- *Rent ceiling* A government regulation that makes it illegal to charge more than a specified rent for housing.
- *Effective rent ceiling* When a rent ceiling is set below the equilibrium rent, the quantity of housing demanded is greater than the equilibrium quantity and the quantity of housing supplied is less than the equilibrium quantity. A housing shortage occurs.

Additional Practice Problems 7.1

1. The figure shows the rental market for apartments in Ocala, Florida. 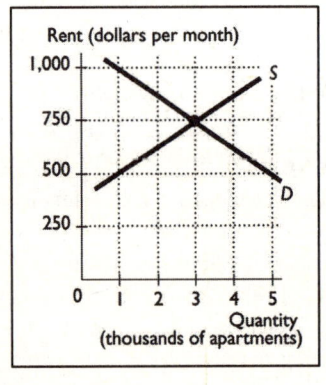
   a. With no government intervention in this market, what is the rent and how many apartments are rented?
   b. If the government imposes a rent ceiling of $500 a month, what is the rent and how many apartments are rented?
   c. Tell why with a strictly enforced $500 rent ceiling the housing market is inefficient. What is the amount of the deadweight loss?
   d. With a strictly enforced $500 rent ceiling, is there a shortage or surplus of apartments?

Price (dollars per round of golf)	Quantity demanded	Quantity supplied
	(rounds per week)	
50	2,000	2,800
40	2,300	2,700
30	2,600	2,600
20	2,900	2,500
10	3,200	2,400

2. The table above gives the supply and demand schedules for rounds of golf at a city owned golf course.
   a. What is the equilibrium price and equilibrium quantity of rounds of golf?
   b. Suppose the city government imposes a price ceiling of $40 a round of golf. What will be the price and quantity of rounds of golf? Is there a shortage?
   c. Suppose the city government imposes a price ceiling of $20 a round of golf. What will be the price and quantity of rounds of golf? Is there a shortage?

Solutions to Additional Practice Problems 7.1

1a. In the figure, the equilibrium rent and the equilibrium quantity are determined at the point where the demand curve and the supply curve intersect. The rent is $750 a month and 3,000 apartments are rented.

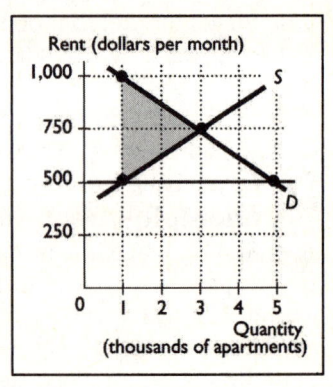

1b. To answer this practice problem remember that a rent ceiling is effective only when it is set below the equilibrium price. The rent ceiling of $500 per month is below the equilibrium rent, so it has an effect. The quantity of apartments rented decreases to 1,000 and the rent is $500.

1c. The market is inefficient because the marginal benefit of the last apartment rented, the 1,000th apartment, exceeds the marginal cost of the apartment. Because the housing market is inefficient a deadweight loss arises. In the figure the deadweight loss is shown by the grey triangle. The amount of the deadweight loss equals the area of the grey triangle. This area is 1/2 × ($1,000 − $500) × (3,000 − 1,000) = $500,000.

1d. There is a shortage of apartments. At the $500 rent ceiling, the quantity of apartments demanded is 5,000 and the quantity supplied is 1,000. So there is a shortage of 4,000 apartments.

2a. The equilibrium price is $30 a round of golf and the equilibrium quantity is 2,600 rounds a week.

2b. The price ceiling is above the equilibrium price, so the price remains at $30 a round and the quantity remains at 2,600 rounds a week. There is no shortage.

2c. The price ceiling is below the equilibrium price. The price falls to $20 a round. The quantity played equals the quantity supplied at $20, which is 2,500 rounds a week. There is a shortage of 400 rounds a week.

■ **Self Test 7.1**

Fill in the blanks

A price ceiling is the ____ (highest; lowest) price at which it is legal to trade a particular good, service, or factor of production. A rent ceiling is effective if it is set ____ (above; below) the equilibrium rent. A rent ceiling can create a housing ____ (shortage; surplus), which leads to ____ (increased; decreased) search activity. Rent ceilings ____ (can result in; do not result in) inefficiency. The ____ (less; more) inelastic the demand or the supply of housing, the smaller the deadweight loss created by a rent ceiling. Rent ceilings ____ (are; are not) fair.

True or false

1. A rent ceiling always lowers the rent paid.
2. When a rent ceiling is higher than the equilibrium rent, a black market emerges.
3. The opportunity cost of a dorm room is equal to its rent plus the value of the search time spent finding the dorm room.
4. Rent ceilings are efficient because they lower the cost of housing to low-income families.
5. The total loss from a rent ceiling exceeds the deadweight loss.

Multiple choice

1. A price ceiling is a government regulation that makes it illegal to charge a price
   a. below the equilibrium price.
   b. above the equilibrium price.
   c. for a good or service.
   d. above some specified level.
   e. that is not equal to the equilibrium price.

2. When a price ceiling is set below the equilibrium price, the quantity supplied ____ the quantity demanded and ____ exists.
   a. is less than; a surplus
   b. is less than; a shortage
   c. is greater than; a surplus
   d. is greater than; a shortage
   e. equals; an equilibrium

3. In a housing market with a rent ceiling set below the equilibrium rent,
   a. some people seeking an apartment to rent will not be able to find one.
   b. the total cost of renting an apartment will decrease for all those seeking housing.
   c. some landlords will not be able to find renters to fill available apartments.
   d. search will decrease because renters no longer need to search for less expensive apartments.
   e. None of the above answers are correct because to have an impact the rent ceiling must be set *above* the equilibrium rent.

4. A rent ceiling on housing creates a problem of allocating the available housing units because
   a. the demand for housing decreases and the demand curve shifts leftward.
   b. the supply of housing increases and the supply curve shifts rightward.
   c. a shortage of apartments occurs.
   d. a surplus of apartments occurs.
   e. it eliminates search, which is one of the major ways housing units are allocated.

■ FIGURE 7.1
Rent (dollars per month)

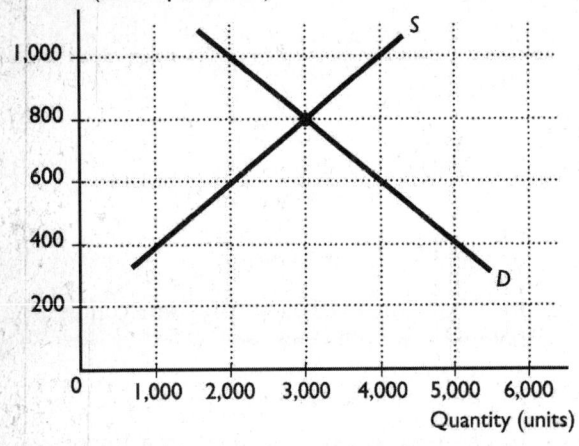

5. Figure 7.1 shows a housing market. If the government imposes a rent ceiling of $1,000 per month, there will be a
   a. surplus of 2,000 units.
   b. shortage of 2,000 units.
   c. surplus of 4,000 units.
   d. shortage of 1,000 units.
   e. neither a shortage nor a surplus of units.

6. Figure 7.1 shows a housing market. If the government imposes a rent ceiling of $400 per month, there will be a
   a. shortage of 1,000 units.
   b. shortage of 2,000 units.
   c. shortage of 3,000 units.
   d. shortage of 4,000 units.
   e. neither a shortage nor a surplus of units.

7. Figure 7.1 shows a housing market. Of the rent ceilings listed below, the deadweight loss from a rent ceiling is largest when the rent ceiling equals ____ per month.
   a. $1,000
   b. $800
   c. $600
   d. $400
   e. More information is needed to determine which of the rent ceilings has the largest deadweight loss.

8. Rent ceilings
   a. increase search activity.
   b. result in surpluses.
   c. are efficient.
   d. benefit producers.
   e. have no effect if they are set below the equilibrium rent.

9. Suppose that the government imposes a price ceiling on gasoline that is below the equilibrium price. The black market for gasoline is ____ market in which the price ____ the ceiling price.
   a. a legal; exceeds
   b. an illegal; exceeds
   c. a legal; is less than
   d. an illegal; is less than
   e. an illegal; equals

10. A rent ceiling creates a deadweight loss
    a. if it is set below the equilibrium rent.
    b. if it is set equal to the equilibrium rent.
    c. if it set above the equilibrium rent.
    d. if it decreases the taxes the government collects in the housing market.
    e. never, because if it did create a deadweight loss, the government would not impose it.

11. Rent ceilings
    a. eliminate the problem of scarcity.
    b. allocate resources efficiently.
    c. ensure that housing goes to the poorer people.
    d. benefit renters living in rent-controlled apartments.
    e. benefit all landlords because the landlords know what rent to charge their renters.

Complete the graph

■ **FIGURE 7.2**

Price (dollars per purse)

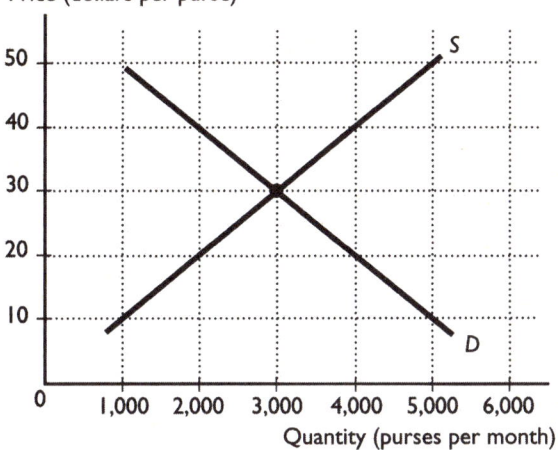

1. Figure 7.2 shows the market for purses.
   a. What is the equilibrium price and quantity of purses?
   b. Suppose the government imposes a $20 price ceiling. With the price ceiling, what is the quantity of purses demanded and the quantity of purses supplied? What is the shortage? Indicate the shortage in the figure.
   c. The price ceiling creates a deadweight loss. Show the deadweight loss in the figure.

Rent (dollars per month)	Quantity demanded	Quantity supplied
	(housing units per month)	
900	200	350
800	300	300
700	400	250
600	500	200
500	600	150

2. The table above gives the demand and supply schedules for housing in a small town. In Figure 7.3, graph the demand and supply curves. Label the axes.
   a. What is the equilibrium rent and quantity of housing?
   b. Suppose the government imposes a $600 a month rent ceiling. With the rent ceiling, what is the quantity of housing demanded and the quantity of housing supplied?

■ **FIGURE 7.3**

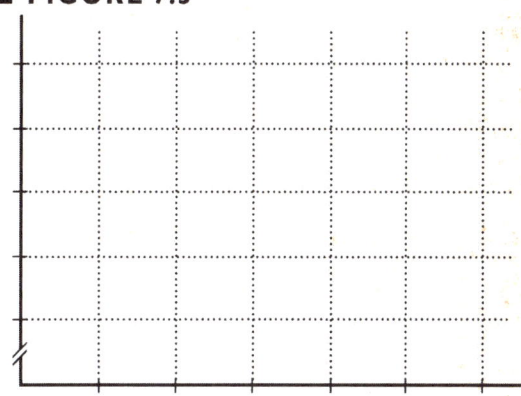

   c. Does the rent ceiling result in a shortage or a surplus of housing? Indicate the shortage or surplus in Figure 7.3.

Short answer and numeric questions

1. What is a price ceiling?

Price (dollars per carton)	Quantity demanded	Quantity supplied
	(cartons per day)	
1.00	200	110
1.25	175	130
1.50	150	150
1.75	125	170
2.00	100	190

2. The table above gives the demand and supply schedules for milk.
   a. What is the market equilibrium in the milk market?
   b. Suppose the government imposes a price ceiling of $1.25 per carton. What is the price of a carton of milk and what quantity is purchased? Is there a shortage or surplus of milk?
   c. Suppose the government imposes a price ceiling of $1.75 per carton. What is the price of a carton of milk and what quantity is purchased? Is there a shortage or surplus of milk?
3. Are rent ceilings efficient?
4. Are rent ceilings fair?

CHECKPOINT 7.2

■ **Explain how a price floor works and show how the minimum wage creates unemployment, inefficiency, and unfairness.**

Quick Review

- *Price floor* A government regulation that places a *lower* limit on the price at which a particular good, service, or factor of production may be traded.
- *Minimum wage law* A government regulation that makes hiring labor services for less than a specified wage illegal.
- *Effective minimum wage law* When the minimum wage is set above the equilibrium wage rate, the quantity of labor demanded is less than the equilibrium quantity and the quantity of labor supplied is greater than the equilibrium quantity. Unemployment occurs.

Additional Practice Problems 7.2

1. The figure shows the market for fast food workers in Lake City Florida. 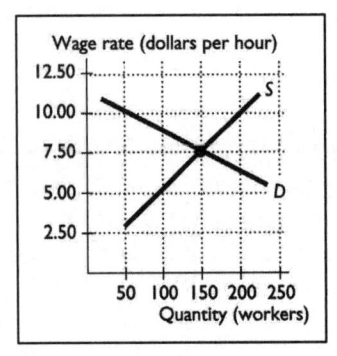
   a. What is the equilibrium wage rate of the workers and what is the equilibrium quantity of workers employed?
   b. If Lake City introduces a minimum wage for fast food workers of $10 an hour, how many fast food workers are employed?
   c. With the minimum wage, is there a surplus or a shortage of fast food workers? Indicate the amount of any shortage or surplus in the figure.
   d. Is the minimum wage of $10 an hour efficient? Is it fair?

Price (cents per pound)	Quantity demanded	Quantity supplied
	(tons of sugar per year)	
10	300	225
15	275	275
20	250	325
25	225	375
30	200	425

2. The above table gives the supply and demand schedules for sugar.
   a. What is the equilibrium price and quantity of sugar?
   b. Suppose the government imposes a price floor of 25¢ a pound. What is the quantity demanded and the quantity supplied? Is there a shortage or surplus and, if so, how much?

Solutions to Additional Practice Problems 7.2

1a. The equilibrium wage rate and the equilibrium quantity of the workers are determined where the labor demand curve and the labor supply curve intersect. The equilibrium wage rate is $7.50 an hour and the equilibrium quantity of workers is 150.

1b. In the figure, 50 fast food workers are employed. This amount equals the quantity of labor demanded when the wage rate is $10 an hour.

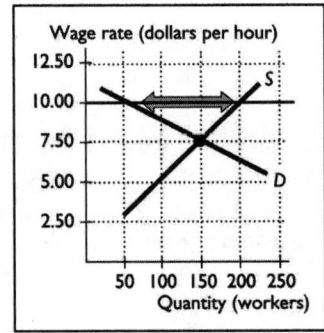

1c. The minimum wage creates a surplus of workers. At the $10 wage rate, 200 workers are willing to work but firms are willing to hire only 50 workers. There is a surplus of 150 workers, that is, there are 150 workers unemployed. In the figure, the length of the arrow shows the 150 unemployed workers.

1d. The minimum wage of $10 an hour is not efficient because the marginal benefit to restaurants who demand workers exceeds the marginal cost borne by the workers who supply work. A deadweight loss is created.

An additional loss arises as unemployed workers search for jobs. The minimum wage is not fair. It violates the "fair-rules" view of fairness because it prevents voluntary exchange. It violates the "fair-results" view of fairness because 100 workers lose their jobs and are made poorer.

2a. The equilibrium price is 15¢ a pound and the equilibrium quantity is 275 tons a year.

2b. The quantity demanded at 25¢ a pound is 225 tons and the quantity supplied is 375 tons. There is a surplus of 150 tons.

■ Self Test 7.2

Fill in the blanks

A minimum wage is a price ____ (ceiling; floor). A price floor is the ____ (highest; lowest) price at which it is legal to trade a particular good, service, or factor of production. If a minimum wage is set above the equilibrium wage rate, the quantity of labor demanded ____ (decreases; increases) and the quantity of labor supplied ____ (decreases; increases). A minimum wage ____ (creates; does not create) unemployment and ____ (decreases; increases) job search activity. An efficient allocation of labor occurs when the marginal ____ (benefit; cost) to firms ____ (equals; is greater than; is less than) the marginal ____ (benefit; cost) borne by workers. The minimum wage is ____ (fair; unfair). Labor unions ____ (do not support; support) the minimum wage.

True or false

1. Firms hire labor, so they determine how much labor to supply in a market.
2. A minimum wage is effective when it is set above the equilibrium wage rate.
3. A minimum wage law can lead to increased job search activity and illegal hiring.
4. When a minimum wage is set above the equilibrium wage rate, the employee's marginal cost of working exceeds the employer's marginal benefit from hiring labor.
5. A minimum wage is fair because low-income workers receive an increase in take-home pay.

Multiple choice

1. A price floor
    a. is the highest price at which it is legal to trade a particular good, service, or factor of production.
    b. is the lowest price at which it is legal to trade a particular good, service, or factor of production.
    c. is an illegal price to charge.
    d. is the equilibrium price when the stock market crashes.
    e. is the lowest price for which the quantity demanded equals the quantity supplied.

2. To be effective in raising people's wages, a minimum wage must be set
    a. above the equilibrium wage rate.
    b. below the equilibrium wage rate.
    c. equal to the equilibrium wage rate.
    d. below $7.
    e. either above or below the equilibrium wage depending on whether the supply curve of labor shifts rightward or leftward in response to the minimum wage.

3. A minimum wage set above the equilibrium wage rate
    a. increases the quantity of labor services supplied.
    b. decreases the quantity of labor services supplied.
    c. has no effect on the quantity of labor services supplied.
    d. shifts the labor supply curve rightward.
    e. shifts the labor supply curve leftward.

4. Suppose the current equilibrium wage rate for lifeguards in Houston is $7.85 an hour. A minimum wage law that creates a price floor of $8.50 an hour leads to
    a. a surplus of lifeguards in Houston.
    b. a shortage of lifeguards in Houston.
    c. no changes in the lifeguard market.
    d. a change in the quantity of lifeguards supplied but no change in the quantity of lifeguards demanded.
    e. an increase in the number of lifeguards employed.

5. An increase in the minimum wage ___ employment and ___ unemployment.
   a. increases; increases
   b. increases; decreases
   c. decreases; increases
   d. decreases; decreases
   e. does not change; increases

■ FIGURE 7.4

Wage rate (dollars per hour)

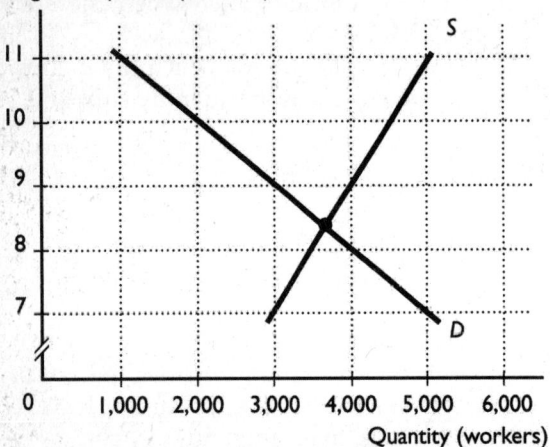

6. Figure 7.4 shows the market for fast food workers in San Francisco. A minimum wage of $11 per hour leads to unemployment of ___ workers.
   a. 1,000
   b. 2,000
   c. 3,000
   d. 4,000
   e. 5,000

7. In Figure 7.4, which of the following minimum wages creates the most unemployment?
   a. $7 an hour
   b. $8 an hour
   c. $9 an hour
   d. $10 an hour
   e. $11 an hour

8. If a minimum wage is introduced that is above the equilibrium wage rate,
   a. the quantity of labor services demanded increases.
   b. job search activity increases.
   c. the supply of labor increases and the supply of labor curve shifts rightward.
   d. unemployment decreases because more workers accept jobs at the higher minimum wage rate.
   e. the quantity of labor supplied decreases because of the increase in unemployment.

9. The minimum wage is set above the equilibrium wage rate. Does the minimum wage create inefficiency?
   a. Yes.
   b. No.
   c. Only if the supply of labor is perfectly inelastic.
   d. Only if the supply of labor is perfectly elastic.
   e. Only if employment exceeds the efficient amount.

10. When the minimum wage is raised, the ___ union labor ___.
    a. demand for; increases
    b. demand for; decreases
    c. supply of; increases
    d. supply of; decreases
    e. demand for; does not change

Complete the graph

Wage rate (dollars per hour)	Quantity demanded	Quantity supplied
	(workers per day)	
6	3,500	2,750
7	3,000	3,000
8	2,500	3,250
9	2,000	3,500
10	1,500	3,750

1. The table above gives the demand and supply schedules for labor in a small town.
   a. In Figure 7.5, on the next page, label the axes. Draw the labor demand and labor supply curves. What is the equilibrium wage rate and employment.

■ FIGURE 7.5

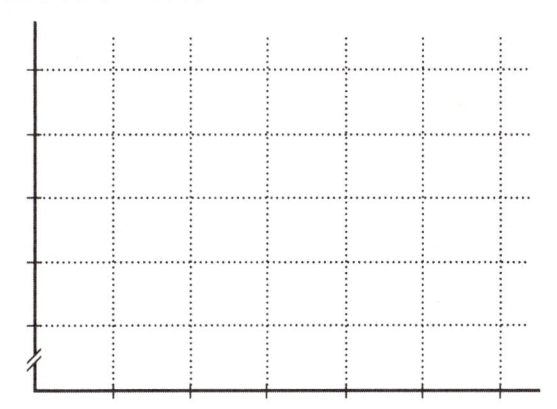

b. Suppose the government imposes a $6 an hour minimum wage. What is the effect on the wage rate and levels of employment and unemployment?

c. Suppose the government raises the minimum wage from $6 an hour to $9 an hour. What is the effect on the wage rate and levels of employment and unemployment? Indicate any unemployment.

■ FIGURE 7.6
Wage rate (dollars per hour)

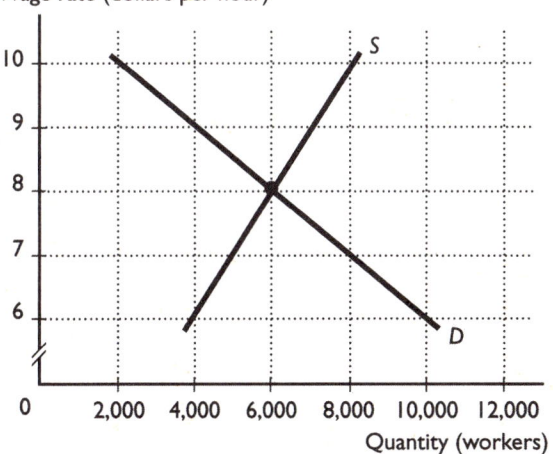

2. Figure 7.6 shows the labor demand and labor supply curves for Rochester, New York. Suppose the city is considering instituting a minimum wage. Indicate the minimum wages that lead to unemployment by darkening the vertical axis for all the minimum wages that create unemployment.

Short answer and numeric questions
1. What is the effect of a minimum wage set below the equilibrium wage rate?
2. How does a minimum wage affect the time needed to find a job?
3. Do all low-wage workers benefit from a minimum wage?

CHECKPOINT 7.3

■ **Explain how a price support in the market for an agricultural product creates a surplus, inefficiency, and unfairness.**

Quick Review
- *Price support* A price support is a price floor in an agricultural market maintained by a government guarantee to buy any surplus output at that price. The price support is the minimum price for which the product may be sold.

Additional Practice Problems 7.3
1. The figure shows the market for sugar. 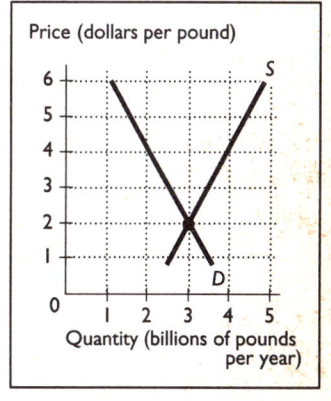
   a. What are the equilibrium price and quantity of sugar?
   b. Suppose the government puts in place a price support for sugar at $4 per pound. In the figure above, indicate this price support.
   c. With the price support, how much sugar is produced? How much sugar is purchased by private consumers? How much is purchased by the government?

d. With the price support, what is the subsidy received by sugar producers?
e. Are consumers made better off or worse off with the price support?
f. Without the price support, is the market efficient? With the price support, is the market efficient?

2. With a price support, the government pays a subsidy to farmers by buying part of the crop. Why is this purchase necessary?

Solutions to Additional Practice Problems 7.3

1a. The equilibrium price and the equilibrium quantity of sugar are determined where the demand curve and the supply curve intersect. The figure shows that the equilibrium price is $2 a pound and the equilibrium quantity is 3 billion pounds a year.

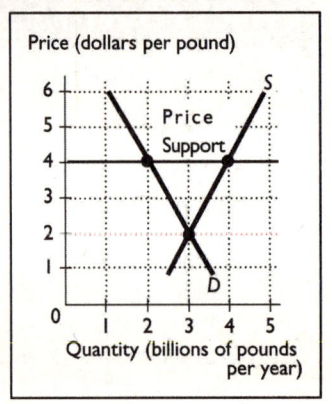

1b. The price support is shown in the figure as the solid line at $4 per pound.

1c. With the price support, the supply curve shows that at $4 per pound, 4 billion pounds of sugar are produced. The demand curve shows that at this price consumers buy 2 billion pounds. The government buys the surplus quantity of sugar, 2 billion pounds.

1d. The government buys 2 billion pounds of sugar at $4 per pound, so the subsidy is 2 billion pounds × $4 per pound, which is $8 billion.

1e. Consumers are worse off with the price support. With the price support the price they must pay for sugar increases, from $2 per pound to $4 per pound. In response consumers decrease the quantity of sugar they consume from 3 billion pounds to 2 billion pounds.

1f. Without the price support, the market is efficient. With the price support, the market is not efficient.

2. The price support leads to a surplus of the crop. If the government did not buy the surplus, the farmers would not be able to cover their costs because there would be part of the crop left unsold.

■ Self Test 7.3

Fill in the blanks

A price support is a ____ (price ceiling; price floor) in an agricultural market. The government maintains the price support by guaranteeing to ____ (buy; sell) the product at the support price. The government gives a ____ to producers to cover part of the costs of production. When the price support is above the equilibrium price, producers ____ (increase; decrease) the quantity supplied and consumers ____ (increase; decrease) the quantity demanded. Farmers ____ (gain; lose) from a price support and consumers ____ (gain; lose) from a price support. A price support ____ (creates; does not create) inefficiency and a deadweight loss.

True or false

1. In order to have an effective price support, the government isolates the domestic market from the world market by restricting imports.

2. A price support sets the maximum price for which farmers may sell their crop.

3. In order to keep the price of a crop above the equilibrium price and equal to the supported price, the government must buy some of the crop.

4. Because they decrease production, price supports decrease farmers' total revenue.

5. Price supports are efficient because they guarantee production of the good.

Multiple choice

1. Price supports are generally used in
   a. labor markets.
   b. industrial markets.
   c. housing markets.
   d. markets for services.
   e. agricultural markets.

2. To have an effective price support program, the government must
   i. isolate the domestic market from the world market
   ii. pay the farmers a subsidy
   iii. introduce a price floor
   a. i only.
   b. ii only.
   c. iii only.
   d. ii and iii.
   e. i, ii, and iii.

3. A price support directly sets the
   a. amount of production.
   b. subsidy the government must receive from producers.
   c. equilibrium quantity.
   d. lowest price for which the good may be sold.
   e. highest price for which the good may be sold.

4. To keep the price at the level set by the price support, the government must
   a. buy some of the good.
   b. sell some of the good.
   c. receive a subsidy from the producers.
   d. insure that imports are readily available.
   e. be careful to always set the price support below the equilibrium price.

5. With a price support program, who receives a subsidy?
   a. only consumers
   b. only producers
   c. the government
   d. importers
   e. both consumers and producers receive a subsidy

6. When a price support is set above the equilibrium price, producers ____ the quantity supplied and consumers ____ the quantity demanded.
   a. increase; increase
   b. increase; decrease
   c. decrease; increase
   d. decrease; decrease
   e. do not change; do not change

■ **FIGURE 7.7**
Price (dollars per ton)

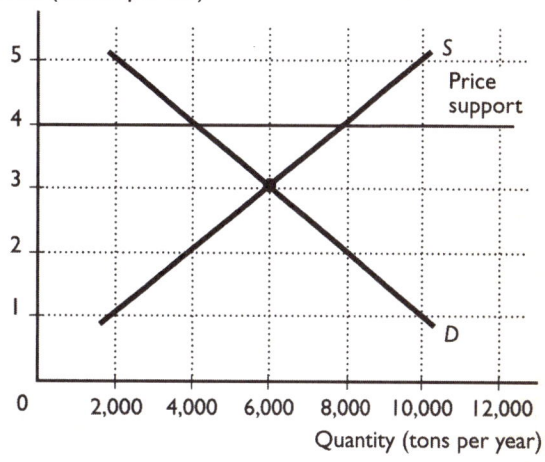

7. Figure 7.7 shows a price support program in an agricultural market. The amount of the subsidy necessary to keep the price at the price support is
   a. $4.
   b. $32,000.
   c. $8,000.
   d. $16,000.
   e. $24,000.

8. A price support ____ producers and ____ a deadweight loss.
   a. has no effect on; does not create
   b. benefits; creates
   c. harms; creates
   d. benefits; does not create
   e. harms; does not create

Complete the graph

Price (dollars per bushel)	Quantity demanded	Quantity supplied
	(millions of bushels per year)	
3	3,500	2,000
4	3,000	3,000
5	2,500	4,000
6	2,000	5,000
7	1,500	6,000

1. The table gives the demand and supply schedules for wheat.
   a. In Figure 7.8 label the axes. Draw the demand curve and supply curve and indicate the equilibrium price and quantity.

FIGURE 7.8

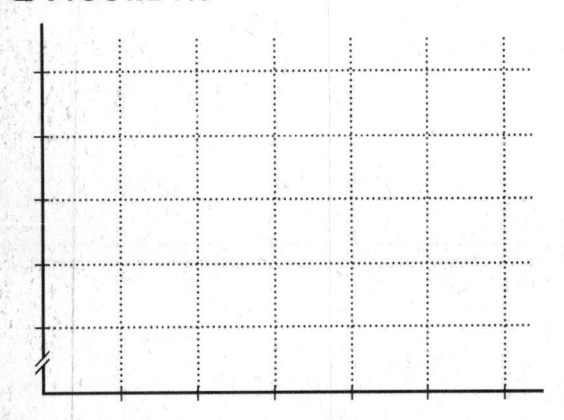

b. Suppose the government imposes a price support of $5 per bushel. What is the effect on the price of wheat, the quantity of wheat produced and the marginal cost of a bushel of wheat? Is there a deadweight loss?

c. With the $5 per bushel price support, how much wheat do consumers buy? What is the subsidy the government must pay to producers?

FIGURE 7.9
Price (dollars per ton)

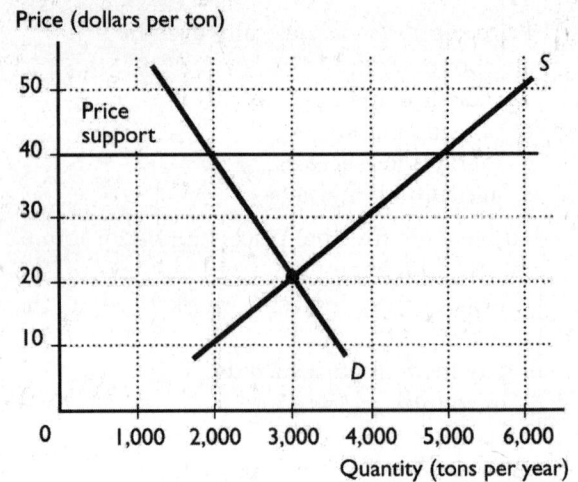

2. Figure 7.9 shows the demand and supply curves for peanuts. There is a price support of $40 per ton of peanuts.
   a. At the support price, what is the quantity of peanuts produced? What is the quantity consumers buy? How many tons of peanuts must the government buy? Indicate the amount the government must buy in Figure 7.9.
   b. How much is the subsidy paid by the government to producers?

Short answer and numeric questions

1. Why must a price support be set above the equilibrium price in order to have an effect?
2. "A price support program benefits producers and harms consumers. But there is no overall net effect on society." Comment on the above assertion. Is it correct or incorrect?

SELF TEST ANSWERS

■ CHECKPOINT 7.1

Fill in the blanks
A price ceiling is the <u>highest</u> price at which it is legal to trade a particular good, service, or factor of production. A rent ceiling is effective if it is set <u>below</u> the equilibrium rent. A rent ceiling can create a housing <u>shortage</u>, which leads to <u>increased</u> search activity. Rent ceilings <u>can result in</u> inefficiency. The <u>more</u> inelastic the demand or the supply of housing, the smaller the deadweight loss created by a rent ceiling. Rent ceilings <u>are not</u> fair.

True or false
1. False; page 168
2. False; pages 168-169
3. True; page 170
4. False; page 172
5. True; page 172

Multiple choice
1. d; page 168
2. b; pages 168-169
3. a; page 169
4. c; page 169
5. e; page 168
6. d; page 169
7. d; page 172
8. a; page 170
9. b; pages 169-170
10. a; page 172
11. d; page 175

Complete the graph
1. a. The equilibrium price is $30 per purse and the equilibrium quantity is 3,000 purses.
   b. The quantity of purses demanded is 4,000, the quantity of purses supplied is 2,000, and the shortage equals 2,000 purses. In Figure 7.10, the shortage equals the length of the double-headed arrow; page 169.
   c. The deadweight loss is shown in the figure; page 172.
2. Figure 7.11 shows the demand curve and supply curve. The equilibrium rent is $800

■ **FIGURE 7.10**
Price (dollars per purse)

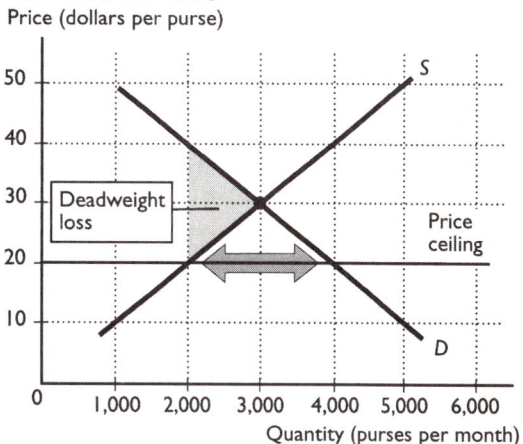

■ **FIGURE 7.11**
Rent (dollars per month)

a month and the quantity is 300 housing units a month.
   a. The quantity of housing demanded is 500 units a month; the quantity supplied is 200 units a month; page 170.
   b. The shortage of 300 units a month is indicated by the arrow; page 170.

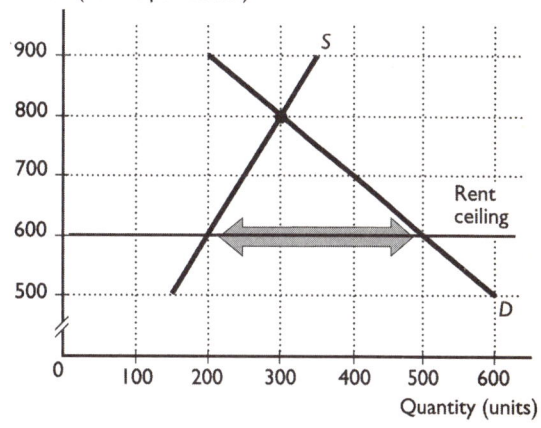

Short answer and numeric questions
1. A price ceiling is the highest price at which it is legal to trade a particular good, service, or factor of production; page 168.
2. a. The equilibrium price is $1.50 a carton and the quantity is 150 cartons a day.
   b. The price is $1.25 a carton and 130 cartons

108 Part 3 · HOW GOVERNMENTS INFLUENCE THE ECONOMY

a day are purchased. There is a shortage of 45 cartons a day; page 169.

c. The price ceiling is above the equilibrium price, and is ineffective. The price is $1.50 a carton, 150 cartons a day are purchased, and there is neither a shortage nor a surplus; page 168.

3. Rent ceilings create a deadweight loss and are not efficient; page 172.

4. Rent ceilings are not fair. They violate both the fair-results view and fair-rules view of fairness; page 175.

■ CHECKPOINT 7.2

Fill in the blanks

A minimum wage is a price <u>floor</u>. A price floor is the <u>lowest</u> price at which it is legal to trade a particular good, service, or factor of production. If a minimum wage is set above the equilibrium wage rate, the quantity of labor demanded <u>decreases</u> and the quantity of labor supplied <u>increases</u>. A minimum wage <u>creates</u> unemployment and <u>increases</u> job search activity. An efficient allocation of labor occurs when the marginal <u>benefit</u> to firms <u>equals</u> the marginal <u>cost</u> borne by workers. The minimum wage is <u>unfair</u>. Labor unions <u>support</u> the minimum wage.

True or false

1. False; page 175
2. True; page 176
3. True; page 177
4. False; page 178
5. False; page 179

Multiple choice

1. b; page 175
2. a; page 176
3. a; page 176
4. a; page 176
5. c; pages 176-177
6. d; page 176
7. e; pages 176-177
8. b; page 177
9. a; page 178
10. a; page 179

Complete the graph

■ **FIGURE 7.12**

Wage rate (dollars per hour)

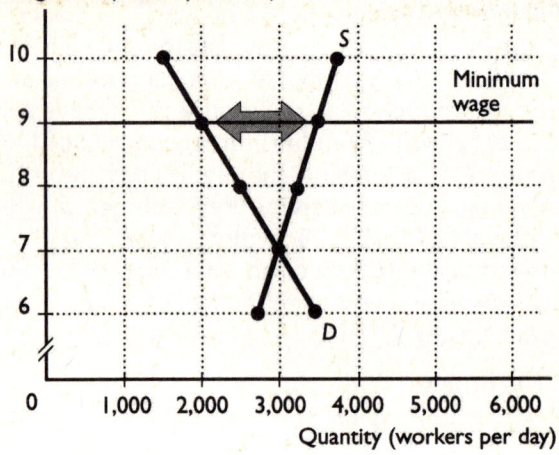

1. a. Figure 7.12 shows the demand and supply curves. The equilibrium wage rate is $7 an hour and the equilibrium employment is 3,000 workers a day.

b. The $6 minimum wage is below the equilibrium wage and has no effect; page 176.

c. The $9 minimum wage raises the wage rate to $9. Employment decreases to 2,000 workers. The number of workers looking for work is 3,500. Unemployment equals 3,500 − 2,000, which is 1,500 people. The amount of unemployment is shown by the arrow in Figure 7.12; pages 176-177.

■ **FIGURE 7.13**

Wage rate (dollars per hour)

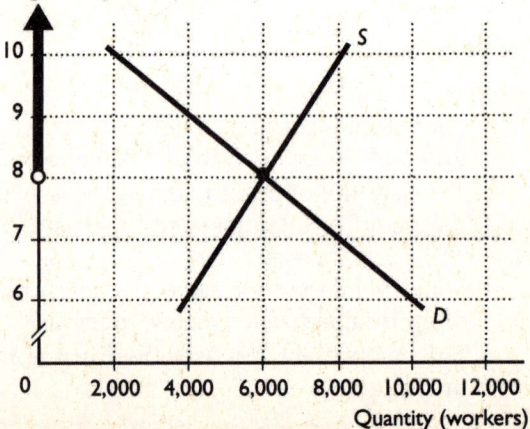

1. In order to have an effect in the market, the

minimum wage must be set above the equilibrium wage. As Figure 7.13 shows, any minimum wage above $8 per hour creates unemployment; page 176.

Short answer and numeric questions
1. A minimum wage set below the equilibrium wage rate has no effect on the wage rate or amount of employment; page 176.
2. By decreasing the quantity of labor demanded and creating unemployment, a minimum wage increases the time spent searching for a job; page 177.
3. A minimum wage harms low-wage workers who lose their jobs or cannot find jobs because of the minimum wage; page 179.

■ CHECKPOINT 7.3

Fill in the blanks

A price support is a <u>price floor</u> in an agricultural market. The government maintains the price support by guaranteeing to <u>buy</u> the product at the support price. The government gives a <u>subsidy</u> to producers to cover part of the costs of production. When the price support is above the equilibrium price, producers <u>increase</u> the quantity supplied and consumers <u>decrease</u> the quantity demanded. Farmers <u>gain</u> from a price support and consumers <u>lose</u> from a price support. A price support <u>creates</u> inefficiency and a deadweight loss.

True or false
1. True; page 181
2. False; page 181
3. True; page 182
4. False; page 183
5. False; page 183

Multiple choice
1. e; page 181
2. e; page 181
3. d; page 181
4. a; page 182
5. b; page 182

6. b; page 182
7. d; page 182
8. b; page 183

Complete the graph

■ **FIGURE 7.14**

Price (dollars per bushel)

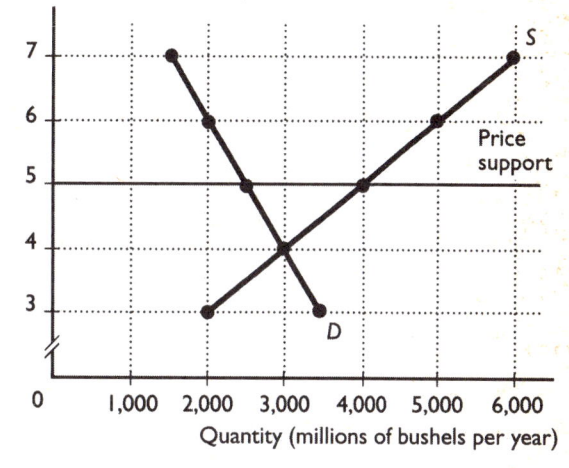

1. a. Figure 7.14 shows the demand and supply curves. The equilibrium price is $4 a bushel and the equilibrium quantity is 3,000 million bushels a year.
   b. The $5 per bushel price support is illustrated in the figure. This price support raises the price of wheat to $5 per bushel. The quantity of wheat produced increases to 4,000 million bushels per year and the marginal cost of the last bushel of wheat produced increases to $5. There is a deadweight loss because the marginal cost exceeds the marginal benefit; page 182.
   c. With the price support, consumers buy only 2,500 million bushels per year. There is a surplus of 1,500 million bushels (4,000 million bushels produced minus $2,500 million purchased by consumers) that the government must buy. The government pays a subsidy of $5 per bushel × 1,500 million bushels, which is $7.5 billion; page 182.

■ FIGURE 7.15

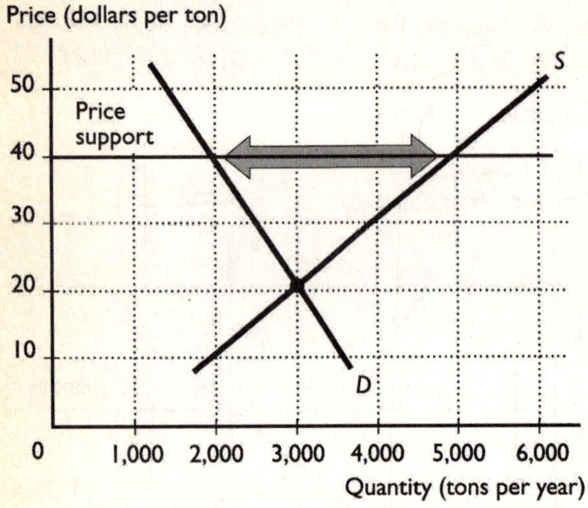

Price (dollars per ton)

2. a. Figure 7.15 shows that at the support price of $40 per ton, 5,000 tons are produced and consumers buy 2,000 tons. The government must buy the surplus, 3,000 tons. The amount the government must buy is equal to the length of the arrow in Figure 7.15; page 182.
   b. To buy the surplus, the government pays a subsidy to producers of $40 per ton × 3,000 tons, which is $120,000; page 182.

Short answer and numeric questions

1. If a price support is set below the equilibrium price, it does not make the equilibrium price illegal and so is ineffective. If a price support is set above the equilibrium price, it makes the equilibrium price illegal and is effective; page 181.

2. The first assertion is correct: a price support program increases producer surplus (which benefits producers) and decreases consumer surplus (which harms consumers). But the second assertion is incorrect. There is a net effect on society because a deadweight loss is created, which harms society; page 182.

Chapter 8: Taxes

CHAPTER CHECKLIST

In Chapter 8 we study how taxes affect markets, who pays a tax, the effect of an income tax and a Social Security tax, and review ideas about the fairness of taxes.

1. Explain how taxes change prices and quantities, are shared by buyers and sellers, and create inefficiency.

Taxes raise the price and decrease the quantity of the good that is taxed. Tax incidence is the division of the burden of a tax between the buyers and the sellers; generally sellers and buyers both pay part of a tax. Tax incidence between the buyers and the sellers depends on the elasticities of demand and supply and *not* upon who sends the government a check. For a given elasticity of supply, the buyers pay a larger share of the tax the more inelastic is the demand for the good. The buyers pay the entire tax when demand is perfectly inelastic or supply is perfectly elastic. Similarly, for a given elasticity of demand, the sellers pay a larger share of the tax the more inelastic is the supply of the good. The sellers pay the entire tax when demand is perfectly elastic or supply is perfectly inelastic. The excess burden of a tax is the amount by which the burden of a tax exceeds the tax revenue received by the government—the deadweight loss from a tax. The more inelastic the demand or supply, the smaller the excess burden of the tax.

2. Explain how income taxes and Social Security taxes change wage rates and create inefficiency.

The marginal tax rate is the percentage of an additional dollar that is paid in tax; the average tax rate is the percentage of income that is paid in tax. With a progressive tax, the average tax rate rises as income increases; with a proportional tax, the average tax rate is constant at all income levels; with a regressive tax, the average tax rate decreases as income increases. A tax on labor income decreases employment and creates a deadweight loss. Both the employer and the worker pay part of the tax. A tax on capital income decreases the quantity of capital and creates a deadweight loss. The supply of capital is highly elastic. If the supply of capital is perfectly elastic, firms, pay the entire tax. A tax on land or other unique resource does not decrease the quantity and creates no deadweight loss because supply is perfectly inelastic. The entire burden of the tax falls on the owner of the resource. The Social Security tax laws are written so that both workers and employers pay equal shares. But the incidence actually depends only on the elasticities of demand and supply and not on who the law says pays the tax.

3. Review ideas about the fairness of the tax system.

The benefits principle is the proposition that people should pay taxes equal to the benefits received from public services. This arrangement is fair because those who benefit the most pay the most. The ability-to-pay principle is the proposition that people should pay taxes according to how easily they can bear the burden. For fairness, the ability-to-pay principle compares people along vertical and horizontal dimensions. The fairness and efficiency of taxes can conflict, leading to the big tradeoff.

CHECKPOINT 8.1

■ **Explain how taxes change prices and quantities, are shared by buyers and sellers, and create inefficiency.**

Quick Review

- *Effect of a sales tax on the supply curve* A sales tax decreases the supply of the good and the supply curve shifts leftward. The vertical distance between the supply curve without the tax and the supply curve with the tax equals the amount of the tax.
- *Tax incidence and elasticities of demand and supply* For a given elasticity of supply, the more inelastic the demand, the larger the share of a tax paid by the buyer. And, for a given elasticity of demand, the more inelastic the supply, the larger the share of a tax paid by the seller.

Additional Practice Problem 8.1

1. The figure illustrates the initial equilibrium in the markets for Coke and Pepsi. The price of a 2 liter bottle of a Coke and a Pepsi are the same, $1.50, and the quantity of each are the same, 12 million bottles a week. The supply of Coke is identical to the supply of Pepsi and both are given by supply curve S in the figure. However, as shown in the figure with the demand curve Dc for Coke and Dp for Pepsi, the demand for Coke is more elastic than the demand for Pepsi. The government now imposes a $1 per bottle sales tax on Coke and Pepsi.

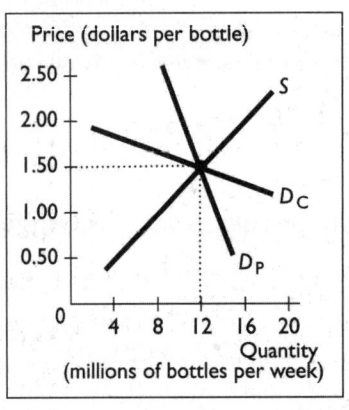

   a. Does the price paid by consumers for a Coke rise by more than, less than, or the same amount as the price paid for a Pepsi?

   b. Do the consumers of Coke pay more of their tax than do consumers of Pepsi? Do the producers of Coke pay more of their tax than do the producers of Pepsi?

   c. Does the quantity of Coke decrease by more than, less than, or the same amount as the quantity of Pepsi?

   d. Does the government collect more than, less than, or the same amount of tax revenue from the tax on Coke as it does from the tax on Pepsi?

   e. Is the deadweight loss from the tax on Coke larger than, less than, or the same amount as the deadweight loss from the tax on Pepsi?

Solution to Additional Practice Problem 8.1

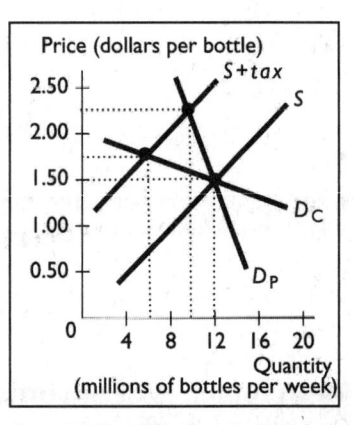

1a. A tax is like an increase in the suppliers' costs, so a tax decreases the supply and shifts the supply curve leftward. The vertical distance between the supply curve with the tax and the supply curve without the tax is equal to the amount of the tax, $1 per bottle in this problem. The figure shows this effect, with the supply curves for Coke and Pepsi both shifting to the curve labeled S+tax. The demand for Coke is more elastic, so the price paid by consumers for a Coke rises only to $1.75, a 25¢ increase. The demand for Pepsi is less elastic, so the price paid for a Pepsi rises to $2.25, a 75¢ increase.

1b. The demand for Coke is more elastic, so consumers play less of the tax imposed on Coke. The price paid by consumers for a Coke rises 25¢, so consumers pay 25¢ of this tax and producers pay the remaining 75¢. The demand for Pepsi is more inelastic, so consumers pay more of a tax imposed on Pepsi. The

price paid by consumers for a Pepsi rises 75¢, so consumers pay 75¢ of this tax and producers pay 25¢.
1c. The quantity of Coke decreases by more than the quantity of Pepsi because the demand for Coke is more elastic than the demand for Pepsi. In the figure, the equilibrium quantity of Coke decreases to 6 million bottles per week and the equilibrium quantity of Pepsi decreases only to 10 million bottles per week.
1d. The total amount of tax revenue equals the tax multiplied by the quantity sold. Because the decrease in the quantity of Coke is greater than the decrease in the quantity of Pepsi, less Coke than Pepsi is sold after the tax is imposed, and the government collects less tax revenue from the tax on Coke.
1e. Because the decrease in the quantity of Coke is greater than the decrease in the quantity of Pepsi, the deadweight loss of the tax is greater for Coke than for Pepsi.

■ Self Test 8.1

Fill in the blanks

The tax ____ (elasticity; incidence) is the division of the burden of a tax between the buyer and the seller. A tax is like ____ (a decrease; an increase) in suppliers' costs. For a given elasticity of supply, the buyer pays a larger share of the tax the more ____ (elastic; inelastic) is the demand for the good. If the supply is perfectly ____ (elastic; inelastic), the seller pays the entire tax. Taxes ____ (create; do not create) a deadweight loss. The excess burden of a tax is the ____ (deadweight loss; surplus) from the tax and is larger the ____ (more; less) elastic the demand for the good being taxed.

True or false

1. When the government imposes a tax on the sale of a good, the burden of the tax falls entirely on the buyer.
2. A tax on fast-food meals does not create a deadweight loss because the elasticity of supply of fast-food meals equals 1.0.
3. The excess burden of a tax is the deadweight loss from the tax.
4. For a given elasticity of supply, the more inelastic the demand for a good, the smaller the share of the tax paid by the buyer.
5. When the government taxes a good that has a perfectly elastic supply, the buyer pays the entire tax.

Multiple choice

1. Tax incidence refers to
   a. how government taxes are spent by the government.
   b. the incidences of tax revolts by the tax payers.
   c. the amount of a tax minus its burden.
   d. the division of the burden of a tax between the buyers and the sellers.
   e. tax revenue minus excess burden.

2. Neither the supply of nor demand for a good is perfectly elastic or perfectly inelastic. So imposing a tax on the good results in a ____ in the price paid by buyers and ____ in the equilibrium quantity.
   a. rise; an increase
   b. rise; a decrease
   c. fall; an increase
   d. fall; a decrease
   e. rise; no change

3. Neither the supply of nor demand for a good is perfectly elastic or perfectly inelastic. So imposing a tax on the good results in a ____ in the price received by sellers and a ____ in the price paid by buyers.
   a. rise; rise
   b. rise; fall
   c. fall; rise
   d. fall; fall
   e. no change; rise

4. A sales tax ____ consumer surplus and ____ producer surplus.
   a. increases; increases
   b. increases; decreases
   c. decreases; increases
   d. decreases; decreases
   e. does not change; does not change

FIGURE 8.1

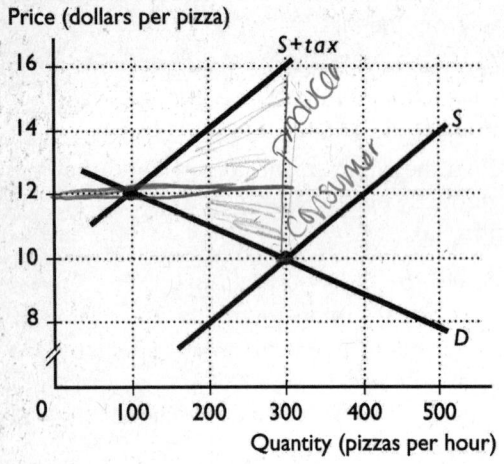

Price (dollars per pizza)

5. Figure 8.1 shows the market for delivered pizza. The government has imposed a tax of ____ per pizza.
   a. $6
   b. $8
   c. $10
   d. $12
   e. $16

6. In Figure 8.1, before the tax was imposed consumers paid ____ for a pizza and after the tax is imposed consumers pay ____ for a pizza.
   a. $10: $16
   b. $12; $16
   c. $10; $12
   d. $12; $16
   e. $10; $6

7. In Figure 8.1, the division of the tax is that consumers pay ____ of the tax and suppliers pay ____ of the tax.
   a. $6; $0
   b. $3; $3
   c. $0; $6
   d. $4; $2
   e. $2; $4

8. The deadweight loss from a tax is called the
   a. marginal benefit of the tax.
   b. marginal cost of the tax.
   c. excess burden of the tax.
   d. net gain from taxation.
   e. net loss from taxation.

9. A sales tax creates a deadweight loss because
   a. there is some paperwork opportunity cost of sellers paying the sales tax.
   b. demand and supply both decrease.
   c. less is produced and consumed.
   d. citizens value government goods less than private goods.
   e. the government spends the tax revenue it collects.

10. To determine who bears the greater share of a tax, we compare
    a. the number of buyers to the number of sellers.
    b. the elasticity of supply to the elasticity of demand.
    c. the size of the tax to the price of the good.
    d. government tax revenue to the revenue collected by the suppliers.
    e. the pre-tax quantity to the post-tax quantity.

11. Suppose the demand for barley is perfectly elastic. The supply curve of barley is upward sloping. If a tax is imposed on barley,
    a. barley sellers pay the entire tax.
    b. barley buyers pay the entire tax.
    c. the government pays the entire tax.
    d. the tax is split evenly between barley buyers and sellers.
    e. who pays the tax depends on whether the government imposes the tax on barley sellers or on barley buyers.

Complete the graph

■ FIGURE 8.2

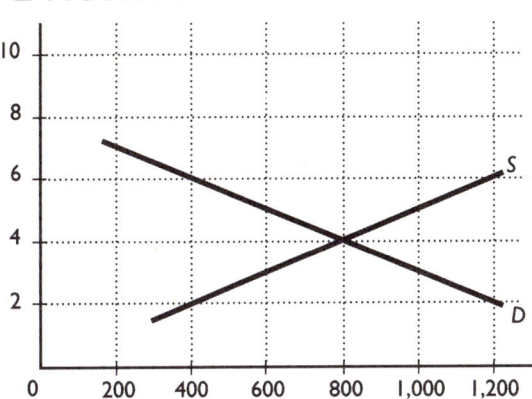

[Graph showing supply curve S and demand curve D, price axis 0-10, quantity axis 0-1,200]

1. The supply curve and the demand curve for pizza slices are shown in Figure 8.2. The price is in dollars per slice and the quantity is pizza slices per day. Label the axes.
   a. What is the equilibrium price and quantity of pizza slices?
   b. Suppose the government imposes a sales tax of $4 a slice of pizza. In Figure 8.2, draw the new supply curve after the tax is imposed.
   c. After the tax is imposed, what is the price paid by buyers for a slice of pizza? What is the price received by sellers for a slice of pizza? What is the incidence of the tax?
   d. In Figure 8.2, darken the area of the deadweight loss from the tax.

2. The supply curve and the demand curve for pizza slices are again shown in Figure 8.3. The price is in dollars per slice and the quantity is pizza slices per day. Once again, label the axes.
   a. Suppose the government imposes a tax on buyers of $4 a slice of pizza. In Figure 8.3, draw the new demand curve after the tax is imposed.
   b. After the tax is imposed, what is the price paid by buyers for a slice of pizza? What is the price received by sellers for a slice of pizza? What is the incidence of the tax?

■ FIGURE 8.3

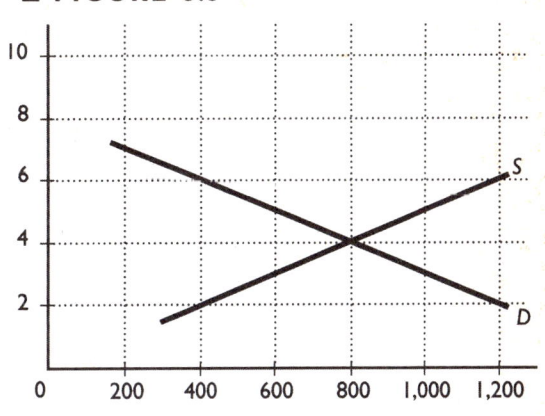

[Graph showing supply curve S and demand curve D, price axis 0-10, quantity axis 0-1,200]

c. How do the prices paid and the tax incidence in this question compare to those in question 1? What general principle does your answer uncover?

Short answer and numeric questions

Price (dollars per golf ball)	Quantity demanded (golf balls)	Before-tax quantity supplied (golf balls)	After-tax quantity supplied (golf balls)
0.50	1,100	600	0
1.00	1,000	620	0
1.50	900	680	0
2.00	700	700	0
2.50	600	850	___
3.00	300	950	___
3.50	60	1,180	680

1. The above table gives the monthly demand and supply schedules for golf balls at the College Hills Golf Shop. With no tax, what is the equilibrium price and quantity? Suppose a $2 per ball tax is imposed.
   a. Complete the last column of the table.
   b. What is the equilibrium price and quantity after the tax is imposed?
   c. How much of the tax is paid by the buyer? How much is paid by the seller?
   d. How much tax revenue does the government collect?

2. The government decides to tax high blood pressure medicine. The supply by drug companies is elastic; the demand by patients is

inelastic. Do the drug companies bear the entire tax burden? Is there much deadweight loss from this tax?
3. What is the relationship between the deadweight loss from a tax and the excess burden of a tax? Why does a tax create a deadweight loss?

CHECKPOINT 8.2

■ **Explain how income taxes and Social Security taxes change wage rates and create inefficiency.**

Quick Review
- *Progressive tax* A tax is progressive if the average tax rate increases as income increases.
- *Proportional tax* A tax is proportional if the average tax rate remains constant at all income levels.
- *Regressive tax* A tax is regressive if the average tax rate decreases as income increases.

Additional Practice Problems 8.2
1. The supply of capital is perfectly elastic. The income from capital is the interest received. If a tax is imposed on the income from capital, who pays the tax: the firms who demand capital or the suppliers of capital? Explain your answer.
2. The supply of land is perfectly inelastic. The income from land is rent. If a tax is imposed on the income from land, who pays the tax: the demanders of land or the suppliers? Explain your answer.
3. In Hong Kong, the marginal tax rates on salaries ranges from 2 percent to 20 percent with a maximum average tax of 15 percent, which is reached on incomes of about $59,000. Compare the tax rates in Hong Kong with the U.S. federal tax rate. In which country is the personal income tax (tax on salaries) more progressive? Why?

Solutions to Additional Practice Problems 8.2
1. Because the supply of capital is perfectly elastic, the suppliers pay none of the tax. The entire tax is paid by the demanders. Supply being perfectly elastic means that the suppliers have a huge number of options where to supply their capital, with all the options paying the same interest rate. If one of these options imposes a tax, suppliers will not supply any capital there unless the interest rate rises to compensate them fully for the tax. When the interest rate rises by the full amount of the tax, suppliers pay none of the tax. The interest rate must rise by the full amount of the tax because that is the only way that the return from supplying capital to this option equals the return from supplying capital to all the other options.

2. Because the supply of land is perfectly inelastic, the suppliers pay all of the tax. The demanders pay none of the tax. Supply being perfectly inelastic means that suppliers have no other choice but to supply their land. Demanders determine the maximum price they are willing to pay for this quantity of land and that is the price. If a tax is imposed on land, demanders will not pay any of the tax because they are already paying the maximum price they are wiling to pay. So suppliers pay the entire tax.

3. The personal income tax in the United States is more progressive because the average tax rate increases to higher levels in the United States. Because Hong Kong's marginal tax rates are lower than U.S. marginal tax rates, Hong Kong's average tax rate remains lower than the U.S. average tax rate.

■ **Self Test 8.2**

Fill in the blanks
The percentage of an additional dollar that is paid in tax is ____ (a progressive tax; a marginal tax; an average tax) rate. A tax is regressive if the average tax rate ____ (increases; decreases) as income increases. A tax on labor income ____ (creates; does not create) a deadweight loss. If

the supply of capital is perfectly elastic, a tax on capital income is paid entirely by the ____ (firms; suppliers of capital) and the tax ____ (creates; does not create) a deadweight loss. If the supply of land is perfectly ____ (inelastic; elastic), a tax on income from land is paid entirely by the landowners and the tax ____ (creates; does not create) a deadweight loss. A Social Security tax imposed on workers and a Social Security tax imposed on firms both ____ (raise; lower) the wage rate that employees receive and ____ (increase; decrease) employment.

True or false
1. When Hank earns an additional dollar, he pays 30 cents in additional tax. Hank's marginal tax rate is 30 percent.
2. If the average tax rate increases as income increases, the tax is a progressive tax.
3. Sam has $40,000 of taxable income and pays $4,000 income tax. Bert has $50,000 of taxable income and pays $4,500 income tax. Sam and Bert live in a country with a progressive income tax.
4. An income tax on labor creates a deadweight loss.
5. If the supply of capital is perfectly elastic, a tax on capital income decreases the demand for capital and decreases the interest rate.

Multiple choice
1. The percentage of an additional dollar of income that is paid in tax is the
   a. sales tax.
   b. excise tax.
   c. marginal tax rate.
   d. personal income tax.
   e. regressive tax.
2. If the average tax rate is constant as income increases, then the tax is called
   a. regressive.
   b. progressive.
   c. proportional.
   d. an average tax.
   e. efficient.

3. If we tax labor income, the tax
   a. increases the quantity employed because the demand for labor increases.
   b. decreases the quantity employed because the supply of labor decreases.
   c. increases the quantity employed because the supply of labor increases.
   d. decreases the quantity employed because the demand for labor increases.
   e. does not change the quantity employed because people must have jobs in order to earn any income.
4. The incidence of an income tax on labor income is generally that the tax is
   a. paid only by workers.
   b. paid only by employers.
   c. shared equally between workers and employers.
   d. shared but not necessarily equally between workers and employers.
   e. funded by the deadweight loss.
5. When governments tax capital income, the equilibrium quantity of capital
   a. increases because of the international mobility of capital.
   b. does not change because the supply of capital is perfectly elastic.
   c. decreases.
   d. does not change because the supply of capital is perfectly inelastic.
   e. might increase or decrease depending on whether the demand for capital is inelastic or elastic.
6. If the supply of capital is perfectly elastic, the incidence of a tax on capital income is
   a. paid entirely by the suppliers of capital.
   b. paid entirely by firms.
   c. shared between firms and the suppliers of capital.
   d. shared but not equally between firms that demand capital and the suppliers of capital.
   e. unknown.

FIGURE 8.4
Interest rate (percent per year)

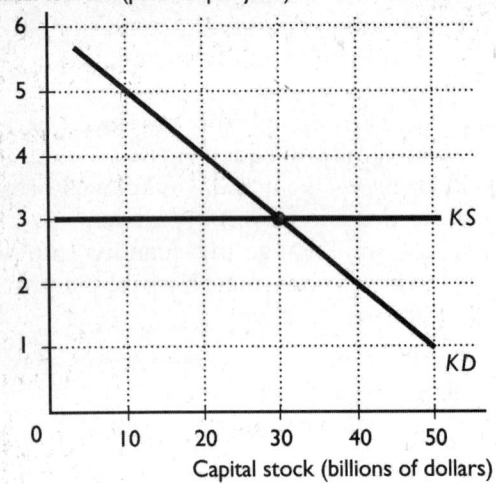

[Graph: KS horizontal line at 3%; KD downward sloping from ~5.5 at Q=0 to 0 at Q=50; equilibrium at 30, 3%]

Capital stock (billions of dollars)

7. Figure 8.4 shows the capital market. If the government imposes a 2 percent tax on capital income, the interest rate ____.
   a. stays at 3 percent.
   b. rises to 4 percent.
   c. rises to 5 percent.
   d. falls to 2 percent.
   e. falls to 1 percent.

8. Figure 8.4 shows the capital market. If the government imposes a 2 percent tax on capital income, the equilibrium quantity of capital becomes
   a. $10 billion.
   b. $20 billion.
   c. $30 billion.
   d. $40 billion.
   e. $50 billion.

9. A tax on income from land in Montana is borne entirely by landowners because the
   a. demand for land is perfectly inelastic.
   b. supply of land is perfectly inelastic.
   c. supply of land is perfectly elastic.
   d. demand for land is perfectly elastic.
   e. deadweight loss from the tax would otherwise be infinite.

10. When a social security tax is imposed on workers, employment ____ and when a social security tax is imposed on employers, employment ____.
    a. increases; increases
    b. increases; decreases
    c. decreases; increases
    d. decreases; decreases
    e. decreases; does not change

Complete the graph
FIGURE 8.5
Wage rate (dollars per hour)

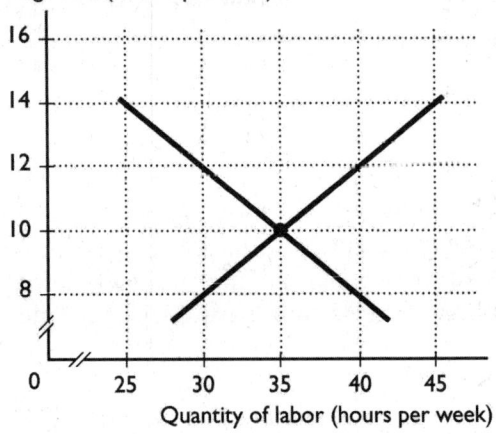

[Graph: supply and demand curves crossing at 35 hours, $10/hour]

Quantity of labor (hours per week)

1. Figure 8.5 shows the labor market.
   a. Label the curves. What is the equilibrium wage rate and quantity of labor?
   b. Suppose the government imposes an income tax of $4 an hour on labor income. Illustrate the effect of this tax in the figure.
   c. After the tax is imposed, what is the wage rate paid by firms and what is the amount received by households?
   d. If a deadweight loss is created, shade its area. If a deadweight loss is not created, explain why not.

FIGURE 8.6
Rent (dollars per acre per year)

[Graph showing vertical Land supply at 30 billion acres, downward-sloping Land demand, equilibrium at $320 and 30 billion acres]

2. Figure 8.6 shows the market for land.
   a. What is the equilibrium rent and quantity of land?
   b. Suppose the government imposes a tax on land income of $10 an acre. What is the new equilibrium rent paid by renters and what is the amount of rent kept by landowners? What is the equilibrium quantity of land?
   c. If a deadweight loss is created, shade its area. If a deadweight loss is not created, explain why not.

FIGURE 8.7
Wage rate (dollars per hour)

[Graph with labor supply curve LS and labor demand curve LD, equilibrium around $32.50 and 8 thousand workers]

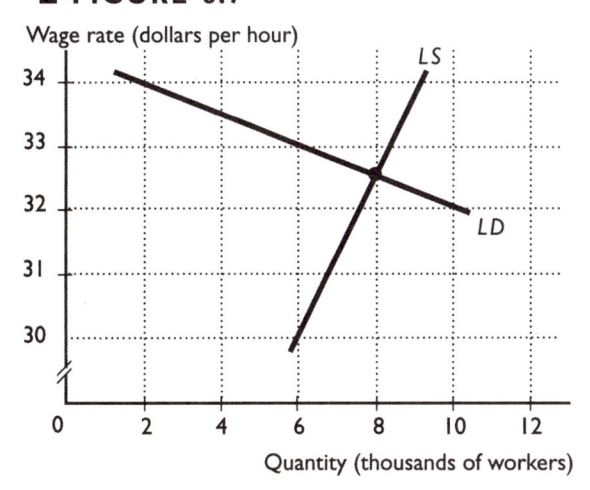

3. Figure 8.7 shows a labor supply curve and labor demand curve. The initial equilibrium wage rate is $32.50 an hour. The government imposes a $3 an hour Social Security tax on firms.
   a. In the figure, show the effect of this tax. What is the wage that workers receive before the tax and after the tax?
   b. Even though the Social Security tax has been imposed on the firms, how is the burden of the tax split?

Short answer and numeric questions

1. Why is the supply of capital highly elastic? Who pays the tax on capital income if the supply of capital is perfectly elastic?
2. The government mandates that half of a Social Security tax has to be paid by the employer and the other half has to be paid by the worker. Does this law mean that the burden of the tax is shared equally by the employer and worker?

CHECKPOINT 8.3

■ **Review ideas about the fairness of the tax system.**

Quick Review
- *Benefits principle* People should pay taxes equal to the benefits they receive from public services.
- *Ability-to-pay principle* People should pay taxes according to how easily they can bear the burden.

Additional Practice Problem 8.3
1. "The only fair taxes are user fees, such as toll roads. The gas tax is fair because the funds raised go for road maintenance. All government-provided services need to be funded through user fees. To pay for parks, we need to charge entrance fees. The cost of garbage collection must be based on how much garbage the household creates. Any tax except a user fee is unfair and must be abolished!" Comment on the fairness principle being used. Is it possible for *all* government programs to be funded through user fees?

Solution to Additional Practice Problem 8.3

1. The speaker is advocating the benefits principle of taxation, which is the proposition that people should pay taxes equal to the benefits they receive from public services. Although user fees have merit, it is not possible to fund all government programs through user fees. First, for public goods such as national defense, everyone consumes the same amount. It is impossible to determine how much any particular person benefits and therefore not possible to determine the proper fee. Second, some programs are designed to redistribute income to poorer people. It would be ludicrous to tax welfare recipients an amount equal to the benefits they received, which is the case under a user-fee arrangement.

■ Self Test 8.3

Fill in the blanks

The ____ (ability-to-pay; benefits) principle is the proposition that people should pay taxes equal to the benefits they receive from public services. Imposing a higher sales tax on the purchase of jewelry than on food is fair according to the ____ (ability-to-pay; benefit) principle. ____ (Horizontal; Vertical) equity requires that taxpayers with the same ability to pay do pay the same taxes. In the United States, the marriage tax problem is that a couple who both work pay often ____ (more; less) taxes when they are married than when they are single.

True or false

1. The benefits principle asserts that those people who are harmed by the deadweight loss of a tax should not pay the tax.
2. If the revenue from gasoline taxes is used to pay for road repairs, the tax reflects the ability-to-pay principle.
3. The U.S. income tax, which uses progressive income taxes, can be considered fair based on the principle of vertical equity.
4. Both vertical and horizontal equity can be achieved and the marriage tax problem eliminated if married couples are taxed as two single persons.
5. The taxes with the largest deadweight loss are taxes on capital income, and the people who pay these taxes generally have the greatest ability to pay taxes.

Multiple choice

1. Which of the following taxes best illustrates the benefits principle of taxation?
   a. sales tax on clothing used to fund food stamps
   b. state income tax used to fund state universities
   c. medicare tax used to fund medical care for the elderly
   d. gasoline tax used to fund road repairs
   e. federal income tax used to fund NASA spending

2. The proposition that people should pay taxes according to how easily they can bear the burden is the ____ principle
   a. regressive tax
   b. benefits
   c. ability-to-pay
   d. fairness principle.
   e. incidence of fairness principle.

3. The government once imposed a luxury tax on very expensive jewelry. This tax followed the ____ principle.
   a. benefits
   b. ability-to-pay
   c. vertical equity
   d. horizontal equity
   e. fair-tax incidence

4. The proposition that taxpayers with the same ability to pay should pay the same taxes is called
   a. the benefits principle.
   b. the ability-to-pay imperative.
   c. vertical equity.
   d. horizontal equity.
   e. fair-tax incidence principle.

5. Vertical equity implies that
   i. tax rates should be equal for all tax payers.
   ii. people with higher incomes should pay more in taxes.
   iii. people with higher incomes should pay a lower average tax rate.
   a. i only.
   b. ii only.
   c. iii only.
   d. i and ii.
   e. ii and iii.

6. Joan's income is $60,000 and she pays $6,000 in taxes. Juan's income is $40,000 and he pays $7,000 in taxes. This situation violates
   a. the benefits principle.
   b. the big tradeoff.
   c. vertical equity.
   d. horizontal equity.
   e. the fair-tax incidence principle.

7. Because the U.S. income tax is a progressive tax, taxing married couples as two single persons can violate
   a. the benefits principle.
   b. the ability-to-pay imperative.
   c. vertical equity.
   d. horizontal equity.
   e. the government's need for more revenue.

8. Compared to taxes on labor income, taxes on capital income generate ____ deadweight loss and are paid by people who generally have the ____ ability to pay.
   a. the greatest; most
   b. the greatest; least
   c. the smallest; most
   d. the smallest; least
   e. no; least

Short answer and numeric questions
1. There are a variety of welfare programs, such as food stamps, designed to boost the income of poor families. Does it make sense to raise the tax revenue necessary to fund these programs by using the benefits principle of taxation?
2. What is the marriage tax problem? If a married couple is taxed as two single individuals, what problem is created?

SELF TEST ANSWERS

■ CHECKPOINT 8.1

Fill in the blanks

The tax <u>incidence</u> is the division of the burden of a tax between the buyer and the seller. A tax is like <u>an increase</u> in suppliers' costs. For a given elasticity of supply, the buyer pays a larger share of the tax the more <u>inelastic</u> is the demand for the good. If the supply is perfectly <u>inelastic</u>, the seller pays the entire tax. Taxes <u>create</u> a deadweight loss. The excess burden of a tax is the <u>deadweight loss</u> from the tax and is larger the <u>more</u> elastic the demand for the good being taxed.

True or false

1. False; pages 190-191
2. False; page 192
3. True; page 192
4. False; page 193
5. True; page 194

Multiple choice

1. d; page 190
2. b; page 191
3. c; page 191
4. d; page 192
5. a; page 191
6. c; page 191
7. e; page 191
8. c; page 192
9. c; page 192
10. b; page 193
11. b; page 193

Complete the graph

1. The axes are labeled in Figure 8.8.
    a. The price is $4 a slice and the quantity is 800 slices a day; pages 191.
    b. Figure 8.8 shows the supply curve after the tax is imposed; page 191.
    c. Buyers pay $6 a slice; sellers receive $2 a slice. The tax is split equally; page 191.
    d. The deadweight loss is the grey triangle in Figure 8.8; page 192.

■ FIGURE 8.8

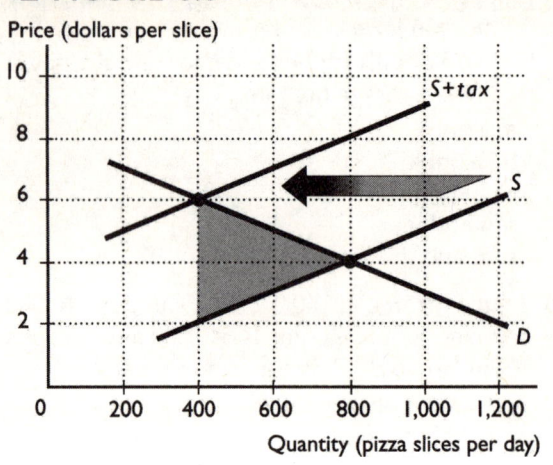

■ FIGURE 8.9

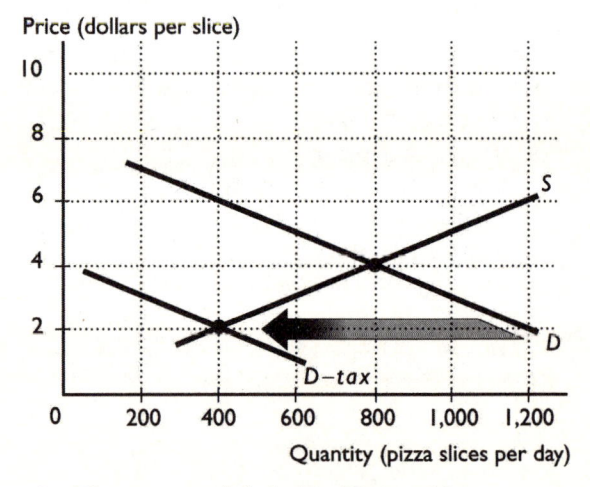

2. The axes are labeled in Figure 8.9.
    a. Figure 8.9 shows the demand curve after the tax is imposed; page 191.
    b. Buyers pay $6 a slice; sellers receive $2 a slice. The tax is split equally; page 191.
    c. The price paid and the tax incidence is the same in problem 1, when the tax is imposed on sellers, and in problem 2, when the tax is imposed on buyers. The general principle is that the tax incidence depends on the elasticity of demand and the elasticity of supply, not on who sends the tax to the government; pages 191, 193.

Short answer and numeric questions

1. The equilibrium price is $2.00 a golf ball and the equilibrium quantity is 700 golf balls.

Price (dollars per golf ball)	After-tax quantity supplied (golf balls per month)
2.50	600
3.00	620

    a. The completed supply schedule is in the table above; page 190.
    b. $2.50 a golf ball and 600 golf balls; page 191.
    c. The buyer pays $0.50 of the tax. The seller pays $1.50 of the tax; page 191.
    d. The tax revenue is $2 a ball × 600 balls, which is $1,200; page 190.

2. The burden of the tax will fall mainly upon buyers, not the drug companies, because demand is inelastic and supply is elastic. Because the demand is inelastic, the decrease in the quantity will not be large and so the deadweight loss from the tax is small; page 193.

3. The excess burden of a tax is the same as the deadweight loss. The deadweight loss arises because the tax leads to less of the good or service being produced and consumed; page 192.

■ CHECKPOINT 8.2

Fill in the blanks

The percentage of an additional dollar that is paid in tax is <u>a marginal tax</u> rate. A tax is regressive if the average tax rate <u>decreases</u> as income increases. A tax on labor income <u>creates</u> a deadweight loss. If the supply of capital is perfectly elastic, a tax on capital income is paid entirely by the <u>firms</u> and the tax <u>creates</u> a deadweight loss. If the supply of land is perfectly <u>inelastic</u>, a tax on income from land is paid entirely by the landowners and the tax <u>does not create</u> a deadweight loss. A Social Security tax imposed on workers and a Social Security tax imposed on firms both <u>lower</u> the wage rate that employees receive and <u>decrease</u> employment.

True or false

1. True; page 197
2. True; page 197
3. False; page 197
4. True; page 198
5. False; page 199

Multiple choice

1. c; page 197
2. c; page 197
3. b; page 198
4. d; page 198
5. c; page 198
6. b; page 198
7. c; page 198
8. a; page 198
9. b; page 199
10. d; pages 200-201

Complete the graph

■ FIGURE 8.10

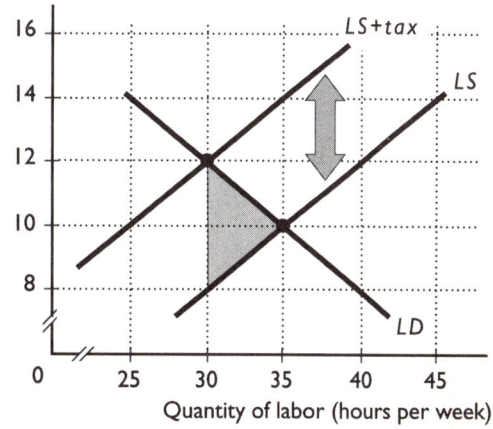

1. a. The curves are labeled *LD* and *LS* in Figure 8.10. The equilibrium wage rate is $10 an hour and the equilibrium quantity of labor is 35 hours a week; page 198.
    b. The income tax decreases the supply of labor services. The labor supply curve shifts leftward from *LS* to *LS + tax*. The vertical distance between the two supply curves, indicated by the arrow, is equal to the $4 tax; page 198.

c. Firms pay a wage rate of $12 an hour; workers receive a wage rate of $8 an hour; page 198.

d. The deadweight loss is the grey triangle in Figure 8.10; page 198.

2. a. The equilibrium rent is $320 an acre per year and the equilibrium quantity of land is 30 billion acres; page 199.

b. After the tax, renters pay $320 an acre and landowners keep $310 an acre. The equilibrium quantity of land is 30 billion acres, the same as before the tax was imposed; page 199.

c. There is no deadweight loss created because the equilibrium quantity does not change. The amount produced remains the efficient quantity; page 199.

■ FIGURE 8.11

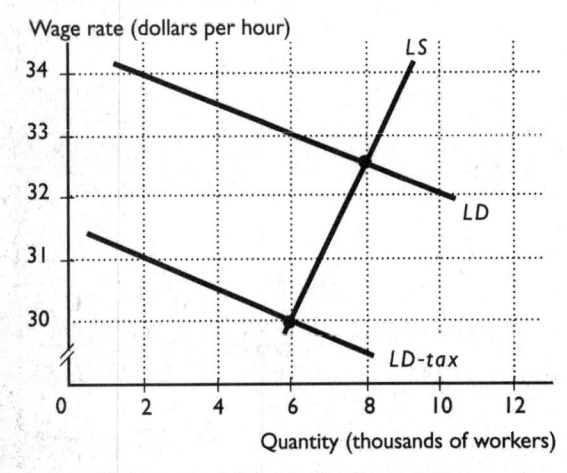

Wage rate (dollars per hour)

3. a. Figure 8.11 shows the effect of the tax. Because the tax is imposed on firms, the tax decreases the demand for labor services and shifts the labor demand curve leftward. The vertical distance between the initial supply curve, LD, and the new supply curve, LD + tax, is the amount of the tax, $3 an hour. The workers received $32.50 per hour before the tax and $30.00 after the tax; page 202.

b. Even though the tax is imposed on firms, the workers pay $2.50 of the $3.00 Social Security tax and the firms pay $0.50; page 202.

Short answer and numeric questions

1. Because capital is internationally mobile, its supply is highly (perhaps perfectly) elastic. If the supply of capital is perfectly elastic, firms pay the entire tax on capital income; page 199.

2. The burden of the Social Security tax is determined by the elasticity of supply and the elasticity of demand of labor, not by the law splitting the tax. If the demand for labor is more elastic than supply, the burden falls more on the worker and less on the employer. The government can legislate how the tax is collected, but cannot legislate the division of the tax's burden; pages 202-203.

■ CHECKPOINT 8.3

Fill in the blanks

The <u>benefits</u> principle is the proposition that people should pay taxes equal to the benefits they receive from public services. Imposing a higher sales tax on the purchase of jewelry than on food is fair according to the <u>ability-to-pay</u> principle. Horizontal equity requires that taxpayers with the same ability to pay do pay the same taxes. In the United States, the marriage tax problem is that a couple who both work often pay <u>more</u> taxes when they are married than when they are single.

True or false

1. False; page 206
2. False; page 206
3. True; page 207
4. False; pages 207-208
5. True; page 208

Multiple choice

1. d; page 206
2. c; page 206
3. b; page 206
4. d; page 206
5. b; page 207
6. c; page 207
7. d; page 207
8. a; page 208

Short answer and numeric questions

1. If the taxes necessary to fund the various welfare programs, such as food stamps, were assessed using the benefits principle of taxation, poor families would be required to pay the tax because they are the ones who benefit from the programs. But this outcome would defeat the purpose of the programs, which are designed to increase these families' incomes. The benefits principle of taxation does not work for government programs designed to increase the incomes of the poor; page 206.

2. The marriage tax problem is that a working couple pays more taxes if they are married than if they are single. Taxing the couple as single taxpayers violates horizontal equity because then two married couples with the same total income could pay different taxes depending on how much each partner earned; pages 207-208.

Chapter 9
Global Markets in Action

CHAPTER CHECKLIST

In Chapter 9 we see that all countries can benefit from free trade but countries nevertheless restrict trade.

1. Explain how markets work with international trade.

The goods and services that we buy from people in other countries are called imports. The goods and services that we sell to people in other countries are called exports. In 2006, the United States accounted for 10 percent of world exports and 15 percent of world imports. Comparative advantage enables countries to gain from trade. A nation has a comparative advantage in producing a good if it can produce that good at a lower opportunity cost than another country. In this case, the domestic no-trade price is lower than the world price. With international trade, the country will export this good.

2. Identify the gains from international trade and its winners and losers.

International trade lowers the prices of the goods and services imported into the country. The lower prices for imported goods mean that consumers gain additional consumer surplus from imports. The lower prices also mean that producers lose producer surplus from imports. The gain to consumers, however, exceeds the loss to producers. International trade raises the prices of the goods and services exported from the country. The higher prices for exported goods mean that producers gain additional producer surplus from exports. The higher prices also mean that consumers lose consumer surplus from exports. The gain to producers, however, exceeds the loss to consumers.

3. Explain the effects of international trade barriers.

A tariff is a tax on a good that is imposed by the importing country when an imported good crosses its international boundary. A tariff on a good reduces imports of that good, increases domestic production of the good, yields revenue for the government, and creates a deadweight loss. A quota is a quantitative restriction on the import of a good that limits the maximum quantity of a good that may be imported in a given period of time. Voluntary export restraints are like a quota given to an exporter of a good. Both quotas and voluntary export restraints reduce imports, increase domestic production, and create deadweight losses. A subsidy is a payment by the government to a producer. Some countries subsidize products which are then exported. These export subsidies increase domestic production of the good or service but create deadweight losses.

4. Explain and evaluate arguments used to justify restricting international trade.

The three main arguments for protection and restriction of trade are the national security argument, the infant-industry argument, and the dumping argument. Each of these arguments is flawed. Other flawed arguments for protection are that protection saves jobs, allows us to compete with cheap foreign labor, brings diversity and stability and penalizes lax environmental standards. Tariffs are imposed in some nations to gain revenue for the government. In addition, trade is restricted is because of rent seeking from those who benefit from trade restrictions.

CHECKPOINT 9.1

■ **Explain how markets work with international trade.**

Quick Review
- *Imports* The goods and services that we buy from people in other countries are called imports.
- *Exports* The goods and services that we sell to people in other countries are called exports.
- *Comparative advantage* A nation has a comparative advantage in a good when its opportunity cost of producing the good is lower than another nation's opportunity cost of producing the good.

Additional Practice Problems 9.1

1. The figure shows the market for CPU chips in the United States with no international trade. The world price for a CPU chip is $150.
   a. Does the United States have a comparative advantage in producing CPU chips? How can you tell?
   b. If international trade is allowed, will the United States import or export CPU chips?
   c. Will the quantity of CPU chips produced in the United States increase or decrease? By how much?
   d. Will the quantity of CPU chips consumed in the United States increase or decrease? By how much?
   e. How many CPU chips will the United States import or export?

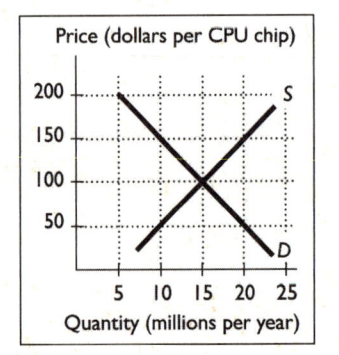

Solutions to Additional Practice Problems 9.1

1a. Because the price of a CPU chip in the United States is lower than the world price, the United States has a comparative advantage in producing CPU chips.

1b. Because the United States has a comparative advantage in producing CPU chips, the United States will export CPU chips.

1c. With international trade, the price of a CPU chip in the United States will be $150. At this price, the supply curve shows that the quantity of chips produced will equal 20 million per year. With no international trade, the equilibrium quantity of CPU chips produced is 15 million, so international trade leads to 5 million more chips being produced.

1d. With international trade, the price of a CPU chip in the United States will be $150. At this price, the demand curve shows that the quantity of chips demanded will equal 10 million per year. With no international trade, the equilibrium quantity of CPU chips consumed is 15 million, so international trade leads to 5 million fewer chips being consumed.

1e. The quantity of CPU chips exported equals the difference between the quantity of CPU chips produced, 20 million per year, and the quantity consumed, 10 million per year. So the United States will export 20 million CPU chips − 10 million CPU chips, which is 10 million CPU chips.

■ **Self Test 9.1**

Fill in the blanks

Global international trade accounts for a bit more than ____ (1/4; 1/2; 2/3) of global production. If a country can produce a good at a lower opportunity cost than any other country, the country has ____ (an export advantage; a comparative advantage) in the production of that good. The United States will export a good if its price in the United States with no international trade is ____ (lower; higher) than its world price. If the United States imports a good, then U.S. production of the good ____ (increases; decreases) and U.S. consumption of the good ____ (increases; decreases).

True or false

1. The United States is the world's largest international trader.
2. If a nation can produce a service at lower opportunity cost than any other nation, the nation has a national comparative advantage in producing that service.
3. If the price of a good in the United States with no international trade is higher than the world price, then with international trade the United States will export that good.
4. As a result of international trade, the U.S. production of goods exported from the Untied States increases and the U.S. production of goods imported into the United States decreases.

Multiple choice

1. Goods and services that we buy from people in other countries are called our
   a. imports.
   b. exports.
   c. inputs.
   d. raw materials.
   e. obligations.

2. If the United States exports planes to Brazil and imports ethanol from Brazil, the price received by U.S. producers of planes ____ and the price received by Brazilian producers of ethanol ____.
   a. does not change; does not change
   b. rises; rises
   c. rises; falls
   d. falls; rises
   e. falls; falls

3. When Italy buys Boeing jets, the price Italy pays is ____ if it produced their own jets and the price Boeing receives is ____ than it could receive from an additional U.S. buyer.
   a. lower than; lower
   b. higher than; higher
   c. lower than; higher
   d. higher than; lower
   e. the same as; higher

4. A nation will import a good if its no-trade, domestic
   a. price is equal to the world price.
   b. price is less than the world price.
   c. price is greater than the world price.
   d. quantity is less than the world quantity.
   e. quantity is greater than the world quantity.

5. When a good is imported, the domestic production ____ and the domestic consumption ____.
   a. increases; increases
   b. increases; decreases
   c. decreases; increases
   d. decreases; decreases
   e. increases; does not change

6. The United States will export a good if its no-trade U.S. price is ____ its world price and with trade, U.S. production of the good will ____ compared to the level of no-trade production.
   a. higher than; not change
   b. higher than; increase
   c. lower than; increase
   d. the same as; increase
   e. the same as; not change

Complete the graph

■ FIGURE 9.1
Price (dollars per bushel)

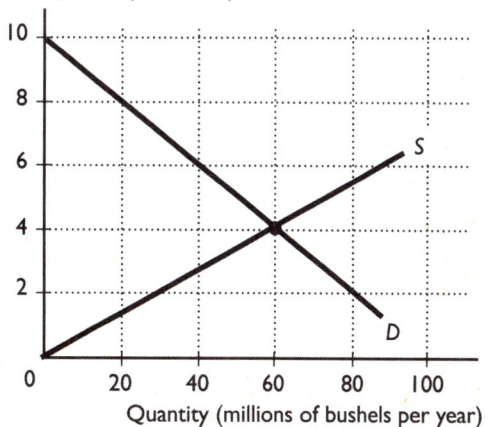

1. Figure 9.1 shows the U.S. demand and sup-

ply curves for wheat.
  a. In the absence of international trade, what is the price of a bushel of wheat in the United States?
  b. If the world price of a bushel of wheat is $6 a bushel, will the United States import or export wheat? Above what world price for wheat will the United States export wheat? Below what world price for wheat will the United States import wheat?

Short answer and numeric questions

1. French cheese is flown to the United States abroad a United Airlines plane. Classify these transactions from the vantage point of the United States and from the vantage point of France.

Price (dollars per ton)	Quantity supplied (tons per year)	Quantity demanded (tons per year)
400	38	58
500	42	52
600	46	46
700	50	40
800	54	34
900	58	28

2. The table above has the U.S. demand and supply schedules for potatoes.
  a. If there is no international trade, what is the equilibrium price and quantity of potatoes?
  b. If the world price of potatoes is $800 a ton, what is the quantity supplied and the quantity demanded in the United States? Does the United States import or export potatoes? What quantity?
  c. If the world price of potatoes rises to $900 a ton, what are the quantity supplied and the quantity demanded in the United States? Does the United States import or export potatoes? What quantity?
  d. Would the United States ever import potatoes?

3. How does international trade affect the domestic production and domestic consumption of goods imported into the country?

CHECKPOINT 9.2

■ **Identify the gains from international trade and its winners and losers.**

Quick Review
- *Consumer surplus* Consumer surplus is the marginal benefit from a good or service minus the price paid for it, summed over the quantity consumed.
- *Producer surplus* The producer surplus of a good equals the price of a good minus the marginal cost of producing it.

Additional Practice Problem 9.2

1. The figure shows the market for CPU chips in the United States with no international trade. The world price for a CPU chip is $150.
  a. Does the United States import or export CPU chips and how many chips are imported or exported?
  b. In the United States, tell who gains and who loses from the international trade and explain why they gain or lose. In the figure show the gains, the losses, and the net gain or net loss.

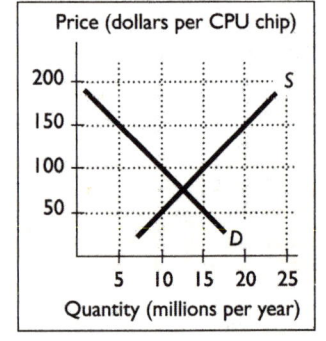

Solution to Additional Practice Problem 9.2

1a. The United States exports 15 million CPU chips per year.

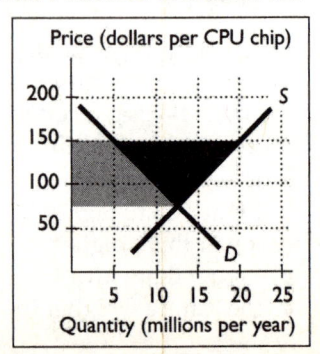

1b. In the United States, producers of CPU chips gains and consumers of CPU chips lose. The gains and loses are in the figure. Producers gain producer surplus and consumers lose consumer surplus. Producers gain because the price of a CPU chip with international trade is higher than the price without international trade, which is why the producer surplus increases. The increase in producer surplus is equal to the sum of the area of the dark grey triangle and the light grey trapezoid. Consumers lose for precisely the same reason producers gain: The price of a CPU chip is higher with international trade than without international trade which is why the consumer surplus decreases. The decrease in consumer surplus is equal to the area of the light grey trapezoid. On net, the economy gains from international trade. The increase in producer surplus is larger than the decrease in consumer surplus, as shown in the figure by the area of the dark grey triangle.

■ **Self Test 9.2**

Fill in the blanks

Imports ____ (decrease; increase) the producer surplus of domestic producers of the product and also ____ (decrease; increase) the consumer surplus of domestic consumers of the product. The consumer surplus from a good that would be exported is larger ____ (with; without) international trade and the consumer surplus from a good that would be imported is larger ____ (with; without) international trade. On net, society ____ (gains; loses) from international trade because the total surplus ____ (increases; decreases) with international trade.

True or false

1. International trade harms the nation.
2. Imports increase consumer surplus and decrease producer surplus.
3. The nation's total surplus increases when goods are exported.
4. Everyone in a nation gains from exports.

Multiple choice

1. International trade is definitely in the social interest if
   a. consumer surplus increases.
   b. producer surplus increases.
   c. consumer surplus does not decrease.
   d. producer surplus does not decrease.
   e. total surplus increases.

2. Imports ____ consumer surplus, ____ producer surplus, and ____ total surplus
   a. decrease; decrease; decrease
   b. increase; increase; increase
   c. increase; decrease; decrease
   d. increase; decrease; increase
   e. decrease; increase; increase

3. When a country imports a good, the ____ in consumer surplus is ____ the ____ in producer surplus.
   a. decrease; larger than; increase
   b. decrease; smaller than; increase
   c. increase; smaller than; decrease
   d. increase; equal to; decrease
   e. increase; larger than; decrease

4. When a country exports a good, the country's producer surplus ____, consumer surplus ____, and the country ____ from the trade.
   a. increases; increases; gains
   b. decreases; increases; gains
   c. increases; decreases; gains
   d. decreases; decreases; loses
   e. increases; decreases; loses

5. Which of the following is correct?
   i. The U.S. total surplus decreases when the United States exports a good.
   ii. The U.S. total surplus decreases when the United States imports a good.
   iii. The U.S. total surplus increases when the United States imports a good and when it exports a good.
   a. i only.
   b. iii only.
   c. i and ii.
   d. ii only.
   e. None of the above because the U.S. total surplus does not change as a result of trade.

Complete the graph

■ FIGURE 9.2

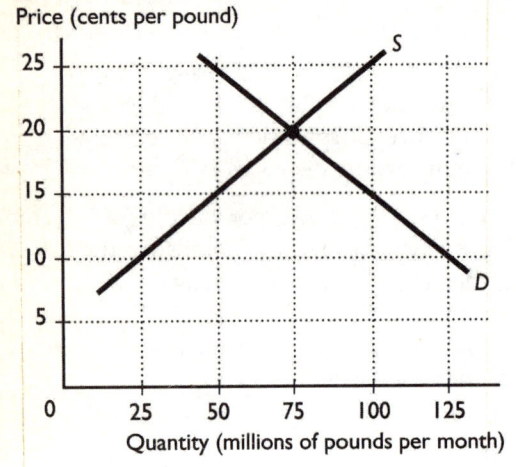

Price (cents per pound)

[Graph showing supply curve S and demand curve D intersecting at price 20¢ and quantity 75 million pounds per month. Price axis ranges 0-25, quantity axis ranges 0-125.]

1. Figure 9.2 shows the supply of and demand for sugar in the United States.
   a. If the world price of sugar is 10¢ a pound, draw the world price line in the figure. What is the quantity consumed in the United States, the quantity produced in the United States, and the quantity imported?
   b. Show the changes in consumer surplus, producer surplus, and total surplus once the United States imports sugar.

■ FIGURE 9.3

Price (dollars per bushel)

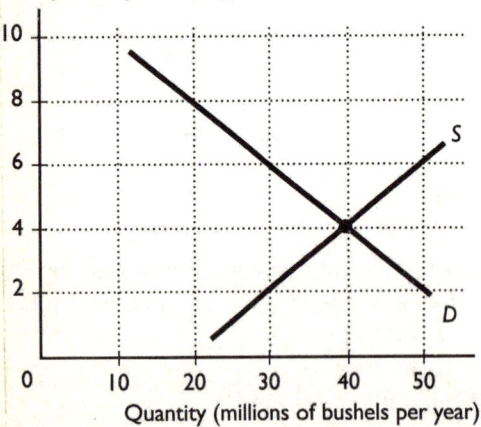

[Graph showing supply curve S and demand curve D intersecting at price $4 and quantity 40 million bushels per year. Price axis ranges 0-10, quantity axis ranges 0-50.]

1. Figure 9.3 shows the supply of and demand for wheat in the United States.
   a. If the world price of wheat is $6 a bushel, draw the world price line in the figure. What is the quantity consumed in the United States, the quantity produced in the United States, and the quantity exported?
   b. Show the changes in consumer surplus, producer surplus, and total surplus once the United States exports wheat.

Short answer and numeric questions

1. How are the gains from international trade measured?
2. Why do consumers gain from imports?
3. Suppose the U.S. price of sugar without any international trade is 30¢ a pound. If the United States then allows international trade, when would the U.S. gain be the largest: when the international price is 20¢ a pound or when the international price is 10¢ a pound? Explain your answer.
4. Why doesn't everyone in a nation gain from exporting a good?

CHECKPOINT 9.3

■ **Explain the effects of international trade barriers.**

Quick Review

- *Tariff* A tariff is a tax on a good that is imposed by the importing country when an imported good crosses its international boundary.
- *Quota* A quota is a quantitative restriction on the import of a good that limits the maximum quantity of a good that may be imported in a given period.

Additional Practice Problems 9.3

Price (dollars per ton of plywood)	U.S. quantity supplied (tons per month)	U.S. quantity demanded (tons per month)
1,000	600	1,400
750	500	1,600
500	300	1,800
250	100	2,000

1. The table above shows the U.S. supply and

demand schedules for plywood. The United States also can buy plywood from Canada at the world price of $500 per ton.

a. If there are no tariffs or other barriers to trade, what is the price of a ton of plywood in the United States? How much plywood is produced in the United States and how much is consumed? How much plywood is imported from Canada?

b. Suppose that the United States imposes a $250 per ton tariff on all plywood imported into the country. What now is the price of a ton of plywood in the United States? How much plywood is produced in the United States and how much is consumed? How much plywood is imported from Canada?

c. Who has gained from the tariff and who has lost?

2. For many years Japan conducted extremely slow, detailed, and costly safety inspections of *all* U.S. cars imported into Japan. In terms of trade, what was the effect of this inspection? How did the inspection affect the price and quantity of cars in Japan?

Solutions to Additional Practice Problems 9.3

1a. With no tariffs or nontariff barriers, the price of a ton of plywood is equal to the world price, $500 per ton. At this price, 300 tons per month are produced in the United States and 1,800 tons per month are consumed. The difference between the quantity consumed and the quantity produced, which is 1,500 tons per month, is imported from Canada.

1b. If a $250 per ton tariff is imposed, the price in the United States rises to $750 per ton. At this price, 500 tons per month are produced in the United States and 1,600 tons per month are consumed. The difference between the quantity consumed and the quantity produced, which is 1,100 tons per month, is imported from Canada.

1c. Gainers from the tariff are U.S. producers of plywood, who have a higher price for plywood and therefore increase their production, and the U.S. government, which gains tariff revenue. Losers are U.S. consumers, who consume less plywood with the tariff, and Canadian producers of plywood, who wind up exporting less plywood to the United States.

2. Japan's safety inspection (which has since been eliminated) was an example of a barrier to trade. It served a role similar to tariffs, quotas, and VERs. The safety inspection added to the cost of selling cars in Japan. It raised the price of U.S. produced cars in Japan and decreased the quantity of U.S. cars sold. The Japanese government, however, received no tariff revenue.

■ Self Test 9.3

Fill in the blanks

A tax on a good that is imposed by the importing country when an imported good crosses its international boundary is a ____ (quota; tariff) and a specified maximum amount of a good that may be imported in a given period of time is a ____ (quota; tariff). A tariff ____ (raises; lowers) the price paid by domestic consumers, ____ (increases; decreases) the quantity produced by domestic producers, and ____ (creates; does not create) a deadweight loss. A quota ____ (raises; lowers) the price paid by domestic consumers and ____ (increases; decreases) the quantity produced by domestic producers.

True or false

1. If the United States imposes a tariff, the price paid by U.S. consumers does not change.

2. If a country imposes a tariff on rice imports, domestic production of rice will increase and domestic consumption of rice will decrease.

3. A tariff increases the gains from trade for the exporting country.

4. A quota on imports of a particular good specifies the minimum quantity of that good that can be imported in a given period.

Multiple choice

1. A tax on a good that is imposed by the importing country when an imported good crosses its international boundary is a
   a. quota.
   b. VER.
   c. tariff.
   d. sanction.
   e. border tax.

2. The average U.S. tariff was highest in the
   a. 1930s.
   b. 1940s.
   c. 1970s.
   d. 1980s.
   e. 1990s.

3. Suppose the world price of a shirt is $10. If the United States imposes a tariff of $5 a shirt, then the price of a shirt in the
   a. United States falls to $5.
   b. United States rises to $15.
   c. world falls to $5.
   d. world rises to $5.
   e. world rises to $15.

4. When a tariff is imposed on a good, the _____ increases.
   a. domestic quantity purchased
   b. domestic quantity produced
   c. quantity imported
   d. quantity exported
   e. world price

5. When a tariff is imposed on a good, domestic consumers of the good _____ and domestic producers of the good _____.
   a. win; lose
   b. lose; win
   c. win; win
   d. lose; lose
   e. lose; neither win nor lose

6. Which of the following parties benefits from a quota but not from a tariff?
   a. the domestic government
   b. domestic producers
   c. domestic consumers
   d. the person with the right to import the good
   e. the foreign government

Complete the graph

■ FIGURE 9.4

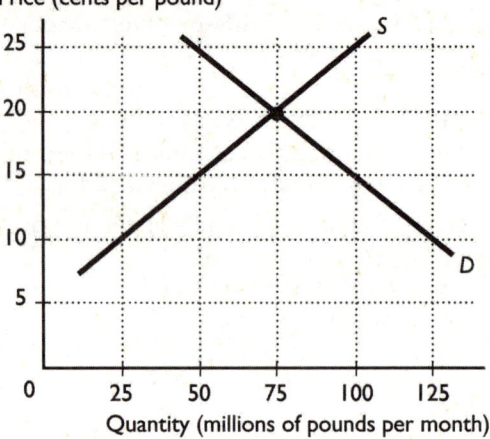

1. Figure 9.4 shows the supply of and demand for sugar in the United States.

   a. If the world price of sugar is 10¢ a pound, draw the world price line in the figure. What is the quantity consumed in the United States, the quantity produced in the United States, and the quantity imported?

   b. Suppose the government imposes a 5¢ a pound tariff on sugar. Show the effect of the tariff in Figure 9.4. After the tariff, what is the quantity consumed in the United States, the quantity produced in the United States, and the quantity imported?

   c. Who wins and who loses from this tariff?

Short answer and numeric questions

Price (dollars per ton of steel)	U.S. quantity supplied (tons per month)	U.S. quantity demanded (tons per month)
1,000	20,000	20,000
750	17,000	22,000
500	14,000	24,000
250	11,000	26,000

1. The table above gives the U.S. supply and the U.S. demand schedules for steel. Suppose the world price of steel is $500 per ton.

   a. If there are no barriers to trade, what is the price of steel in the United States, the quantity of steel consumed in the United

States, the quantity produced in the United States, and the quantity imported into the United States?

b. If the U.S. government imposes a tariff of $250 per ton of steel, what is the price of steel in the United States, the quantity of steel consumed in the United States, the quantity produced in the United States, and the quantity imported into the United States?

c. Instead of a tariff, if the U.S. government imposes a quota of 5,000 tons of steel per month, what is the price of steel in the United States, the quantity of steel consumed in the United States, the quantity produced in the United States, and the quantity imported into the United States?

d. Comparing your answers to parts (b) and (c), are U.S. consumers better off with the tariff or the quota? Are U.S. producers better off with the tariff or the quota?

2. Suppose the U.S. government imposes a tariff on sugar. How does the tariff affect the price of sugar? How does it affect U.S. sugar consumers? U.S. sugar producers?

3. Suppose the U.S. government imposes a quota on sugar. How does the quota affect the price of sugar? How does it affect U.S. sugar consumers? U.S. sugar producers?

4. Why do consumers lose from a tariff?

CHECKPOINT 9.4

■ **Explain and evaluate arguments used to justify restricting international trade.**

Quick Review
- *Rent seeking* Lobbying and other political activity that seeks to capture the gains from trade.

Additional Practice Problems 9.4

1. Canada has limits on the amount of U.S. television shows that can be broadcast in Canada. What are Canada's arguments for restricting imports of U.S. television shows? Are these arguments correct? Who loses from this restriction of trade?

2. The United States has, from time to time, limited imports of lumber from Canada. What is the argument that the United States has used to justify this quota? Who wins from this restriction? Who loses?

3. In each of the first two additional Practice Problems, identify who is rent seeking.

Solutions to Additional Practice Problems 9.4

1. Canada has used a number of arguments, but they are all incorrect. Canada has argued that Canadian television shows are of a higher quality than U.S. shows, but if Canadian consumers can detect a quality difference, they can watch Canadian shows rather than U.S. shows. Canada also has argued that these limitations are necessary to save Canadian culture, but if Canadian consumers want to protect this part of their heritage, they can watch exclusively Canadian shows rather than U.S. shows. The major losers from the Canadian limitations are Canadian consumers who can watch only a limited number of popular U.S. television shows.

2. In past decades, the United States asserted that the lumber industry was needed because it played a major role in national defense. With the use of more exotic materials in defense armaments, the national defense argument has passed into history. More recently, the United States has set quotas and tariffs allegedly for environmental reasons and allegedly because the Canadian government was subsidizing the production of lumber. Both of these arguments are likely not the true reason for the quotas. The quotas and limitations are the result of political lobbying by lumber producers and lumber workers. The winners from the quotas and tariffs are the lumber producers and lumber workers. The losers are all U.S. lumber consumers.

3. Rent seeking is lobbying and other political activity that seeks to capture the gains from trade. In Practice Problem 1, the Canadian pro-

ducers of television shows are rent seeking. In Practice Problem 2, the U.S. lumber producers and U.S. lumber workers are rent seeking. It is important to keep in mind that free trade promotes prosperity for all countries. Protection reduces the potential gains from trade

■ **Self Test 9.4**

Fill in the blanks

The assertion that it is necessary to protect a new industry to enable it to grow into a mature industry that can compete in world markets is the ____ (infant-industry; maturing-industry) argument. Dumping occurs when ____ (U.S. jobs are lost to cheap foreign labor; a foreign firm sells its exports at a lower price than its cost of production). Protection ____ (is; is not) necessary to bring diversity and stability to our economy. Protection ____ (is; is not) necessary to penalize countries with lax environmental standards. The major reason why international trade is restricted is because ____ (foreign countries protect their industries; of rent seeking).

True or false

1. The national security argument is the only valid argument for protection.
2. Dumping by a foreign producer is easy to detect.
3. Protection saves U.S. jobs at no cost.
4. International trade is an attractive source for tax collection in developing countries

Multiple choice

1. The national security argument is used by those who assert they want to
   a. increase imports as a way of strengthening their country.
   b. increase exports as a way of earning money to strengthen their country.
   c. limit imports that compete with domestic producers important for national defense.
   d. limit exports to control the flow of technology to third world nations.
   e. limit all imports.

2. The argument that it is necessary to protect a new industry to enable it to grow into a mature industry that can compete in world markets is the
   a. national security argument.
   b. diversity argument.
   c. infant-industry argument.
   d. environmental protection argument.
   e. national youth protection argument.

3. ____ occurs when a foreign firm sells its exports at a lower price than its cost of production.
   a. Dumping
   b. The trickle-down effect
   c. Rent seeking
   d. Tariff avoidance
   e. Nontariff barrier protection

4. The United States
   a. needs tariffs to allow us to compete with cheap foreign labor.
   b. does not need tariffs to allow us to compete with cheap foreign labor.
   c. should not trade with countries that have cheap labor.
   d. will not benefit from trade with countries that have cheap labor.
   e. avoids trading with countries that have cheap labor.

5. Why do governments in less-developed nations impose tariffs?
   a. The government gains revenue from the tariff.
   b. The government's low-paid workers are protected from high-paid foreign workers.
   c. The nation's total income is increased.
   d. The national security of the country definitely is improved.
   e. The government protects its national culture.

6. What is a major reason international trade is restricted in developed countries?
   a. rent seeking
   b. to allow competition with cheap foreign labor
   c. to save jobs
   d. to prevent dumping
   e. to protect national culture

Short answer and numeric questions

1. What is the dumping argument for protection? What is its flaw?
2. How do you respond to a speaker who says that we need to limit auto imports from Japan in order to save U.S. jobs?
3. Why is it incorrect to assert that trade with countries that have lax environmental standards needs to be restricted?
4. The Eye on Your Life discusses the role international trade plays in your life. Suppose you get a job working for Frito Lay, the maker of corn chips (and other snacks). Frito Lay is a big user of corn. Corn can also be used to produce ethanol and increasingly more ethanol is being used as a replacement (or additive) fuel for gasoline. Currently the U.S. government places a hefty tariff on ethanol imported from Brazil. As a representative of Frito Lay, would you be in favor of this tariff? Explain your answer.

SELF TEST ANSWERS

■ CHECKPOINT 9.1

Fill in the blanks

Global international trade accounts for a bit more than 1/4 of global production. If a country can produce a good at a lower opportunity cost than any other country, the country has a comparative advantage in the production of that good. The United States will export a good if its price in the United States with no international trade is lower than its world price. If the United States imports a good, then U.S. production of the good decreases and U.S. consumption of the good increases.

True or false

1. True; page 214
2. True; page 214
3. False; pages 216-217
4. True; page 216

Multiple choice

1. b; page 214
2. b; page 214
3. c; page 214
4. c; page 216
5. c; page 216
6. b; page 217

Complete the graph

1. a. In the absence of international trade, the equilibrium price of a bushel of wheat in the United States is $4; pages 216-217.
   b. If the world price of a bushel of wheat is $6 a bushel, the United States will export wheat because the world price exceeds the no-trade price. If the price of wheat exceeds $4 a bushel, the United States will export wheat. If the price of wheat is less than $4 a bushel, the United States will import wheat; pages 216-217.

Short answer and numeric questions

1. From the U.S. vantage, the cheese is an imported good and the air transportation is an exported service. From the French vantage, the cheese is an exported good and the air transportation is an imported service; page 214.

2. a. In the absence of international trade, the equilibrium price is $600 a ton and the equilibrium quantity is 46 tons; pages 216-217.
   b. In the United States, the quantity supplied is 54 tons and the quantity demanded is 34 tons. The United States exports 20 tons of potatoes; pages 217.
   c. In the United States, the quantity supplied is 58 tons and the quantity demanded is 28 tons. The United States exports 30 tons of potatoes; pages 217.
   d. The United States would import potatoes if the world price is less than $600 a ton; pages 216.

3. International trade lowers the domestic price of imported goods. The lower price increases the quantity domestic demanders consume and decreases the quantity domestic suppliers produce; page 216.

■ CHECKPOINT 9.2

Fill in the blanks

Imports decrease the producer surplus of domestic producers of the product and also increase the consumer surplus of domestic consumers of the product. The consumer surplus from a good that would be exported is larger without international trade and the consumer surplus from a good that would be imported is larger with international trade. On net, society gains from international trade because the total surplus increases with international trade.

True or false

1. False; pages 220-221
2. True; page 220
3. True; page 221
4. False; page 221

Multiple choice

1. e; page 219

2. d; page 220
3. e; page 220
4. c; page 221
5. b; pages 220-221

Complete the graph

■ **FIGURE 9.5**
Price (cents per pound)

■ **FIGURE 9.6**
Price (dollars per bushel)

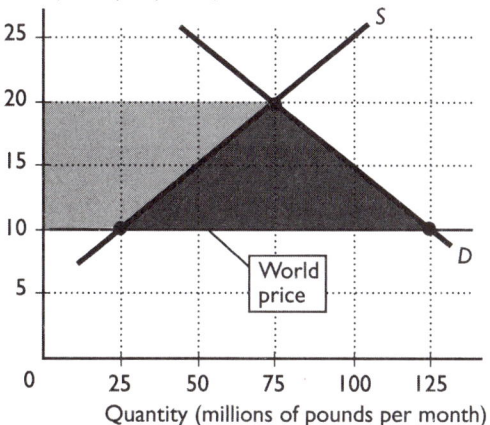

1. a. Figure 9.5 shows the world price line. At this price, 125 million pounds of sugar per month are consumed in the United States and 25 million pounds of sugar are produced in the United States. The difference, 100 million pounds of sugar per month, is imported into the United States; page 220.

   b. Consumer surplus increases. The increase in consumer surplus is equal to the sum of the area of the lighter grey trapezoid plus the area of the dark grey triangle in Figure 9.5. The producer surplus decreases. The decrease is equal to the area of the light grey trapezoid. On net, total surplus increases. The net increase is equal to the area of the dark grey triangle; page 220.

2. a. Figure 9.6 shows the world price line. At this price, 30 million bushels of wheat per year are consumed in the United States and 50 million bushels of wheat are produced in the United States. The difference, 20 million bushels of wheat per year, is exported from the United States; page 221.

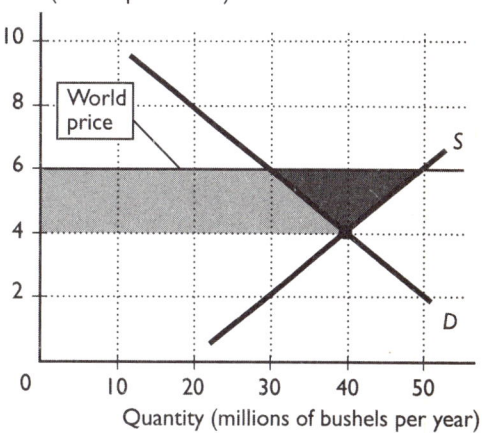

   b. Consumer surplus decreases. The decrease in consumer surplus is equal to the area of the lighter grey trapezoid in Figure 9.6. The producer surplus increases. The increase is equal to the sum of the area of the light grey trapezoid plus the area of the dark grey triangle. On net, total surplus increases. The increase is equal to the area of the dark grey triangle; page 221.

Short answer and numeric questions

1. The gains from international trade are measured as increases in consumer surplus or in producer surplus. The net gain from international trade is measured as the gain in the total surplus; page 219.

2. Consumers gain from imports because international trade lowers the prices of imported goods and services. Consumer surplus increases because the price is lower and because The lower price leads consumers to buy more of the good or service; page 220.

3. Consumers are the group in the economy that gain from imports. They gain because international trade lowers the prices of imported goods and services, which then increases their consumer surplus. The increase in consumer surplus will be larger the lower the price. So the United States gains more if the international price of sugar is 10¢ a pound rather than 20¢ a pound; page 220.

140 Part 3 · HOW GOVERNMENTS INFLUENCE THE ECONOMY

4. When a good is exported, its domestic price rises. Producers gain from the higher price but consumers lose. (The gain to the producers, however, is larger than the loss to consumers.) So not everyone gains when a good is exported because consumers of that good lose; page 221.

■ CHECKPOINT 9.3

Fill in the blanks

A tax on a good that is imposed by the importing country when an imported good enters its boundary is called a tariff and a specified maximum amount of a good that may be imported is called a quota. A tariff raises the price paid by domestic consumers, increases the quantity produced by domestic producers, and creates a deadweight loss. A quota raises the price paid by domestic consumers and increases the quantity produced by domestic producers.

True or false

1. False; pages 224
2. True; pages 224
3. False; pages 226
4. False; page 227

Multiple choice

1. c; page 223
2. a; page 223
3. b; page 224
4. b; page 224
5. b; pages 225-226
6. d; page 227

Complete the graph

1. a. The world price line is shown in Figure 9.7. 125 million pounds of sugar are consumed in the United States, 25 million pounds are produced in the United States, and 100 million pounds are imported into the United States; page 224.
   b. The tariff increases the domestic price, as shown in the figure. The quantity con-

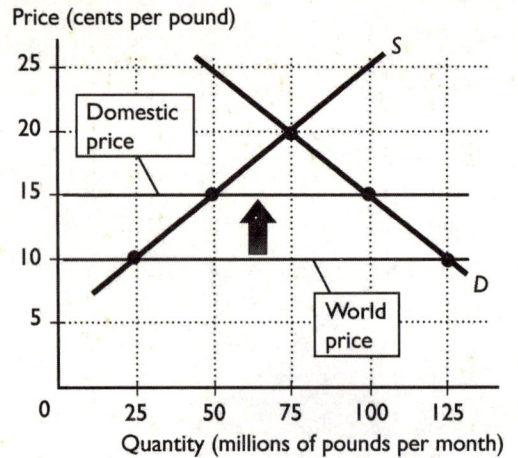

■ **FIGURE 9.7**
Price (cents per pound)

sumed in the United States decreases to 100 million pounds, the quantity produced in the United States increases to 50 million pounds, and the amount imported decreases to 50 million pounds; page 224.
   c. Consumers lose because consumer surplus decreases. Producers win because producer surplus increases. The government also wins because it raises revenue from the tariff; page 226.

Short answer and numeric questions

1. a. The price is the world price, $500 per ton. At this price, the quantity consumed in the United States is 24,000 tons per month, the quantity produced in the United States is 14,000 tons per month, and the quantity imported is the difference, 10,000 tons per month; page 224.
   b. With a $250 per ton tariff, the price is $750 per ton. At this price, the quantity consumed in the United States is 22,000 tons per month, the quantity produced in the United States is 17,000 tons per month, and the quantity imported is the difference, 5,000 tons per month; page 224.
   c. With a quota of 5,000 tons per month, the total supply schedule equals the U.S. supply schedule plus 5,000 tons per month. The price of steel is $750 per ton because this is the price that sets the U.S. quantity demanded (22,000 tons) equal to the U.S.

quantity supplied (17,000 tons) plus the quantity that can be imported (5,000 tons). At this price, the quantity consumed in the United States is 22,000 tons per month and the quantity produced in the United States is 17,000 tons per month; page 227.

d. U.S. consumers are no better off or worse off with the tariff or the quota because both raise the price to $750 per ton and decrease the quantity consumed to 22,000 tons. U.S. producers are no better off or worse off with the tariff or the quota because both raise the price to $750 per ton and increase the quantity produced to 17,000 tons; page 227.

2. The tariff raises the price of sugar. U.S. sugar consumers decrease the quantity they purchase and U.S. sugar producers increase the quantity they produce; pages 224-226.

3. The quota has the same effects as the tariff in the previous question. The quota raises the price of sugar. U.S. sugar consumers decrease the quantity purchased and U.S. sugar producers increase the quantity produced; page 227.

4. Consumers lose from a tariff because the tariff raises the price they pay and the quantity bought decreases. The tariff makes people pay more than the opportunity cost of the good. Society also loses because the tariff creates a deadweight loss; page 226.

■ CHECKPOINT 9.4

Fill in the blanks

The assertion that it is necessary to protect a new industry to enable it to grow into a mature industry that can compete in world markets is the <u>infant-industry</u> argument. Dumping occurs when <u>a foreign firm sells its exports at a lower price than its cost of production</u>. Protection <u>is not</u> necessary to bring diversity and stability to our economy. Protection <u>is not</u> necessary to penalize countries with lax environmental standards. The major reason why international trade is restricted is because <u>of rent seeking</u>.

True or false
1. False; page 231
2. False; page 232
3. False; page 233
4. True; page 234

Multiple choice
1. c; page 231
2. c; page 231
3. a; page 232
4. b; page 233
5. a; page 234
6. a; page 235

Short answer and numeric questions
1. Dumping occurs when a foreign firm sells its exports at a lower price than its cost of production. The dumping argument is flawed for the following reasons. First, it is virtually impossible to detect dumping because it is hard to determine a firm's costs and the fair market price. Second, it is hard to think of a good that is produced by a global natural monopoly. Third, if a firm truly was a global natural monopoly, the best way to deal with it would be by regulation; page 232.

2. Saving jobs is one of the oldest arguments in favor of protection. It is also incorrect. Protecting a particular industry will likely save jobs in that industry but will cost many other jobs in other industries. The cost to consumers of saving a job is many times the wage rate of the job saved; page 233.

3. The assertion that trade with developing countries that have lax environmental standards should be restricted to "punish" the nation for its lower standards is weak. Everyone wants a clean environment, but not every country can afford to devote resources toward this goal. The rich nations can afford this expenditure of resources, but for many poor nations protecting the environment takes second place to more pressing problems such as feeding their people. These nations must develop and grow economically in order to be able to afford to protect their

environment. One important way to help these nations grow is by trading with them. Through trade these nations' incomes will increase and with this increase will also increase their ability and willingness to protect the environment; page 234.

4. The tariff on ethanol imported from Brazil severely limits the quantity of ethanol that can be imported and so serves to keep the price of ethanol high in the United States. The high price for ethanol increases the demand for U.S. corn to be processed into ethanol. As a result, the tariff on ethanol keeps the price of corn in the United States higher than it would be in the absence of the tariff. As a representative of Frito Lay, your interest lies in lowering the price of corn. So you would be in favor of lowering or eliminating entirely this tariff; page 224.

Chapter 10

Externalities

CHAPTER CHECKLIST

An externality in an unregulated market leads to inefficiency and creates a deadweight loss. Chapter 9 explains the role of the government in markets where an externality is present and how government intervention can result in an efficient level of production.

1. Explain why negative externalities lead to inefficient overproduction and how property rights, pollution charges, and taxes can achieve a more efficient outcome.

Marginal private cost is the cost of producing an additional unit of a good or service that is borne by the producer of that good or service. Marginal external cost is the cost of producing an additional unit of a good or service that falls on people other than the producer. And marginal social cost, which is the marginal cost incurred by the entire society, is the sum of marginal private cost and marginal external cost. Producers take account only of marginal private cost and overproduce when there is a marginal external cost. Sometimes it is possible to reduce the inefficiency arising from an externality by establishing a property right where one does not currently exist. The Coase theorem is the proposition that if property rights exist, only a small number of parties are involved, and transactions costs are low, then private transactions are efficient and the outcome is not affected by who is assigned the property right. When property rights cannot be assigned, the three main methods that governments can use to cope with externalities are emission charges (which set a price per unit of pollution that a firm must pay), marketable permits (each firm is issued permits that allow a certain amount of pollution and firms can buy and sell the permits), and taxes (the government imposes a tax equal to the marginal external cost).

2. Explain why positive externalities lead to inefficient underproduction and how public provision, subsidies, vouchers, and patents can achieve a more efficient outcome.

Marginal private benefit is the benefit from an additional unit of a good or service that the consumer of that good or service receives. Marginal external benefit is the benefit from an additional unit of a good or service that people other than the consumer of the good or service enjoy. And marginal social benefit, which is the marginal benefit enjoyed by society, is the sum of marginal private benefit and marginal external benefit. External benefits from education arise because better-educated people are better citizens, commit fewer crimes, and support social activities. External benefits from research arise because once someone has worked out a basic idea, others can copy it. When people make decisions about how much schooling to obtain, they neglect its external benefit. The result is that if education were provided only by private schools that charged full-cost tuition, we would produce too few graduates. Four devices that governments can use to overcome the inefficiency created by external benefits are public provision, private subsidies, vouchers, and patents and copyrights.

CHECKPOINT 10.1

■ **Explain why negative externalities lead to inefficient overproduction and how property rights, pollution charges, and taxes can achieve a more efficient outcome.**

Quick Review
- *Marginal external cost* The cost of producing an additional unit of a good or service that falls on people other than the producer.
- *Efficiency* Efficiency is achieved when the marginal social benefit equals the marginal social cost.
- *Coase theorem* If property rights exist, only a small number of parties are involved, and transactions costs are low, then private transactions are efficient and the outcome is not affected by who is assigned the property right.

Additional Practice Problems 10.1

1. The figure illustrates the unregulated market for paper. When the factories produce paper, they also create air pollution. The cost of the pollution is $1,500 per ton. The pollution is a marginal external cost.
   a. What is the quantity of paper produced in an unregulated market? What is the price of a ton of paper?
   b. Draw the marginal social cost curve in the figure. What is the efficient quantity of paper to produce?
   c. If the government imposed a tax on the firms, what must the tax equal to have the efficient quantity of paper produced? With this tax imposed, what is the equilibrium price of a ton of paper?

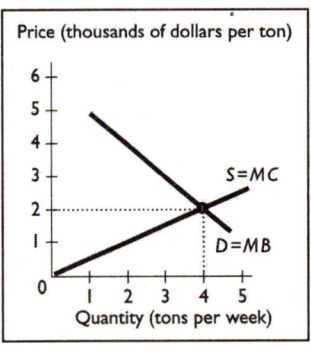

2. Two factories each emit 10 tons of the pollutant sulfur dioxide a week. The cost to eliminate a ton of sulfur dioxide to Factory A is $4 and the cost to Factory B is $2. The government wants to eliminate 10 tons of sulfur dioxide a week.
   a. If the government requires that Firm A decrease emissions by 10 tons a week, what is the cost of eliminating the pollution?
   b. If the government requires that Firm B decrease emissions by 10 tons a week, what is the cost of the eliminating the pollution?
   c. If the government gives each firm 5 marketable permits, each good for 1 ton of pollution, what will occur?

Solutions to Additional Practice Problems 10.1

1a. The equilibrium is determined by the intersection of the demand and supply curves. So the equilibrium quantity is 4 tons of paper per week and the equilibrium price is $2,000 per ton.

1b. The figure shows the marginal social cost curve, labeled MSC. At 1 ton of paper this curve lies $1,500 above the supply curve; at 2 tons of paper it lies $3,000 above the supply curve; and so on. The efficient quantity is where the marginal social cost equals the marginal benefit, which the figure shows is 2 tons of paper.

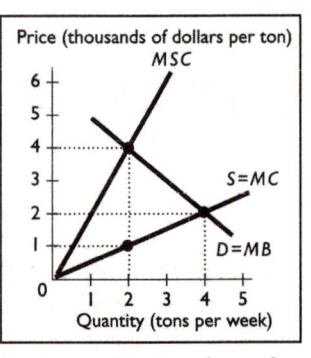

1c. To lead to efficiency, the tax must equal the marginal external cost. So the tax should be $1,500 per ton. At the efficient quantity of 2 tons, the tax is $3,000. With this tax, the equilibrium price is $4,000 per ton of paper.

2a. The cost for Firm A to decrease emissions is $4 a ton multiplied by 10 tons, which is $40 a week.

2b. The cost for Firm B to decrease emissions is $2 a ton multiplied by 10 tons, which is $20 a week.

2c. Firm A is willing to buy permits from Firm B for any price less than $4 per permit; Firm B is willing to sell permits to Firm A for any price greater than $2 per permit. The two companies will settle on a price and Firm A will buy 5 permits from Firm B. Only Firm B will decrease its pollution and incur a cost of $20 a week.

■ Self Test 10.1

Fill in the blanks

Marginal social cost equals marginal private cost ____ (minus; plus) marginal external cost. A pollution externality creates an ____ (efficient; inefficient) equilibrium. According to the Coase theorem, if property rights exist, then private transactions are efficient and the outcome ____ (is; is not) affected by who is assigned the property right. By setting the tax rate equal to the marginal ____ (external; private; social) cost, firms can be made to behave in the same way as they would if they bore the cost of the externality directly.

True or false

1. All externalities are negative.
2. Smoking on a plane creates a negative externality.
3. Marginal social cost equals marginal private cost minus marginal external cost.
4. Copper mining creates land pollution. If the copper mining industry is unregulated, then the quantity of copper mined is less than the efficient quantity.
5. The Coase theorem concludes that if property rights to a polluted river are assigned to the polluter, the quantity of pollution will increase.
6. Emission charges allow the government to set the price for a unit of pollution.
7. By issuing marketable permits, the government sets the price for each unit of pollution produced.
8. If the government imposes a pollution tax on lead mining equal to its marginal external cost, the quantity of lead mined will be the efficient quantity.

Multiple choice

1. Which of the following best describes an externality?
   a. something that is external to the economy
   b. a sales tax on a good in addition to the market price
   c. an effect of a transaction felt by someone other than the consumer or producer
   d. anything produced in other countries
   e. a change from what is normal

2. Pollution is an example of a ____ externality.
   a. negative production
   b. positive production
   c. negative consumption
   d. positive consumption
   e. Coasian

3. The cost of producing one more unit of a good or service that is borne by the producer of that good or service
   a. always equals the benefit the consumer derives from that good or service.
   b. equals the cost borne by people other than the producer.
   c. is the marginal private cost.
   d. is the external cost.
   e. is the marginal social cost.

4. The cost of producing an additional unit of a good or service that falls on people other than the producer is
   a. the marginal cost.
   b. represented by the demand curve.
   c. represented by the supply curve.
   d. the marginal external cost.
   e. the marginal social cost.

5. Which of the following is an example of something that creates an external cost?
   i. second-hand smoke
   ii. sulfur emitting from a smoke stack
   iii. garbage on the roadside
   a. i only.
   b. ii only.
   c. iii only.
   d. ii and iii.
   e. i, ii, and iii.

6. The marginal cost of production that is borne by the entire society is the marginal
   a. private cost.
   b. social cost.
   c. external cost.
   d. public cost.
   e. user cost.

7. If the marginal private cost of producing one kilowatt of power in California is five cents and the marginal social cost of each kilowatt is nine cents, then the marginal external cost equals ____ a kilowatt.
   a. five cents
   b. nine cents
   c. four cents
   d. zero cents
   e. fourteen cents

8. When the production of a good has a marginal external cost, which of the following will occur in an unregulated market?
   i. Overproduction relative to the efficient level will occur
   ii. The market price will be less than the marginal social cost at the equilibrium quantity
   iii. A deadweight loss will occur
   a. i only.
   b. ii only.
   c. iii only.
   d. i and ii.
   e. i, ii, and iii.

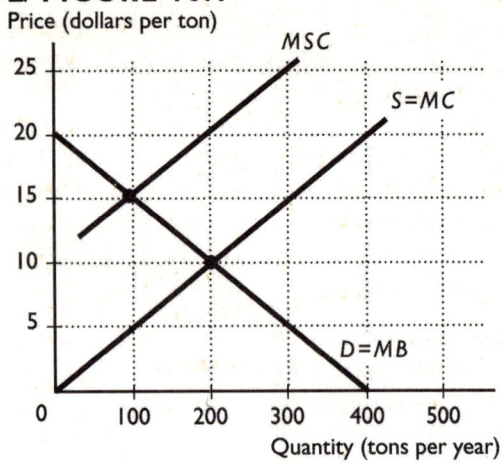

■ FIGURE 10.1

9. Figure 10.1 shows the market for a good with an external cost. The external cost equals ____ per ton.
   a. $5
   b. $10
   c. $15
   d. $20
   e. $25

10. Figure 10.1 shows the market for a good with an external cost. If the market is unregulated, the equilibrium quantity is ____ tons per year.
    a. 0
    b. 100
    c. 200
    d. 300
    e. 400

11. Figure 10.1 shows the market for a good with an external cost. The efficient quantity is ____ tons per year.
    a. 0
    b. 100
    c. 200
    d. 300
    e. 400

12. The Coase theorem is the proposition that if property rights exist and are enforced, private transactions are
    a. inefficient.
    b. efficient.
    c. inequitable.
    d. illegal.
    e. unnecessary.

13. A marketable permit
    a. allows firms to pollute all they want without any cost.
    b. allows firms to buy and sell the right to pollute at government controlled prices.
    c. eliminates pollution by setting the price of pollution permits above the marginal cost of polluting.
    d. allows firms to buy and sell the right to pollute.
    e. is the Coase solution to pollution.

14. If we compare air pollution today to air pollution in 1980, we see that
    a. pollution of all forms has increased.
    b. pollution of all forms has been substantially reduced.
    c. pollution of most types has been decreased.
    d. pollution from lead has increased.
    e. pollution of most types has not changed.

15. If a polluting producer is forced to pay an emission charge or a tax on its output, what is the effect on the supply and demand curves for the product?
    a. The quantity supplied along the firm's supply curve will increase.
    b. The firm's demand curve shifts leftward.
    c. The firm's supply curve shifts rightward.
    d. The firm's supply curve shifts leftward.
    e. *Both* the supply curve and the demand curve shift leftward.

Complete the graph

Quantity (megawatts per day)	Marginal private cost (dollars)	Marginal social cost (dollars)	Marginal benefit (dollars)
1	5	10	50
2	10	20	40
3	15	30	30
4	20	40	20

1. The table above shows the marginal private cost, marginal social cost, and marginal benefit schedules for generating electricity.
   a. In Figure 10.2, label the axes and then plot the marginal private cost curve, the marginal social cost curve, and the marginal benefit curve.

■ **FIGURE 10.2**

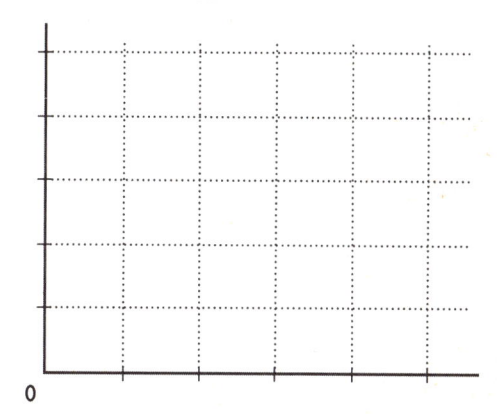

   b. How much electricity will an unregulated market produce? What is the marginal external cost at this amount of production?
   c. What is the efficient amount of electricity? Illustrate the deadweight loss resulting from the market equilibrium.
   d. At the efficient quantity of electricity, what is the marginal external cost? If the government imposes a tax on producing electricity to produce the efficient quantity, what should be the amount of tax? How much electricity is generated and what is its price?

148 Part 3 · HOW GOVERNMENTS INFLUENCE THE ECONOMY

Quantity (tons per day)	Marginal private cost (dollars)	Marginal benefit (dollars)
1	200	600
2	300	500
3	400	400
4	500	300

2. The table above shows the marginal private cost and marginal benefit schedules for producing PBDE, a chemical flame retardant. Suppose that there is an external cost of $100 per ton of PBDE produced.

   a. In Figure 10.3, label the axes and then plot the marginal private cost curve, the marginal social cost curve, and the marginal benefit curve.

   ■ FIGURE 10.3

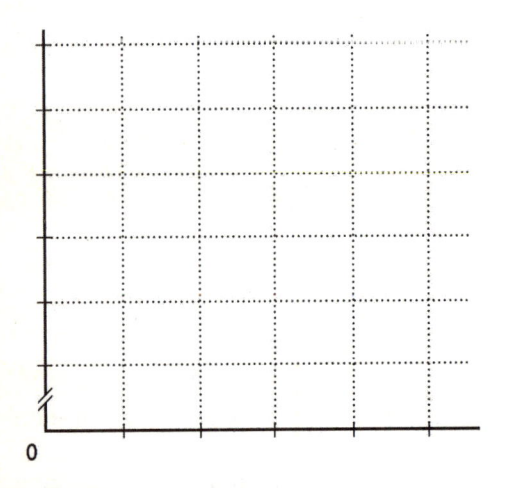

   b. How much PBDE will an unregulated market produce? What is the equilibrium price? What is the amount of the marginal external cost at the equilibrium quantity of production?

   c. What is the efficient amount of PBDE? At the efficient quantity, what is the amount of the marginal external cost?

   d. If the government set an emission charge for producing PBDE, what must the charge equal to lead to the efficient quantity of PBDE?

Short answer and numeric questions

1. If the marginal social cost curve lies above the marginal private cost curve, is there an external cost or benefit from production of the good or service?

Quantity (tons of pesticide per day)	Marginal private cost (dollars per ton)	Marginal external cost (dollars per ton)	Marginal social cost (dollars per ton)
1	100	—	130
2	120	40	—
3	—	60	210
4	190	—	280
5	240	120	—

2. The table above shows the costs of producing pesticide. Complete the table.

3. According to the Coase theorem, when are private transactions efficient?

4. What is a marketable permit? What advantage do marketable permits have over the government assigning each firm a limit on how much it can pollute?

5. The production of fertilizer creates water pollution. How do emission charges and taxes result in an efficient quantity of production? What information must the government possess to use emission charges and taxes effectively?

CHECKPOINT 10.2

■ **Explain why positive externalities lead to inefficient underproduction and how public provision, subsidies, vouchers, and patents can achieve a more efficient outcome.**

Quick Review
- *Marginal external benefit* The benefit from an additional unit of a good or service that people other than the consumer of the good or service enjoy.

Additional Practice Problems 10.2

1. The figure shows the marginal private benefit, marginal social benefit, and marginal cost of a college education.

    a. How much does the marginal external benefit equal?
    b. If colleges are private and government has no involvement in college education, how many people will undertake a college education and what will be the tuition?
    c. What is the efficient number of students?
    d. If the government decides to provide public colleges, what tuition will these colleges charge to achieve the efficient number of students? What is the marginal cost of educating this many students? Why is it justified to charge a tuition that is less than the marginal cost?

2. A vaccine for chicken pox was recently developed. The company that developed the vaccine, Merck Incorporated, was required to submit a document comparing the costs and benefits of vaccinating children. The government would approve the drug only if the benefit of vaccination exceeded the cost. The producer reports that the marginal cost of a dose of vaccine is $80. The marginal benefit to the child being vaccinated is estimated to be $30 and an additional marginal benefit to the child's parents is estimated at $60.

    a. How much is the marginal private benefit and the marginal external benefit?
    b. Based on these data, should the government have approved the vaccine?

Solutions to Additional Practice Problems 10.2

1a. The marginal external benefit equals the vertical distance between the marginal social benefit curve, *MSB*, and the marginal private benefit curve, *MB*. In the figure the difference is $8,000, so the marginal external benefit equals $8,000.

1b. If the government has no involvement, the equilibrium tuition and number of students is determined by the equilibrium between supply and demand. The supply curve is the marginal private cost curve, S = MC, and the demand curve is the marginal private benefit curve, *MB*. The figure shows that the equilibrium tuition equals $8,000 a year and the equilibrium enrollment is 200,000 students a year.

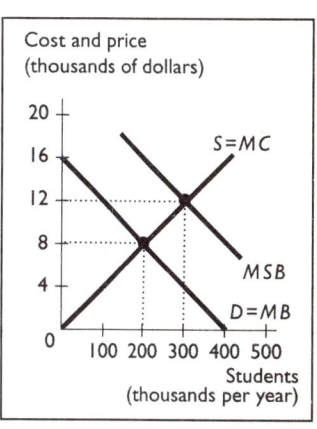

1c. The efficient number of students is 300,000 because this the quantity at which the marginal cost equals the marginal social benefit.

1d. The demand curve, which is the same as the marginal private benefit curve, shows that tuition must be $4,000 in order for 300,000 students to attend college. The marginal cost of educating 300,000 students is $12,000 students per year. It is justified to charge a tuition that is less than the marginal cost because education has external benefits so that society as well as the student benefits from the college education.

2a. The marginal private benefit is the benefit to the child being vaccinated and is $30. The marginal external benefit is the benefit to the child's parents and is $60.

2b. Based on the data that were submitted, the government should have approved the vaccine. The marginal social benefit equals the marginal private benefit to the child of $30 plus the marginal external benefit to the parent of $60, which is $90. The marginal social benefit from the vaccine is greater than the marginal cost.

■ Self Test 10.2

Fill in the blanks

Marginal ____ (social; external) benefit is the benefit enjoyed by society from one more unit of a good or service. If the government leaves education to the private market, ____ (overproduction; underproduction) occurs. A payment that the government makes to private producers that depends on the level of output is ____ (a subsidy; public provision). The property rights of the creators of knowledge and other discoveries are ____ (intellectual property; patent property) rights.

True or false

1. The marginal private benefit from a good or service must exceed the marginal external benefit.
2. The expanded job opportunities from a college degree is a marginal private benefit enjoyed by college graduates.
3. A flu vaccination has an external benefit, so the marginal private benefit curve for flu vaccinations lies above the marginal social benefit curve for flu vaccinations.
4. An unregulated market underproduces products with external benefits, such as education.
5. A public community college is an example of public provision of a good that has an external benefit.
6. To overcome the inefficiency in the market for a good with an external benefit, the government can either tax or subsidize the good.
7. Vouchers can help overcome the inefficiency created by a good with an external cost but not the inefficiency created by a good with an external benefit.
8. A patent protects intellectual property rights by giving the patent holder a monopoly.

Multiple choice

1. The benefit the consumer of a good or service receives is the
   a. social benefit.
   b. external benefit.
   c. private benefit.
   d. public benefit.
   e. consumption benefit.

2. An external benefit is a benefit from a good or service that someone other than the ____ receives.
   a. seller of the good or service
   b. government
   c. foreign sector
   d. consumer
   e. market maker

3. When Ronald takes another economics class, other people in society benefit. The benefit to these other people is called the marginal ____ benefit of the class.
   a. social
   b. private
   c. external
   d. opportunity
   e. extra

4. Marginal social benefit equals
   a. marginal external benefit.
   b. marginal private benefit.
   c. marginal private benefit minus marginal external benefit.
   d. marginal private benefit plus marginal external benefit
   e. marginal external benefit minus marginal private benefit.

5. If an external benefit is present, then the
   a. marginal private benefit curve lies above the marginal private cost curve.
   b. marginal social benefit curve lies above the marginal private benefit curve.
   c. marginal social cost curve lies above the marginal private benefit curve.
   d. marginal social benefit is equal to the marginal social cost.
   e. marginal social benefit curve is the same as the marginal private benefit curve.

6. In an unregulated market with an external benefit, the
   a. quantity produced is greater than the efficient quantity.
   b. price charged is too high for efficiency.
   c. quantity produced is less than the efficient quantity.
   d. producer is causing pollution but not paying for it.
   e. government might impose a tax to help move the market toward the efficient amount of production.

■ **FIGURE 10.4**

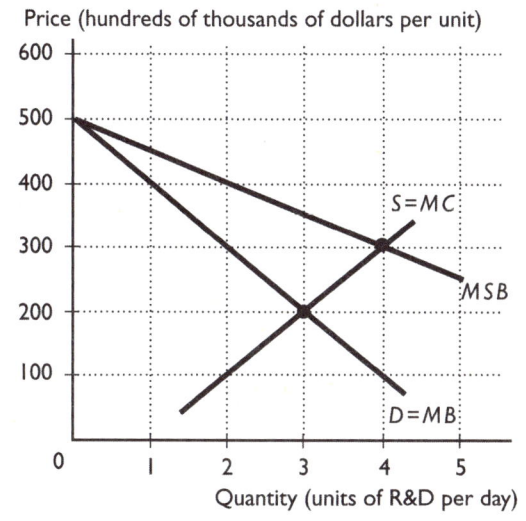

Price (hundreds of thousands of dollars per unit)

7. Figure 10.4 shows the market for research and development, which has ____.
   a. only external costs
   b. only external benefits
   c. both external costs and external benefits
   d. neither external costs nor external benefits
   e. might have external benefits or external costs, but more information is needed

8. Figure 10.4 shows the market for research and development. If the market is unregulated, the equilibrium quantity of R&D is ____ units per day.
   a. 0
   b. 2
   c. 3
   d. 4
   e. 5

9. Figure 10.4 shows the market for research and development. The efficient quantity of R&D is ____ units per day.
   a. 0
   b. 2
   c. 3
   d. 4
   e. 5

10. If all education in the United States were provided by private, tuition-charging schools,
    a. too much education would be consumed.
    b. too little education would be consumed.
    c. the efficient level of education would be provided.
    d. the government would provide *both* students and schools with vouchers.
    e. education would no longer have an external benefit.

11. Which of the following is a method used by government to cope with the situation in which production of a good creates an external benefit?
    a. removing property rights
    b. paying subsidies
    c. issuing marketable permits
    d. running a lottery
    e. imposing a Coasian tax

12. If tuition at a college is $30,000 and the external benefit of graduating from this college is $10,000, then
    i. in the absence of any government intervention, the number of students graduating is less than the efficient number
    ii. the government could increase the number of graduates by giving the college a $10,000 subsidy per student
    iii. the government could increase the number of graduates by giving the students $10,000 vouchers
    a. i only.
    b. i and ii.
    c. i and iii.
    d. ii and iii.
    e. i, ii, and iii.

13. Public universities are a service that is an example of
    a. patent protection.
    b. vouchers.
    c. private subsidies.
    d. public provision.
    e. an emission charge.

14. Which of the following is an example of a voucher?
    a. the postal service
    b. police services
    c. social security
    d. food stamps
    e. a patent on a pharmaceutical drug

15. Which government device is associated with intellectual property rights?
    a. public provision
    b. private subsidies
    c. vouchers
    d. patents and copyrights
    e. taxes

Complete the graph

■ FIGURE 10.5

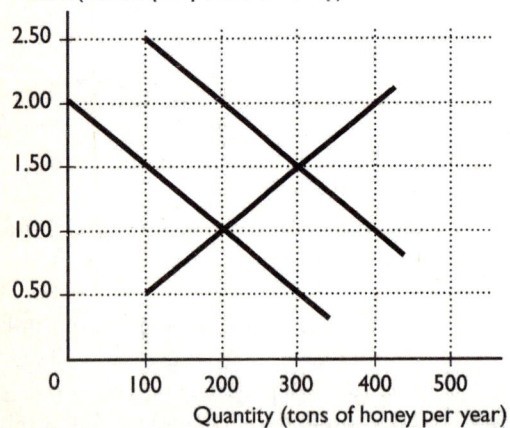

1. Figure 10.5 illustrates the market for honey.
   a. Label the curves in the figure.
   b. Based on Figure 10.5, does the production of honey create an external cost? An external benefit?
   c. What is the efficient quantity of honey? What is the quantity that will be produced in an unregulated market?
   d. Shade the area that equals the deadweight loss in an unregulated market.

Short answer and numeric questions

Quantity (units of R&D per day)	Marginal private cost (dollars per unit of R&D)	Marginal private benefit (dollars per unit of R&D)	Marginal social benefit (dollars per unit of R&D)
100	100	250	340
200	120	200	290
300	150	150	240
400	190	100	190
500	240	50	140

1. The table above shows the benefits and costs of research and development, R&D.
   a. Based on the table, what is the amount of the marginal external benefit?
   b. If the market for R&D was left unregulated, what would be the competitive amount of R&D?
   c. What is the efficient amount of R&D?
   d. Would a subsidy or a tax be the proper government policy to make the market for R&D more efficient?

2. Is efficiency guaranteed when production is such that the marginal private benefit equals the marginal private cost? Or does efficiency require that the marginal social benefit equal the marginal social cost?

3. Most elementary schools require that children be vaccinated before allowing the child to attend school. Can this policy be justified using economic analysis?

4. Is a private subsidy or a tax the correct government policy for a product that has an external benefit?

5. What is a voucher? How do vouchers work? Why is a voucher a proper policy to deal with the inefficiency created by a good or service that has an external benefit?

SELF TEST ANSWERS

■ CHECKPOINT 10.1

Fill in the blanks

Marginal social cost equals marginal private cost <u>plus</u> marginal external cost. A pollution externality creates an <u>inefficient</u> equilibrium. According to the Coase theorem, if property rights exist, then private transactions are efficient and the outcome <u>is not</u> affected by who is assigned the property right. By setting the tax rate equal to the marginal <u>external</u> cost, firms can be made to behave in the same way as they would if they bore the cost of the externality directly.

True or false

1. False; page 242
2. True; page 243
3. False; page 244
4. False; page 246
5. False; page 248
6. True; page 250
7. False; page 250
8. True; page 251

Multiple choice

1. c; page 242
2. a; page 242
3. c; page 244
4. d; page 244
5. e; page 244
6. b; page 244
7. c; page 244
8. e; page 246
9. b; page 245
10. c; page 246
11. b; page 246
12. b; page 248
13. d; page 250
14. c; page 249
15. d; page 251

Complete the graph

1. a. Figure 10.6 shows the *MSC*, *MC*, and *MB* curves; page 246.

■ FIGURE 10.6

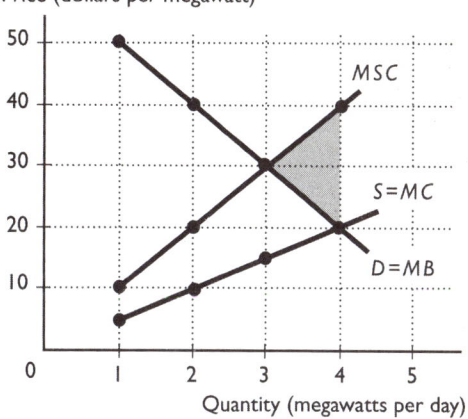

b. An unregulated market will produce 4 megawatts of electricity a day. The marginal external cost at this production is $20 per megawatt; page 246.
c. The efficient amount of electricity is 3 megawatts a day. The deadweight loss is illustrated in the figure; page 246.
d. At the efficient quantity of electricity, the marginal external cost is $15 a megawatt. The tax is $15 a megawatt. With the tax, 3 megawatts of electricity are produced and the price is $30 per megawatt; page 251.

■ FIGURE 10.7

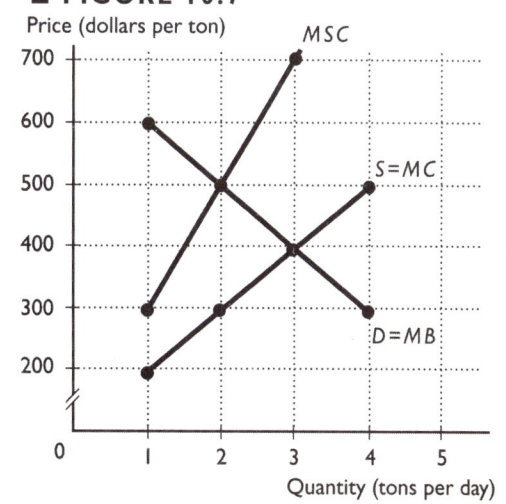

2. a. Figure 10.7 shows the *MSC*, *MC*, and *MB* curves; page 246.

154 Part 3 · HOW GOVERNMENTS INFLUENCE THE ECONOMY

b. An unregulated market will produce 3 tons of PBDE a day. At this quantity the marginal external cost is $300; pages 245-246.
c. The efficient quantity of PBDE is 2 tons per day. At this quantity the marginal external cost is $200; pages 245-246.
d. The emission charge will equal $100 per ton of PBDE; page 250.

Short answer and numeric questions

1. If the marginal social cost curve lies above the marginal private cost curve, production of the good creates an external cost; page 245.

Quantity (tons of pesticide per day)	Marginal private cost (dollars per ton)	Marginal external cost (dollars per ton)	Marginal social cost (dollars per ton)
1	100	30	130
2	120	40	160
3	150	60	210
4	190	90	280
5	240	120	360

2. The completed table is above; page 244.
3. According to the Coase theorem, if property rights are assigned, the number of people involved is small, and transactions costs are low, then private transactions are efficient; page 248.
4. A marketable permit is a government-issued permit given to firms that allows the company to pollute up to the limit of the permit. Permits can be bought and sold amongst firms. The advantage marketable permits have over assigning each firm a limit for its pollution is information. In order to assign each firm a limit and achieve efficiency, the government must know each firm's marginal cost schedule. Marketable permits do not require that the government know this information; page 250.
5. Emission charges and taxes are designed to charge polluting firms the cost of their pollution. By forcing a firm to pay this cost, the firm's marginal private cost becomes equal to the marginal social cost. To use emission charges or taxes to overcome the problem of pollution, the government must know the marginal external cost at different levels of output; page 250.

■ CHECKPOINT 10.2

Fill in the blanks

Marginal <u>social</u> benefit is the benefit enjoyed by society from one more unit of a good or service. If the government leaves education to the private market, <u>underproduction</u> occurs. A payment that the government makes to private producers that depends on the level of output is <u>a subsidy</u>. The property rights of the creators of knowledge and other discoveries are <u>intellectual property</u> rights.

True or false

1. False; page 254
2. True; page 254
3. False; page 254
4. True; page 255
5. True; page 256
6. False; page 256
7. False; page 258
8. True; page 259

Multiple choice

1. c; page 254
2. d; page 254
3. c; page 254
4. d; page 254
5. b; page 254
6. c; page 255
7. b; page 254
8. c; page 255
9. d; page 255
10. b; page 255
11. b; page 256
12. e; pages 256-258
13. d; page 256
14. d; page 258
15. d; page 259

Complete the graph

FIGURE 10.8

Price (dollars per pound of honey)

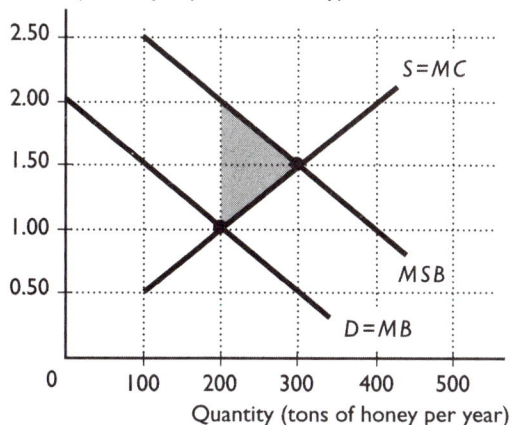

(Graph showing S=MC curve, D=MB curve, and MSB curve. Equilibrium at 200 tons, $1.00; efficient quantity at 300 tons, $1.50. Deadweight loss shaded between quantities 200 and 300.)

1. a. Figure 10.8 labels the curves; page 255.
   b. The production of honey has an external benefit but no external cost; page 255.
   c. The efficient quantity of honey is 300 tons, a year, at the intersection of the *MSB* curve and the *S = MC* curve. In an unregulated market, the equilibrium quantity is 200 tons a year, at the intersection of the *D = MB* curve and the *S = MC* curve; page 255.
   d. Figure 10.8 shades the deadweight loss; page 255.

Short answer and numeric questions

1. a. The marginal external benefit equals the difference between the marginal social benefit and the marginal social cost, so it is $90 per unit of R&D; page 254.
   b. The competitive equilibrium is where the marginal private cost (which determines the supply) equals the marginal private benefit (which determines the demand), so the equilibrium amount of R&D is 300 units per day; page 255.
   c. The efficient quantity is produced when the marginal social benefit equals the marginal cost, so the efficient amount is 400 units of R&D per day; page 255.
   d. A subsidy would be a proper government policy; page 257.

2. Efficiency is not guaranteed when production sets the marginal private benefit equal to the marginal cost. The efficient quantity is produced when the marginal social benefit equals marginal cost; page 255.

3. Vaccination protects not only the child who is vaccinated, but also makes it less likely for classmates to catch the disease. So a vaccination has an external benefit. Although the marginal cost of a vaccination can be greater than the marginal private benefit of a vaccination, the marginal social benefit exceeds the marginal private benefit. The market might be efficient when vaccination is required; page 255.

3. The correct government action to deal with a good or service that has an external benefit is a private subsidy, not a tax; page 256.

4. A voucher is a token that the government gives to households which they can use to buy specified goods or services. Vouchers increase the demand for the product and shift the demand curve (which is the same as the marginal private benefit curve, or *MB* curve) rightward, closer to the marginal social benefit curve. Vouchers reduce the inefficiency created by a good or service with an external benefit; page 258.

Chapter 11
Public Goods and Common Resources

CHAPTER CHECKLIST

Chapter 11 studies the types of goods and services provided by the government.

1 Distinguish among private goods, public goods, and common resources.

An excludable good, service, or resource is one for which it is possible to prevent someone from benefiting from it; a nonexcludable good, service, or resource is one for which it is impossible to prevent someone from benefiting from it. A rival good, service, or resource is one for which its consumption by one person decreases the quantity available for someone else; a nonrival good, service, or resource is one for which its consumption by one person does not decrease the quantity available to someone else. A private good is excludable and rival. A public good is a good or service that can be consumed simultaneously by everyone and from which no one can be excluded. A public good is nonexcludable and nonrival. A common resource is a resource that is nonexcludable and rival.

2 Explain the free-rider problem and how public provision might help to overcome that problem.

Public goods create a free-rider problem, a person who enjoys the benefits of a good or service without paying for it. The economy's marginal benefit curve of a public good is the vertical sum of the individual marginal benefit curves. The efficient quantity of a public good is the quantity where marginal benefit equals marginal cost. Because of the free-rider problem, public goods are under-provided by private firms so public provision of public goods might lead efficiency. The tendency for political parties to propose identical policies to appeal to the maximum number of voters is an example of the principle of minimum differentiation. Rational ignorance is the decision not to acquire information because the marginal cost of doing so exceeds the expected marginal benefit. Rational ignorance, combined with the bureaucratic desire to maximize budgets, can lead to inefficient overprovision of public goods.

3 Explain the tragedy of the commons and review the possible solutions to that problem.

Common resources suffer from the tragedy of the commons, which is the absence of incentives to prevent the overuse and depletion of a commonly owned resource. Fish are an example of a common resource. The marginal private benefit of an additional boat is that boat's catch. But the quantity of fish caught by each boat decreases as more boats fish. The marginal social benefit of an additional boat is the change in the total catch that results from that additional boat. Efficiency occurs when the marginal social benefit from a resource equals its marginal cost. But the marginal private benefit is more than the marginal social benefit, so in an unregulated market overuse of the resource occurs. The government can help bring about an efficient use of the common resource by assigning property rights to the resource, or by setting quotas on the amount of the resource that can be used, or by creating a program of individual transferable quotas (ITQ). An individual transferable quota is a production limit that the owner can transfer to someone else.

CHECKPOINT 11.1

■ **Distinguish among private goods, public goods, and common resources.**

Quick Review
- *Public good* A public good is nonrival and nonexcludable.
- *Private good* A private good is rival and excludable.
- *Common resource* A common resource is rival and nonexcludable.

Additional Practice Problem 11.1
1. It's a balmy, pleasant Sunday afternoon on a fall day on Long Island, where the U.S. Open Tennis Men's Singles Finals are being played. A variety of goods and services are being consumed. Classify each of the list of goods and services as rival, nonrival, excludable, and nonexcludable. State if they are a public good, a private good, or a common resource.
    - a. U.S. Lawn Tennis Association membership
    - b. tennis lessons
    - c. racquets
    - d. watching the Men's Singles Championship
    - e. a pleasant, sunny afternoon
    - f. sunset seen over Fire Island
    - g. shrimp eaten at a tailgate party

Solution to Additional Practice Problem 11.1
1a. Membership in the U.S. Lawn Tennis Association is nonrival and excludable.

1b. Tennis lessons are rival and excludable and are a private good.

1c. Racquets are rival and excludable and hence are a private good.

1d. Watching the Men's Singles Championship is excludable. Whether it is rival depends on whether the match is a sell out. If it is a sell out, then watching the championship is rival and it is a private good; in the event that it is not sold out and seats remain available, it is nonrival.

1e. The pleasant afternoon is nonrival and nonexcludable and so is a public good.

1f. The sunset is nonrival and nonexcludable and so is a public good.

1g. The shrimp are rival and excludable and so are a private good.

■ **Self Test 11.1**

Fill in the blanks
A good is ____ (rival; nonrival; excludable) if it is possible to prevent someone from enjoying its benefits. A good is ____ (rival; nonrival; excludable) if its use by one person does not decrease the quantity available for someone else. A good that is nonrival and nonexcludable is a ____ (private; public; common) good and a good that is rival and excludable is a ____ (private; public; common) good. A common resource is ____ (rival; nonrival) and ____ (excludable; nonexcludable).

True or false
1. A good is nonexcludable if it is impossible to prevent someone from benefiting from it.
2. A private good is nonrival and nonexcludable.
3. A taco from Taco Bell is a public good.
4. A common resource is nonrival and excludable.
5. Fish in the ocean are rival and nonexcludable.

Multiple choice
1. The fact that Heidi's enjoyment of a sunset on Saint Simon's Island does not preclude Mounette from enjoying the same sunset is an example of
    - a. a good that is nonrival.
    - b. a good that is excludable.
    - c. a private good.
    - d. the rival nature of consumption.
    - e. a common resource.

2. When use of a good decreases the quantity available for someone else, the good is
   a. rival.
   b. nonrival.
   c. excludable.
   d. nonexcludable.
   e. a public good.

3. A private good is ____ and ____.
   a. rival; excludable
   b. rival; nonexcludable
   c. nonrival; excludable
   d. nonrival; nonexcludable
   e. scarce; expensive

4. If I order a pizza and invite my neighbors to eat it, the pizza is
   a. a private good.
   b. a common resource.
   c. a public good because many people ate it.
   d. either a common resource or a public good depending on whether it is overused.
   e. produced by a natural monopoly.

5. A public good is ____ and ____.
   a. rival; excludable
   b. rival; nonexcludable
   c. nonrival; excludable
   d. nonrival; nonexcludable
   e. cheap; available

6. A public good
   a. can only be consumed by one person at a time.
   b. can be consumed simultaneously by many people.
   c. is any good provided by a company owned by a member of the public.
   d. is any good provided by government.
   e. is both rival and excludable.

7. Which of the following is the best example of a public good?
   a. national defense
   b. a Ford Thunderbird
   c. Yosemite national park
   d. a Mountain Dew
   e. a satellite radio

8. Which of the following is the best example of a common resource?
   a. national defense
   b. a Ford Thunderbird
   c. Yosemite national park
   d. a can of Mountain Dew
   e. a cable television network

Short answer and numeric questions

1. What does it mean for a good to be nonexcludable? Nonrival?
2. Goods can be excludable or nonexcludable, rival or nonrival. Using these criteria, what is a public good, a private good, and a common resource?

CHECKPOINT 11.2

■ **Explain the free-rider problem and how public provision might help to overcome that problem.**

Quick Review
- *Free rider* A free rider enjoys the benefits of a good or service without paying for the good or service.

Additional Practice Problems 11.2

Quantity (square miles per day)	Abe's marginal benefit (dollars per day)	Bee's marginal benefit (dollars per day)	Kris's marginal benefit (dollars per day)
1	20	20	30
2	35	35	50
3	48	42	60
4	60	45	65
5	70	47	68

1. A (small) city that is exactly 5 square miles in size has three people in it, Abe, Bee, and Kris. The table above gives the marginal benefit of each from a mosquito control program.
   a. Is mosquito spraying a public good or a private good? Explain your answer.
   b. Calculate the marginal social benefit for spraying 1, 2, 3, 4, and 5 square miles a day.

c. If the marginal cost of spraying was constant at $150 for a square mile, what it is the efficient number of miles that should be sprayed?
d. How many square miles would the bureau head of the city's mosquito control project lobby the city commissioners to spray?

2. How do rational ignorance and bureaucrats' goal of budget maximization combine to lead to inefficient overprovision of public goods?

Solutions to Additional Practice Problems 11.2

1a. Mosquito spraying is a public good because it's both nonrival—everyone can simultaneously enjoy not being bitten—and nonexcludable—even if one of the residents does not pay, the mosquitoes still do not bite that resident.

1b. The marginal social benefit is equal to the sum of the benefits of all the residents for each quantity. So the marginal social benefit for spraying 1 square mile is equal to $20 + $20 + $30 = $70. The rest of the answers in the table are calculated similarly.

Quantity (square miles per day)	Marginal social benefit (dollars per day)
1	70
2	120
3	150
4	170
5	185

1c. The marginal social cost equals the marginal social benefit when 3 square miles are sprayed, so 3 square miles is the efficient quantity of spraying.

1d. The head of the city's mosquito control commission wants to maximize the budget of the commission, so the head will lobby to spray 5 square miles.

2. If voters knew the marginal social benefit and marginal social cost of a public good, they could elect politicians who would deliver the efficient quantity. But voters generally are rationally ignorant about the marginal social benefit and marginal social cost of most public goods. So bureaucrats, who want to increase their budget, and special interest groups, such as the producers of a public good, lobby politicians to provide more than the efficient amount of public goods. Politicians accede to the lobbying because they know that (rationally ignorant) voters will not realize that too much of the public good is provided.

■ Self Test 11.2

Fill in the blanks

A person who enjoys the benefit of a good or service without paying for it is a ____. The marginal benefit curve for a public good is the ____ (horizontal; vertical) sum of the individual marginal benefit curves. The efficient quantity of a public good is the quantity at which the marginal benefit ____ the marginal cost. ____ (Rational ignorance; The principle of minimum differentiation) is the decision to not acquire information because the marginal cost of doing so exceeds the expected marginal benefit. Bureaucrats try to ____ (maximize; minimize) their budgets.

True or false
1. Beth is a free rider when she is protected by the nation's military but does not pay anything for the protection.
2. The marginal benefit curve for a public good slopes downward.
3. The efficient quantity of a public good is the quantity at which marginal benefit equals marginal cost.
4. A private firm would produce too much of a public good.
5. Rational ignorance can lead to the provision of more than the efficient amount of a public good.

Multiple choice
1. When someone enjoys the benefit of a good or service but does not pay for it, that person
    a. is a free range consumer.
    b. is a free rider.
    c. receives no marginal benefit from the good.
    d. must be consuming an excludable good
    e. is contributing to the tragedy of the commons.

2. The marginal benefit of a public good is the
   a. sum of the marginal benefits of all the individuals at each quantity.
   b. marginal benefit of the individual person who places the lowest value on the good, multiplied by the number of people in the economy.
   c. marginal benefit of the individual person who places the highest value on the good, multiplied by the number of people in the economy.
   d. benefit of the last person's consumption.
   e. average of the marginal benefits of all the individuals at each quantity.

3. The marginal benefit curve of a public good
   a. slopes downward.
   b. slopes upward.
   c. is vertical.
   d. is horizontal.
   e. is U-shaped.

4. Sue and Mark are the only two members of a community. Sue's marginal benefit from one lighthouse is $2,000 and Mark's marginal benefit is $1,000. If the marginal cost of one lighthouse is $2,500 and if a lighthouse is a public good, then for efficiency the lighthouse should
   a. be built but only Sue should be allowed to use it.
   b. be built but only Mark should be allowed to use it.
   c. be built and both Sue and Mark should be allowed to use it.
   d. not be built because its marginal cost exceeds Sue's marginal benefit.
   e. not be built because its marginal cost exceeds both Sue's and Mark's marginal benefit.

5. The efficient quantity of a public good is
   a. the quantity produced by private firms.
   b. the quantity at which the marginal benefit equals the marginal cost.
   c. impossible to determine because each person's marginal benefit is different.
   d. the quantity at which the marginal benefit exceeds the marginal cost by as much as possible.
   e. where the demand curve and supply curve of the good intersects.

6. The efficient quantity of a public good can't be produced by private firms because
   a. only government has the necessary resources.
   b. it is impossible to determine the efficient amount.
   c. consumers have an incentive to free ride and not pay for their share of the good.
   d. private firms aren't large enough.
   e. the price would be too high if private firms produced the goods.

7. If the two political parties propose similar or identical policies, they are following the principle of
   a. rational ignorance.
   b. inefficient overprovision.
   c. free riding.
   d. minimum differentiation.
   e. the commons.

8. ____ is the decision not to acquire information because the marginal cost of doing so exceeds expected marginal benefit.
   a. Rational ignorance
   b. The principle of minimum differentiation
   c. A free rider
   d. Consumer ignorance
   e. The tragedy of the commons

9. Government bureaucracies over-provide public goods and grow larger because of their goal of ____ combined with ____ of the voters.
   a. budget maximization; rational ignorance
   b. budget minimization; irrational intelligence
   c. budget maximization; minimum differentiation
   d. budget maximization; irrational exuberance
   e. minimum differentiation; budget maximization

Complete the graph

Quantity (lighthouses)	Marginal benefit, Firm A (dollars)	Marginal benefit, Firm B (dollars)	Marginal benefit, Firm C (dollars)
1	50,000	50,000	50,000
2	45,000	45,000	45,000
3	40,000	40,000	40,000
4	35,000	35,000	35,000

1. Three shipping firms serve the west coast of a nation. The table has the firms' marginal benefit schedules for lighthouses. Lighthouses are a public good and the marginal cost of constructing a lighthouse is constant at $120,000.

   a. Complete the table below. Then graph the economy's marginal benefit and marginal cost curves in Figure 11.1.

Quantity (lighthouses)	Marginal benefit, (dollars per lighthouse)
1	
2	
3	
4	

   b. What is the efficient number of lighthouses to build?

   c. If all three firms agree to split the cost of building lighthouses equally, how much would each firm pay per lighthouse and how many lighthouses will be built?

   d. Suppose that one firm decides to free ride and not pay for the construction of any lighthouses. How much would each of the two other firms pay per lighthouse and how many lighthouses will be built?

■ FIGURE 11.1

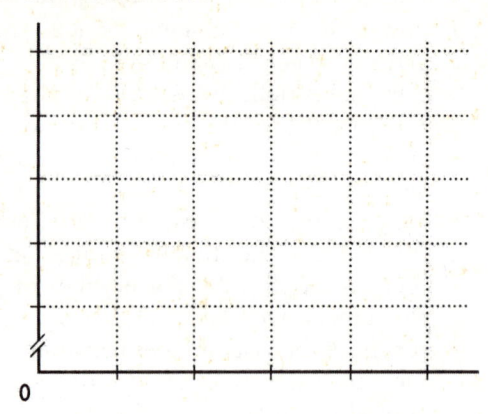

   e. In the situation described in part (d), how might government action overcome the problem?

Short answer and numeric questions

1. What is a free rider? Why is free riding not a problem for private goods?

2. A very small (!) nation has 10 citizens. Each resident has a $10 marginal benefit from 1 unit of a private good. In addition, each has a $10 marginal benefit from 1 unit of a public good. What is one combination of marginal benefit and quantity on the economy's marginal benefit curve for the private good and what is one combination on the economy's marginal benefit curve for the public good? Explain the difference.

3. How does free riding affect the private provision of a public good? How does rational ignorance affect the public provision of a public good?

4. The Eye on Your Life in the book explains how MP3 files have a free rider problem. One of the most common instances of free riding amongst students comes when a group of students are assigned to complete a project. Explain how free riding can occur in this situation. Occasionally instructors grade a group project by basing each student's grade, in part, on the group member's evaluations of each other. Explain how this technique can overcome the free rider problem.

CHECKPOINT 11.3

■ **Explain the tragedy of the commons and review the possible solutions to that problem.**

Quick Review
- *Tragedy of the commons* The absence of incentives to prevent the overuse and depletion of a commonly owned resource.
- *Marginal private benefit* The benefit received by an individual from using a common resource.
- *Marginal social benefit* The benefit received by society when an individual uses a common resource.

Additional Practice Problem 11.3
1. Suppose Tom, Dick, and Harry are three potential fishermen. If Tom fishes by himself, the total catch is 50 fish. If Dick joins Tom fishing, the total catch is 90 fish, split evenly between the two. If Harry joins Tom and Dick fishing, the total catch is 120 fish, split evenly between the three.
    a. What is Dick's marginal private benefit from fishing? What is the marginal social benefit from Dick's fishing?
    b. What is Harry's marginal private benefit from fishing? What is the marginal social benefit from Harry's fishing?
    c. The fish that Tom, Dick, and Harry are catching are a common resource. For a common resource, why is the marginal social benefit less than the marginal private benefit?
    d. If fishing is unregulated, will the amount of fish caught equal the efficient quantity, be more than the efficient quantity, or be less that the efficient quantity?

Solution to Additional Practice Problem 11.3
1a. Dick's marginal private benefit is 45 fish, the quantity that he catches. The marginal social benefit of Dick's fishing is 40 fish, the difference in the total catch with Tom and Dick fishing (90 fish) versus Tom alone fishing (50 fish).
1b. Harry's marginal private benefit is 40 fish, the quantity that he catches. The marginal social benefit of Harry's fishing is 30 fish, the difference in the total catch with Tom, Dick, and Harry fishing (120 fish) versus just Tom and Dick fishing (90 fish).
1c. The marginal private benefit measures *only* the benefit going to an individual from his or her use of a common resource. But when someone uses a common resource, he or she decreases the benefit going to other users. The marginal social benefit takes account of this decrease. In the case at hand, when Dick goes fishing, while he catches 45 fish, 5 of these fish would already have been caught when Tom alone fished. So Dick's marginal social benefit is his marginal private benefit (45 fish) minus the decrease in Tom's catch (5 fish), or 40 fish. Dick adds only 40 *new* fish to the total catch. Dick's marginal social benefit from the common resource is less than his marginal private benefit.
1d. The amount of fish caught will exceed the efficient quantity because people will fish until their marginal private benefit equals the marginal cost. Since the marginal private benefit exceeds the marginal social benefit, more than the efficient quantity of fish will be caught; the fish will be subject to the tragedy of the commons.

■ Self Test 11.3
Fill in the blanks
The problem of the commons is the absence of incentives to prevent the ____ (overuse; under use) of a commonly owned resource. The marginal private benefit of an additional fishing boat is the ____ (increase in the total fish catch; quantity of fish that one boat can catch). The marginal social benefit of an additional fishing boat is the ____ (increase in the total fish catch; quantity of fish that one boat can catch). The marginal private benefit curve for a common resource lies ____ (above; below) the marginal

social benefit curve. To use a common resource efficiently, establishing property rights ____ (is; is not) a potential solution. The price of an individual transferable quota equals the marginal ____ (private; social) benefit of the resource at the efficient quantity ____ (plus; minus) the marginal cost of using the resource.

True or false

1. The tragedy of the commons is the absence of incentives that prevent the overuse and depletion of a commonly owned resource.
2. The marginal benefit curve of a common resource slopes upward.
3. The efficient use of a common resource occurs when the marginal private benefit equals the marginal cost.
4. At the efficient level of use, the marginal private benefit of a common resource exceeds the marginal social benefit.
5. Property rights and quotas are potential solutions to the problem of the commons.

Multiple choice

1. The tragedy of the commons is the absence of incentives to
   a. correctly measure the marginal cost.
   b. prevent under use of the common resource.
   c. prevent overuse and depletion of the common resource.
   d. discover the resource.
   e. prevent the free-rider problem.

2. For a common resource such as fish, the marginal private benefit of an additional boat is the ____ and the marginal social benefit is the ____.
   a. catch per boat; quantity of fish that one more boat catches
   b. quantity of fish that one more boat catches; change in the total catch from an additional boat
   c. change in the total catch from an additional boat; catch per boat
   d. change in the total catch from an additional boat; change in the total catch from an additional boat
   e. quantity of fish that one more boat catches; catch per boat

3. For a common resource, the equilibrium with no government intervention is such that ____ equals ____.
   a. marginal private benefit; marginal cost
   b. marginal social benefit; marginal cost
   c. marginal private benefit; marginal social benefit
   d. social benefit; cost
   e. total social benefit; total social cost

4. For a common resource, the marginal private benefit of the resource is
   a. greater than the marginal social benefit.
   b. equal to the marginal social benefit.
   c. less than the marginal social benefit.
   d. not comparable to the marginal social benefit.
   e. not defined because the resource is nonexcludable.

FIGURE 11.2

Sustainable harvest per logger (tons per month)

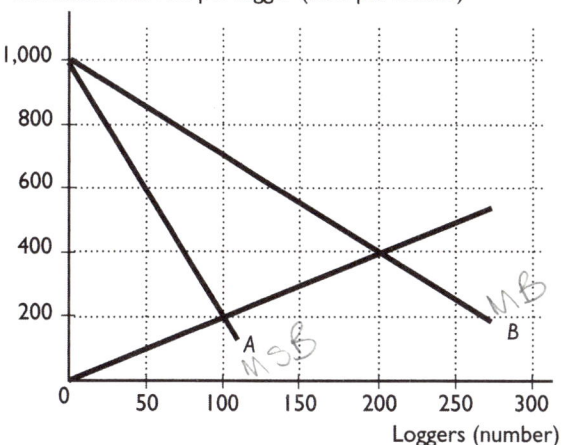

[Graph showing two curves: Curve A (MSB) slopes downward steeply from 1,000 at 0 loggers; Curve B (MB) slopes downward gradually. Axes: vertical 0–1,000, horizontal 0–300 loggers.]

5. Figure 11.2 shows a market for logging in a tropical rainforest, which is a common resource. In the figure, curve A is the ____ and curve B is the ____.
   a. MSB; MC
   b. MSB; MB
   c. MB; MSB
   d. MC; MSB
   e. MC; MB

6. Figure 11.2 shows a market for logging in a tropical rainforest, which is a common resource. The efficient number of loggers is ____ and if the market is unregulated, the equilibrium number of loggers is ____.
   a. 0; 100
   b. 0; 250
   c. 250; 100
   d. 100; 0
   e. 100; 250

7. For a common resource, the marginal private benefit curve ____ and the marginal social benefit curve ____.
   a. slopes upward; slopes upward
   b. slopes upward; slopes downward
   c. slopes downward; slopes upward
   d. slopes downward; slopes downward
   e. is vertical; is horizontal

8. For a common resource, efficiency requires that the ____ equals the ____.
   a. marginal private benefit; marginal cost
   b. marginal social benefit; marginal cost
   c. marginal private benefit; marginal social benefit
   d. marginal social cost; marginal cost
   e. marginal private benefit; marginal social cost

9. If the government assigns private property rights to a common resource, then the
   a. resource is under-utilized.
   b. marginal private benefit becomes equal to the marginal social benefit.
   c. government needs to set a quota to achieve efficiency.
   d. resource becomes subject to the free riding problem.
   e. resource cannot be utilized.

10. The market price of an individual transferable quota is equal to the
    a. marginal private benefit.
    b. marginal social benefit.
    c. marginal private benefit minus the marginal cost.
    d. marginal social benefit minus the marginal cost.
    e. marginal private benefit plus the marginal cost.

Complete the graph

1. Figure 11.3 (on the next page) shows the marginal cost, marginal private benefit, and marginal social benefit curves for swordfish, a common resource. Label each curve.
   a. What is the equilibrium number of boats and sustainable catch? What is the efficient number of boats and sustainable catch?
   b. If the government sets a quota, what quota achieves the efficient outcome?
   c. If the government issues individual transferable quotas (ITQ), what is the market price of an ITQ?

FIGURE 11.3
Sustainable catch per boat (tons per month)

FIGURE 11.4
Meat output (pounds per year)

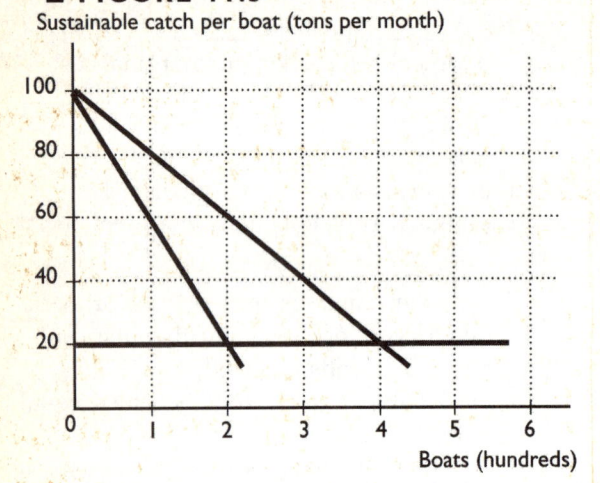

Number of sheep	Meat (pounds per year)	Marginal private benefit (pounds per year)	Marginal social benefit (pounds per year)
0	0		
10	2,000	___	150
20	3,000	___	50
30	3,000	___	−50
40	2,000	___	−150
50	0	___	

3. The table above gives the quantity of meat per year and marginal social benefit of grazing sheep on a common pasture. The marginal cost of raising a sheep is 50 pounds of meat per year.

   a. Complete the table by calculating the marginal private benefit.

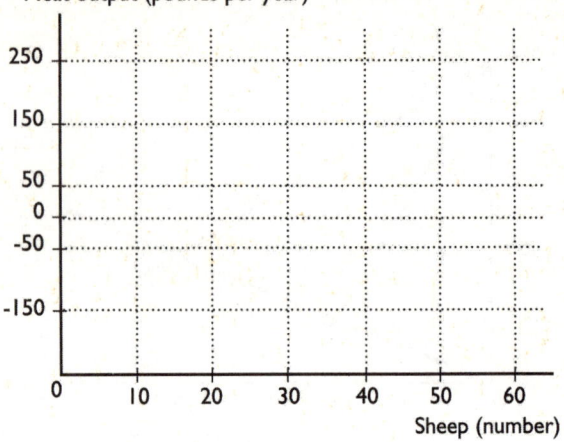

   b. In Figure 11.4, plot the marginal cost curve, the marginal private benefit curve, and the marginal social cost curve.

   c. What is the equilibrium number of sheep and the equilibrium quantity of meat?

   d. What is the efficient number of sheep and the efficient quantity of meat?

   e. If the government issues the efficient quantity of individual transfer quotas (ITQ), each of which allows 1 sheep to be grazed on the pasture, how many ITQs does the government issue and what is the market price of an ITQ?

Short answer and numeric questions

1. What is the problem of the commons and why does it occur? Give an example of how the problem of the commons affects the world's fisheries.

2. For a common resource, why does the marginal private benefit not equal the marginal social benefit? Which is smaller?

SELF TEST ANSWERS

■ CHECKPOINT 11.1

Fill in the blanks

A good is <u>excludable</u> if it is possible to prevent someone from enjoying its benefits. A good is <u>nonrival</u> if its use by one person does not decrease the quantity available for someone else. A good that is nonrival and nonexcludable is a <u>public</u> good and a good that is rival and excludable is a <u>private</u> good. A common resource is <u>rival</u> and <u>nonexcludable</u>.

True or false

1. True; page 266
2. False; page 266
3. False; pages 266-267
4. False; page 267
5. True; page 267

Multiple choice

1. a; page 266
2. a; page 266
3. a; pages 266-267
4. a; page 266
5. d; page 267
6. b; page 267
7. a; page 267
8. c; page 267

Short answer and numeric questions

1. A good is nonexcludable if it is impossible (or extremely costly) to prevent someone from benefiting from it. For example, the national defense provided by a fighter plane benefits everyone and so is nonexcludable. A good is nonrival if its use by one person does not decrease the quantity available for someone else. For example, the national defense provided by a fighter plane to you does not decrease the amount of defense it provides to your neighbor and so is nonrival; page 266.
2. A public good is nonrival and nonexcludable. A private good is rival and excludable. A common resource is rival and nonexcludable; pages 266-267.

■ CHECKPOINT 11.2

Fill in the blanks

A person who enjoys the benefit of a good or service without paying for it is a <u>free rider</u>. The marginal benefit curve for a public good is the <u>vertical</u> sum of the individual marginal benefit curves. The efficient quantity of a public good is the quantity at which the marginal benefit <u>equals</u> the marginal cost. <u>Rational ignorance</u> is the decision to not acquire information because the marginal cost of doing so exceeds the expected marginal benefit. Bureaucrats try to <u>maximize</u> their budgets.

True or false

1. True; page 269
2. True; pages 270-271
3. True; page 272
4. False; page 272
5. True; page 275

Multiple choice

1. b; page 269
2. a; pages 270-271
3. a; page 271
4. c; page 272
5. b; page 272
6. c; page 272
7. d; page 274
8. a; page 275
9. a; page 276

Complete the graph

Quantity (lighthouses)	Economy's marginal benefit (dollars)
1	150,000
2	135,000
3	120,000
4	105,000

1. a. The complete table is above and the completed figure is Figure 11.5 (on the next page); pages 270-271.

FIGURE 11.5
Marginal benefit (thousands of dollars per lighthouse)

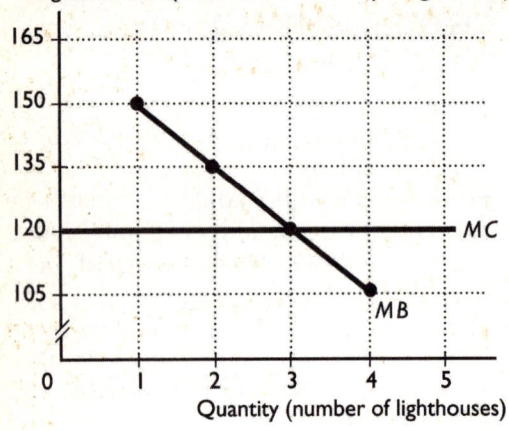

b. The efficient number of lighthouses to build is 3; page 272.
c. Each firm pays $40,000 per lighthouse and three lighthouses are built; page 272.
d. If one firm free rides, the other firms would need to pay $60,000 a lighthouse. No lighthouses would be built because $60,000 exceeds each firm's marginal benefit from any lighthouse; page 272.
e. The government could tax each firm $40,000 per lighthouse and use the tax revenue to build three lighthouses; page 273.

Short answer and numeric questions

1. A free rider is a person who enjoys the benefits of a good or service without paying for it. Free riding is not a problem for private goods because private goods are excludable; page 269.
2. For the private good, one combination on the economy's marginal benefit curve is: $10 marginal benefit and 10 units. For the public good, one combination is: $100 marginal benefit and 1 unit. The difference occurs because for the rival private good, all residents need their own unit of the good in order to consume it, whereas for the nonrival public good, each citizen will consume the same unit. So to obtain the economy's marginal benefit curve for a private good, we sum the quantities demanded at each price. To obtain the economy's marginal benefit curve for a public good, we sum the marginal benefits of all individuals at each quantity; pages 268-271.
3. Because everyone can consume the same quantity of a public good and no one can be excluded from enjoying its benefits, no one has an incentive to pay for it. Everyone has an incentive to free ride. Because of the free-rider problem, the market would provide too small a quantity of a public good.
   Bureaucrats who maximize their budgets and voters who work in the industry exert a larger influence on public policy than voters who are rationally ignorant. This set of circumstances leads to overprovision; pages 272 and 276.
4. The free rider problem in student groups is that a student might try to avoid all work and rely on the other students to complete the assignment. The grading technique in which group members assign grades to other members can overcome this free rider problem because each of the other group members can assign the free rider a grade of F. In order to avoid this grade, the potential free rider now is given the incentive to work and not free ride.

■ CHECKPOINT 11.3

Fill in the blanks

The problem of the commons is the absence of incentives to prevent the <u>overuse</u> of a commonly owned resource. The marginal private benefit of an additional fishing boat is the <u>quantity of fish that one boat can catch</u>. The marginal social benefit of an additional fishing boat is the <u>increase in the total fish catch</u>. The marginal private benefit curve for a common resource lies <u>above</u> the marginal social benefit curve. To use a common resource efficiently, establishing property rights <u>is</u> a potential solution. The price of an individual transferable quota equals the marginal <u>private</u> benefit of the resource at the efficient quantity <u>minus</u> the marginal cost of using the resource.

True or false
1. True; page 278
2. False; page 279
3. False; pages 280-281
4. True; page 281
5. True; page 282

Multiple choice
1. c; page 278
2. b; pages 279-280
3. a; page 279
4. a; page 280
5. b; pages 280-281
6. e; pages 279-281
7. d; page 281
8. b; pages 280-281
9. b; page 282
10. c; page 283

Complete the graph

■ **FIGURE 11.6**
Sustainable catch per boat (tons per month)

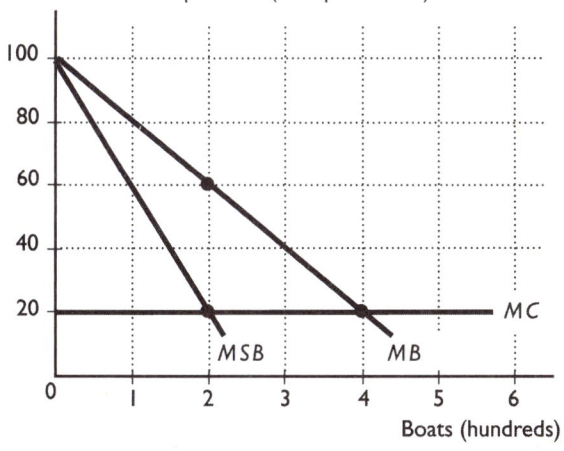

1. Figure 11.6 labels the curves.; page 279.
    a. The equilibrium number of boats is determined by the intersection of the marginal cost curve, MC, and the marginal private benefit curve, MB, so the equilibrium number of boats is 400. The sustainable catch is 20 tons of swordfish a month. The efficient number of boats is determined by the intersection of the marginal cost curve and the marginal social benefit curve, so the efficient number of boats is 200. The sustainable catch is 60 tons of swordfish a month, determined from the marginal private benefit curve; pages 279-281.
    b. If the government sets the quota at the efficient quantity, the quota for total production is set at the quantity at which marginal social benefit equals marginal cost. Here, that quantity is the production from 200 boats; page 282.
    c. The market price of an individual transferable quota (ITQ) equals the marginal private benefit minus the marginal cost at the quota level of fish. The government issues ITQs to 200 boats. The market price of an ITQ is 60 tons a month, the marginal private benefit, minus 20 tons a month, the marginal cost, which equals a market price of 40 tons a month; page 283.

Short answer and numeric questions
1. The problem of the commons is that there is no incentive to prevent the overuse and depletion of a commonly used resource. As more boats fish, the quantity of fish that one boat can catch decreases. But no individual takes account of the *decrease* in the average catch because each person is concerned about what he or she catches As a result, additional boats continue to fish until their marginal private benefit equals the marginal cost of fishing. Each boat considers only its marginal private benefit. With this many boats fishing, marginal cost is greater than marginal social benefit and the fish stock is depleted; pages 278-279.
2. The marginal private benefit of using a common resource does not equal the marginal social benefit because the marginal private benefit does not take account of the effect that using the resource has on others. As a common resource is used more intensively, each additional person's use decreases everyone else's benefit from the resource. But the marginal private benefit ignores the de-

crease in other people's benefit. The marginal social benefit takes account of *both* the added benefit to the new user (the marginal private benefit) *and* the decrease in everyone else's benefit. So the marginal social benefit is less than the marginal private benefit; pages 280-281.

Number of sheep	Meat (pounds per year)	Marginal private benefit (pounds per year)	Marginal social benefit (pounds per year)
0	0		
10	2,000	200	150
20	3,000	150	50
30	3,000	100	−50
40	2,000	50	−150
50	0	0	

3. a. The completed table is above. The marginal private benefit of a sheep is the quantity of meat per sheep. For 10 sheep the marginal private benefit is 2,000 pounds ÷ 10 sheep, which is 200 pounds; page 279.

■ FIGURE 11.7

Meat output (pounds per year)

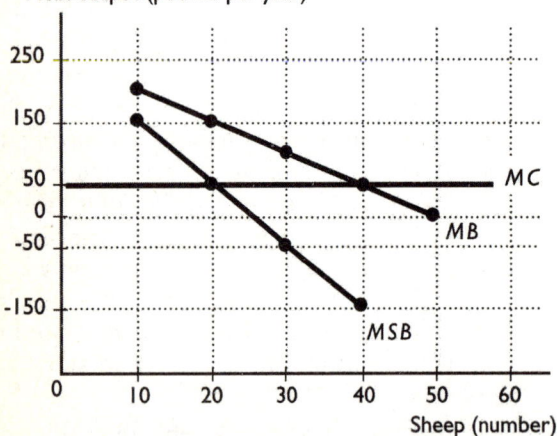

b. Figure 11.7 shows the marginal cost curve, MSC; the marginal private benefit curve, MB; and the marginal social benefit curve, MSB; page 281.

c. The equilibrium number of sheep is determined by the intersection of the marginal private benefit curve and the marginal cost curve. The equilibrium number of sheep is 40 sheep. The equilibrium quantity of meat with 40 sheep is 2,000 pounds a year; page 279.

d. The efficient number of sheep is determined by the intersection of the marginal social benefit curve and the marginal cost curve. The equilibrium number of sheep is 20 sheep. The equilibrium quantity of meat with 20 sheep is 3,000 pounds a year; pages 280-281.

e. The government issues 20 ITQs because 20 sheep is the efficient number of sheep. The market price of an ITQ is the marginal private benefit at the quantity of ITQs issued minus the marginal cost. The marginal private benefit with 20 ITQs is 150 pounds of meat a year. The marginal cost is 50 pounds of meat a year. The market price of an ITQ is equal to 150 pounds of meat − 50 pounds of meat, which is 100 pounds of meat a year; page 283.

Chapter 12
Consumer Choice and Demand

CHAPTER CHECKLIST

Chapter 12 presents a model of consumer choice based on marginal utility and the fundamental idea that people make rational choices. We use marginal utility theory to derive a demand curve and explain the paradox of value.

1 Calculate and graph a budget line that shows the limits to a person's consumption possibilities.

The budget line describes the limits to a consumer's consumption possibilities. A consumer can afford any combination on the budget line and inside it, but cannot afford any combination outside the budget line. When the price of a good changes, the slope of the budget line changes. The relative price is the price of one good in terms of another good—an opportunity cost. It equals the price of one good divided by the price of another good. The slope of the budget line equals the relative price of the good plotted on the *x*-axis. An increase in the budget shifts the budget line rightward, and a decrease in the budget shifts the budget line leftward.

2 Explain marginal utility theory and use it to derive a consumer's demand curve.

Utility is the benefit or satisfaction a person gets from the consumption of a good or service. Total utility is the total benefit that a person gets from the consumption of a good or service; marginal utility is the change in total utility that results from a one-unit increase in the quantity of a good consumed. As the quantity of a good consumed increases, its total utility increases but its marginal utility decreases. A consumer maximizes total utility when he or she allocates his or her entire available budget and makes the marginal utility per dollar the same for all goods. The marginal utility per dollar is the increase in total utility that comes from the last dollar spent on a good. If the price of a good falls, the marginal utility per dollar for that good rises at the current consumption level and the consumer buys more of that good. So when the price of a good falls, there is an increase in the quantity demanded and a movement down along the demand curve.

3 Use marginal utility theory to explain the paradox of value: why water is vital but cheap while diamonds are relatively useless but expensive.

The paradox of value is that water, which is essential to life, is cheap, while diamonds, which are relatively useless, are expensive. We solve this puzzle by distinguishing between total utility and marginal utility. The total utility from water is enormous. But we use so much water that its marginal utility is a small value. The total utility from diamonds is small. But we have few diamonds so their marginal utility is high. Diamonds have a high price and a high marginal utility while water has a low price and a low marginal utility. When the high marginal utility of diamonds is divided by the high price of a diamond, the result is a number that equals the low marginal utility of water divided by the low price of water. Water is cheap but provides a large consumer surplus, while diamonds are expensive but provide a small consumer surplus.

CHECKPOINT 12.1

■ **Calculate and graph a budget line that shows the limits to a person's consumption possibilities.**

Quick Review
- *Budget line* A line that describes the limits to consumption choices and that depends on a consumer's budget and the prices of goods and services.

Additional Practice Problems 12.1
1. Mark, a chemistry major at Cal State East Bay, dines by himself at the local Olive Garden. He has $30 per week to spend. Pizza is $15 and a salad is $5.
   a. List the combinations of pizza and salads he can buy.
   b. Graph Mark's budget line in the figure to the right.
   c. What is the opportunity cost of a pizza?
   d. What is the relative price of a pizza?

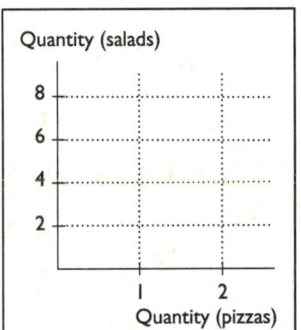

2. Sue is a student at Chabot Junior College. She has a budget of $240 that she will spend on purses and/or shoes. The price of a purse is $40 and the price of a pair of shoes is $60.
   a. Draw a graph of Sue's budget line in the figure to the right.
   b. If purses rise in price to $60, in the figure show what happens to Sue's budget line.

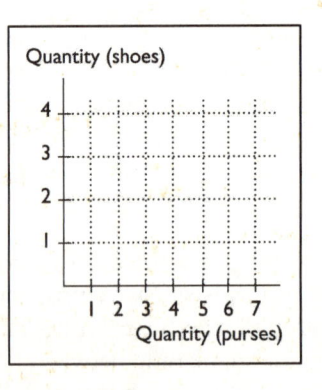

Solutions to Additional Practice Problems 12.1
1a. The combinations of pizza and salads that Mark can afford are listed in the table. To construct this table, select the combinations of pizza and salads that spend all of Mark's $30 budget.

Pizza	Salads
0	6
1	3
2	0

1b. The figure shows Mark's budget line. The maximum number of pizzas he can buy is 2 and the maximum number of salads he can buy is 6.

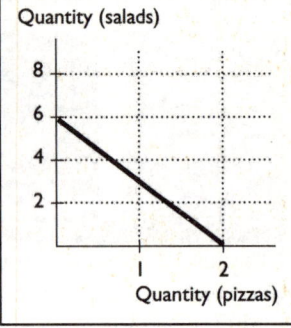

1c. The slope of the budget line is the opportunity cost of a pizza. The slope is (6 salads) ÷ (2 pizzas), which equals 3 salads per pizza. So consuming 1 pizza means Mark forgoes 3 salads.

1d. The opportunity cost of a pizza is also its relative price. The relative price of a pizza is 3 salads per pizza.

2a. The figure shows Sue's budget line as the grey line. The maximum number of purses Sue can buy is 6, where the budget line intersects the x-axis, and the maximum number of shoes Sue can buy is 4, where the budget line intersects the y-axis.

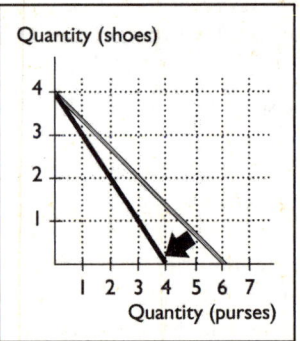

2b. When the price of a purse rises, the maximum number of purses that can be purchased decreases to 4 but the maximum number of shoes is unchanged. The budget line rotates inward as shown in the figure by the dark budget line.

■ **Self Test 12.1**

Fill in the blanks
A ____ shows the limits to consumption possibilities. The budget line becomes ____ (less

steep; steeper) when the price of the good measured on the *x*-axis increases and everything else remains the same. The slope of the budget line is equal to a ____ price. When a consumer's budget increases, the budget line shifts ____ (inward; outward).

True or false
1. Dian's budget line shows the limits to what Dian can consume.
2. When Stan's budget increases, his budget line shifts outward.
3. A fall in the price of the good measured along the *x*-axis, all other things remaining the same, rotates the budget line inward.
4. The slope of the budget line measures the opportunity cost of one more unit of the good plotted on the *x*-axis.
5. The price of one good plus the price of another good equals the relative price.

Multiple choice
1. A budget line shows the
   a. limits to production possibilities.
   b. limits to production opportunities.
   c. the slope of the demand curve.
   d. limits to consumption possibilities.
   e. way the demand curve shifts if the consumer's budget changes.
2. A budget line
   a. represents combinations of goods a consumer desires.
   b. marks the boundary between what a consumer can and cannot afford.
   c. has a positive slope.
   d. is the same as the production possibilities frontier.
   e. is the same as a demand curve.
3. Linda has $10 a month to spend on ice cream cones and chocolate bars. If the price of an ice cream cone is $2 a cone and the price of a chocolate bar is $1 a bar, which of the following is a point on Linda's budget line?
   a. 4 cones and 0 chocolate bars
   b. 1 cone and 8 chocolate bars
   c. 3 cones and 1 chocolate bar
   d. 5 cones and 10 chocolate bars
   e. 0 cones and 0 chocolate bars
4. If a consumer's budget increases, the budget line
   a. rotates outward and its slope changes.
   b. rotates inward and its slope changes.
   c. shifts outward and its slope does not change.
   d. shifts inward and its slope does not change.
   e. does not change.
5. Reb buys fishing lures and steaks. If his budget increases, the maximum number of fishing lures he can purchase ____ and the maximum number of steaks he can purchase ____.
   a. increases; increases
   b. increases; decreases
   c. decreases; increases
   d. decreases; decreases
   e. does not change; does not change
6. If a budget line rotates inward and becomes steeper, then the
   a. consumer's budget decreased.
   b. consumer's budget increased.
   c. price of one of the goods decreased.
   d. price of one of the goods increased.
   e. price of both of the goods must have decreased.

■ FIGURE 12.1
Quantity (movies per month)

Quantity (hours playing paintball per month)

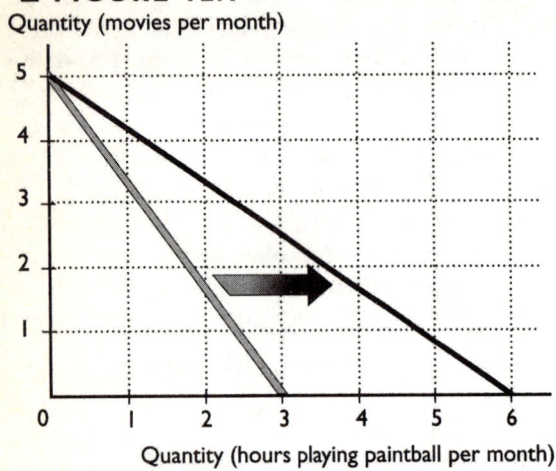

7. ____ will change Bobby's budget line as shown by the change from the gray budget line to the black budget line in Figure 12.1.
   a. An increase in Bobby's budget
   b. A decrease in Bobby's budget
   c. A fall in the price of playing paintball
   d. A rise in the price playing paintball
   e. A rise in the price of a movie

8. If the budget line rotates inward and becomes steeper, there is a
   a. higher opportunity cost of the good measured on the *x*-axis.
   b. lower opportunity cost of the good measured on the *x*-axis.
   c. larger budget.
   d. higher price for the good measured on the *y*-axis.
   e. lower price for the good measured on the *x*-axis.

9. A relative price is the
   a. price of a substitute.
   b. price of a related good.
   c. price of one good divided by the price of another.
   d. absolute price of a good.
   e. price of one good multiplied by the price of another.

Complete the graph
■ FIGURE 12.2
Quantity (magazines per week)

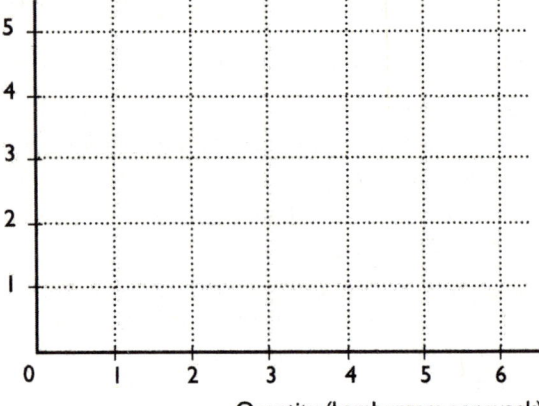

Quantity (hamburgers per week)

1. Jack buys two things: magazines, which have a price of $3 each, and hamburgers, which have a price of $4 each. Jack's income is $12.
   a. In Figure 12.2, draw Jack's budget line.
   b. What does the slope of the budget line equal? What is the interpretation of this slope?
   c. Can Jack buy 2 magazines and 1 hamburger? Can he buy 2 magazines and 3 hamburgers?
   d. Suppose the price of a hamburger falls to $2. In Figure 12.2, draw Jack's new budget line.
   e. What does the slope of the new budget line equal? How does the slope compare to your answer to part (b)?
   f. Can Jack now buy 2 magazines and 1 hamburger? Can he now buy 2 magazines and 3 hamburgers?

Short answer and numeric questions
1. How is a budget line similar to a production possibilities frontier? How is it dissimilar?
2. If a consumer's budget increases, what happens to his or her budget line? Does its slope change?

3. What does the slope of a budget line equal?
4. What is the relationship between the relative price of a good and its opportunity cost?

CHECKPOINT 12.2

■ **Explain marginal utility theory and use it to derive a consumer's demand curve.**

Quick Review
- *Marginal utility* The change in total utility that results from a one-unit increase in the quantity of a good consumed.
- *Marginal utility per dollar* The increase in total utility that comes from the last dollar spent on the good.

Additional Practice Problems 12.2

Orange juice		Cookies	
Quantity per week	Total utility	Quantity per week	Total utility
0	0	0	0
1	20	1	60
2	32	2	100
3	40	3	120
4	44	4	130
5	46	5	145

1. The table above shows Tommy's total utility from orange juice and cookies.

   a. Calculate Tommy's marginal utility schedule from orange juice and from cookies by completing the table below.

Orange juice		Cookies	
Quantity per week	Marginal utility	Quantity per week	Marginal utility
0	XX	0	XX
1	___	1	___
2	___	2	___
3	___	3	___
4	___	4	___
5	___	5	___

   b. If the price of a carton of orange juice is $2, what is Tommy's marginal utility per dollar for orange juice when Tommy buys 2 cartons of orange juice a week?

   c. If the price of a box of cookies is $4, what is Tommy's marginal utility per dollar for cookies when Tommy buys 3 boxes of cookies a week?

   d. If Tommy's budget for orange juice and cookies is $10 per week and orange juice is $2 per carton and cookies are $4 per box, what combination of orange juice and cookies will Tommy buy? Why does Tommy buy this combination? What is his total utility?

   e. Tommy could afford to buy 5 cartons of orange juice a week. Why does he not buy 5 cartons?

2. If Jenny is allocating her entire available budget on movies and popcorn, explain the rule she follows to maximize her total utility.

Solutions to Additional Practice Problems 12.2

Orange juice		Cookies	
Quantity per week	Marginal utility	Quantity per week	Marginal utility
0	XX	0	XX
1	20	1	60
2	12	2	40
3	8	3	20
4	4	4	10
5	2	5	5

1a. The completed table is above. Marginal utility equals the change in total utility from a one-unit increase in the quantity of the good consumed. So the marginal utility of the second box of cookies equals 100 − 60, which is 40.

1b. The marginal utility per dollar is 12 ÷ $2 = 6.

1c. The marginal utility per dollar is 20 ÷ $4 = 5.

1d. Tommy buys 2 boxes of cookies and 1 carton of orange juice. This combination allocates his entire budget and the marginal utility per dollar for orange juice, 10, equals the marginal utility per dollar for cookies, 10. This combination gives Tommy total utility of 120.

1e. Tommy does not buy 5 cartons of orange juice because his total utility would be only 46, well less than his total utility from the utility-maximizing combination derived in the answer to part (d).

2. If the marginal utility per dollar from movies exceeds the marginal utility per dollar from popcorn, then Jenny sees more movies and buys less popcorn because this action increases her total utility; if the marginal utility per dollar from popcorn exceeds the marginal utility per dollar from movies, Jenny buys more popcorn and sees fewer movies because this action increases her total utility. More generally, if the marginal gain from an action exceeds the marginal loss, take the action. Jenny is maximizing her total utility when the marginal utility per dollar from movies equals the marginal utility per dollar from popcorn.

■ Self Test 12.2

Fill in the blanks
The total benefit a person gets from the consumption of a good or service is ____ (marginal; total) utility. The change in total utility that results from a one-unit increase in the consumption of a good or service is ____ (marginal; elastic) utility. As the quantity of a good consumed increases, total utility ____ (increases; decreases) and marginal utility ____ (increases; decreases). The marginal utility per dollar equals the marginal utility of a good ____ (multiplied; divided) by the price of the good. When total utility is maximized, the marginal utility per dollar ____ (equals 1; is equal) for all goods. Marginal utility theory implies that, other things remaining the same, the ____ (higher; lower) the price of a good, the smaller is the quantity demanded of that good.

True or false
1. As Katie consumes more sushi, her total utility from sushi increases.
2. As Katie consumes more sushi, her marginal utility from sushi increases.
3. Bobby maximizes his utility whenever he allocates his entire available budget.
4. Tommy is allocating his entire available budget. If Tommy's marginal utility per dollar for tacos is 8 and the marginal utility per dollar from burritos is 10, then Tommy is NOT maximizing his total utility.
5. Diminishing marginal utility theory implies that other things remaining the same, the higher the price of a good, the greater is the quantity demanded of that good.

Multiple choice
1. In economics, utility
   a. always decreases as income increases.
   b. equals opportunity cost.
   c. is an index of satisfaction.
   d. is measured by the same units as relative price.
   e. and relative price are the same thing.

2. Marginal utility is the
   a. change in total utility that results from a one-unit increase in the quantity of a good consumed.
   b. total benefit from the consumption of a good or service.
   c. quantity of a good a consumer prefers.
   d. average utility per unit consumed.
   e. change in total utility that results from a one dollar change in the price of a good consumed.

3. Sushi costs $3 per piece. Cynthia's total utility after eating one piece is 30 and her total utility after eating 2 pieces is 51, so her marginal utility from the second piece is
   a. 17.
   b. 10.
   c. 51.
   d. 7.
   e. 21.

4. As Shaniq drinks additional cups of tea at breakfast, Shaniq's
   a. marginal utility from tea decreases.
   b. total utility from tea increases.
   c. total utility from tea decreases.
   d. Both answers (a) and (b) are correct.
   e. Both answers (b) and (c) are correct.

Chapter 12 · Consumer Choice and Demand

5. Marginal utility per dollar is calculated by ____ the price of the good.
   a. multiplying the marginal utility from a good by
   b. dividing the marginal utility from a good by
   c. multiplying the total utility from a good by
   d. dividing the total utility from a good by
   e. averaging the marginal utility from the good with

6. Sushi costs $3 per piece. Cynthia's total utility after eating one piece is 30 and her total utility after eating 2 pieces is 51, so her marginal utility per dollar from the second piece is
   a. 17.
   b. 10.
   c. 51.
   d. 7.
   e. 21.

7. When a household maximizes its total utility, then its entire available budget is allocated in such a way that the
   a. marginal utility from all goods is equal.
   b. marginal utility per dollar is equal for all goods.
   c. marginal utility is as large as possible for goods.
   d. marginal utility will start decreasing if it consumes fewer goods.
   e. quantities consumed of each good are equal.

8. Suppose that Misty likes pizza and hotdogs. If her marginal utility per dollar from pizza is 6 and from hotdogs is 5, Misty
   a. is maximizing her total utility.
   b. could increase her total utility by buying more hotdogs and less pizza.
   c. could increase her total utility by buying more pizza and fewer hotdogs.
   d. is maximizing her marginal utility.
   e. must obtain more income in order to reach her consumer equilibrium.

9. You can use marginal utility theory to find the demand curve by changing
   a. only the price of one good.
   b. only income.
   c. the utility schedule.
   d. only the prices of both goods.
   e. income and the prices of both goods.

10. Suppose that Hank consumes only Mountain Dew and pizza. If Hank's total utility from all amounts of both Mountain Dew and pizza double from what they were before, then Hank's demand for
    a. both goods must double.
    b. one of the goods must double.
    c. both goods must decrease by one-half.
    d. one of the goods must decrease by one-half.
    e. neither good changes.

Complete the graph

Pizza			Soda		
Quantity (slices per day)	Total utility, pizza	Marginal utility, pizza	Quantity (cans per day)	Total utility, soda	Marginal utility, soda
0	0		0	0	
1	45	___	1	25	___
2	85	___	2	45	___
3	120	___	3	60	___
4	150	___	4	70	___
5	175	___	5	75	___
6	195	___	6	76	___

1. Bertha consumes only soda and pizza. The table above gives Bertha's total utility from soda and pizza slices.
   a. Complete the marginal utility columns of the table.
   b. The price of a can of soda is $1 and the price of a slice of pizza is $2. If Bertha's budget is $6, how many cans of soda and slices of pizza will she consume?
   c. Suppose the price of a slice of pizza rises to $3, while the price of a can of soda and Bertha's budget does not change. Now how many cans of soda and slices of pizza will she consume?

FIGURE 12.3

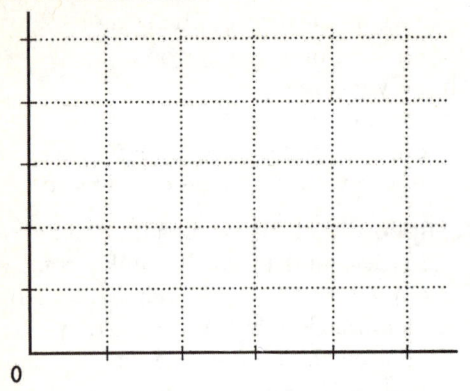

[Graph with unlabeled axes, origin at 0]

d. What are two points on Bertha's demand curve for slices of pizza? Assuming her demand curve is a straight line, label the axes and then draw her demand curve in Figure 12.3.

Short answer and numeric questions

Quantity (bottles of Aquafina per day)	Total utility	Marginal utility
0	0	——
1	25	——
2	45	——
3	60	——
4	70	——
5	75	——
6	76	——

1. Carlos drinks Aquafina bottled water. The table above gives his total utility from this water. Calculate his marginal utility.

Quantity (tacos per week)	Marginal utility	Quantity (hamburgers per week)	Marginal utility
0	0	0	0
1	50	1	80
2	40	2	40
3	30	3	20
4	20	4	10
5	10	5	5

2. Lisa eats tacos and hamburgers. The quantities and marginal utilities from each are in the table above. Lisa's budget is $8.

   a. If the price of taco is $1 and the price of a hamburger is $2, what quantity of tacos and hamburgers will Lisa purchase?

   b. If the price of a taco rises to $2 while neither Lisa's income nor the price of a hamburger change, what quantity of tacos and hamburgers will Lisa purchase?

   c. How does Lisa respond to a change in the price of a taco?

3. What does it mean to "allocate the entire available budget?" How does saving fit into the picture?

4. What is marginal analysis? Why is making the marginal utility per dollar necessary for a consumer to maximize his or her utility?

CHECKPOINT 12.3

■ **Use marginal utility theory to explain the paradox of value: why water is vital but cheap while diamonds are relatively useless but expensive.**

Quick Review

- *The paradox of value* Why is water, which is essential to life, cheap, but diamonds, which are useless compared to water, expensive?

Additional Practice Problem 12.3

1. Anthony buys 30,000 gallons of water a month. His marginal utility from a gallon of water is 100 units. The price of a gallon of water is $0.001. Anthony also buys 4 boxes of Krispy Kreme doughnuts a month. He pays $5 for a box. Anthony is maximizing his utility.

   a. What is the marginal utility from a box of Krispy Kreme doughnuts?

   b. Why does Anthony receive a lower marginal utility from his consumption of water?

Solution to Additional Practice Problem 12.3

1a. Because Anthony is maximizing his utility, the marginal utility per dollar he spends on water equals the marginal utility per dollar he spends on doughnuts. The marginal utility per dollar for water equals 100 units ÷ $0.001 = 100,000. So the marginal utility of a box of doughnuts divided by the price of a box of doughnuts ($5) must equal 100,000. In terms of a formula, $MU \div 5 = 100{,}000$, so the marginal utility of a box of doughnuts equals $5 \times 100{,}000$, which is 500,000.

1b. Anthony buys 30,000 gallons of water a month and (only) 4 boxes of doughnuts a month. As the quantity of a good consumed increases, the marginal utility decreases. Because Anthony is consuming much more water than doughnuts, his total utility from water is almost surely greater than his total utility from doughnuts, but his marginal utility from water is much less than his marginal utility from doughnuts.

■ Self Test 12.3

Fill in the blanks
Marginal benefit is the maximum price a consumer is willing to pay for an extra unit of a good or service when ____. The paradox of value is resolved by noting that diamonds have a high price, a ____ (high; low) total utility, and a ____ (high; low) marginal utility. Water provides ____ (more; less) consumer surplus than diamonds.

True or false
1. Susan's demand curve for curry shows the quantity of curry she demands at each price when her total utility is maximized.
2. Marginal benefit is the maximum price a consumer is willing to pay for an extra unit of a good or service when total utility is maximized.
3. The paradox of value is that water, which is essential to life, is plentiful, while diamonds, which are not essential to life, are much less plentiful.
4. The paradox of value is solved by noting that the total utility from water is small while the marginal utility from water is large.
5. The consumer surplus from water is greater than the consumer surplus from diamonds.

Multiple choice
1. At all points on a demand curve, the
   i. consumer's budget has been allocated to maximize total utility.
   ii. quantity describes the quantity demanded at each price when total utility is maximized.
   iii. price represents the marginal benefit the consumer gets from an extra unit of a good.
   a. i only.
   b. ii only.
   c. i and ii.
   d. i and iii.
   e. i, ii, and iii.

2. As more of a good is consumed, the marginal utility of an additional unit ____, so consumers are willing to pay ____ for an additional unit.
   a. decreases; less
   b. increases; less
   c. decreases; more
   d. increases; more
   e. does not change; less

3. The paradox of value refers to the
   a. utility maximizing rule.
   b. fact that water is vital but cheap while diamonds are relatively useless but expensive.
   c. fact that consumers have different preferences and utility schedules.
   d. law of demand.
   e. issue of why the consumer surplus from water equals the consumer surplus from diamonds.

4. One reason why water is cheap compared to diamonds is because the
   a. marginal utility of water is enormous.
   b. marginal utility of water is small.
   c. total utility of water is enormous.
   d. total utility of water is small.
   e. total utility of water and diamonds must be equal but the marginal utility of water is much lower than the marginal utility of diamonds.

5. In the paradox of value between expensive diamonds and inexpensive water, we see that
   a. the consumer surpluses are very high for both goods.
   b. diamonds have a low consumer surplus while water has a high consumer surplus.
   c. diamonds have a high consumer surplus while water has a low consumer surplus.
   d. the consumer surpluses are very low for both goods.
   e. the consumer surpluses for the two goods cannot be compared.

Complete the graph

■ FIGURE 12.4
Price (dollars per thousand gallons)

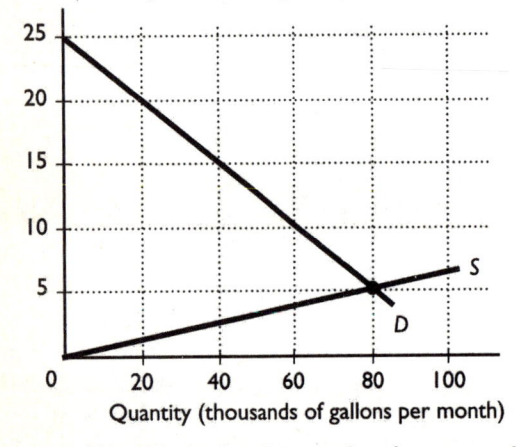

1. Figure 12.4 shows the market for water. Indicate the equilibrium price and then shade in the area of the consumer surplus.

■ FIGURE 12.5
Price (thousands of dollars per carat)

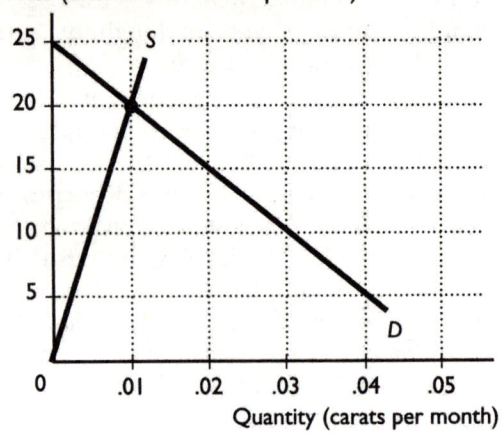

2. Figure 12.5 shows the market for rubies. Indicate the equilibrium price and then shade in the area of the consumer surplus.

3. Based on Figures 12.4 and 12.5, is there more consumer surplus for water or rubies? Which is larger: the marginal utility of a gallon of water or a carat of rubies?

Short answer and numeric questions

1. Bobby consumes potato chips and Gatorade and is maximizing his utility. His marginal utility from the last bag of chips he eats is 40 and his marginal utility from the last bottle of Gatorade he drinks is 60. The price of a bag of chips is $2. What must be the price of a bottle of Gatorade?

2. Does the price Bianca is willing to pay for another purse depend on her total utility from purses or her marginal utility? Explain your answer.

3. What is the paradox of value and what is its solution?

SELF TEST ANSWERS

■ CHECKPOINT 12.1

Fill in the blanks

A <u>budget line</u> shows the limits to consumption possibilities. The budget line becomes <u>steeper</u> when the price of the good measured on the *x*-axis increases and everything else remains the same. The slope of the budget line is equal to a <u>relative</u> price. When a consumer's budget increases, the budget line shifts <u>outward</u>.

True or false

1. True; page 290
2. True; page 291
3. False; page 292
4. True; page 293
5. False; page 294

Multiple choice

1. d; page 290
2. b; page 290
3. b; page 290
4. c; page 291
5. a; page 291
6. d; page 292
7. c; page 292
8. a; page 294
9. c; page 294

Complete the graph

1. a. The budget line in Figure 12.6 labeled "hamburgers $4" is Jack's budget line; page 290.
   b. The slope of the budget line equals (−4 magazines/3 hamburgers), which is −1 1/3 of a magazine per hamburger. The slope is the opportunity cost of a hamburger, which is the relative price of a hamburger; page 293.
   c. Jack can buy 2 magazines and 1 hamburger. Jack cannot buy 2 magazines and 3 hamburgers because that combination is outside his budget line; page 290.
   d. The new budget line is in Figure 12.6, labeled "Hamburgers $2"; page 290.

■ **FIGURE 12.6**

Quantity (magazines per week)

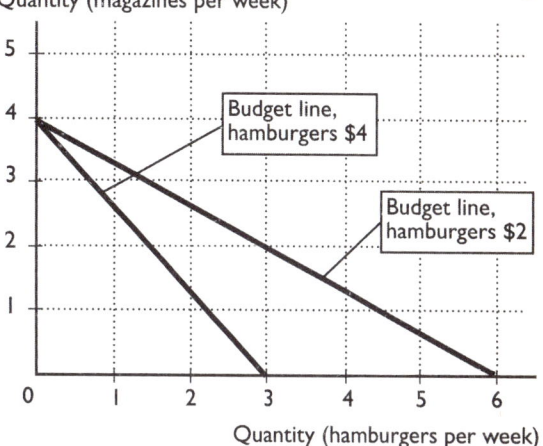

[Graph showing two budget lines: "Budget line, hamburgers $4" going from (0,4) to (3,0), and "Budget line, hamburgers $2" going from (0,4) to (6,0). X-axis: Quantity (hamburgers per week), 0 to 6. Y-axis: 0 to 5.]

   e. The slope of the new budget line is −2/3 of a magazine per hamburger. Compared to the slope in part (b), the opportunity cost of a hamburger is lower when its price falls; page 294.
   f. Jack can buy 2 magazines and 1 hamburger. Jack also can buy 2 magazines and 3 hamburgers because that combination is now on his budget line; page 290.

Short answer and numeric questions

1. A budget line is similar to the production possibilities frontier. Both curves show a limit to what is feasible. The *PPF* is a technological limit that does not depend on prices. But the budget line does depend on prices. Consumption possibilities change when prices or the available budget change; page 290.
2. The budget line shifts outward. Its slope does not change; page 291.
3. The slope of the budget line equals the opportunity cost and the relative price of the good measured along the *x*-axis; page 293.
4. The relative price is the price of one good in terms of another good. The relative price is an opportunity cost. It equals the price of one good divided by the price of another good; page 294.

■ CHECKPOINT 12.2

Fill in the blanks

The total benefit a person gets from the consumption of a good or service is <u>total</u> utility. The change in total utility that results from a one-unit increase in the consumption of a good or service is <u>marginal</u> utility. As the quantity of a good consumed increases, total utility <u>increases</u> and marginal utility <u>decreases</u>. The marginal utility per dollar equals the marginal utility of a good <u>divided</u> by the price of the good. When total utility is maximized, the marginal utility per dollar <u>is equal</u> for all goods. Marginal utility theory implies that, other things remaining the same, the <u>higher</u> the price of a good, the smaller is the quantity demanded of that good.

True or false

1. True; page 296
2. False; page 297
3. False; page 300
4. True; page 301
5. False; page 303

Multiple choice

1. c; page 296
2. a; page 297
3. e; page 297
4. d; page 297
5. b; page 301
6. d; page 301
7. b; page 301
8. c; page 301
9. a; page 303
10. e; page 304

Complete the graph

Pizza			Soda		
Quantity (slices per day)	Total utility, pizza	Marginal utility, pizza	Quantity (cans per day)	Total utility, soda	Marginal utility, soda
0	0		0	0	
1	45	<u>45</u>	1	25	<u>25</u>
2	85	<u>40</u>	2	45	<u>20</u>
3	120	<u>35</u>	3	60	<u>15</u>
4	150	<u>30</u>	4	70	<u>10</u>
5	175	<u>25</u>	5	75	<u>5</u>
6	195	<u>20</u>	6	76	<u>1</u>

1. a. The completed table is above; page 297.
   b. Bertha will consume 2 cans of soda and 2 slices of pizza. This combination allocates all her budget and equalizes the marginal utility per dollar from soda and pizza at 20 units; page 302.
   c. Bertha will now consume 3 cans of soda and 1 slice of pizza. This combination allocates all of her budget and equalizes the marginal utility per dollar from soda and pizza at 15 units; page 302.

■ FIGURE 12.7

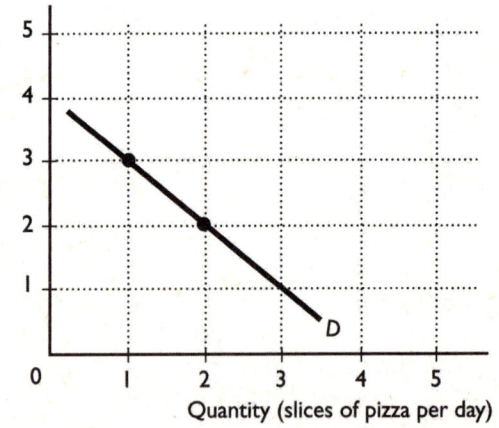

   d. One point on her demand curve is $2 and 2 slices of pizza; another point is $3 and 1 slice of pizza. Figure 12.7 shows Bertha's demand curve; page 303.

Short answer and numeric questions

Quantity (bottles of Aquafina per day)	Total utility	Marginal utility
0	0	
1	25	25
2	45	20
3	60	15
4	70	10
5	75	5
6	76	1

1. The completed table is above; page 297.

2. a. Lisa will buy 4 tacos and 2 hamburgers because this combination allocates her entire budget and sets the marginal utility per dollar from tacos equal to the marginal utility per dollar from hamburgers; page 302.

   b. Lisa will buy 2 tacos and 2 hamburgers because this combination allocates all her budget and equalizes the marginal utility per dollar from tacos and hamburgers at 20 units; page 302.

   c. When the price of a taco rises, the quantity of tacos demanded decreases; page 303.

3. To "allocate the entire available budget" means that we use the entire available budget. Using the entire budget doesn't mean not saving anything. The available budget is the amount available after choosing how much to save; page 300.

4. Marginal analysis compares the marginal gain from having more of one good with the marginal loss from having less of another good. The "equalize the marginal utility per dollar" rule is the result of marginal analysis. Suppose the marginal utility per dollar for a blouse exceeds that of a dollar for a purse. Marginal analysis indicates that the consumer can increase her total utility by spending a dollar less on purses and spending a dollar more on blouses because the gain in utility from the dollar spent on blouses exceeds the loss in utility from the dollar reduction on purses; page 304.

■ CHECKPOINT 12.3

Fill in the blanks

Marginal benefit is the maximum price a consumer is willing to pay for an extra unit of a good or service when <u>total utility is maximized</u>. The paradox of value is resolved by noting that diamonds have a high price, a <u>low</u> total utility, and a <u>high</u> marginal utility. Water provides <u>more</u> consumer surplus than diamonds.

True or false

1. True; page 306
2. True; page 306
3. False; page 306
4. False; page 306
5. True; page 307

Multiple choice

1. e; page 306
2. a; page 306
3. b; page 306
4. b; page 306
5. b; page 307

Complete the graph

■ FIGURE 12.8

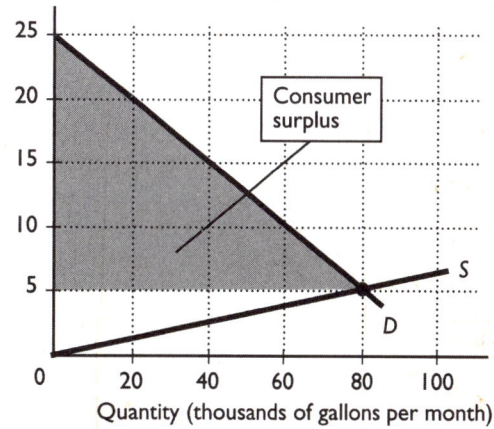

1. The equilibrium price is $5 per thousand gallons of water. The consumer surplus is the gray triangle in Figure 12.8; page 307.

184 Part 4 · A CLOSER LOOK AT DECISION MAKERS

■ **FIGURE 12.9**

Price (thousands of dollars per carat)

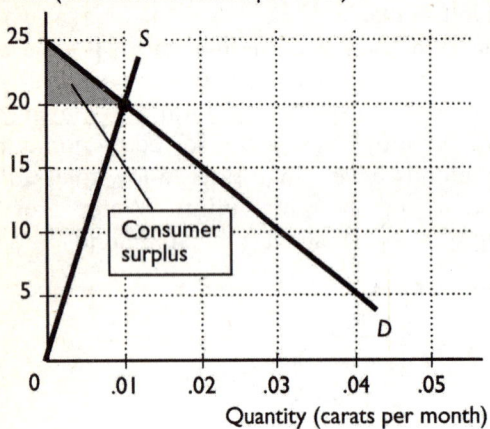

[Graph showing supply curve S and demand curve D intersecting at approximately (.01, 20). Consumer surplus is the shaded triangle above the equilibrium price and below the demand curve. Vertical axis: 0 to 25 in increments of 5. Horizontal axis: Quantity (carats per month), 0 to .05 in increments of .01.]

2. The equilibrium price is $20,000 a carat. Figure 12.8 shows the consumer surplus; page 307.

3. There is more consumer surplus for water than rubies. Because the price of a carat of rubies is much greater than the price of a gallon of water, it must be the case that the marginal utility of a carat of rubies is much greater than the marginal utility of a gallon of water; page 307.

Short answer and numeric questions

1. Bobby maximizes his total utility by consuming the combination of chips and Gatorade such that the marginal utility per dollar for chips equals the marginal utility per dollar for Gatorade. The marginal utility from the last bag of chips is 40 and the price of a bag of chips is $2, so the marginal utility per dollar is 40 ÷ $2 = 20. Because the marginal utility of the Gatorade is 60, the price is $3 to make the marginal utility per dollar equal to 20; page 306.

2. The price Bianca is willing to pay for another purse depends on her marginal utility. Bianca maximizes her total utility by making her marginal utility per dollar equal for all goods. If her marginal utility from an additional purse is high, she is willing to pay a high price for the purse; page 306.

3. The paradox of value is that water, which is essential for life, is cheap while diamonds are relatively useless but expensive. The solution to the paradox is that people consume a lot of water, so the marginal utility of an additional gallon of water is very low. People consume only a few diamonds, so the marginal utility of an additional diamond is quite high. A household maximizes its total when the marginal utility per dollar is equal for all goods. So water has a low marginal utility and a low price and diamonds have a high marginal utility and a high price; page 306.

Chapter 12

Appendix: Indifference Curves

APPENDIX CHECKLIST

The appendix uses indifference curves and budget lines to derive a demand curve.

1 Indifference curves

An indifference curve is a line that shows combinations of goods among which a consumer is indifferent. All combinations above the indifference curve are preferred to those on the indifference curve and all combinations on the indifference curve are preferred to those below the indifference curve. The marginal rate of substitution, MRS, is the rate at which the consumer will give up the good y (the good measured on the y-axis) to get more of the good x (the good measured on the x-axis) and at the same time remain on the same indifference curve. The magnitude of the slope of the indifference curve equals the marginal rate of substitution. The marginal rate of substitution diminishes as the consumer moves along an indifference curve, increasing consumption of the good measured on the x-axis and decreasing consumption of the good measured on the y-axis. The consumer equilibrium is at the best affordable point so that the consumer is on the budget line, is on the highest attainable indifference curve, and has a marginal rate of substitution equal to the relative price of the two goods. We can use the indifference curve model to generate a demand curve.

CHECKPOINT 1

■ **Indifference curves.**

Additional Practice Problems 1

1. Figure A12.1 shows one of Maria's indifference curves between ice cream cones and milkshakes. Lightly shade combinations of cones and milkshakes that are more preferred to those on the indifference curve. More heavily shade combinations that are less preferred to those on the indifference curve.

2. In Figure A12.1, what is Maria's marginal rate of substitution when she is consuming 4 ice cream cones and 2 milkshakes?

■ **FIGURE A12.1**

Milkshakes (quantity per week)

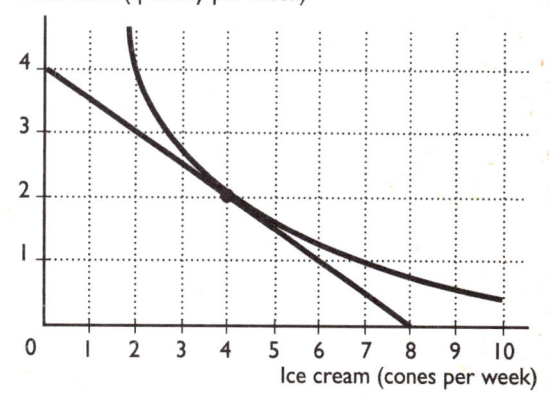

■ FIGURE A12.2
Milkshakes (number per week)

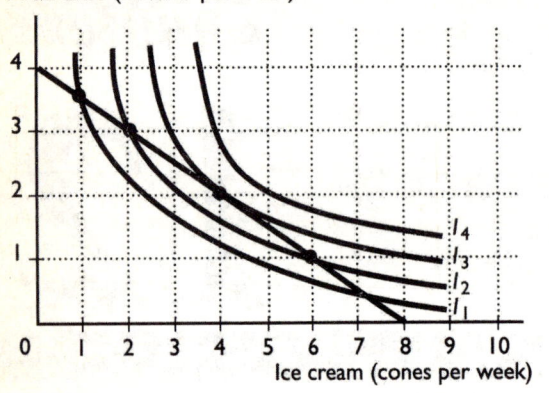

3. Figure A12.2 shows Maria's budget line and several of her indifference curves.
   a. What is Maria's best affordable point?
   b. If Maria consumed 3 milkshakes and 2 ice creams, how would her marginal rate of substitution between cones and shakes compare to the relative price of cones and shakes?

Solutions to Additional Practice Problems 1

■ FIGURE A12.3
Milkshakes (number per week)

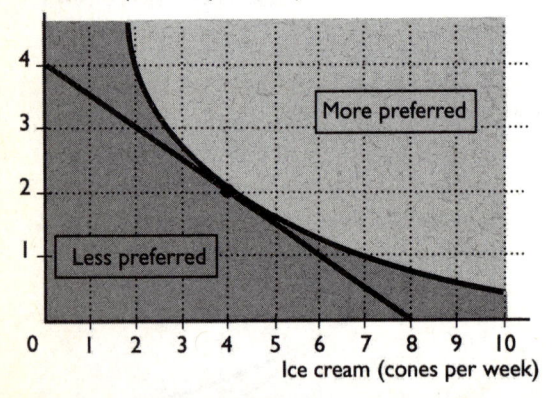

1. Figure A12.3 shows that all combinations above the indifference curve are more preferred to those on it and all combinations below the indifference curve are less preferred to those on it.

2. Maria's marginal rate of substitution equals the magnitude of the slope of the indifference curve. Use the straight line that goes through the combination of 4 ice cream cones and 2 milkshakes and touches the indifference curve at only that point. The magnitude of the slope of this line is 1/2 of a milkshake per ice cream cone, so Maria's marginal rate of substitution is 1/2 of a milkshake per ice cream cone. This marginal rate of substitution means that when Maria is consuming 4 ice cream cones and 2 milkshakes, she is willing to give up only 1/2 of a milkshake in order to get another ice cream cone.

■ FIGURE A12.4
Milkshakes (number per week)

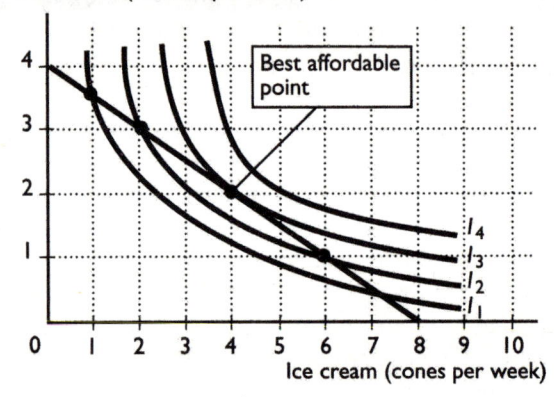

3a. Figure A12.4 shows Maria's best affordable point. This point is on Maria's budget line and also on the highest attainable indifference curve, I_3. At this point, Maria's marginal rate of substitution between cones and shakes equals the relative price of cones and shakes.

3b. If Maria consumed 3 milkshakes and 2 ice cream cones, she would be on indifference curve I_3. The slope of this indifference curve at that point equals Maria's marginal rate of substitution. So Maria's marginal rate of substitution between cones and shakes at this consumption possibility is greater than the relative price of cones and shakes.

■ Self Test 1

Fill in the blanks

An ____ is a curve that shows combinations of goods among which a consumer is indifferent. A consumer prefers being on a ____ (lower;

higher) indifference curve. The magnitude of the slope of an indifference curve equals the ____. If an indifference curve is steep, the marginal rate of substitution is ____ (high; low). The best affordable point occurs at the point on the budget line where the magnitude of the slope of the budget line ____ (is greater than; equals; is less than) the marginal rate of substitution.

True or false
1. A consumer is indifferent among combinations of goods that are on his or her indifference curve.
2. A consumer is indifferent among combinations on different indifference curves.
3. The marginal rate of substitution is the rate at which a person will give up the good measured on the y-axis to get more of the good measured on the x-axis and at the same time remain indifferent.
4. The only requirement for a consumer to be at his best affordable point is that the consumer be on the budget line.
5. Along a demand curve that is derived using indifference curves, the quantity of the good demanded increases when the price rises.

Multiple choice
1. An indifference curve is a line that shows combinations of goods among which a consumer
   a. prefers one over the other.
   b. places no value on any of the items.
   c. can afford to buy all the combinations.
   d. is indifferent.
   e. believes that all combinations have the same marginal rate of substitution.

2. What is the difference between a budget line and an indifference curve?
   a. One is measured in dollars while the other is measured in units of goods.
   b. One shows what is possible while the other shows what is preferred.
   c. One shows a positive relationship and the other shows a negative relationship.
   d. The budget line is bowed in toward the origin and the indifference curves are linear.
   e. There is no difference.

3. In a preference map, consumption combinations on higher indifference curves
   a. always cost more than any combination on a lower indifference curve.
   b. always are preferred to combinations on lower indifference curves.
   c. always cost less than any combination on a lower indifference curve.
   d. always are less preferred than combinations on lower indifference curves.
   e. are sometimes more preferred, sometimes less preferred, and sometimes equally preferred than any combination on a lower indifference curve.

4. The marginal rate of substitution for the good on the horizontal axis is
   a. the consumer surplus.
   b. the same as the consumer's budget line.
   c. equal to the magnitude of the slope of the indifference curve.
   d. equal to the magnitude of the slope of the consumer surplus curve.
   e. equal to 1.0 if the indifference curves are linear.

FIGURE A12.5

Slices of pizza (quantity per week) vs Tacos (quantity per week)

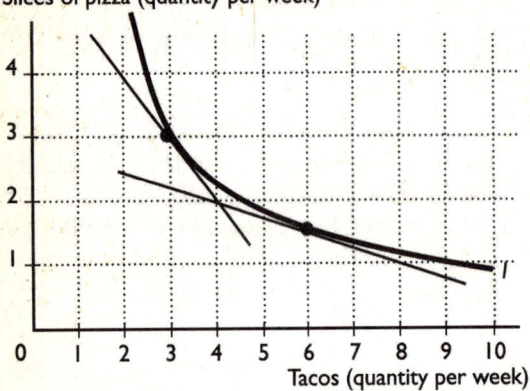

5. When the consumer whose indifference curve is illustrated in the figure above is consuming 3 slices of pizza and 3 tacos per week, the marginal rate of substitution is ____ of pizza per taco
   a. 3 slices
   b. 9 slices
   c. 0 slices
   d. 1 slice
   e. More information is needed about the consumer's budget line to determine the marginal rate of substitution.

6. When the consumer whose indifference curve is illustrated in the figure above is consuming 1½ slices of pizza and 6 tacos per week, the marginal rate of substitution is ____ of pizza per taco
   a. 6 slices
   b. 1½ of a slice
   c. 1/4 of a slice
   d. 1 slice
   e. More information is needed about the consumer's budget line to determine the marginal rate of substitution.

7. When the consumer whose indifference curve is illustrated in the figure consumes more tacos, the marginal rate of substitution is of slices of pizza for tacos
   a. stays the same.
   b. increases.
   c. decreases.
   d. changes randomly.
   e. More information is needed about the consumer's budget line to determine how the marginal rate of substitution changes.

8. At her best affordable point, Kris
   i. is on her budget line.
   ii. is on the highest attainable indifference curve.
   iii. has a marginal rate of substitution equal to the relative price of the goods.
   a. i only.
   b. ii only.
   c. iii only.
   d. i, and ii.
   e. i, ii, and iii.

9. When Bo is at his best affordable consumption point, his marginal rate of substitution is
   a. greater than the relative price.
   b. equal to the relative price.
   c. less than the relative price.
   d. is equal to one.
   e. maximized.

10. To derive a demand curve using the indifference curve model, you must change the
    a. consumer's preferences.
    b. consumer's income.
    c. price of one good, holding the price of the other good and income constant.
    d. price of both goods simultaneously but by different amounts.
    e. price of both goods simultaneously but by the same percentage.

Complete the graph

■ FIGURE A12.6
Movies (number per month)

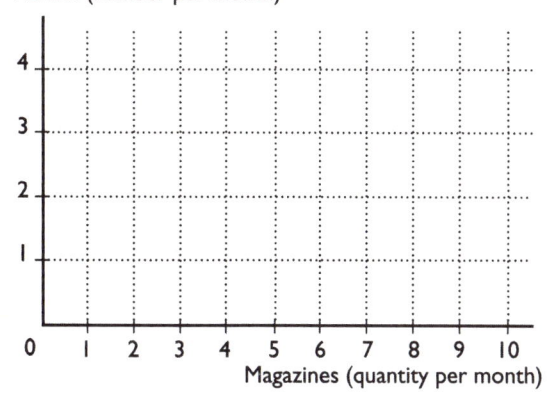

1. For entertainment, Laura goes to the movies and buys magazines. Laura devotes a monthly budget of $24 per month for entertainment. The price of a movie is $8 and the price of a magazine is $4.
   a. In Figure A12.6, draw Laura's budget line and label it BL_1.
   b. Suppose magazines rise in price to $6. Draw Laura's new budget line in Figure A12.6 and label it BL_2.
   c. Finally suppose that magazines fall in price to $3. Draw Laura's new budget line in Figure A12.6 and label it BL_3.

■ FIGURE A12.7
Movies (number per month)

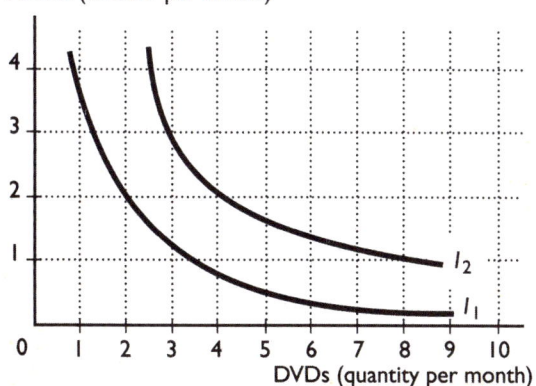

2. Brent goes to the movies and buys DVDs. Figure A12.7 shows two of his indifference curves.
   a. Initially, the price of a movie is $10 and the price of a DVD is also $10. Brent's income is $40 per month. Draw Brent's budget line in Figure A12.7. How many DVDs does Brent buy per month?
   b. DVDs fall in price to $5. Brent's income remains at $40 and the price of a movie remains at $10. Draw Brent's new budget line in Figure A12.7. How many DVDs does Brent now buy per month?

■ FIGURE A12.8
Price (dollars per DVD)

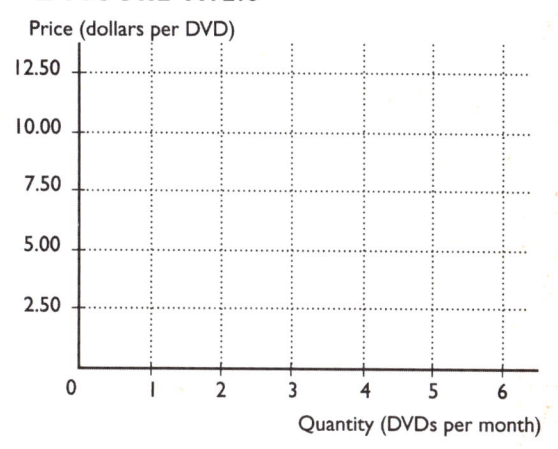

   c. You have two points on Brent's demand curve for DVDs. What are these two points? Assuming Brent's demand curve is linear, plot these points in Figure A12.8 and draw his demand curve. How does a fall in the price of a DVD affect the quantity of DVDs Brent buys?

Short answer and numeric questions

1. What is the defining characteristic of the points on an indifference curve?
2. If Alberto's marginal rate of substitution between shirts and pants is 2 shirts per pair of pants, what does this number mean? As Alberto obtains more pants, what happens to his marginal rate of substitution?
3. What is the difference between an indifference curve and a demand curve?

SELF TEST ANSWERS

■ CHECKPOINT 1

Fill in the blanks

An <u>indifference curve</u> is a curve that shows combinations of goods among which a consumer is indifferent. A consumer prefers being on a <u>higher</u> indifference curve. The magnitude of the slope of an indifference curve equals the <u>marginal rate of substitution</u>. If an indifference curve is steep, the marginal rate of substitution is <u>high</u>. The best affordable point occurs at the point on the budget line where the magnitude of the slope of the budget line <u>equals</u> the marginal rate of substitution.

True or false

1. True; page 313
2. False; page 313
3. True; page 314
4. False; page 315
5. False; page 317

Multiple choice

1. d; page 313
2. b; page 313
3. b; page 313
4. c; page 314
5. d; page 315
6. c; page 315
7. c; page 314
8. e; page 315
9. b; page 316
10. c; page 317

Complete the graph

1. a. Figure A12.9 shows the budget line;. page 317.
   b. Figure A12.9 shows the budget line;. page 317.
   c. Figure A12.9 shows the budget line;. page 317.

■ FIGURE A12.9
Movies (number per month)

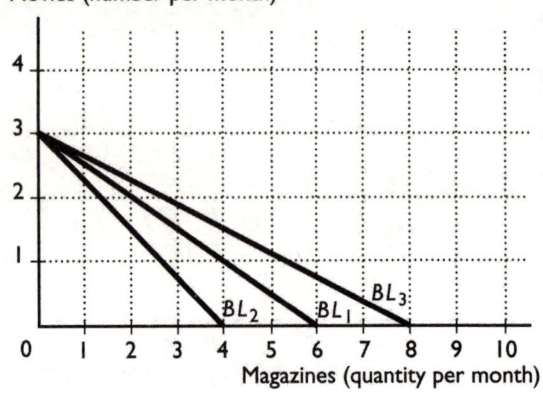

■ FIGURE A12.10
Movies (number per month)

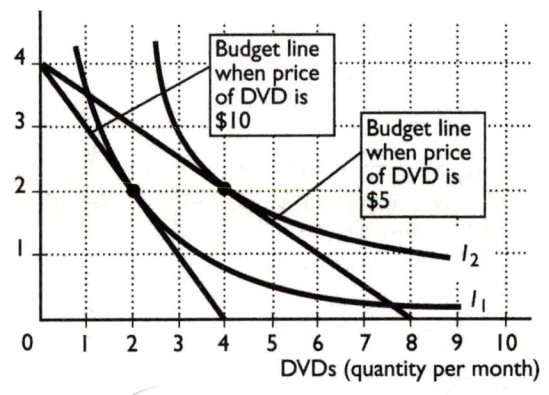

1. a. Figure A12.10 shows the budget line. Brent buys 2 DVDs a month; page 316.
   b. Figure A12.10 shows the new budget line. Brent now buys 4 DVDs a month; page 316.

■ FIGURE A12.11

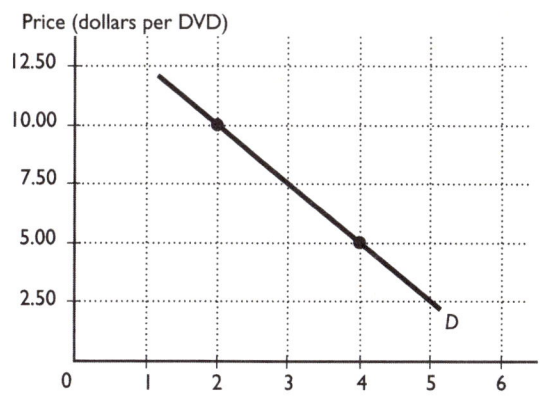

Price (dollars per DVD) vs Quantity (DVDs per month). Demand curve D passes through (2, $10.00) and (4, $5.00).

c. One point on Brent's demand curve is from part (a). When the price of a DVD rental is $10, the quantity of DVDs Brent buys is 2 a month. The other point is from part (b). When the price of a DVD is $5, Brent buys 4 DVDs a month. Figure A12.11 plots these two points and draws Brent's demand curve. A fall in the price of a DVD increases the quantity of DVDs Brent buys; page 317.

Short answer and numeric questions

1. The defining characteristic of points on an indifference curve is that the consumer is indifferent about which combination he or she consumes. Of all the possible combinations on an indifference curve, the consumer does not care which combination he or she receives; page 313.

2. The marginal rate of 2 shirts per pair of pants means that Alberto is willing to give up 2 shirts in order to get another pair of pants. As Alberto obtains more pants, his marginal rate of substitution decreases; page 314.

3. An indifference curve and a demand curve are quite different. An indifference curve shows combinations of goods among which a consumer is indifferent. A demand curve shows the relationship between the price of a good and the quantity demanded. An indifference curve, along with a budget line, can be used to derive a demand curve. Hence the demand curve can be viewed as a result of using an indifference curve; pages 313 and 317.

Chapter 13

Production and Cost

CHAPTER CHECKLIST

In Chapter 13 we study how a firm's costs are determined and how these costs vary as the firm varies its output.

1 Explain how economists measure a firm's cost of production and profit.

The firm's goal is to maximize its profit. The highest-valued alternative forgone is the opportunity cost of a firm's production. A cost paid in money is an explicit cost. A firm incurs an implicit cost when it uses a factor of production but does not make a direct money payment for its use. The return to entrepreneurship is normal profit and is part of the firm's costs because it compensates the entrepreneur for not running another business. A firm's economic profit equals total revenue minus total cost, which is the sum of explicit costs and implicit costs and is the opportunity cost of production.

2 Explain the relationship between a firm's output and labor employed in the short run.

The short run is the time frame in which the quantities of some resources are fixed; the long run is the time frame in which the quantities of all resources can be varied. Marginal product is the change in total product that results from a one-unit increase in the quantity of labor employed. As firms hire labor, initially increasing marginal returns occur but eventually decreasing marginal returns set in. Average product is total product divided by the quantity of an input. When marginal product exceeds the average product, the average product curve slopes upward and average product increases as more labor is employed. And when marginal product is less than average product, the average product curve slopes downward and average product decreases as more labor is employed.

3 Explain the relationship between a firm's output and costs in the short run.

Total cost is the sum of total fixed cost and total variable cost. Marginal cost is the change in total cost that results from a one-unit increase in total product. Average total cost is the sum of average fixed cost and average variable cost. The U-shape of the average total cost curve arises from the influence of two opposing forces: spreading total fixed cost over a larger output and decreasing marginal returns. The marginal cost curve intersects the average variable cost and average total cost curves at their minimum points. The average cost curve and the marginal cost curve shift when technology changes or when the price of a factor of production changes.

4 Derive and explain a firm's long-run average cost curve.

In the long run, all costs are variable. When a firm changes its plant size, it might experience economies of scale, diseconomies of scale, or constant returns to scale. The long-run average cost curve is a curve that shows the lowest average cost at which it is possible to produce each output when the firm has had sufficient time to change both its plant size and labor employed. The long-run average cost curve slopes downward with economies of scale and upward with diseconomies of scale.

CHECKPOINT 13.1

■ **Explain how economists measure a firm's cost of production and profit.**

Quick Review
- *Explicit cost* A cost paid in money.
- *Implicit cost* A cost incurred by using a factor of production but for which no direct money payment is made.
- *Economic profit* Total revenue minus total opportunity cost.

Additional Practice Problem 13.1
1. Gary manufactures toy gliders made of balsa wood. Each week, Gary pays $200 in wages, buys balsa wood for $400, pays $50 to lease saws and sanders, and pays $150 in rent for the workspace. To fund his operations, Gary withdrew his life's savings, $162,500, from his savings account at the bank, which paid interest of $250 a week. The normal profit for a glider company is $250 a week. Gary sells $1,500 worth of gliders a week.
   a. How much are the weekly explicit costs?
   b. How much are the weekly implicit costs?
   c. What does an accountant compute for the weekly profit?
   d. What does an economist compute for the weekly economic profit?

Solution to Additional Practice Problem 13.1
1a. The explicit costs are the wages, the balsa wood, the leased saws and sanders, and rent. The weekly explicit costs are $200 + $400 + $50 + $150, which equals $800.
1b. The implicit costs are the forgone interest and the normal profit. The weekly implicit costs are $250 + $250, which equals $500.
1c. Accountants calculate profit as total revenue minus explicit costs, which is $1,500 − $800 = $700.
1d. Economic profit is total revenue minus total cost. Total cost is the sum of explicit and implicit costs. So Gary's total cost is $800 + $500, which is $1,300. Gary's economic profit equals $1,500 − $1,300, which is $200.

■ Self Test 13.1

Fill in the blanks
The firm's goal is to maximize ____ (growth; market share; profit). A cost paid in money is an ____ (explicit; implicit) cost; a cost incurred when a firm uses a factor of production for which it does not make a direct money payment is an ____ (explicit; implicit) cost. The return to entrepreneurship is ____ (normal; economic) profit and ____ (is; is not) part of the firm's opportunity cost. A firm's total revenue minus total opportunity cost is ____ (normal; economic) profit.

True or false
1. The firm's goal is to maximize profit.
2. An accountant measures profit as total revenue minus opportunity cost.
3. All of a firm's costs must be paid in money.
4. If a firm earns an economic profit, the return to the entrepreneur exceeds normal profit.

Multiple choice
1. The paramount goal of a firm is to
   a. maximize profit.
   b. maximize sales.
   c. maximize total revenue.
   d. minimize its costs.
   e. force its competitors into bankruptcy.

2. For a business, opportunity cost measures
   a. only the cost of labor and materials.
   b. only the implicit costs of the business.
   c. the cost of all the factors of production the firm employs.
   d. only the explicit costs the firm must pay.
   e. all of the firm's costs including its normal profit *and* its economic profit.

3. Costs paid in money to hire a resource is
   a. normal profit.
   b. an implicit cost.
   c. an explicit cost.
   d. an alternative-use cost.
   e. economic profit.

4. Which of the following is an example of an implicit cost?
   a. wages paid to employees
   b. interest paid to a bank on a building loan
   c. the cost of using capital an owner donates to the business
   d. dollars paid to a supplier for materials used in production
   e. liability insurance payments made only once a year

5. The opportunity cost of a firm using its own capital is
   a. economic depreciation.
   b. standard ownership depreciation.
   c. economic loss.
   d. normal loss.
   e. capital loss.

6. The difference between a firm's total revenue and its total cost is its ____ profit.
   a. explicit
   b. normal
   c. economic
   d. accounting
   e. excess

Short answer and numeric questions
1. What is likely to happen to a firm that does not maximize profit?
2. Bobby quits his job as a veterinarian to open a model train store. Bobby made $80,000 a year as a veterinarian. The first year his train store is open, Bobby pays a helper $26,000. He also pays $24,000 in rent, $10,000 in utilities, and buys $200,000 of model trains. Bobby had a good year because he sold all of his model trains for $300,000. Bobby's normal profit is $30,000.
   a. What would an accountant calculate as Bobby's profit?
   b. What is Bobby's total opportunity cost? What is his economic profit?
3. Why are wages a cost to a business? Why is a normal profit a cost to a business?

CHECKPOINT 13.2

■ **Explain the relationship between a firm's output and labor employed in the short run.**

Quick Review
- *Marginal product* The change in total product that results from a one-unit increase in the quantity of labor employed.
- *Formula for the marginal product* The marginal product equals:

Change in total product ÷ change in quantity of labor

Additional Practice Problems 13.2
1. Bobby runs a cat grooming service. Bobby hires students to groom the cats. The table to the right shows how many cats Bobby's service can groom when Bobby changes the number of students he hires.

Labor (students per day)	Total product (cats groomed per day)
0	0
1	5
2	12
3	18
4	22
5	25

Labor (students per day)	Average product (cats groomed per day)	Marginal product (cats groomed per day)
1	____	____
2	____	____
3	____	____
4	____	____
5	____	____

   a. Complete the table above.
   b. Draw Bobby's average product curve and his marginal product curve. When does the marginal product equals the average product?

2. The first five members of the men's basketball squad are each 6 feet tall. A sixth player, whose height is 7 feet, is added. Has the average height increased or decreased with the addi-

tion of this player? A seventh player, whose height is 5 feet, is added. What happens to the team's average height? An eighth player, whose height is 6 feet, is added. What is the effect on the average height? What is the general rule about how the marginal player's height changes the average height of the team?

Solutions to Additional Practice Problems 13.2

Labor (students per day)	Average product (cats groomed per day)	Marginal product (cats groomed per day)
1	5.0	5.0
2	6.0	7.0
3	6.0	6.0
4	5.5	4.0
5	5.0	3.0

1a. The completed table is above. The average product equals: total product ÷ total labor and the marginal product equals: change in total product ÷ change in quantity of labor.

1b. The figure is to the right. The marginal product equals the average product when the average product is at its maximum. Both equal 6 cats groomed per day.

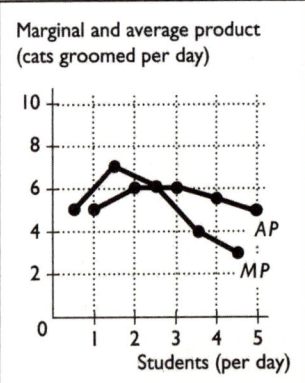

2. The 7-foot player is above the average height, so adding him to the team increases the average height. The 5-foot player is below the average height, so adding him decreases the average height. When the 6-foot player is added, the team's average height equals 6 feet, so his addition has no effect on the average height. The general rule is that when a marginal value lies above the average, the average rises. When the marginal value is below the average, the average falls. And when the marginal value equals the average, the average does not change.

■ Self Test 13.2

Fill in the blanks

The time frame in which the quantities of some resources are fixed is the ____ (long; market; short) run and the time frame in which the quantities of *all* resources can be varied is the ____ (long; market; short) run. Marginal product equals ____ (total product; the change in total product) divided by the ____ (quantity of labor; increase in the quantity of labor). Average product equals the ____ (total product; change in total product) divided by the ____ (quantity of labor; change in quantity of labor). When the marginal product of an additional worker is less than the marginal product of the previous worker, the firm experiences decreasing ____ (marginal; fixed) returns. The law of decreasing returns states that as a firm uses more of a ____ (fixed; variable) input, with a given quantity of ____ (fixed; variable) inputs, the marginal product of the ____ (fixed; variable) input eventually decreases. If the marginal product exceeds the average product, the average product curve slopes ____ (downward; upward).

True or false

1. In the short run, the firm's fixed inputs cannot be changed.
2. Points on and below the total product curve are efficient.
3. Most production processes initially have decreasing marginal returns followed eventually by increasing marginal returns.
4. When the marginal product of labor exceeds the average product of labor, the average product curve is downward sloping.

Multiple choice

1. The short run is a time period during which
   a. some of the firm's resources are fixed.
   b. all of the firm's resources are fixed.
   c. all of the firm's resources are variable.
   d. the fixed cost equals zero.
   e. the firm cannot increase its output.

2. In the short run, firms can increase output by
   a. only increasing the size of their plant.
   b. only decreasing the size of their plant.
   c. only increasing the amount of labor used.
   d. only decreasing the amount of labor used.
   e. either increasing the amount of labor used or increasing the size of their plant.

3. Which of the following is correct?
   a. The short run for a firm can be longer than the long run for the same firm.
   b. The short run is the same for all firms.
   c. The long run is the time frame in which the quantities of all resources can be varied.
   d. The long run is the time frame in which all resources are fixed.
   e. The long run does not exist for some firms.

4. Marginal product equals
   a. the total product produced by a certain amount of labor.
   b. the change in total product that results from a one-unit increase in the quantity of labor employed.
   c. total product divided by the total quantity of labor.
   d. the amount of labor needed to produce an increase in production.
   e. total product minus the quantity of labor.

5. If 5 workers can wash 30 cars a day and 6 workers can wash 33 cars a day, then the marginal product of the 6th worker equals
   a. 30 cars a day.
   b. 33 cars a day.
   c. 5 cars a day.
   d. 5.5 cars a day.
   e. 3 cars a day.

6. Increasing marginal returns occur when the
   a. average product of an additional worker is less than the average product of the previous worker.
   b. marginal product of an additional worker exceeds the marginal product of the previous worker.
   c. marginal product of labor is less than the average product of labor.
   d. total output of the firm is at its maximum.
   e. total product curve is horizontal.

7. If 25 workers can pick 100 flats of strawberries an hour, then average product is
   a. 100 flats an hour.
   b. 125 flats an hour.
   c. 75 flats an hour.
   d. 4 flats an hour.
   e. More information is needed about how many flats 24 workers can pick.

Complete the graph

Quantity of labor (workers)	Total product (turkeys per day)	Average product (turkeys per worker)	Marginal product (turkeys per worker)
0	0	xx	
			100
1	100	100	
			___
2	300	___	
			___
3	450	___	
			30
4	___	___	
			___
5	___	100	

1. The table gives the total product schedule at Al's Turkey Town Farm.
   a. Complete this table. (The marginal product is entered midway between rows to emphasize that it is the result of changing inputs, that is, moving from one row to the next.)

■ FIGURE 13.1

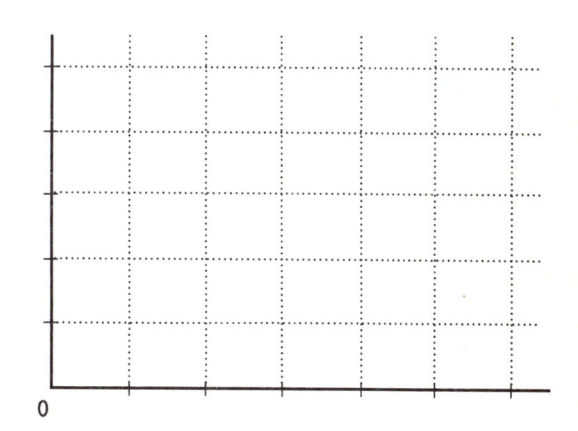

   b. In Figure 13.1 label the axes and plot the marginal product (MP) and average product (AP) curves. (Plot the MP curve midway between the quantities of labor.) Where do the two curves intersect?

c. When the MP curve is above the AP curve, is the AP curve rising or falling? When the MP curve is below the AP curve, is the AP curve rising or falling?

Short answer and numeric questions

1. What is the difference between the short run and the long run?
2. Pizza Hut opens a new store nearby. As the owner adds workers, what happens to their marginal product? Why?
3. What is the law of decreasing returns?
4. If the marginal product of a new worker exceeds the average product, what happens to the average product?

CHECKPOINT 13.3

■ **Explain the relationship between a firm's output and costs in the short run.**

Quick Review
- *Total cost* The cost of all the factors of production used by a firm. Total cost equals the sum of total fixed cost and total variable cost.
- *Marginal cost* The cost that arises from a one-unit increase in output.
- *Average total cost* Total cost per unit of output, which equals average fixed cost plus average variable cost as well as total cost divided by output.

Additional Practice Problems 13.3

1. Pearl owns a company that produces pools. Pearl has total fixed cost of $2,000 a month and pays each of her workers $2,500 a month. The table in the next column shows the number of pools Pearl's company can produce in a month.
   a. Complete the left side of the table.
   b. Suppose that the wage Pearl pays her

Labor	Output	TC	MC	TC	MC
0	0	___		___	
			___		___
1	1	___		___	
			___		___
2	5	___		___	
			___		___
3	9	___		___	
			___		___
4	12	___		___	
			___		___
5	14	___		___	
			___		___
6	15	___		___	

workers increases to $3,000 a month. Complete the right side of the table.

c. What was the effect of the wage hike on Pearl's marginal cost?

2. In the figure to the right is an ATC curve. In this figure sketch an AVC curve and a MC curve. Tell what relationships these curves must obey so that they are drawn correctly.

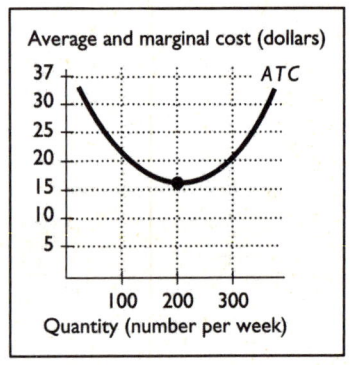

Solutions to Additional Practice Problems 13.3

Labor	Output	TC	MC	TC	MC
0	0	2,000		2,000	
			2,500		3,000
1	1	4,500		5,000	
			625		750
2	5	7,000		8,000	
			625		750
3	9	9,500		11,000	
			833		1,000
4	12	12,000		14,000	
			1,250		1,500
5	14	14,500		17,000	
			2,500		3,000
6	15	17,000		20,000	

1a. The completed table is above. Total cost, TC, equals the sum of total fixed cost and total variable cost. For example, when Pearl hires 6 workers, total cost is ($2,000) + (6 × $2,500), which is $17,000. Marginal cost equals the change in the total cost divided by the change in output. For example, when output increases from 14 to 15 pools, marginal cost is ($17,000 − $14,500) ÷ (15 − 14), which is $2,500.

1b. The completed table is above.

1c. The increase in the wage rate increased Pearl's marginal cost at every level of output.

2. The completed figure is to the right. To be drawn correctly, there are three requirements: First, the *AVC* curve must reach its minimum at a lower level of output than does the *ATC* curve. Second, the vertical distance between the *ATC* and *AVC* curves must decrease as output increases. Finally the *MC* curve must go through the minimum points on both the *AVC* and *ATC* curves.

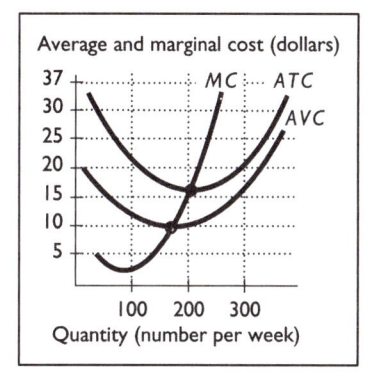

■ Self Test 13.3

Fill in the blanks

Total cost equals total fixed cost ____ (plus; minus; times) total variable cost. ____ (Marginal; Average) cost is the change in total cost that results from a one-unit increase in output. Average total cost equals average fixed cost ____ (plus; minus; times) average variable cost. The average total cost curve is ____ (S-shaped; U-shaped). When the firm hires the quantity of labor so that the marginal product is at its maximum, marginal cost is at its ____ (maximum; minimum).

True or false

1. In the short run, total fixed cost does not change when the firm changes its output.

2. Marginal cost is always less than average total cost.

3. The average total cost curve is U-shaped.

4. An increase in the wage rate shifts the marginal cost curve upward.

Multiple choice

1. Total cost is equal to the sum of
   a. total revenue and total cost.
   b. total variable cost and total product.
   c. total variable cost and total fixed cost.
   d. total fixed cost and total product.
   e. the marginal cost plus the total fixed cost plus the total variable cost.

2. Total fixed cost is the cost of
   a. labor.
   b. production.
   c. a firm's fixed factors of production.
   d. only implicit factors of production.
   e. only explicit factors of production.

3. Jay set up his hot dog stand near the business district. His total variable cost includes the
   a. annual insurance for the hot dog stand.
   b. cost of buying the hot dog stand.
   c. cost of the hot dogs and condiments.
   d. interest he pays on the funds he borrowed to pay for advertising.
   e. revenue he gets when he sells his first hot dog each day.

4. Marginal cost is equal to
   a. the total cost of a firm's production.
   b. the difference between total cost and fixed cost.
   c. a cost that is not related to the quantity produced.
   d. the change in total cost that results from a one-unit increase in output.
   e. the change in fixed cost that results from a one-unit increase in output.

5. To produce 10 shirts, the total cost is $80; to produce 11 shirts, the total cost is $99. The marginal cost of the 11th shirt is equal to
   a. $8.
   b. $9.
   c. $80.
   d. $99.
   e. $19.

6. Average total cost equals
   a. marginal cost divided by output.
   b. average fixed cost plus average variable cost.
   c. total fixed cost plus total variable cost.
   d. marginal cost plus opportunity cost.
   e. marginal cost multiplied by the quantity of output.

7. To produce 10 shirts, the total cost is $80; to produce 11 shirts, the total cost is $99. The average total cost of the 11th shirt is equal to
   a. $8.
   b. $9.
   c. $80.
   d. $99.
   e. $19.

8. One of the major reasons for the U-shaped average total cost curve is the fact that
   a. there are increasing returns from labor regardless of the number of workers employed.
   b. there eventually are decreasing returns from labor as more workers are employed.
   c. prices fall as output increases.
   d. the average fixed cost increases as more output is produced.
   e. the variable cost decreases as more output is produced.

Complete the graph

Labor	Output	TC	ATC	MC
0	0	___	xx	___
1	10	___	___	___
2	25	___	___	___
3	35	___	___	___
4	40	___	___	___
5	43	___	___	___
6	45	___	___	___

1. Sue hires workers to produce subs at Sue's Super Supper Sub Shop. Sue pays her workers $10 an hour and has fixed costs of $30 an hour. The table shows Sue's total product schedule.

   a. Complete the table above the question in the previous column.
   b. Using the completed table, plot Sue's ATC and MC curves in figure 13.2. (Plot the MCs midway between the quantities.)

■ FIGURE 13.2

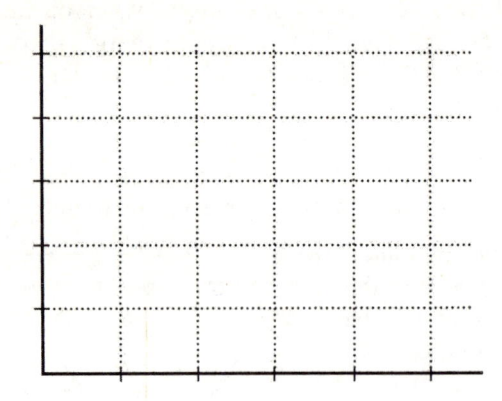

Labor	Output	TC	ATC	MC
0	0	___	xx	___
1	10	___	___	___
2	25	___	___	___
3	35	___	___	___
4	40	___	___	___
5	43	___	___	___
6	45	___	___	___

   c. Sue's rent increases so her fixed cost rises to $75 an hour. Complete the table above and then plot Sue's new ATC and MC curves in Figure 13.2.
   d. How does the increase in fixed cost change Sue's average total cost curve? Her marginal cost curve?

Chapter 13 • Production and Cost

■ **FIGURE 13.3**
Total cost (dollars per unit)

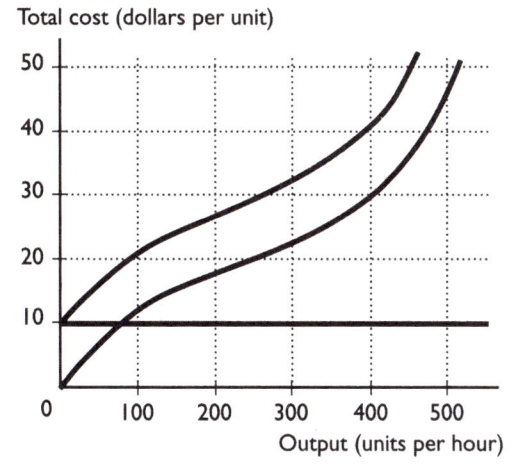

2. Label the cost curves in Figure 13.3.

Short answer and numeric questions
1. If a firm closes and produces nothing, does it still have any costs?
2. What is the difference between marginal cost and average total cost?
3. Why is the average total cost curve U-shaped?
4. Where does the marginal cost curve intersect the average variable cost and average total cost curves?
5. What two factors shift the cost curves?

CHECKPOINT 13.4

■ **Derive and explain a firm's long-run average cost curve.**

Quick Review
- *Long-run average cost curve* The long-run average cost curve shows the lowest average cost at which it is possible to produce each output when the firm has had sufficient time to adjust its labor force and its plant.

Additional Practice Problem 13.4a
1. The figure shows three average total cost curves for A1 Sewing, a company that sells sewing machines. The company can use three different sized stores, which account for the different cost curves. 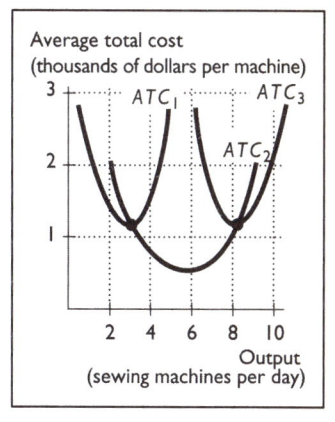
   a. Which average cost curve occurs when A-1 uses the smallest store? The largest store?
   b. Indicate A1's long-run average cost curve, *LRAC* in the figure.
   c. If A1 plans to sell 6 sewing machines per day, what sized store will A1 use?
   d. Over what range of output does A1 Sewing have economies of scale? Diseconomies of scale?

2. Describe economies of scale and diseconomies of scale along a long-run average total cost curve.

Solutions to Additional Practice Problems 13.4
1a. When A1 uses the smallest store, its plant size is the smallest and so its average total cost curve is ATC_1 in the figure. When A1 uses the largest store, its plant size is the largest and so its average total cost curve is ATC_2 in the figure.

1b. The long-run average cost curve is the curve that shows the lowest average total cost to produce each output. In the figure to the right, the *LRAC* curve is the darkened parts of the three average total cost curves.

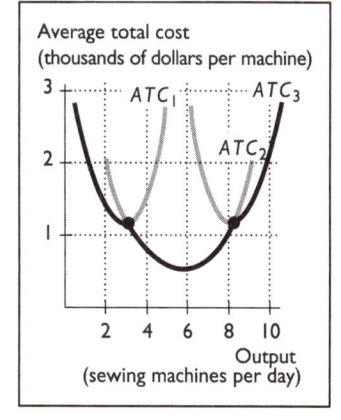

1c. If A1 plans to sell 6 sewing machines, it will use the middle sized store because that is the store that gives it the lowest average total cost when selling 6 sewing machines a day.

1d. A1 has economies of scale when selling from 0 to 6 sewing machines per day. It has diseconomies of scale when it sells more than 6 sewing machines per day.

2. When economies of scale are present, the *LRAC* curve slopes downward. When the *LRAC* curve is horizontal, constant returns to scale are present. And when the *LRAC* curve slopes upward, diseconomies of scale are present.

■ **Self Test 13.4**

Fill in the blanks

In the long run, a firm ____ (can; cannot) vary its quantity of labor and ____ (can; cannot) vary its quantity of capital. Economies of scale occur if, when a firm increases its plant size and labor employed by the same percentage, the firm's average total cost ____ (increases; decreases). When the firm has ____ (economies; diseconomies) of scale, its long-run average cost curve slopes upward.

True or false
1. All costs are fixed in the long run.
2. When a firm increases its plant size and labor, greater specialization of capital and labor can lead to economies of scale.
3. Constant returns to scale occur when the firm increases its plant size and labor employed by the same percentage and output increases by the same percentage.
4. The long-run average cost curve is derived from the marginal cost curves for different possible plant sizes.

Multiple choice
1. Economies of scale occur whenever
   a. marginal cost decreases as production increases.
   b. total cost increases as production is increased by increasing all inputs by the same percentage.
   c. marginal product increases as labor increases and capital decreases.
   d. a firm increases its plant size and labor employed, and its output increases by a larger percentage.
   e. marginal product decreases as labor increases and capital increases.

2. The main source of economies of scale is
   a. better management.
   b. constant returns to plant size.
   c. specialization.
   d. long-run cost curves eventually sloping downward.
   e. increases in the labor force not matched by increases in the plant size.

3. Diseconomies of scale can occur as a result of which of the following?
   a. increasing marginal returns as the firm increases its size
   b. lower total fixed cost as the firm increases its size
   c. management difficulties as the firm increases its size
   d. greater specialization of labor and capital as the firm increases its size
   e. increases in the labor force not matched by increases in the plant

4. Constant returns to scale occur when an equal percentage increase in plant size and labor
   a. increases total cost.
   b. does not change total cost.
   c. increases average total cost.
   d. does not change average total cost.
   e. does not change production.

5. A firm's long-run average cost curve shows the ____ average cost at which it is possible to produce each output when the firm has had ____ time to change both its labor force and its plant.
   a. highest; sufficient
   b. lowest; sufficient
   c. lowest; insufficient
   d. highest insufficient
   e. average; sufficient

6. Economies of scale and diseconomies of scale explain
   a. cost behavior in the short run.
   b. profit maximization in the long run.
   c. the U-shape of the long-run cost curve.
   d. the U-shape of the short-run cost curves.
   e. the U-shape of the marginal cost curves.

■ FIGURE 13.4
Average total cost (dollars per unit)

7. Figure 13.4 shows four of a firm's ATC curves. If the firms produces 2,000 units per day, it will use the plant size that corresponds to
   a. ATC_1.
   b. ATC_2.
   c. ATC_3.
   d. ATC_4.
   e. either ATC_1 or ATC_4.

Complete the graph

■ FIGURE 13.5
Average total cost (dollars per unit)

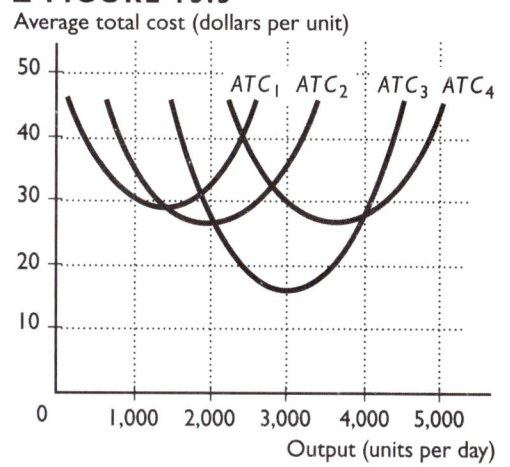

1. In Figure 13.5, darken the firm's long-run average total cost curve. Show over which range of output the firm has economies of scale and over which range of output the firm has diseconomies of scale.

Short answer and numeric questions
1. Describe how a long-run average cost curve is constructed.
2. What are economies of scale? What leads to economies of scale?

SELF TEST ANSWERS

■ CHECKPOINT 13.1

Fill in the blanks

The firm's goal is to maximize <u>profit</u>. A cost paid in money is an <u>explicit</u> cost; a cost incurred when a firm uses a factor of production for which it does not make a direct money payment is an <u>implicit</u> cost. The return to entrepreneurship is <u>normal</u> profit and <u>is</u> part of the firm's opportunity cost. A firm's total revenue minus total opportunity cost is <u>economic</u> profit.

True or false
1. True; page 320
2. False; page 320
3. False; page 321
4. True; pages 321-322

Multiple choice
1. a; page 320
2. c; page 320
3. c; page 321
4. c; page 321
5. a; page 321
6. c; page 321

Short answer and numeric questions
1. A firm that does not seek to maximize profit is either driven out of business or bought by firms that do seek that goal; page 320.
2. a. An accountant calculates profit as total revenue minus explicit costs. Bobby's explicit costs are $26,000 + $24,000 + $10,000 + $200,000, which equals $260,000. The accountant calculates profit as $300,000 − $260,000, which is $40,000; page 320.
   b. Bobby's opportunity cost is the sum of his explicit costs and his implicit costs. Bobby's explicit costs are $260,000. His implicit costs are the sum of his income forgone as a veterinarian, $80,000, and normal profit, $30,000. So Bobby's implicit costs are $110,000. His total opportunity cost is $260,000 + $110,000, which is $370,000. Bobby's economic profit is his total revenue minus his opportunity cost, which is $300,000 − $370,000 = −$70,000. Bobby incurs an economic loss; pages 319-322.
3. Wages are a cost because they are paid to hire a factor of production, labor. A normal profit is a cost because it is paid to obtain the use of another factor of production, entrepreneurship; page 321.

■ CHECKPOINT 13.2

Fill in the blanks

The time frame in which the quantities of some resources are fixed is the <u>short</u> run and the time frame in which the quantities of *all* resources can be varied is the <u>long</u> run. Marginal product equals <u>the change in total product</u> divided by the <u>increase in the quantity of labor</u>. Average product equals the <u>total product</u> divided by the <u>quantity of labor</u>. When the marginal product of an additional worker is less than the marginal product of the previous worker, the firm has experienced decreasing <u>marginal</u> returns. The law of decreasing returns states that as a firm uses more of a <u>variable</u> input, with a given quantity of <u>fixed</u> inputs, the marginal product of the <u>variable</u> input eventually decreases. If the marginal product exceeds the average product, the average product curve slopes <u>upward</u>.

True or false
1. True; page 324
2. False; page 326
3. False; page 326
4. False; pages 328-329

Multiple choice
1. a; page 324
2. c; page 324
3. c; page 324
4. b; pages 326-327
5. e; pages 326-327
6. b; page 326
7. d; page 328

Complete the graph

1. a. The completed table is below; pages 325-328.

Quantity of labor	Total product (turkeys per day)	Average product (turkeys per worker)	Marginal product (turkeys per worker)
0	0	xx	
			100
1	100	100	
			200
2	300	150	
			150
3	450	150	
			30
4	480	120	
			20
5	500	100	

■ **FIGURE 13.6**
Total product (turkeys per day)

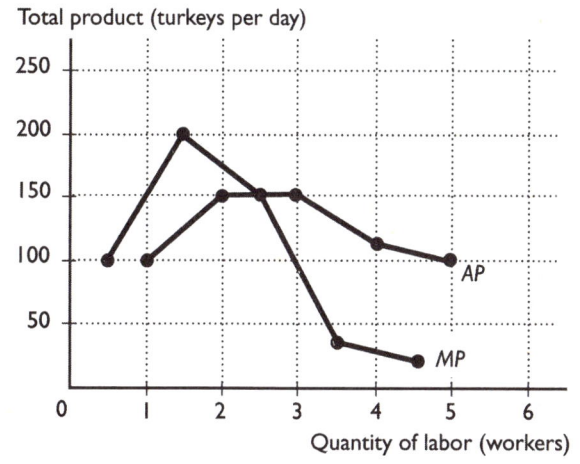

b. Figure 13.6 plots the *MP* and *AP* curves. The curves intersect where the *AP* curve is at its maximum; page 328.

c. When the *MP* curve is above the *AP* curve, the *AP* curve is rising. When the *MP* curve is below the *AP* curve, the *AP* curve is falling; pages 328-329.

Short answer and numeric questions

1. The short run is the time frame in which the quantities of some resources (the plant) are fixed. The long run is the time frame in which the quantities of *all* resources can be changed; page 324.

2. As Pizza Hut initially adds workers, the marginal product of each additional worker exceeds the marginal product of the previous worker. The marginal product increases because the workers can specialize. Some workers can make the pizzas and others can deliver them. As more workers are added, eventually the marginal product of each additional worker is less than the marginal product of the previous worker. The marginal product decreases because more workers are using the same equipment, so there is less productive work for each new worker; page 326.

3. The law of decreasing returns states that as a firm uses more of a variable input, with a given quantity of fixed inputs, the marginal product of the variable input eventually decreases; page 328.

4. If the marginal product of a worker exceeds the average product, then hiring the worker will increase the average product; page 329.

■ **CHECKPOINT 13.3**

Fill in the blanks

Total cost equals total fixed cost plus total variable cost. Marginal cost is the change in total cost that results from a one-unit increase in output. Average total cost equals average fixed cost plus average variable cost. The average total cost curve is U-shaped. When the firm hires the quantity of labor so that the marginal product is at its maximum, marginal cost is at its minimum.

True or false

1. True; page 331
2. False; page 334
3. True; page 334
4. True; page 337

Multiple choice

1. c; page 331
2. c; page 331
3. c; page 331
4. d; page 332

5. e; page 332
6. b; page 333
7. b; page 333
8. b; page 335

Complete the graph

Labor	Output	TC	ATC	MC
0	0	30	xx	
				1.00
1	10	40	4.00	
				0.67
2	25	50	2.00	
				1.00
3	35	60	1.71	
				2.00
4	40	70	1.75	
				3.33
5	43	80	1.86	
				5.00
6	45	90	2.00	

■ **FIGURE 13.7**
Average and marginal cost (dollars per sub)

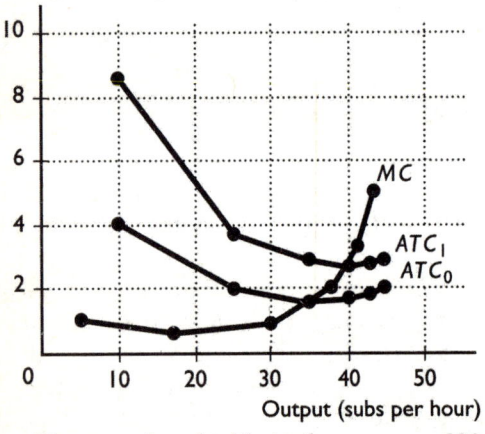

Labor	Output	TC	ATC	MC
0	0	75	xx	
				1.00
1	10	85	8.50	
				0.67
2	25	95	3.80	
				1.00
3	35	105	3.00	
				2.00
4	40	115	2.88	
				3.33
5	43	125	2.91	
				5.00
6	45	135	3.00	

■ **FIGURE 13.8**
Total cost (dollars per unit)

2. The labeled figure, Figure 13.8, is above; page 332.

1. a. The completed table is above; page 333.
   b. Figure 13.7 plots the curves as ATC_0 and MC.
   c. The completed table after the change in costs is at the top of the next column and Figure 13.7 plots the new curves as ATC_1 and MC; page 333.
   d. The average cost curve shifts upward; the marginal cost curve does not change; page 336.

Short answer and numeric questions

1. Yes, even a closed firm might still have fixed costs. So even if zero output is produced, the firm might have (fixed) costs such as interest payments on a loan or rent on a lease that has not expired; page 331

2. Marginal cost is the change in total cost that results from a one-unit increase in output. Average total cost is total cost per unit of output, which equals average fixed cost plus average variable cost; pages 332-333.

3. When output increases, the firm spreads its total fixed cost over a larger output and its average fixed cost decreases—its average fixed cost curve slopes downward.

Decreasing marginal returns means that as output increases, ever larger amounts of labor are needed to produce an additional unit of output. So average variable cost eventually increases, and the *AVC* curve eventually slopes upward.

Initially as output increases, both average fixed cost and average variable cost decrease, so average total cost decreases and the *ATC* curve slopes downward. But as output increases further and decreasing marginal returns set in, average variable cost begins to increase. Eventually, average variable cost increases more quickly than average fixed cost decreases, so average total cost increases and the *ATC* curve slopes upward; page 335.

4. The marginal cost curve intersects the average variable cost curve and the average total cost curve at the point where they are the minimum; page 334.
5. Cost curves shift if there is a change in technology or a change in the price of a factor of production; pages 336-337.

■ **CHECKPOINT 13.4**

Fill in the blanks

In the long run, a firm <u>can</u> vary its quantity of labor and <u>can</u> vary its quantity of capital. Economies of scale occur if, when a firm increases its plant size and labor employed by the same percentage, the firm's average total cost <u>decreases</u>. When the firm has <u>diseconomies</u> of scale, its long-run average cost curve slopes upward.

True or false
 1. False; page 339
 2. True; page 339
 3. True; page 340
 4. False; page 340

Multiple choice
 1. d; page 339
 2. c; page 339
 3. c; page 340
 4. d; page 340

 5. b page 340
 6. c; page 340
 7. c; page 341

Complete the graph

■ **FIGURE 13.9**

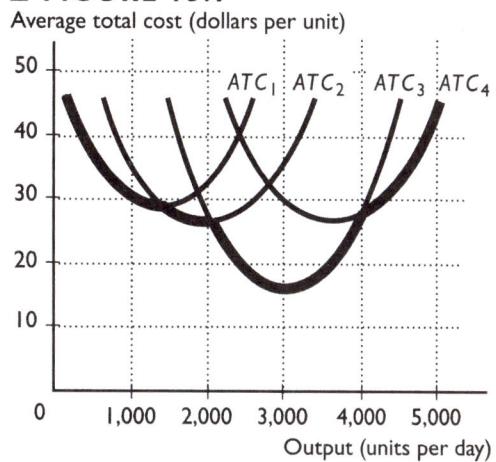

1. Figure 13.9 darkens the firm's long-run average total cost curve. As indicated by the dotted line, the firm has economies of scale at all output levels less than 3,000 and has diseconomies of scale at all output levels greater than 3,000; page 341.

Short answer and numeric questions

1. A long-run average cost curve is a curve that shows the lowest average total cost at which it is possible to produce each output when the firm has had sufficient time to change both its plant size and labor employed. Suppose a newspaper publisher can operate with four different plant sizes. The segment of each of the four average total cost curves for which that plant has the lowest average total cost is the scallop-shaped curve that is the long-run average cost curve; page 339.

2. Economies of scale is a condition in which, when a firm increases its plant size and labor force by the same percentage, its output increases by a larger percentage and its long-run average cost decreases. The main source of economies of scale is greater specialization of both labor and capital; page 339.

Chapter 14

Perfect Competition

CHAPTER CHECKLIST

In Chapter 14 we study perfect competition, the market that arises when the demand for a product is large relative to the output of a single producer.

1 Explain a perfectly competitive firm's profit-maximizing choices and derive its supply curve.

Perfect competition exists when: many firms sell an identical product to many buyers; there are no restrictions on entry into (or exit from) the market; established firms have no advantage over new firms; and sellers and buyers are well informed about prices. A firm in perfect competition is a price taker—it cannot influence the price of its product. The market demand curve is downward sloping. A perfectly competitive firm faces a perfectly elastic demand so its demand curve is horizontal. Marginal revenue is the change in total revenue that results from a one-unit increase in the quantity sold. In perfect competition, marginal revenue equals price. A firm maximizes its profit at the output level at which total revenue exceeds total cost by the largest amount. Another way to find the profit-maximizing output is to use marginal analysis. A firm maximizes its profit at the output level at which marginal revenue equals marginal cost. The shutdown point is the output and price at which the firm just covers its total variable cost. If a firm shuts down, it incurs a loss equal to its total fixed cost. A firm's supply curve is its marginal cost curve above minimum average variable cost.

2 Explain how output, price, and profit are determined in the short run.

The market supply curve in the short run shows the quantity supplied at each price by a fixed number of firms. Market demand and market supply determine the price and quantity bought and sold. Each firm takes the price as given and produces its profit-maximizing output. When price equals the average total cost, a perfectly competitive firm earns a normal profit. The firm earns an economic profit when price exceeds average total cost and incurs economic loss when price is less than average total cost.

3 Explain how output, price, and profit are determined in the long run and explain why perfect competition is efficient.

Economic profit is an incentive for new firms to enter a market, but as they do so, the price falls and the economic profit of each existing firm decreases. Economic loss is an incentive for firms to exit a market, and as they do so the price rises and the economic loss of each remaining firm decreases. In the long run, a firm earns a normal profit and there is no entry or exit. A In a market undergoing technological change, firms that adopt the new technology make an economic profit. Firms that stick with the old technology incur economic losses. They either exit the market or switch to the new technology. Competition eliminates economic profit in the long run. Perfect competition is efficient because in a perfectly competitive market the market demand curve is the same as the marginal benefit curve and the market supply curve is the same as the entire market's marginal cost curve.

Part 5 · PRICES, PROFITS, AND INDUSTRY PERFORMANCE

CHECKPOINT 14.1

■ **Explain a perfectly competitive firm's profit-maximizing choices and derive its supply curve.**

Quick Review
- *MC = MR* Profit is maximized when production is such that marginal cost equals marginal revenue.
- *A firm's short-run supply curve* At prices less than its minimum average variable cost, the firm shuts down. At prices above the minimum average variable cost, the supply curve is the marginal cost curve.
- *Shutdown point* The output and price at which price equals the minimum average variable cost.

Additional Practice Problem 14.1
1. Patricia is a perfectly competitive wheat farmer. Her average variable cost curve and her marginal cost are shown in the figure. 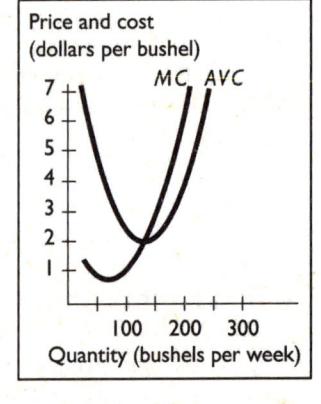
   a. If the price of a bushel of wheat is $6 per bushel, how much wheat will Patricia produce?
   b. If the price of a bushel of wheat falls to $4 per bushel, how much wheat will Patricia produce?
   c. What are two points on Patricia's supply curve?
   d. What is the lowest price for which Patricia will produce wheat rather than shut down?
   e. Suppose that when the price of a bushel of wheat is $6, Patricia produces a quantity of wheat such that her marginal revenue is greater than marginal cost. Explain why she is not maximizing her profit.

Solution to Additional Practice Problem 14.1
1a. When the price of a bushel of wheat is $6 per bushel, Patricia's marginal revenue curve is shown in the figure as MR_1. To maximize her profit, Patricia produces 200 bushels of wheat, the quantity at which marginal revenue equals marginal cost.

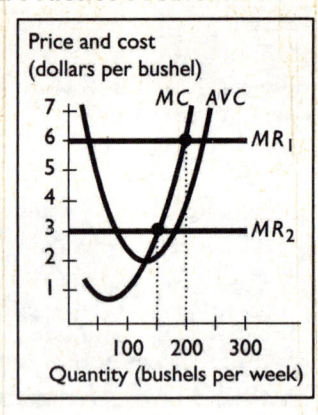

1b. If the price of wheat falls to $3 per bushel, Patricia's marginal revenue curve is shown in the figure as MR_2. She decreases the quantity of wheat she produces to 150 bushels per week because that is the quantity at which marginal revenue equals marginal cost.

1c. One point on Patricia's supply curve is a price of $6 and 200 bushels. Another point is a price of $3 and a quantity of 150 bushels.

1d. The lowest price for which Patricia produces rather than shuts down is the price equal to her minimum average variable cost. The figure shows that this price is equal to $2 per bushel.

1e. If marginal revenue exceeds marginal cost, then the extra revenue from selling one more bushel of wheat exceeds the extra cost incurred to produce it. So if Patricia produces one more bushel of wheat, the marginal revenue that she receives from selling that bushel is greater than the cost to produce that bushel and this bushel increases her profit. To maximize profit, Patricia must increase her output until she reaches the point where the marginal revenue equals the marginal cost.

■ **Self Test 14.1**

Fill in the blanks

The conditions that define perfect competition arise when the market demand for the product is ____ (large; small) relative to the output of a single producer. A perfectly competitive firm faces a perfectly ____ (elastic; inelastic) demand. The change in total revenue that results from a one-unit increase in the quantity sold is the marginal ____ (cost; price; revenue). When a perfectly competitive firm maximizes profit, marginal revenue equals ____ (average variable; marginal) cost. When a firm shuts down, it incurs a loss equal to its total ____ (variable; fixed) cost. A firm will shut down if price is less than minimum ____ (marginal; average total; average variable) cost. A perfectly competitive firm's supply curve is its marginal ____ (cost; revenue) curve above the minimum ____ (average total; average variable) cost.

True or false
1. A perfectly competitive market has many firms.
2. A firm in perfect competition is a price taker.
3. When a perfectly competitive firm is maximizing its profit, the vertical difference between the firm's marginal revenue curve and its marginal cost curve is as large as possible.
4. Stan's U-Pick blueberry farm, a perfectly competitive firm, will shut down if its total revenue is less than its total cost.
5. A perfectly competitive firm's short-run supply curve is its average total cost above minimum average variable cost.

Multiple choice
1. The four market types are
   a. perfect competition, imperfect competition, monopoly, and oligopoly.
   b. oligopoly, monopsony, monopoly, and imperfect competition.
   c. perfect competition, monopoly, monopolistic competition, and oligopoly.
   d. oligopoly, oligopolistic competition, monopoly, and perfect competition.
   e. perfect competition, imperfect competition, monopoly, and duopoly.

2. A requirement of perfect competition is that
   i. many firms sell an identical product to many buyers.
   ii. there are no restrictions on entry into (or exit from) the market, and established firms have no advantage over new firms.
   iii. sellers and buyers are well informed about prices.
   a. i only.
   b. i and ii.
   c. iii only.
   d. i and iii.
   e. i, ii, and iii.

3. A perfectly competitive firm is a price taker because
   a. many other firms produce the same product.
   b. only one firm produces the product.
   c. many firms produce a slightly differentiated product.
   d. a few firms compete.
   e. it faces a vertical demand curve.

4. The demand curve faced by a perfectly competitive firm is
   a. horizontal.
   b. vertical.
   c. downward sloping.
   d. upward sloping.
   e. U-shaped.

5. For a perfectly competitive corn grower in Nebraska, the marginal revenue curve is
   a. downward sloping.
   b. the same as the demand curve.
   c. upward sloping.
   d. U-shaped.
   e. vertical at the profit maximizing quantity of production.

6. A perfectly competitive firm maximizes its profit by producing at the point where
   a. total revenue equals total cost.
   b. marginal revenue is equal to marginal cost.
   c. total revenue is equal to marginal revenue.
   d. total cost is at its minimum.
   e. total revenue is at its maximum.

FIGURE 14.1
Price and cost (dollars per shirt)

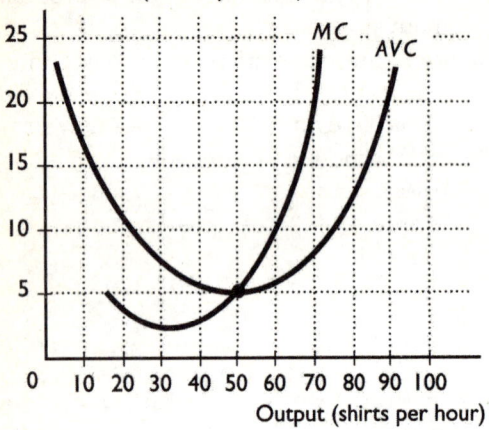

[Graph showing MC and AVC curves, with AVC minimum at approximately (50, 5) and MC intersecting AVC at that point. Output on x-axis from 0 to 100 shirts per hour, Price/cost on y-axis from 0 to 25.]

7. Figure 14.1 shows cost curves for Wring Around the Collar, a perfectly competitive dry cleaner. If the price of dry cleaning a shirt is $20 per shirt, the firm will dry clear ____ shirts per hour.
   a. 0
   b. between 1 and 49
   c. 50
   d. 60
   e. 61 or more. *(circled)*

8. In Figure 14.1, if the price of dry cleaning a shirt is $10 per shirt, the firm will dry clear ____ shirts per hour.
   a. 0
   b. between 1 and 49
   c. 50
   d. 60 *(circled)*
   e. 61 or more.

9. Based on Figure 14.1, the lowest price for which the company might remain open is
   a. $25 per shirt.
   b. $20 per shirt.
   c. $15 per shirt.
   d. $10 per shirt.
   e. $5 per shirt. *(circled)*

10. If the market price is lower than a perfectly competitive firm's average total cost, the firm will
    a. immediately shut down.
    b. continue to produce if the price exceeds the average fixed cost.
    c. continue to produce if the price exceeds the average variable cost. *(circled)*
    d. shut down if the price exceeds the average fixed cost.
    e. shut down if the price is less than the average fixed cost.

11. One part of a perfectly competitive trout farm's supply curve is its
    a. marginal cost curve below the shutdown point.
    b. entire marginal cost curve.
    c. marginal cost curve above the shutdown point. *(circled)*
    d. average variable cost curve above the shutdown point.
    e. marginal revenue curve above the demand curve.

Complete the graph

FIGURE 14.2
Price and cost (dollars per unit)

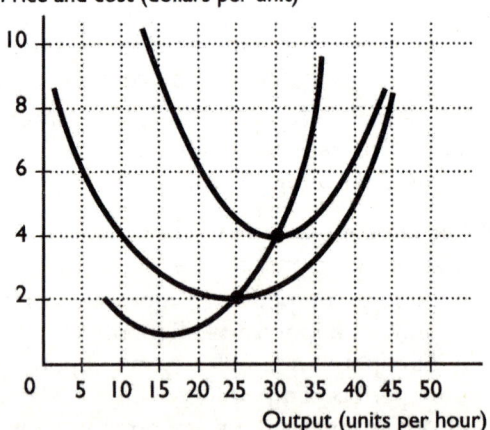

[Graph showing three cost curves with intersection points around (25, 2) and (35, 4). Output on x-axis from 0 to 50 units per hour, Price/cost on y-axis from 0 to 10.]

1. Figure 14.2 shows a perfectly competitive firm's cost curves.
   a. Label the curves.
   b. If the market price is $8, what is the firm's equilibrium output and price?

c. If the market price is $4, what is the firm's equilibrium output and price?
d. What is the firm's shutdown price?
e. Darken the firm's supply curve.

Short answer and numeric questions
1. What are the conditions that define perfect competition?
2. What is a "price taker?" Why are perfectly competitive firms price takers?
3. What is the difference between a perfectly competitive firm's demand curve and the market demand curve?
4. Willy, a perfectly competitive wheat farmer, can sell 999 bushels of wheat for $3 per bushel or 1,000 bushels for $3 per bushel. What is Willy's marginal revenue and total revenue if he sells 1,000 bushels of wheat?

Quantity (hogs)	Total cost (dollars)	Total revenue (dollars)	Economic profit (dollars)
0	300	___	___
1	350	___	___
2	425	___	___
3	575	___	___
4	825	___	___
5	1,200	___	___

5. Peter owns Peter's Porkers, a small hog farm. The above table gives Peter's total cost schedule. Peter is in a perfectly competitive market and can sell each hog for $200.
   a. Complete the table.
   b. What is Peter's profit-maximizing number of hogs and what price will Peter set?
   c. When Peter increases his production from 2 hogs to 3 hogs, what is the marginal cost? Is the third hog profitable for Peter?
   d. When Peter increases his production from 3 hogs to 4 hogs, what is the marginal cost? Is the fourth hog profitable for Peter?
   e. What is the marginal cost of the third hog?
6. When will a firm temporarily shut down?

CHECKPOINT 14.2

■ **Explain how output, price, and profit are determined in the short run.**

Quick Review
- *Economic profit* If the price exceeds the average total cost, the firm earns an economic profit.
- *Economic loss* If the price is less than the average total cost, the firm incurs an economic loss.

Additional Practice Problem 14.2

Quantity (roses per week)	Average total cost (dollars per rose)	Marginal cost (dollars per rose)
100	2.00	1.50
200	1.50	1.50
300	1.67	2.50
400	2.00	5.00

1. Growing roses is a perfectly competitive industry. There are 100 rose growers and all have the same cost curves. The above table gives the costs of one of the growers, Rosita's Roses. The market demand schedule for roses is in the table to the right.

Price (dollars per rose)	Quantity (roses per week)
1.00	50,000
1.50	45,000
2.00	40,000
2.50	30,000
3.00	20,000

   a. Plot the market supply curve and the market demand curve in the figure.
   b. What is the equilibrium price of a rose?
   c. How many roses does Rosita produce? What is her economic profit or loss?

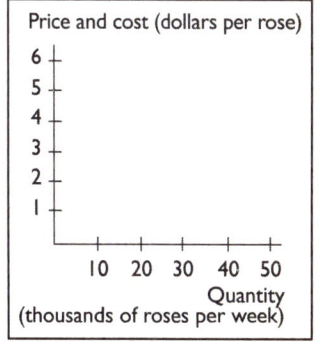

Solution to Additional Practice Problem 14.2

1a. The market demand curve and market supply curve are plotted in the figure. The quantity supplied in the market at any price is the sum of the quantities supplied by each firm at that price. Because each firm is identical, the market quantity supplied is 100 times the quantity supplied by any one firm. The firm's supply curve is its marginal cost curve above the minimum average variable cost. For instance, when the price is $2.50 a rose, Rosita's marginal cost schedule shows she will supply 300 roses a week. So the quantity supplied in the market equals 100 × (300 roses a week), which is 30,000 roses a week.

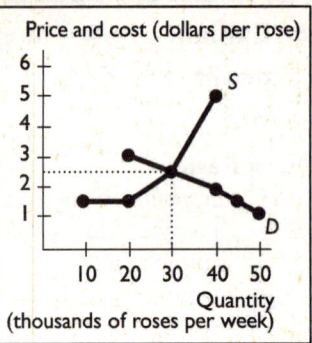

1b. The figure shows that the equilibrium price of a rose is $2.50.

1c. In the short run, a firm can make an economic profit or incur an economic loss. A firm earns an economic profit when price exceeds average total cost and incurs an economic loss when price is less than average total cost. In the case at hand, Rosita produces 300 roses. Rosita earns an economic profit. Rosita's economic profit per rose equals the price of a rose minus the average total cost, which is $2.50 − $1.67 = $0.83. She produces 300 roses, a week so her total economic profit is (300 roses a week) × ($0.83) = $249 a week.

■ Self Test 14.2

Fill in the blanks

In a perfectly competitive industry, the quantity supplied in the market at any price is ____ (determined by the market demand curve; equal to the sum of the quantities supplied by all firms at that price). A firm earns an economic profit when price exceeds ____ (marginal revenue; average total cost). A firm ____ (can; cannot) incur an economic loss in the short run.

True or false

1. The market supply curve in the short run shows the quantity supplied at each price by a fixed number of firms.
2. Market supply in a perfectly competitive market is perfectly elastic at all prices.
3. A perfectly competitive firm earns an economic profit if price equals average total cost.
4. In a perfectly competitive industry, a firm's economic profit is equal to price minus marginal revenue multiplied by quantity.
5. A perfectly competitive firm has an economic loss if price is less than the marginal cost.

Multiple choice

1. If the market supply curve and market demand curve for a good intersect at 600,000 units and there are 10,000 identical firms in the market, then each firm is producing
   a. 600,000 units.
   b. 60,000,000,000 units.
   c. 60,000 units.
   d. 60 units.
   e. 10,000 units.

2. A perfectly competitive firm definitely earns an economic profit in the short run if price is
   a. equal to marginal cost.
   b. equal to average total cost.
   c. greater than average total cost.
   d. greater than marginal cost.
   e. greater than average variable cost.

3. If a perfectly competitive firm is maximizing its profit and earning an economic profit, which of the following is correct?
   i. price equals marginal revenue
   ii. marginal revenue equals marginal cost
   iii. price is greater than average total cost
   a. i only.
   b. i and ii only.
   c. ii and iii only.
   d. i and iii only.
   e. i, ii, and iii.

FIGURE 14.3
Price and cost (dollars per unit)

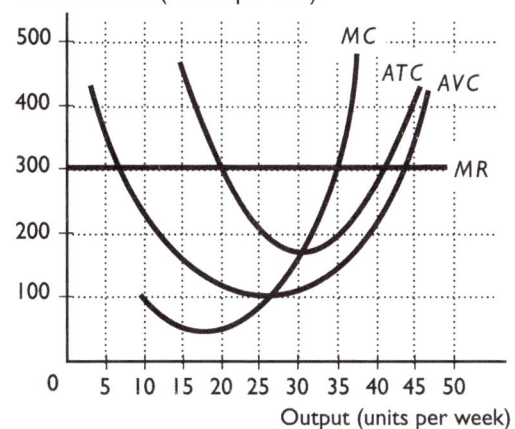

[Graph showing MC, ATC, AVC curves with horizontal MR line at 300, Output (units per week) on x-axis from 0 to 50]

4. Figure 14.3 shows the marginal revenue and cost curves for a perfectly competitive firm. The firm
   a. is incurring an economic loss.
   b. will shut down and will incur an economic loss.
   c. will shut down and will earn zero economic profit.
   d. is earning zero economic profit.
   e. is earning an economic profit.

5. The market for watermelons in Alabama is perfectly competitive. A watermelon producer earning a normal profit could earn an economic profit if the
   a. average total cost of selling watermelons does not change.
   b. average total cost of selling watermelons increases.
   c. average total cost of selling watermelons decreases.
   d. marginal cost of selling watermelons does not change.
   e. marginal cost of selling watermelons does not change.

6. Juan's Software Service Company is in a perfectly competitive market. Juan has total fixed cost of $25,000, average variable cost for 1,000 service calls is $45, and marginal revenue is $75. Juan's makes 1,000 service calls a month. What is his economic profit?
   a. $5,000
   b. $25,000
   c. $45,000
   d. $75,000.
   e. $50,000

7. If a perfectly competitive firm finds that price is less than its *ATC*, then the firm
   a. will raise its price to increase its economic profit.
   b. will lower its price to increase its economic profit.
   c. is earning an economic profit.
   d. is incurring an economic loss.
   e. is earning zero economic profit.

8. A perfectly competitive video-rental firm in Phoenix incurs an economic loss if the average total cost of each video rental is
   a. greater than the marginal revenue of each rental.
   b. less than the marginal revenue of each rental.
   c. equal to the marginal revenue of each rental.
   d. equal to zero.
   e. less than the price of each video.

9. In the short run, a perfectly competitive firm
   a. must make an economic profit.
   b. must suffer an economic loss.
   c. must earn a normal profit.
   d. might make an economic profit, incur an economic loss, or make a normal profit.
   e. must earn an economic profit.

Complete the graph

■ **FIGURE 14.4**
Price and cost (dollars per lawn)

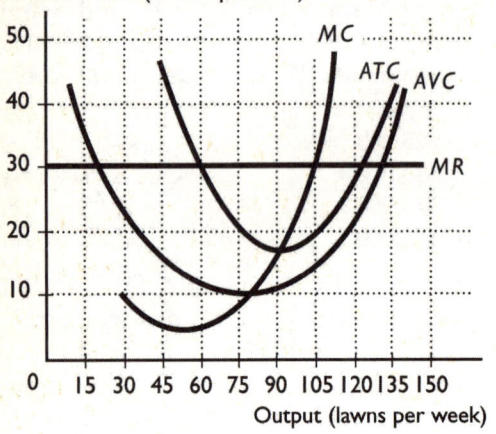

1. Moe's Mowers is a perfectly competitive lawn mowing company. Moe's costs and marginal revenue are illustrated in Figure 14.4.
   a. How many lawns does Moe mow?
   b. Is Moe earning an economic profit or incurring an economic loss? Darken the area that shows the economic profit or loss. What is the amount of economic profit or loss?

■ **FIGURE 14.5**
Price and cost (dollars per lawn)

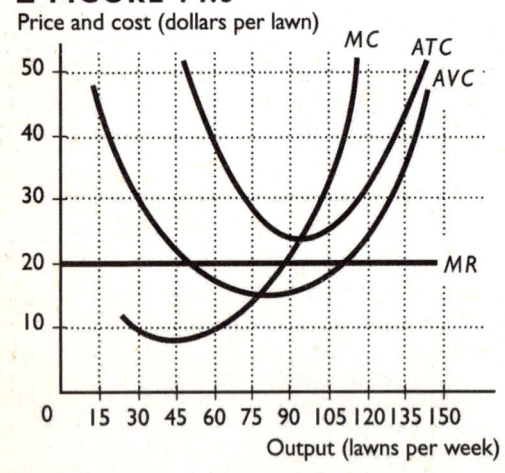

2. Larry's Lawns is (another) perfectly competitive lawn mowing company in another city. Larry's costs and marginal revenue are illustrated in Figure 14.5.
   a. How many lawns does Larry mow?
   b. Is Larry earning an economic profit or incurring an economic loss? Darken the area that shows the economic profit or loss. In the short run, will Larry remain open or shut down?

Short answer and numeric questions
1. In a perfectly competitive market, how is the market supply calculated?
2. If price is less than average total cost, is the firm earning an economic profit or incurring an economic loss?

CHECKPOINT 14.3

■ **Explain how output, price, and profit are determined in the long run and explain why perfect competition is efficient.**

Quick Review
- *Entry* Economic profit is an incentive for new firms to enter a market, but as they do so, the price falls and the economic profit of each existing firm decreases.
- *Exit* Economic loss is an incentive for firms to exit a market, but as they do so, the price rises and the economic loss of each remaining firm decreases.

Additional Practice Problem 14.3

Quantity (roses per week)	Average total cost (dollars)	Marginal cost (dollars)
100	2.00	1.50
200	1.50	1.50
300	1.67	2.50
400	2.00	5.00

1. Growing roses is a perfectly competitive industry. Initially there are 100 rose growers and all have the same cost curves. The above table gives the costs of one of the growers, Rosita's Roses. The table to the right has the market demand schedule for roses.

Price (dollars per rose)	Quantity (roses per week)
1.00	50,000
1.50	45,000
2.00	40,000
2.50	30,000
3.00	20,000

The equilibrium price for a rose initially is $2.50.

a. Plot Rosita's marginal cost curve and her marginal revenue curve in the figure to the right. Is Rosita earning an economic profit or is Rosita incurring an economic loss?

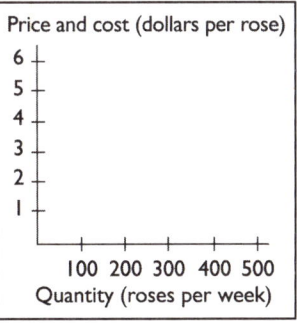

b. As time passes, what takes place in the market?

c. What will be the long-run price of a rose? What will be Rosita's profit in the long run? In the long run, how many growers will be in the market?

Solution to Additional Practice Problem 14.3

1a. The figure shows Rosita's marginal cost curve and marginal revenue curve. The figure shows that she is producing 300 roses a week. Rosita is earning an economic profit because the price of a rose, $2.50, exceeds her average total cost of producing 300 roses, $1.67.

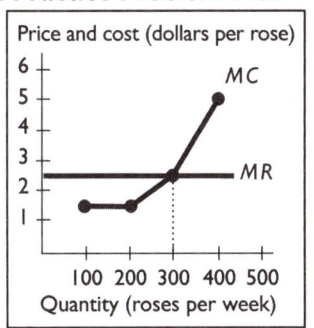

1b. A perfectly competitive firm earns a normal profit in the long run. A firm will not incur an economic loss in the long run because it will shut down. And a perfectly competitive firm cannot earn an economic profit in the long run because the presence of an economic profit attracts entry, which drives down the price and eliminates economic profit. Competitive firms cannot prevent entry into their market and so they cannot protect any economic profit.

In the case of the rose growers, rose growers are earning an economic profit, so more rose growers enter the market. The supply of roses increases and the market supply curve shifts rightward. The equilibrium price of a rose falls and the market equilibrium quantity increases.

1c. The long-run price of a rose will be $1.50 because that is the minimum average total cost. At that price, all rose growers, including Rosita, earn a normal profit. Indeed, the fact that they are earning only a normal profit is what removes the incentive for further firms to enter the industry. When the price of a rose is $1.50, the demand schedule shows that the quantity demanded is 45,000 roses. At a price of $1.50, each grower produces 200 roses. There will be 225 growers, each producing 200 roses.

■ Self Test 14.3

Fill in the blanks

In the long run, a perfectly competitive firm ____ (can; cannot) earn an economic profit, ____ (can; cannot) incur an economic loss, and ____ (can; cannot) earn a normal profit. In the long run, a perfectly competitive firm ____ (produces; does not produce) at minimum average total cost. Entry into an industry shifts the market ____ (demand; supply) curve ____ (rightward; leftward). Firms exit an industry when they are ____ (making a normal profit; incurring an economic loss). A technological change results in perfectly competitive firms ____ (temporarily; permanently) earning an economic profit.

True or false

1. When price equals average total cost, the firm earns a normal profit.
2. Entry into a perfectly competitive market lowers the price.
3. In the long run, firms respond to an economic loss by exiting a perfectly competitive market.
4. New technology shifts a firm's cost curves upward and the market supply curve leftward.

5. Perfect competition is efficient because it results in the efficient quantity being produced.

Multiple choice

1. In the long run, new firms enter a perfectly competitive market when
   a. normal profits are greater than zero.
   b. economic profits are equal to zero.
   c. normal profits are equal to zero.
   d. economic profits are greater than zero.
   e. the existing firms are weak because they are incurring economic losses.

2. In a perfectly competitive market, if firms are earning an economic profit, the economic profit
   a. attracts entry by more firms, which lowers the price.
   b. can be earned both in the short run and the long run.
   c. is less than the normal profit.
   d. leads to a decrease in market demand.
   e. generally leads to firms exiting as they seek higher profit in other markets.

3. If firms in a perfectly competitive market are earning an economic profit, then
   a. the market is in its long-run equilibrium.
   b. new firms enter the market and the equilibrium profit of the initial firms decreases.
   c. new firms enter the market and the equilibrium profit of the initial firms increases.
   d. firms exit the market and the equilibrium profit of the remaining firms decreases.
   e. firms exit the market and the equilibrium profit of the remaining firms increases.

4. Firms exit a competitive market when they incur an economic loss. In the long run, this exit means that the economic losses of the surviving firms
   a. increase.
   b. decrease until they equal zero.
   c. decrease until economic profits are earned.
   d. do not change.
   e. might change but more information is needed about what happens to the price of the good as the firms exit.

5. If firms in a perfectly competitive market have economic losses, then as time passes firms ____ and the market ____.
   a. enter; demand curve shifts leftward
   b. enter; supply curve shifts rightward
   c. exit; demand curve shifts leftward
   d. exit; supply curve shifts rightward
   e. exit; supply curve shifts leftward

6. As a result of firms leaving the perfectly competitive frozen yogurt market in the 1990s, the market
   a. supply curve shifted leftward.
   b. supply curve did not change.
   c. demand curve shifted rightward.
   d. supply curve shifted rightward.
   e. demand curve shifted rightward.

7. In the long run, a firm in a perfectly competitive market will
   a. earn zero economic profit, that is, it will earn a normal profit.
   b. earn zero normal profit but it will earn an economic profit.
   c. remove all competitors and become a monopolistically competitive firm.
   d. incur an economic normal loss but not earn a positive economic profit.
   e. remove all competitors and become a monopoly.

8. Technological change brings a ____ to firms that adopt the new technology.
   a. permanent economic profit
   b. temporary economic profit
   c. permanent economic loss
   d. temporary economic loss
   e. temporary normal profit

Complete the graph

■ **FIGURE 14.6**
Price and cost (dollars per unit)

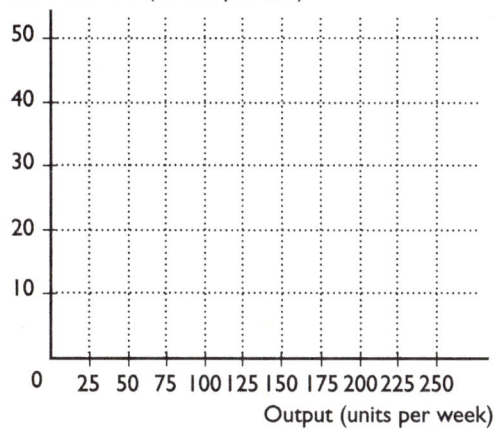

1. In Figure 14.6, suppose that the price of the good is $20. Show the long-run equilibrium for a perfectly competitive firm that produces 150 units per week.

■ **FIGURE 14.7**
Price and cost (dollars per unit)

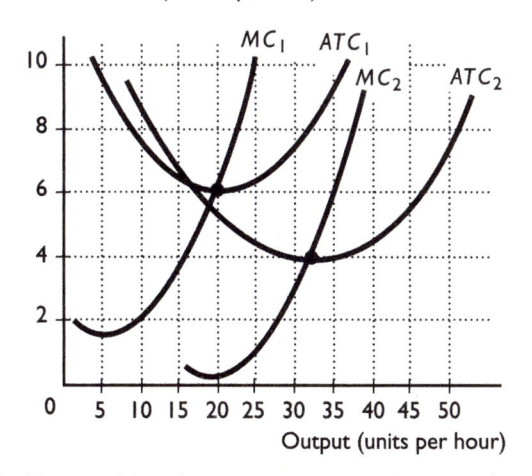

2. Figure 14.7 shows cost curves for two firms in an industry undergoing technological change. Firm 1 uses the old technology and has an average total cost curve ATC_1 and marginal cost curve MC_1. Firm 2 uses the new technology and has an average total cost curve ATC_2 and marginal cost curve MC_2. Initially the price of the product was $6.
   a. At the price of $6, do firm 1 and firm 2 earn an economic profit, normal profit, or incur economic loss?
   b. As more firms adopt the new technology, what happens to market supply and price? Do firms 1 and 2 earn an economic profit, normal profit, or incur an economic loss?
   c. In the long run, what will be the new price? Will firm 1 earn an economic profit, a normal profit, or incur an economic loss? Will firm 2 earn an economic profit, a normal profit, or incur an economic loss?

Short answer and numeric questions
1. Why are perfectly competitive firms unable to earn an economic profit in the long run? Why won't they incur an economic loss in the long run?
2. Is perfect competition efficient?
3. The Eye on Your Life discusses how competition benefits you by leading to the production of the vast array of goods and services you consume. Competition also benefits you by affecting the prices you pay for goods and services. The market for home delivered pizza is extremely competitive. How does this competition affect the price you pay for home delivered pizza?

SELF TEST ANSWERS

■ CHECKPOINT 14.1

Fill in the blanks

The conditions that define perfect competition arise when the market demand for the product is <u>large</u> relative to the output of a single producer. A perfectly competitive firm faces a perfectly <u>elastic</u> demand. The change in total revenue that results from a one-unit increase in the quantity sold is the marginal <u>revenue</u>. When a perfectly competitive firm maximizes profit, marginal revenue equals <u>marginal</u> cost. When a firm shuts down, it incurs a loss equal to its total <u>fixed</u> cost. A firm will shut down if price is less than minimum <u>average variable</u> cost. A perfectly competitive firm's supply curve is its marginal <u>cost</u> curve above the minimum <u>average variable</u> cost.

True or false

1. True; page 348
2. True; page 349
3. False; page 352
4. False; page 353
5. False; pages 354-355

Multiple choice

1. c; page 348
2. e; page 348
3. a; page 349
4. a; page 350
5. b; page 350
6. b; page 352
7. e; page 352
8. d; page 352
9. e; pages 353-354
10. c; pages 353-354
11. c; pages 354-355

Complete the graph

1. a. Figure 14.8 labels the curves; page 354.
   b. Output is 35 units and the price is $8; page 352.
   c. Output is 30 units and the price is $4; page 352.

■ **FIGURE 14.8**
Price and cost (dollars per unit)

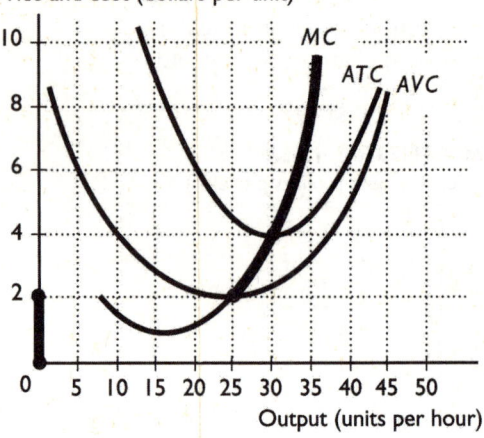

   d. The shutdown price is $2; pages 353-354.
   e. The firm's supply curve is darkened in Figure 14.8; page 355.

Short answer and numeric questions

1. Perfect competition exists when many firms sell an identical product to many buyers; there are no restrictions on entry into (or exit from) the market; established firms have no advantage over new firms; and sellers and buyers are well informed about prices; page 348.

2. A price taker is a firm that cannot influence the price of the good or service it produces. Perfectly competitive firms are price takers because there are many competing firms selling an identical product. Any individual firm is such a small part of the market that its actions cannot affect the price; page 349.

3. A perfectly competitive firm's demand is perfectly elastic because all sellers produce goods that are perfect substitutes. So the firm's demand curve is horizontal. The market demand curve is downward sloping; page 350.

4. Willy's marginal revenue equals the price of a bushel of wheat, which is $3. His total revenue equals price multiplied by quantity, which is $3,000; page 351.

Chapter 14 · Perfect Competition

Quantity (hogs)	Total cost (dollars)	Total revenue (dollars)	Economic profit (dollars)
0	300	0	−300
1	350	200	−150
2	425	400	−25
3	575	600	25
4	825	800	−25
5	1,200	1,000	−200

5. a. The completed table is above; page 351.

   b. The profit-maximizing number of hogs is 3. Peter charges $200 a hog; page 351.

   c. The marginal cost is the change in total cost that results from producing the third hog. So marginal cost is $150. This is a profitable hog because the marginal revenue from the hog exceeds its marginal cost; page 352.

   d. The marginal cost is $250. This hog is not profitable; page 352.

   e. The marginal cost of the third hog is $200, which is the average of the marginal cost of increasing production from 2 to 3 hogs and of increasing production from 3 to 4 hogs. The marginal cost of the third hog equals the marginal revenue so 3 hogs is the profit-maximizing output; page 352.

6. If a firm shuts down, it incurs an economic loss equal to total fixed cost. If the firm produces some output, it incurs an economic loss equal to total fixed cost plus total variable cost minus total revenue. If total revenue exceeds total variable cost, the firm's economic loss is less than total fixed cost. It pays the firm to produce. But if total revenue is less than total variable cost, the firm's economic loss exceeds total fixed cost. The firm shuts down; pages 353-354.

■ CHECKPOINT 14.2

Fill in the blanks

In a perfectly competitive industry, the market supply at any price is <u>equal to the sum of the quantities supplied by all firms at that price</u>. A perfectly competitive firm earns an economic profit if the price exceeds <u>average total cost</u>. A firm <u>can</u> incur an economic loss in the short run.

True or false
1. True; page 357
2. False; page 357
3. False; page 358
4. False; page 359
5. False; page 360

Multiple choice
1. d; page 357
2. c; page 359
3. e; page 359
4. e; page 359
5. c; page 359
6. a; page 359
7. d; page 360
8. a; page 360
9. d; pages 358-360

Complete the graph

■ **FIGURE 14.9**
Price and cost (dollars per lawn)

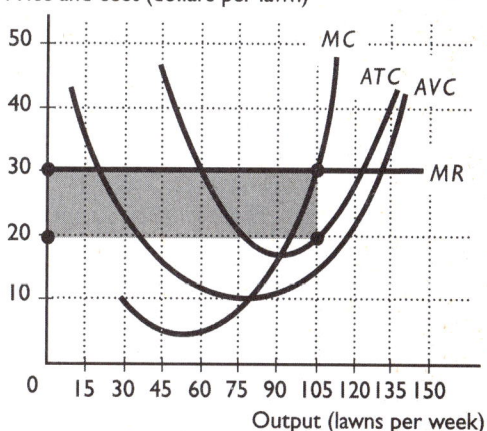

1. a. Moe mows 105 lawns per week because that is the quantity at which marginal revenue equals marginal cost; page 352.

   b. Moe is earning an economic profit. Figure 14.9 illustrates the economic profit. The economic profit per lawn equals price minus average total cost, which is $30 − $20 = $10 per lawn. The quantity is 105 lawns, so the total economic profit equals ($10 per lawn) × (105 lawns), which is $1,050 a week; page 359.

FIGURE 14.10
Price and cost (dollars per lawn)

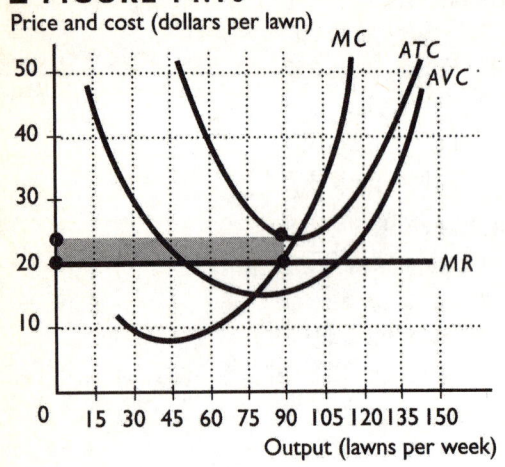

2. a. Larry mows 90 lawns per day because that is the quantity at which marginal revenue equals marginal cost; page 352.
   b. Larry has an economic loss. Figure 14.10 illustrates the economic loss as the darkened rectangle. Even though he has an economic loss, Larry remains open in the short run because the price exceeds his average variable cost; page 360.

Short answer and numeric questions
1. The market supply in the short run is the quantity supplied at each price by a fixed number of firms. The quantity supplied at a given price is the sum of the quantities supplied by all firms at that price. For example, if there are 100 firms in the geranium market and each produces 50 geraniums when the price is $3, then the quantity supplied in the market at $3 is 5,000 geraniums; page 357.

2. The firm is suffering an economic loss. If the price is less than average total cost, the firm is incurring an economic loss on each unit produced and has an overall economic loss; page 360.

■ CHECKPOINT 14.3
Fill in the blanks

In the long run, a perfectly competitive firm <u>cannot</u> earn an economic profit, <u>cannot</u> incur an economic loss, and <u>can</u> earn a normal profit. In the long run, a perfectly competitive firm <u>produces</u> at minimum average total cost. Entry into an industry shifts the market <u>supply</u> curve <u>rightward</u>. Firms exit an industry when they are <u>incurring an economic loss</u>. A technological change results in perfectly competitive firms <u>temporarily</u> earning an economic profit.

True or false
1. True; page 362
2. True; pages 363-364
3. True; pages 363-364
4. False; pages 366-367
5. True; page 368

Multiple choice
1. d; page 363
2. a; pages 363-364
3. b; pages 363-364
4. b; page 365
5. e; pages 364-365
6. a; page 364
7. a; pages 363-365
8. b; pages 366-367

Complete the graph
1. Figure 14.11 (on the next page) shows a perfectly competitive firm in long-run equilibrium. The marginal revenue curve is horizontal at the price of $20. The firm produces 150 units because that is the quantity at which marginal revenue equals marginal cost. The firm has zero economic profit because the price, $20 per unit, equals the average total cost, also $20 per unit; page 362.

■ FIGURE 14.11
Price and cost (dollars per unit)

[Graph showing MC and ATC curves intersecting at approximately output 150, price $20, with horizontal MR line at $20. Output axis: 0 to 250 units per week. Price axis: 0 to 50.]

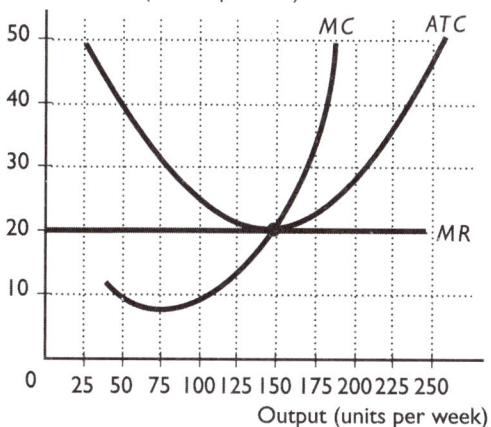

■ FIGURE 14.12
Price and cost (dollars per unit)

[Graph showing MC_1, ATC_1, MC_2, ATC_2 curves with horizontal MR_1 line at $6. Output axis: 0 to 50 units per hour. Price axis: 0 to 10.]

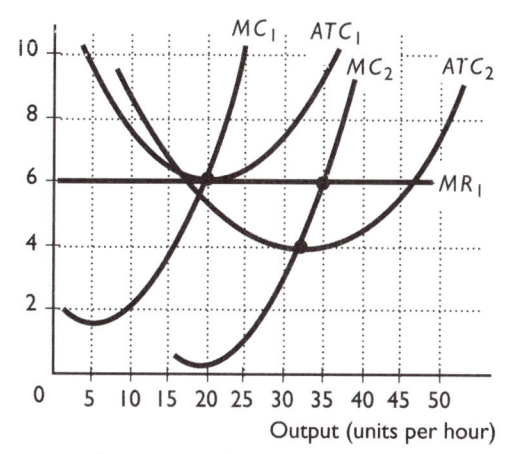

2. a. At the price of $6, the marginal revenue curve is MR_1 in Figure 14.12. Firm 1 produces 20 units and earns a normal profit because the $6 price equals average total cost. Firm 2 produces 35 units and earns an economic profit because the $6 price exceeds average total cost; pages 366-367.

   b. Market supply increases and the price falls. Firm 1 now incurs an economic loss and Firm 2 earns a smaller economic profit; pages 366-367.

   c. In the long run, the new price will $4 because that is the minimum of the new average total cost. Firm 1 will either have adopted the new technology and be earning a normal profit or will have exited the industry. Firm 2 will earn a normal profit; pages 366-367.

Short answer and numeric questions

1. Perfectly competitive firms cannot earn an economic profit in the long run because the existence of an economic profit invites entry by new firms. As these new firms enter, the market supply increases, driving down the price and eventually eliminating the economic profit. No firm will incur an economic loss in the long run because it will close; pages 363-365.

2. Perfect competition is efficient. In a perfectly competitive market, equilibrium occurs at the intersection of the supply and demand curves. Key, however, the facts that the supply curve also is the marginal cost curve and the demand curve also is the marginal benefit curve. So the equilibrium quantity also is the quantity at which the marginal cost equals the marginal benefit, which is the efficient quantity; pages 368-369.

3. Competition in the market for home delivered pizza keeps the price of home delivered pizza low. The producers of pizza would like to charge the highest price they can. However their price is limited by competition and it is this competition that protects you by keeping the price of home delivered pizza low.

Monopoly

Chapter 15

CHAPTER CHECKLIST

In Chapter 15 we study how a monopoly chooses its price and quantity, discuss whether a monopoly is efficient or fair, and investigate how monopolies can be regulated.

1 Explain how monopoly arises and distinguish between single-price monopoly and price-discriminating monopoly.

A monopoly is a market with a single supplier of a good or service that has no close substitutes and in which natural, ownership, or legal barriers to entry prevent competition. A single-price monopoly is a monopoly that sells each unit of its output for the same price to all its customers. A price-discriminating monopoly is a monopoly that is able to sell different units of a good or service for different prices.

2 Explain how a single-price monopoly determines its output and price.

The demand curve for a monopoly is the downward sloping market demand curve. For a single-price monopoly, marginal revenue is less than price, so the marginal revenue curve lies below the demand curve. A monopoly maximizes profit by producing the quantity at which marginal revenue equals marginal cost and finding the highest price at which it can sell this output on the demand curve.

3 Compare the performance of a single-price monopoly with that of perfect competition.

Compared to perfect competition, a single-price monopoly produces a smaller output and charges a higher price. A monopoly is inefficient because it creates a deadweight loss. A monopoly redistributes consumer surplus so that the producer gains and the consumers lose. Rent seeking is the act of obtaining special treatment by the government to create an economic profit or divert consumer surplus or producer surplus away from others. Rent seeking restricts competition and can create a monopoly.

4 Explain how price discrimination increases profit.

To be able to price discriminate, a firm must be able to identify and separate different types of buyers and sell a product that cannot be resold. Price discrimination converts consumer surplus into economic profit so price discrimination increases the firm's profit. Perfect price discrimination leaves no consumer surplus but is efficient.

5 Explain why natural monopoly is regulated and the effects of regulation.

Regulation generally sets the prices a regulated firm can charge. The social interest theory of regulation is that regulation seeks an efficient use of resources; the capture theory is that regulation helps producers maximize economic profit. Natural monopolies are usually regulated. A marginal cost pricing rule sets price equal to marginal cost and achieves an efficient level of output but the regulated firm incurs an economic loss. An average cost pricing rule sets price equal to average total cost. The firm earns a normal profit but there is a deadweight loss. Rate of return regulation sets the price so that the firm can earn a target rate of return on its capital. Price cap regulation specifies the highest price the firm can set.

CHECKPOINT 15.1

■ **Explain how monopoly arises and distinguish between single-price monopoly and price-discriminating monopoly.**

- *Barrier to entry* Any constraint that protects a firm from competitors.

Additional Practice Problem 15.1

1. What is the source of the monopoly for each of the following situations? What sort of barrier to entry protects these producers?
    a. The U.S. Postal Service has a monopoly on first class mail delivery.
    b. DeBeer's, while not truly a monopoly, nonetheless controls about 80 percent of the world's diamond sales.
    c. Tampa Electric is the only electric utility company supplying power to Tampa, Florida.

Solution to Additional Practice Problem 15.1

1a. The U.S. Postal Service derives its monopoly status by a government franchise to deliver first class mail. So the U.S. Postal Service is protected by a legal barrier to entry. Though it retains its franchise on first class mail delivery, it faces competition from the overnight services provided by FedEx, United Parcel Service, and others.

1b. DeBeers gained its monopoly power in diamond sales by buying up supplies of diamonds from sources throughout the world. So DeBeers is protected by an ownership barrier to entry.

1c. Tampa Electric has been granted a public franchise to be the only distributor of electricity in Tampa. Although Tampa Electric might be a natural monopoly, the public franchise, a legal barrier to entry, is perhaps the most immediate source of monopoly.

■ **Self Test 15.1**

Fill in the blanks

One of the requirements for monopoly is that there ____ (are; are no) close substitutes for the good. A ____ (legal; natural) monopoly exists when one firm can meet the entire market demand at a lower average total cost than two or more firms could. A monopoly that is able to sell different units of a good or service for different prices is a ____ (legal-price; natural-price; price-discriminating) monopoly.

True or false

1. A legal barrier creates a natural monopoly.
2. A firm experiences economies of scale along a downward-sloping long-run average total cost curve.
3. A monopoly always charges all customers the same price.

Multiple choice

1. A monopoly market has
    a. a few firms.
    b. a single firm.
    c. two dominating firms in the market.
    d. only two firms in it.
    e. some unspecified number of firms in it.

2. Two of the three types of barriers to entry that can protect a firm from competition are
    a. legal and illegal.
    b. natural and legal.
    c. natural and illegal.
    d. natural and rent seeking.
    e. ownership and rent seeking.

3. A natural monopoly is one that arises from
    a. patent law.
    b. copyright law.
    c. a firm buying up all of a natural resource.
    d. economies of scale.
    e. ownership of a natural resource.

4. A legal barrier is created when a firm
    a. has economies of scale, which allow it to produce at a lower cost than two or more firms.
    b. is granted a public franchise, government license, patent, or copyright.
    c. produces a unique product or service.
    d. produces a standardized product or service.
    e. has an ownership barrier to entry.

5. Pizza producers charge one price for a single pizza and almost give away a second one. This is an example of
   a. monopoly.
   b. a barrier to entry.
   c. behavior that is not profit-maximizing.
   d. price discrimination.
   e. rent seeking.

Short answer and numeric questions
1. What conditions define monopoly?
2. What are the two types of barriers to entry?
3. What are the two pricing strategies a monopoly can use? Why don't perfectly competitive firms have these same strategies?

CHECKPOINT 15.2

■ **Explain how a single-price monopoly determines its output and price.**

Quick Review
- *Marginal revenue* The change in total revenue resulting from a one-unit increase in the quantity sold.
- *Maximize profit* A single-price monopoly maximizes its profit by producing where $MR = MC$ and then using the demand curve to determine the price for this quantity of output.

Additional Practice Problems 15.2

Quantity (pizzas per hour)	Total cost (dollars per pizza)	Average total cost (dollars per pizza)	Marginal cost (dollars per pizza)
0	1.00		
1	6.00	___	___
2	13.00	___	___
3	22.00	___	___
4	33.00	___	___

1. In a small town, Leonardo's Pizza is the sole restaurant. The table above gives Leonardo's total cost schedule. Complete the table.

Quantity demanded (pizzas per hour)	Price (dollars per pizza)	Marginal revenue (dollars per pizza)
0	16.00	
1	14.00	___
2	12.00	___
3	10.00	___
4	8.00	___

2. The table above gives the demand schedule for Leonardo's pizzas. Complete the table.
3. In a figure, plot Leonardo's demand curve, average total cost curve, marginal cost curve, and marginal revenue curve.
   a. What is Leonardo's equilibrium quantity and price?
   b. What is Leonardo's economic profit or loss? In the figure show the economic profit or loss.

Solutions to Additional Practice Problems 15.2

Quantity (pizzas per hour)	Total cost (dollars per pizza)	Average total cost (dollars per pizza)	Marginal cost (dollars per pizza)
0	1.00		
			5.00
1	6.00	6.00	
			7.00
2	13.00	6.50	
			9.00
3	22.00	7.33	
			11.00
4	33.00	8.25	

1. The completed table is above.

Quantity demanded (pizzas per hour)	Price (dollars per pizza)	Marginal revenue (dollars per pizza)
0	16.00	
		14.00
1	14.00	
		10.00
2	12.00	
		6.00
3	10.00	
		2.00
4	8.00	

2. The completed table is above.

228 Part 5 · PRICES, PROFITS, AND INDUSTRY PERFORMANCE

3. The figure shows Leonardo's demand curve, average total cost curve, marginal cost curve, and marginal revenue curve.

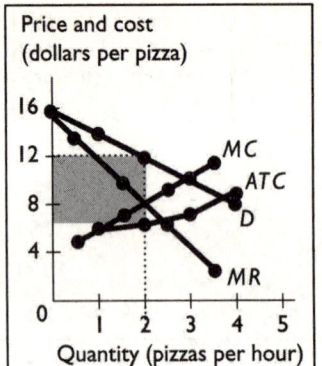

3a. Both a monopoly and a perfectly competitive firm maximize their profit by producing the quantity at which marginal revenue equals marginal cost. So Leonardo's maximizes its profit by producing 2 pizzas per hour. The price, from the demand curve, is $12 per pizza.

3b. Leonardo's sells each pizza for $12.00. The average total cost for 2 pizzas is $6.50. So for each pizza Leonardo's earns an economic profit of $5.50 for a total economic profit of $5.50 per pizza × 2 pizzas, or $11.00. This economic profit is equal to the area of the darkened rectangle in the figure.

■ **Self Test 15.2**

Fill in the blanks

For each level of output, marginal revenue for a single-price monopoly is ____ (greater than; equal to; less than) price. When demand is inelastic, marginal revenue is ____ (positive; negative). A single-price monopoly maximizes profit by producing the quantity at which marginal revenue ____ (is greater than; equals; is less than) marginal cost and then finds the highest price for which it can sell that output by using the ____ (demand; marginal revenue; average total cost) curve.

True or false

1. For a single-price monopoly, marginal revenue exceeds price.
2. Marginal revenue is always positive for a monopoly.
3. A single-price monopoly maximizes profit by producing the quantity at which marginal revenue equals marginal cost.

Multiple choice

1. For a single-price monopoly, price is
   a. greater than
   b. one half of marginal revenue
   c. equal to
   d. unrelated to marginal revenue.
   e. always less than average total cost when the firm maximizes its profit.

2. A single-price monopoly can sell 1 unit for $9.00. To sell 2 units, the price must be $8.50 per unit. The marginal revenue from selling the second unit is
   a. $17.50.
   b. $17.00.
   c. $8.50.
   d. $8.00.
   e. $9.00.

3. When demand is elastic, marginal revenue is
   a. positive.
   b. negative.
   c. zero.
   d. increasing as output increases.
   e. undefined.

4. To maximize profit, a single-price monopoly produces the quantity at which
   a. the difference between marginal revenue and marginal cost is as large as possible.
   b. marginal revenue is equal to marginal cost.
   c. average total cost is at its minimum.
   d. the marginal cost curve intersects the demand curve.
   e. the marginal revenue curve intersects the horizontal axis.

5. Once a monopoly has determined how much it produces, it will charge a price that
   a. is determined by the intersection of the marginal revenue and marginal cost curves.
   b. minimizes marginal cost.
   c. is determined by its demand curve.
   d. is independent of the amount produced.
   e. is equal to its average total cost.

Complete the graph

Quantity (hamburgers per hour)	Price (dollars)	Marginal revenue (dollars)
1	8.00	
2	7.00	___
3	6.00	___
4	5.00	___
5	4.00	___

1. The table above gives the demand schedule for Bud's Burgers, a monopoly seller of hamburgers in a small town. Complete the table by calculating the marginal revenue.

■ FIGURE 15.1
Price and marginal revenue (dollars per hamburger)

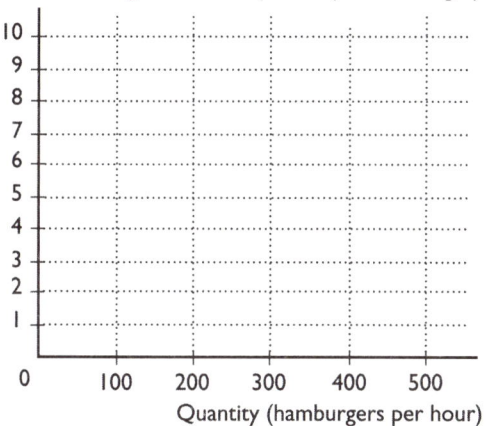

a. In Figure 15.1 draw the demand curve and marginal revenue curve.
b. Suppose the marginal cost is $3 no matter how many hamburgers Bud's produces. Draw the marginal cost curve in the figure. To maximize his profit, how many burgers will Bud grill in an hour and what will be their price?

■ FIGURE 15.2
Price and cost (dollars per unit)

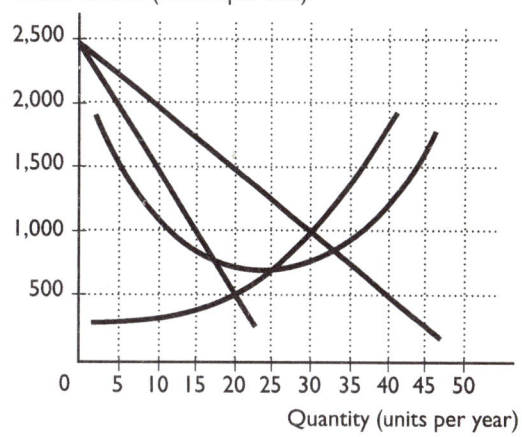

2. Figure 15.2 shows a monopoly's cost curves and demand and marginal revenue curves. Label the curves. Identify the profit-maximizing quantity price. Is the monopoly earning an economic profit or incurring an economic loss? Darken the area that shows the economic profit or economic loss.

Short answer and numeric questions
1. What is the relationship between the elasticity of demand and marginal revenue?
2. Both perfectly competitive and monopoly firms maximize their profit by producing where $MR = MC$. Why do both use the same rule?
3. Why can a monopoly earn an economic profit in the long run?

CHECKPOINT 15.3

■ **Compare the performance of a single-price monopoly with that of perfect competition.**

Quick Review
- *Monopoly and competition compared* Compared to perfect competition, a single-price monopoly produces a smaller output and charges a higher price.

Additional Practice Problems 15.3

1. In River Bend, Mississippi, suppose that the owners of the Acme cab company have convinced the city government to grant it a public franchise so it is the only cab company in town. Prior to this, the cab market in River Bend was perfectly competitive. The figure shows the market demand and marginal revenue curves for cab rides as well as the marginal cost curve.

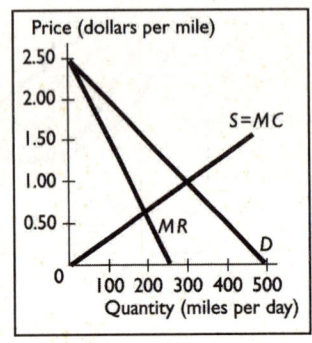

    a. Before the government granted Acme its monopoly, how many miles of taxi rides were driven and what was the price?
    b. As a monopoly, how many miles of taxi rides will Acme drive? What is the price Acme sets?
    c. What is the efficient number of miles?
    d. On the graph, show the deadweight loss that results from Acme's monopoly.

2. Suppose that Acme is put up for sale. Looking at the entire future, say Acme's total economic profit is $2 million. If the bidding for Acme is a competitive process, what do you expect will be the price for which the company is sold? What result are you illustrating?

Solutions to Additional Practice Problems 15.3

1a. Before the monopoly was granted, the equilibrium number of miles and price were determined by the demand and supply curves. As the figure shows, the equilibrium number of miles was 300 miles per day and the price was $1.00 per mile.

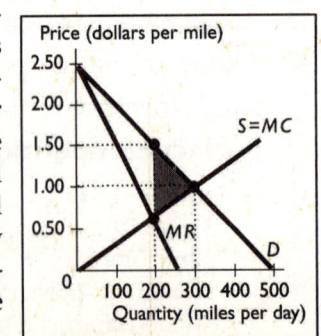

1b. To maximize its profit, the figure shows that Acme drives 200 miles per day because that is the quantity at which marginal revenue equals marginal cost. The price is set from the demand curve and is $1.50 per mile.

1c. The efficient quantity is the quantity at which marginal benefit equals marginal cost. The demand curve is the marginal benefit curve, so the figure shows that the efficient quantity is 300 miles a day.

1d. Single-price monopolies create a deadweight loss because a monopoly produces where $MR = MC$ but efficiency requires production where $MB = MC$. The figure illustrates the deadweight loss as the darkened triangle.

2. Bidders are willing to pay up to $2 million for Acme because if they can buy it for any price less than $2 million, they receive an economic profit. Because the bidding is competitive, the price of Acme will be bid up to $2 million, so that the winning bidder earns a normal profit. This result demonstrates rent-seeking equilibrium in which the rent-seeking costs exhaust the economic profit.

■ **Self Test 15.3**

Fill in the blanks

Compared to perfect competition, a single-price monopoly produces a ____ (larger; smaller) output and charges a ____ (higher; lower) price. A single-price monopoly ____ (creates; does not create) a deadweight loss. The act of obtaining special treatment by the government to create an economic profit is called ____ (government surplus; rent seeking). Rent seeking ____ (decreases; increases) the amount of deadweight loss.

True or false

1. A monopoly charges a higher price than a perfectly competitive industry would charge.
2. A monopoly redistributes consumer surplus so that the consumers gain and the producer loses.
3. The buyer of a monopoly always makes an economic profit.

Multiple choice

1. If a perfectly competitive industry is taken over by a single firm that operates as a single-price monopoly, the price will ____ and the quantity will ____.
   a. fall; decrease
   b. fall; increase
   c. rise; decrease
   d. rise; increase
   e. not change; decrease

FIGURE 15.3
Price and costs (dollars per gallon)

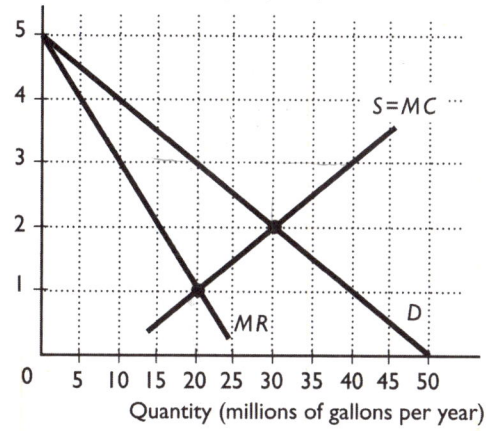

2. Figure 15.3 shows the market for gasoline in a town. If the market is perfectly competitive, the price is ____ per gallon and if the market is taken over by a firm that operates as a single-price monopoly, the price is ____.
   a. $1; $2
   b. $1; $3
   c. $1; $1
   d. $2; $1
   e. $2; $3

3. Figure 15.3 shows the market for gasoline in a town. If the market is perfectly competitive, the quantity is ____ million gallons a year and if the market is taken over by a firm that operates as a single-price monopoly, the quantity is ____ million gallons a year.
   a. 50; 20
   b. 50; 30
   c. 30; 20
   d. 50; 10
   e. 20; 30

4. Comparing single-price monopoly to perfect competition, monopoly
   a. increases the amount of consumer surplus.
   b. has the same amount of consumer surplus.
   c. has no consumer surplus.
   d. decreases the amount of consumer surplus.
   e. decreases the amount of economic profit.

5. Is a single-price monopoly efficient?
   a. Yes, because it creates a deadweight loss.
   b. No, because it creates a deadweight loss.
   c. Yes, because consumers gain and producers lose some of their surpluses.
   d. Yes, because consumers lose and producers gain some of their surpluses.
   e. Yes, because it produces the quantity at which $MR=MC$.

6. Monopolies
   a. are always fair but are not efficient.
   b. might or might not be fair and are always efficient.
   c. might or might not be fair and are generally inefficient.
   d. are always fair and are always efficient.
   e. are never fair and are always efficient.

7. In equilibrium, rent seeking eliminates the
   a. deadweight loss.
   b. economic profit.
   c. consumer surplus.
   d. demand for the product.
   e. opportunity to price discriminate.

Complete the graph

FIGURE 15.4
Price and costs (dollars per ostrich)

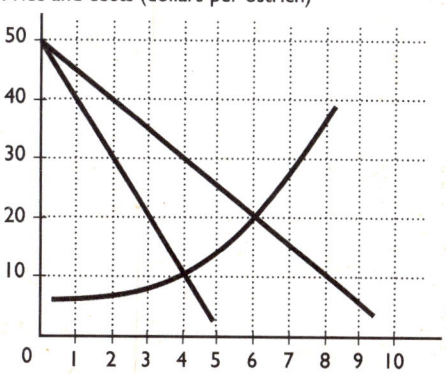

1. Figure 15.4 shows the market for ostrich

farming, an industry that is initially perfectly competitive. Then one farmer buys all the other farms and operates as a single-price monopoly. In the figure, label the curves. What was the competitive price and quantity? What is the monopoly price and quantity? Darken the deadweight loss area.

Short answer and numeric questions

1. How does the quantity produced and the price set by a single-price monopoly compare to those in a perfectly competitive market?
2. What happens to consumer surplus with a single-price monopoly?
3. What is rent seeking? How does rent seeking affect society?

CHECKPOINT 15.4

■ **Explain how price discrimination increases profit.**

Quick Review
- *Price discrimination* Price discrimination is selling a good at a number of different prices.
- *Consumer surplus* The consumer surplus of a good is its marginal benefit, which equals the maximum price the consumer is willing to pay, minus the price paid for it summed over the quantity consumed.

Additional Practice Problems 15.4

1. Frequently the price of the first scoop of ice cream in a cone is less than the price of the second scoop. Why is this the case?
2. Why is the price to attend a movie less on a weekday afternoon than on a weekend evening?
3. How does price discrimination affect the amount of consumer surplus? The amount of the firm's economic profit?

Solutions to Additional Practice Problems 15.4

1. The ice cream store is price discriminating among units of the good by charging different prices for different scoops of ice cream. The store knows that consumers' marginal benefits from ice cream decrease, so that the consumer is willing to pay less for the second scoop than for the first scoop. By charging less for the second scoop, the store will sell more scoops and increase its profit.
2. When the price to attend a movie is less on a weekday afternoon than on a weekend evening, the movie theater is practicing price discrimination among two groups of buyers. Each group has a different average willingness to pay to see a movie. By having two different prices, the movie theater maximizes profit by converting consumer surplus into economic profit.
3. Price discrimination decreases consumer surplus because it allows the business to set a price that is closer to the maximum the consumer is willing to pay. Price discrimination increases the firm's profit, which is why firms price discriminate.

■ **Self Test 15.4**

Fill in the blanks

It is ____ (sometimes; never) possible for a monopoly to charge different customers different prices. The key idea behind price discrimination is to convert ____ (consumer surplus; producer surplus) into economic profit. Price discrimination results in consumers with a higher willingness paying a ____ (higher; lower) price than consumers with a lower willingness to pay. Perfect price discrimination results in ____ (the maximum; zero) consumer surplus and ____ (creates; does not create) a deadweight loss.

True or false

1. Price discrimination lowers a firm's profit.
2. Price discrimination converts producer surplus into consumer surplus.
3. With perfect price discrimination, the firm produces the efficient quantity of output and has a larger profit than it would if it did not price discriminate.

Multiple choice

1. Which of the following must a firm be able to do to successfully price discriminate?
   i. divide buyers into different groups according to their willingness to pay
   ii. prevent resale of the good or service
   iii. identify into which group (high willingness to pay or low willingness to pay) a buyer falls
   a. ii only.
   b. i and ii.
   c. i and iii.
   d. iii only.
   e. i, ii, and iii.

2. Which of the following is (are) price discrimination?
   i. charging different prices based on differences in production cost
   ii. charging business flyers a higher airfare than tourists
   iii. charging more for the first pizza than the second
   a. i only.
   b. ii only.
   c. ii and iii.
   d. i and iii.
   e. i, ii, and iii.

3. When a monopoly price discriminates, it
   a. increases the amount of consumer surplus.
   b. decreases its economic profit.
   c. converts consumer surplus into economic profit.
   d. converts economic profit into consumer surplus.
   e. has no effect on the deadweight loss.

4. If a monopoly is able to perfectly price discriminate, then consumer surplus is
   a. equal to zero.
   b. maximized.
   c. unchanged from what it is with a single-price monopoly.
   d. unchanged from what it is in a perfectly competitive industry.
   e. not zero but is less than with a single-price monopoly.

5. With perfect price discrimination, the quantity of output produced by the monopoly is ____ the quantity produced by a perfectly competitive industry.
   a. greater than but not equal to
   b. less than
   c. equal to but not greater than
   d. not comparable to
   e. either greater than or equal to

Complete the graph

■ FIGURE 15.5

Price and cost (dollars per article of clothing)

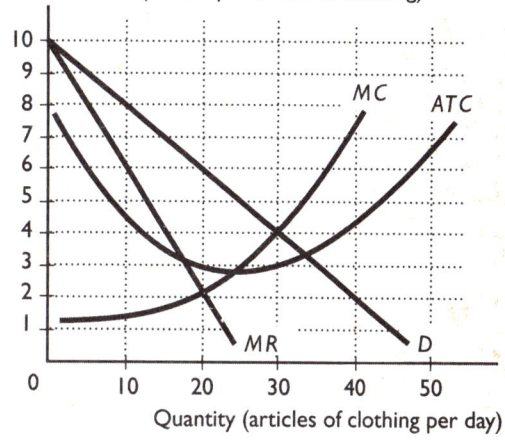

Quantity (articles of clothing per day)

1. Figure 15.5 shows the cost and demand curves for a dry-cleaner that has a monopoly in a small town.
   a. In the figure, lightly darken the area of the economic profit for a single-price monopoly. What is the amount of economic profit this firm earns?
   b. Suppose the firm can price discriminate and set one price for the first 10 articles of clothing and another price for the second 10 articles of clothing. What prices would it set? Darken the additional economic profit the firm earns. What is the amount of the firms economic profit now?
   c. Suppose the firm is able to perfectly price discriminate. More heavily darken the additional economic profit the firm now earns. What is the amount of the firm's economic profit now?

Short answer and numeric questions

1. Explain the effect of price discrimination on consumer surplus and economic profit.
2. When does a price discriminating monopoly produce the efficient quantity of output?

CHECKPOINT 15.5

■ **Explain why natural monopoly is regulated and the effects of regulation.**

- *Marginal cost pricing rule* A price rule for a natural monopoly that sets price equal to marginal cost.
- *Average cost pricing rule* A price rule for a natural monopoly that sets price equal to average cost.

Additional Practice Problems 15.5

1. The figure shows the demand and cost curves for the local water distributing company. The company is a natural monopoly.
   a. If the company is unregulated, what price does it charge for water and how much is distributed? Does the firm earn an economic profit, a normal profit, or an economic loss?
   b. If the company is regulated using an average cost pricing rule, what price does it charge for water and how much is distributed? Does the firm earn an economic profit, a normal profit, or an economic loss?
   c. If the company is regulated using a marginal cost pricing rule, what price does it charge for water and how much is distributed? Does the firm earn an economic profit, a normal profit, or an economic loss?

2. The Airmail Act of 1934 awarded airline routes on the basis of competitive bidding. The airlines bid for routes (the bids were the fares the airline would charge) and the low bidder won. The Interstate Commerce Commission regulated the fares. Frequently, after having won a route, an airline was allowed to raise its fare to a profitable level.

   The Civil Aeronautics Act was passed in 1938 and served to regulate airlines for the next four decades. There was complete control over entry and exit, as well as fare and route structure. Over this period of time, virtually no new airlines were allowed to enter the market. For two decades after World War II, utilization continued to decline until less than half of seating capacity was being utilized.

   In 1978, the airlines opposed deregulation but nonetheless deregulation occurred. Airlines were free to enter or exit and were also free to determine the fare they would charge. Since deregulation in 1978, passenger airline miles have more than doubled, prices have fallen, and mergers have occurred.

   Which theory, the social interest or capture theory, best describes each of these three periods of the airline industry history?

Solutions to Additional Practice Problems 15.5

1a. An unregulated monopoly produces the quantity where marginal revenue equals marginal cost and the price is determined by the demand curve. In the figure, marginal revenue equals marginal cost when 2 thousand gallons of water per day are distributed. The price is $6 per thousand gallons. The firm earns an economic profit.

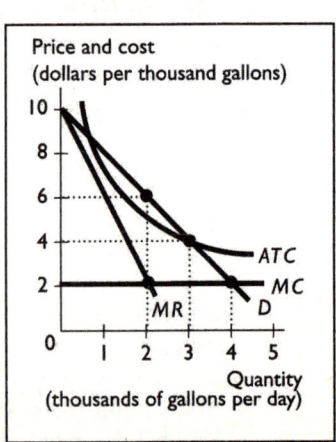

1b. If an average cost pricing rule is used, price and quantity are determined by where the average total cost curve intersects the demand curve. From the figure, the price is $4 per thousand gallons and the quantity is 3 thousand gallons per day. The firm earns a normal profit.

1c. If a marginal cost pricing rule is used, price and quantity are determined by where the marginal cost curve intersects the demand curve. From the figure, the price is $2 per thousand gallons and the quantity is 4 thousand gallons per day. The firm incurs an economic loss.

2. From 1934 to 1938, the competitive bidding suggests that social interest might have been more important than in the 1938 to 1978 period. But during the early four-year period, airlines were learning to expect a handout from government regulators.

During the four-decade era of the Civil Aeronautics Act, the industry is best described by the capture theory. Airlines were protected from competition by new entrants. They also faced little competition from existing airlines because fares were fixed. Competition took the form of frills, such as fancy dinners, champagne, and attractive accommodations and services.

Since 1978 airline behavior more typically resembles social interest theory and has as its legacy lower prices, higher capacity utilization, new low-fare entrants, bankruptcies, and mergers.

■ Self Test 15.5

Fill in the blanks
The theory that regulation seeks an efficient use of resources is the ____ (capture; social interest) theory, and the theory that regulation helps producers maximize economic profit is the ____ (capture; social interest) theory. With ____ (an average; a marginal) cost pricing rule, a natural monopoly incurs an economic loss. Regulated firms have an incentive to inflate their costs under ____ (rate of return; price cap) regulation.

True or false
1. Social interest theory assumes that the political process introduces regulation that eliminates deadweight loss.
2. A regulated natural monopoly produces the efficient quantity of output when it is regulated to use a marginal cost pricing rule.
3. Price cap regulation is designed to give firms the incentive to raise the price of their output, provided competition in the market increases.

Multiple choice
1. The theory that regulation seeks an efficient use of resources is the
   a. social interest theory.
   b. producer surplus theory.
   c. consumer surplus theory.
   d. capture theory.
   e. deadweight loss theory.

2. Which of the following best describes the capture theory of regulation?
   i. Regulation seeks an efficient use of resources
   ii. Regulation is aimed at keeping prices as low as possible
   iii. Regulation helps firms maximize economic profit
   a. i only.
   b. ii only.
   c. iii only.
   d. i and ii.
   e. i, ii, and iii.

3. At a level of output when regulators require a natural monopoly to set a price that is equal to marginal cost, the firm
   a. earns a normal profit.
   b. earns an economic profit.
   c. incurs an economic loss.
   d. earns a normal-economic profit.
   e. earns either a normal profit or an economic profit, depending on whether the firm's average total cost equals or is less than the marginal cost.

4. If a natural monopoly is told to set price equal to average cost, then the firm
   a. is not able to set marginal revenue equal to marginal cost.
   b. automatically also sets price equal to marginal cost.
   c. will earn a substantial economic profit.
   d. will incur an economic loss
   e. sets a price that is lower than its marginal cost.

■ FIGURE 15.6
Price and cost (dollars per month)

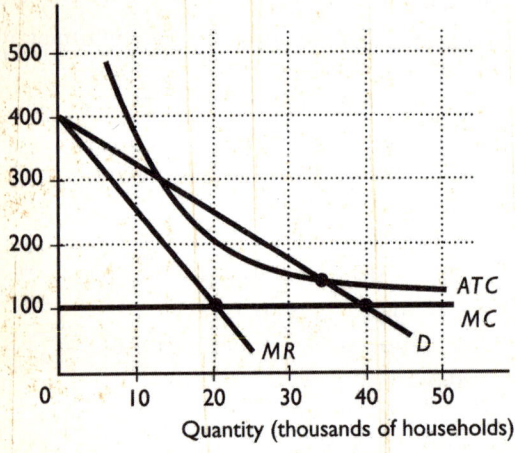

5. If the natural monopoly illustrated in Figure 15.6 was regulated using a marginal cost pricing rule, the price would be ____.
   a. $100
   b. between $100.01 and $200.00
   c. between $200.01 and $300.00
   d. between $300.01 and $400.00
   e. more than $400.01

6. If the natural monopoly illustrated in Figure 15.6 was regulated using an average total cost pricing rule, the price would be ____.
   a. $100
   b. between $100.01 and $200.00
   c. between $200.01 and $300.00
   d. between $300.01 and $400.00
   e. more than $400.01

7. If the natural monopoly illustrated in Figure 15.6 was unregulated, the price would be ____.
   a. $100
   b. between $100.01 and $200.00
   c. between $200.01 and $300.00
   d. between $300.01 and $400.00
   e. more than $400.01

Complete the graph

■ FIGURE 15.7
Price and cost (dollars per month)

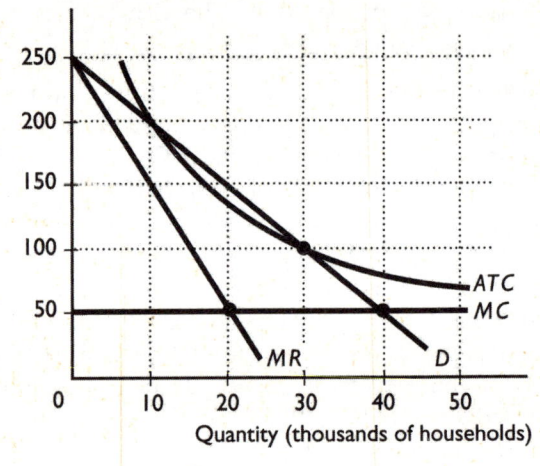

1. Figure 15.7 shows both the average total cost curves of a cable TV company that is a regulated monopoly. Also given are the demand curve and marginal revenue curve.
   a. What price would the regulator set using the marginal cost pricing rule?
   b. What price would the regulator set using the average cost pricing rule?
   c. What price would the firm set if it was unregulated?

Short answer and numeric questions

1. Why doesn't the government regulate all industries?
2. What is the social interest theory of regulation? The capture theory?
3. What is the advantage of using a marginal cost pricing rule to regulate a natural monopoly? The disadvantage?
5. What is the goal of price cap regulation?

SELF TEST ANSWERS

■ CHECKPOINT 15.1

Fill in the blanks
One of the requirements for monopoly is that there <u>are no</u> close substitutes for the good. A <u>natural</u> monopoly exists when one firm can meet the entire market demand at a lower average total cost than two or more firms could. A monopoly that is able to sell different units of a good or service for different prices is a <u>price-discriminating</u> monopoly.

True or false
1. False; pages 376-377
2. True; page 377
3. False; page 378

Multiple choice
1. b; page 376
2. b; page 376
3. d; page 376
4. b; page 377
5. d; page 378

Short answer and numeric questions
1. Monopoly occurs when there is a market with a single firm selling a good or service that has no close substitutes and in which the firm is protected by either a natural, ownership, or a legal barrier to entry; page 376.
2. Barriers to entry are anything that protects a firm from the entry of new competitors. Barriers to entry are either natural barriers, ownership barriers, or legal barriers; pages 376-377.
3. A monopoly can sell each unit of its output for the same price to all its customers or it can price discriminate by selling different units of its good or service at different prices. A perfectly competitive firm cannot affect the price so it must charge a single price determined by market demand and market supply; page 378.

■ CHECKPOINT 15.2

Fill in the blanks
For each level of output, marginal revenue for a single-price monopoly is <u>less than</u> price. When demand is inelastic, marginal revenue is <u>negative</u>. A single-price monopoly maximizes profit by producing the quantity at which marginal revenue <u>equals</u> marginal cost and then finds the highest price for which it can sell that output by using the <u>demand</u> curve.

True or false
1. False; page 380
2. False; page 381
3. True; page 383

Multiple choice
1. a; page 380
2. d; page 380
3. a; page 381
4. b; page 383
5. c; page 383

Complete the graph

Quantity (hamburgers per hour)	Price (dollars)	Marginal revenue (dollars)
1	8.00	
		6.00
2	7.00	
		4.00
3	6.00	
		2.00
4	5.00	
		0.00
5	4.00	

1. The completed table is above
    a. Figure 15.8 (on the next page) plots the demand and marginal revenue curves; page 383.
    b. Figure 15.8 shows the marginal cost curve. To maximize his profit, Bud produces the quantity at which marginal revenue equals marginal cost. So Bud prepares 300 hamburgers per hour. From the demand curve, the price of a hamburger is $6; pages 382-383.

■ FIGURE 15.8
Price and marginal revenue (dollars per hamburger)

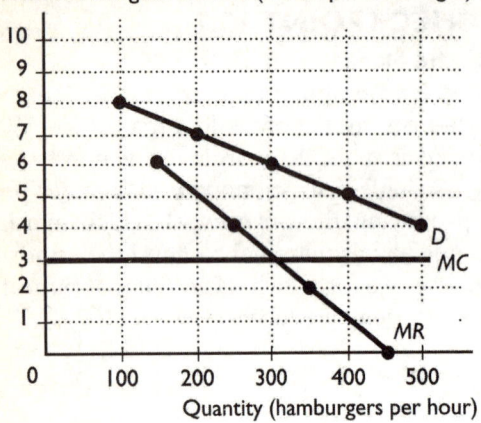

■ FIGURE 15.9
Price and cost (dollars per unit)

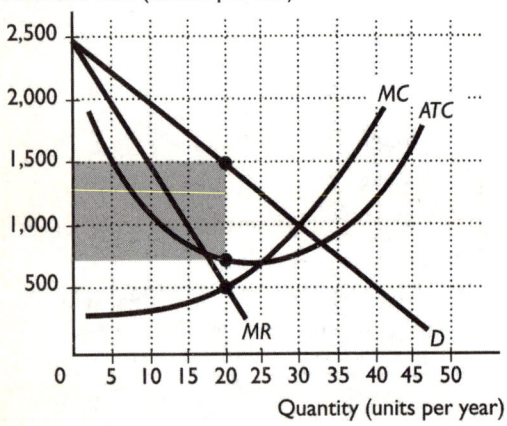

2. The curves are labeled in Figure 15.9. The profit-maximizing quantity is 20 units and the price is $1,500. The economic profit equals the area of the dark rectangle; page 383.

Short answer and numeric questions
1. If demand is elastic, marginal revenue is positive; if demand is unit elastic, marginal revenue is zero; and if demand is inelastic, marginal revenue is negative; page 381.
2. Both perfectly competitive and monopoly firms maximize profit by producing where $MR = MC$ because for *any* firm, a unit of output is produced if $MR > MC$ and is not produced if $MR < MC$. As long as $MR > MC$, *any* firm increases its total profit by continuing to produce additional output until it reaches the point at which $MR = MC$; pages 382-383.
3. A monopoly can earn an economic profit in the long run because it is protected by a barrier to entry. Other firms want to enter the market in order also to earn some economic profit, but they cannot do so; page 383.

■ CHECKPOINT 15.3
Fill in the blanks
Compared to perfect competition, a single-price monopoly produces a <u>smaller</u> output and charges a <u>higher</u> price. A single-price monopoly <u>creates</u> a deadweight loss. The act of obtaining special treatment by the government to create an economic profit is called <u>rent seeking</u>. Rent seeking <u>increases</u> the amount of deadweight loss.

True or false
1. True; page 385
2. False; page 386
3. False; page 387

Multiple choice
1. c; page 385
2. e; page 385
3. c; page 385
4. d; page 386
5. b; page 386
6. c; page 387
7. b; page 388

Complete the graph
■ FIGURE 15.10
Price and cost (dollars per ostrich)

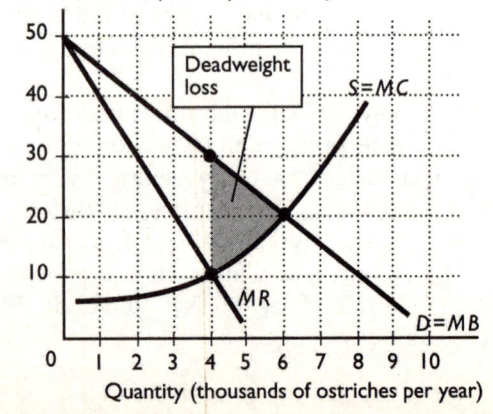

1. Figure 15.10 shows that the perfectly com-

petitive price is $20 an ostrich and the quantity is 3,000 ostriches. The monopoly price is $30 an ostrich and the quantity is 2,000 ostriches a year. The deadweight loss is the dark triangular area; page 386.

Short answer and numeric questions
1. The price set by a monopoly exceeds the price in a competitive market and the quantity produced by a monopoly is less than the quantity produced in a competitive market; page 386.
2. Consumer surplus decreases with a single-price monopoly. Consumer surplus decreases because the monopoly produces less output and charges a higher price; page 386.
3. Rent seeking is the act of obtaining special treatment by the government to create economic profit or to divert consumer surplus or producer surplus away from others. Rent seeking harms society because in a competitive rent-seeking equilibrium, the amount of the deadweight loss increases; page 387.

■ CHECKPOINT 15.4
Fill in the blanks
It is <u>sometimes</u> possible for a monopoly to charge different customers different prices. The key idea behind price discrimination is to convert <u>consumer surplus</u> into economic profit. Price discrimination results in consumers with a higher willingness paying a <u>higher</u> price than consumers with a lower willingness to pay. Perfect price discrimination results in <u>zero</u> consumer surplus and <u>does not create</u> a deadweight loss.

True or false
1. False; pages 390-392
2. False; page 390
3. True; page 393

Multiple choice
1. e; page 390
2. c; page 390
3. c; pages 390-392
4. a; pages 393
5. c; page 393

Complete the graph
■ **FIGURE 15.11**
Price and cost (dollars per article of clothing)

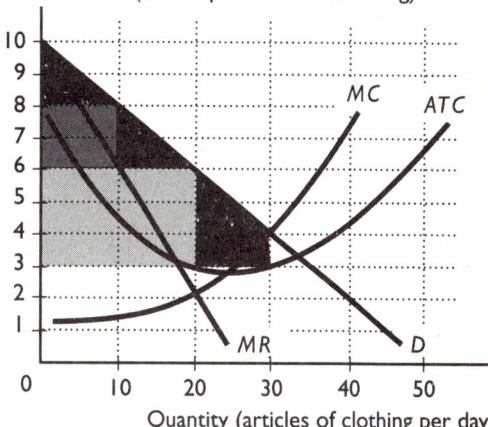

1. a. The economic profit is the light gray rectangle in Figure 15.11. The economic profit equals the area of the rectangle, which is $60 a day; page 391.
   b. The firm will set a price of $8 for each of the first 10 articles and $6 for each of the second 10 articles. The added profit is the darker gray rectangle for the first 10 articles. The total economic profit the firm now earns is $80 a day; page 392.
   c. The economic profit is increased by the addition of the three very dark gray areas. The economic profit is now $120 a day; page 393.

Short answer and numeric questions
1. Price discrimination decreases consumer surplus and increases economic profit. Price discrimination allows the firm to charge a price closer to the maximum the consumer is willing to pay, which is the marginal benefit of the good. Consumer surplus is converted into economic profit; page 390.
2. With perfect price discrimination, the monopoly increases output to the point at which price equals marginal cost. This output is identical to that of perfect competition. Deadweight loss with perfect price discrimination is zero. So perfect price discrimination produces the efficient quantity; page 393.

■ CHECKPOINT 15.5

Fill in the blanks

The theory that regulation seeks an efficient use of resources is the <u>social interest</u> theory, and the theory that regulation helps producers maximize economic profit is the <u>capture</u> theory. With <u>a marginal</u> cost pricing rule, a natural monopoly incurs an economic loss. Regulated firms have an incentive to inflate their costs under <u>rate of return</u> regulation.

True or false

1. True; page 397
2. True; page 398
3. False; page 401

Multiple choice

1. a; page 397
2. c; page 397
3. c; page 398
4. a; page 399
5. a; page 398
6. b; page 399
7. c; page 383

Complete the graph

1. a. Using marginal cost pricing, the regulator sets a price of $50 a month; pages 397.
   b. Using average cost pricing, the regulator sets a price of $100 a month; page 399.
   c. The firm serves 20,000 household, where marginal revenue equals marginal cost, and sets the price at $150 a month.

Short answer and numeric questions

1. The government does not regulate all industries because not all industries need to be regulated. Competitive industries do not need regulation because competition produces an efficient outcome. But a natural monopoly is not a competitive industry and so government regulation might help move the monopoly toward efficiency; pages 396-401.

2. The social interest theory of regulation is that the regulators pursue the public's interest by devising regulation that achieves an efficient use of resources. The capture theory of regulation is that the producers have "captured the regulators" and, as a result, the regulation helps producers maximize their economic profit; page 397.

3. The advantage of using a marginal cost pricing rule is that the firm produces the efficient quantity of output. The disadvantage is that the firm incurs an economic loss; page 398.

4. Price cap regulation gives regulated firms the incentive to cut their costs and produce efficiently, without exaggerating their costs or wasting resources; page 401.

Chapter 16

Monopolistic Competition

CHAPTER CHECKLIST

In Chapter 16 we study a market structure that lies between the extremes of perfect competition and monopoly: monopolistic competition.

1 Describe and identify monopolistic competition.

Monopolistic competition is a market structure in which a large number of firms compete; each firm produces a differentiated product; firms compete on product quality, price, and marketing; and firms are free to enter and exit. Product differentiation is making a product that is slightly different from the products of competing firms. Product differentiation allows the firm to compete on product quality, price, and marketing. There are no barriers to entry in monopolistic competition. The four-firm concentration ratio and the Herfindahl-Hirschman Index (HHI) measure the extent to which a market is dominated by a small number of firms. The four-firm concentration ratio is the percentage of the value of the sales accounted for by the four largest firms in the industry. The Herfindahl-Hirschman Index is the square of the percentage market share of each firm summed over the 50 largest firms in the market.

2 Explain how a firm in monopolistic competition determines its output and price in the short run and the long run.

A firm in monopolistic competition has a downward-sloping demand curve. A firm in monopolistic competition makes its output and price decisions just like a monopoly firm does. It maximizes profit by producing the output at which marginal revenue equals marginal cost. The price is determined from the demand curve and is the highest price for which the firm can sell the quantity it produces. In the short run, the firm might have an economic profit or an economic loss. Entry and exit result in zero economic profit in the long run. In the long run a firm in monopolistic competition has excess capacity because it produces less than the efficient scale. In monopolistic competition price exceeds marginal cost, which indicates inefficiency, but the inefficiency arises from product variety, a gain for consumers.

3 Explain why advertising costs are high and why firms use brand names in monopolistic competition.

To maintain economic profit, firms in monopolistic competition innovate and develop new products, and incur huge costs to ensure that buyers appreciate the differences between their own products and those of their competitors. Selling costs, such as advertising, increase a firm's *total* cost, but they might lower *average* total cost if they increase the quantity sold by a large enough amount. Firms advertise to send a signal to the consumer that the product is high quality. Brand names also send a signal to the consumer about the product's quality. They also give the firm the incentive to maintain the expected level of product quality. Advertising and brand names provide consumers with information, but the opportunity cost of the additional information must be weighed against the gain to the consumer. So the efficiency of monopolistic competition is ambiguous.

CHECKPOINT 16.1

■ **Describe and identify monopolistic competition.**

Quick Review

- *Four-firm concentration ratio* The four-firm concentration ratio is the percentage of the value of sales accounted for by the four largest firms in the industry.
- *Herfindahl-Hirschman Index (HHI)* The HHI is the square of the percentage market share of each firm summed over the 50 largest firms (or summed over all the firms if there are fewer than 50) in a market.

Additional Practice Problem 16.1

Firm	Total revenue (millions of dollars)	Percent of total revenue (percent)
McDonald's	1,200	____
Burger King	600	____
Wendy's	600	____
Hardee's	300	____
Checker's	180	____
Other 20 smaller firms	720	____

1. The table gives some hypothetical data on sales in the fast-food hamburger market. Suppose that the total revenue of each of the 20 smallest firms is the same and each has total revenue of $36 million.
   a. Complete the table.
   b. Calculate the four-firm concentration ratio.
   c. Calculate the Herfindahl-Hirschman Index.
   d. Based on the hypothetical concentration ratios, in what market structure would you classify the fast-food hamburger market?

Solution to Additional Practice Problem 16.1

1a. The total revenue shares are in the table above. To calculate the total revenue shares, first determine the total revenue within the market, which is $3,600 million. A firm's total revenue equals its total revenue divided by $3,600 million and then multiplied by 100.

Firm	Total revenue (millions of dollars)	Percent of total revenue (percent)
McDonald's	1,200	33.3
Burger King	600	16.7
Wendy's	600	16.7
Hardee's	300	8.3
Checker's	180	5.0
Other 20 smaller firms	720	20.0

1b. The four-firm concentration ratio is the percentage of the total revenue accounted for by the four largest firms in the industry, which is 33.3 percent + 16.7 percent + 16.7 percent + 8.3 percent = 75.0 percent.

1c. To calculate the Herfindahl-Hirschman Index (HHI), we need to square and then sum the market shares of the firms. The market shares are equal to each firm's percentage of total revenue. Each of the 20 smaller firms has total revenue of $36 million, so each has a 1 percentage point market share. So the HHI = $(33.3)^2 + (16.7)^2 + (16.7)^2 + (8.3)^2 + (5.0)^2 + (1.0)^2 \times 20 = 1,108.89 + 278.89 + 278.89 + 68.89 + 25.00 + 20.00$, which is 1,780.56.

1d. Based on concentration ratios, the fast-food hamburger market is just on the borderline between monopolistic competition and oligopoly. To make a decision whether this industry is monopolistically competitive or an oligopoly, information about the presence or absence of barriers to entry is needed.

■ **Self Test 16.1**

Fill in the blanks

In monopolistic competition there are a ____ (large; small) number of firms producing ____ (identical; differentiated) products. Firms in monopolistic competition ____ (do; do not) compete on product quality. In monopolistic competition, barriers to entry ____ (do not exist; exist). The square of the percentage market share of each firm summed over the 50 largest firms (or summed over all firms if there are fewer than 50) is the ____ (50-firm concentration ratio; Herfindahl-Hirschman Index). Concentration ratios ____ (do; do not) measure barriers to entry.

True or false

1. Firms in monopolistic competition are free to enter or exit the market.
2. Each firm in monopolistic competition constantly tries to collude with its competitors.
3. The goods and services produced by firms in monopolistic competition all have virtually the same, if not identical, quality.
4. The larger the four-firm concentration ratio, the more competitive the industry.
5. Concentration ratios might overstate the degree of competition within an industry because concentration ratios take a national view of the market.

Multiple choice

1. In monopolistic competition there
   a. are a large number of firms.
   b. are several large firms.
   c. is one large firm.
   d. might be many, several, or one firm.
   e. are many firms but only a few buyers.

2. A firm in monopolistic competition has a ____ market share and ____ influence the price of its good or service.
   a. large; can
   b. large; cannot
   c. small; can
   d. small; cannot
   e. large; might be able to

3. Product differentiation means
   a. making a product that has perfect substitutes.
   b. making a product that is entirely unique.
   c. the inability to set your own price.
   d. making a product that is slightly different from products of competing firms.
   e. making your demand curve horizontal.

4. A firm in monopolistic competition has ____ demand curve.
   a. a downward-sloping
   b. an upward-sloping
   c. a vertical
   d. a horizontal
   e. a U-shaped

5. Firms in monopolistic competition compete on
   i. quality.
   ii. price.
   iii. marketing.
   a. i and ii.
   b. ii only.
   c. ii and iii.
   d. i and iii.
   e. i, ii, and iii.

6. The absence of barriers to entry in monopolistic competition means that in the long run firms
   a. earn an economic profit.
   b. earn zero economic profit.
   c. incur an economic loss.
   d. earn either an economic profit or a normal profit.
   e. earn either a normal profit or suffer an economic loss.

7. Each of the ten firms in an industry has 10 percent of the industry's total revenue. The four-firm concentration ratio is
   a. 80.
   b. 100.
   c. 1,000.
   d. 40.
   e. 10.

8. Each of the four firms in an industry has a market share of 25 percent. The Herfindahl-Hirschman Index equals
   a. 3,600.
   b. 100.
   c. 625.
   d. 25.
   e. 2,500.

9. If the four-firm concentration ratio for the market for pizza is 28 percent, then this industry is best characterized as
   a. a monopoly.
   b. monopolistic competition.
   c. an oligopoly.
   d. perfect competition.
   e. oligoplistic competition.

10. The larger the four-firm concentration ratio, the ____ competition within an industry; the larger the Herfindahl-Hirschman Index, the ____ competition within an industry.
   a. more; more
   b. more; less
   c. less; more
   d. less; less
   e. The premise of the question is wrong because the four-firm concentration ratio applies only to markets with four firms in it and these markets are, by definition, not competitive.

Short answer and numeric questions
1. What conditions define monopolistic competition?

Firm	Total revenue (millions of dollars)	Percent of total revenue (percent)
Dell	1,000	____
HP	800	____
IBM	500	____
Toshiba	400	____
Other 46 smaller firms	2,300	____

2. The table gives some hypothetical data on sales in the desktop computer market. Suppose that the total revenue of each of the 46 smallest firms is the same and each has total revenue of $50 million.
   a. Complete the table.
   b. Calculate the four-firm concentration ratio.
   c. Calculate the Herfindahl-Hirschman Index.

3. Industry A has 1 firm with a market share of 57 percent and 43 other firms, each with a market share of 1 percent. Industry B has 4 firms, each with a market share of 15 percent, and 40 other firms, each with a market share of 1 percent.
   a. Calculate the four-firm concentration ratio for the two industries.
   b. Calculate the Herfindahl-Hirschman Index for the two industries.

CHECKPOINT 16.2

■ **Explain how a firm in monopolistic competition determines its output and price in the short run and the long run.**

Quick Review
- *Profit maximization* A firm in monopolistic competition produces where marginal revenue equals marginal cost. The price is determined from the demand curve.

Additional Practice Problems 16.2
1. The figure shows the demand and costs for Bernie's Burger barn, a firm in monopolistic competition.
   a. To maximize its profit, how many burgers does Bernie produce in an hour? What is the price of a hamburger?
   b. Is the firm earning an economic profit or loss and, if so, how much?
   c. Does this figure show the firm in the short run or the long run? Explain your answer.

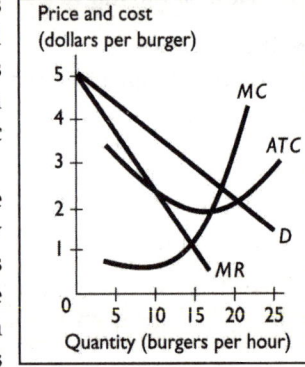

2. The Piece A' Pie company is a pizza restaurant in competition with many other pizza restaurants. Piece A' Pie produces 50 pizzas an hour.
   a. If Piece A' Pie's average total cost is $10 a pizza and its price is $12 a pizza, what is its economic profit?
   b. If Piece A' Pie's average total cost is $12 a pizza and its price is $12 a pizza, what is its economic profit?
   c. If Piece A' Pie's average total cost is $15 a pizza and its price is $12 a pizza, what is its economic profit?
   d. Which of the three situations outlined in parts (a), (b), and (c) can represent a short-run equilibrium? A long-run equilibrium? Why?

Solutions to Additional Practice Problems 16.2

1a. To maximize its profit, Bernie's will produce where $MR = MC$. So Bernie's produces 15 burgers per hour. Bernie's demand curve shows that Bernie will set a price of $3 for a burger.

1b. Bernie's is earning an economic profit, because its price is greater than its average total cost. Its economic profit equals the area of the darkened rectangle in the figure. Bernie's earns an economic profit of $1 (its price, $3, minus its average total cost, $2) on each burger and so its total economic profit is $1 × 15 = $15.

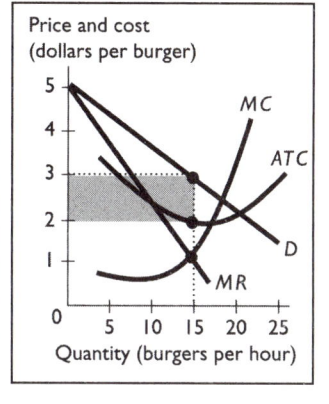

1c. Bernie's is in its short-run equilibrium. It is not in its long-run equilibrium because the firm is earning an economic profit. Firms in monopolistic competition cannot earn an economic profit in the long run; they can earn an economic profit only in the short run.

1b. The figure shows the marginal social cost curve, labeled MSC. At 1 ton of paper this curve lies $1,500 above the supply curve; at 2 tons of paper it lies $3,000 above the supply curve; and so on. The efficient quantity is where the marginal social cost equals the marginal benefit, which the figure shows is 2 tons of paper.

2a. Piece A' Pie's economic profit on a pizza is equal to price minus average total cost. So Piece A' Pie earns an economic profit of $12 a pizza minus $10 a pizza, which is $2 a pizza. Piece A' Pie produces 50 pizzas an hour, so its total economic profit is $2 a pizza × 50 pizzas an hour, which is $100 an hour.

2b. Piece A' Pie's economic profit on a pizza is equal to price minus average total cost. So Piece A' Pie earns an economic profit of $12 a pizza minus $12 a pizza, which is zero dollars a pizza. Piece A' Pie earns zero economic profit so it earns a normal profit.

2c. Piece A' Pie's economic profit on a pizza is equal to price minus average total cost. So Piece A' Pie earns an economic profit of $12 a pizza minus $15 a pizza, which is –$3 a pizza. Piece A' Pie produces 50 pizzas an hour, so its total economic profit is –$3 a pizza × 50 pizzas an hour, which is –$150 an hour. So Piece A' Pie incurs an economic loss of $150 an hour.

2d. In the short run, depending on market conditions, a firm in monopolistic competition can earn an economic profit, can earn zero economic profit, or can incur an economic loss. Only the situation in part (b) can represent a long-run equilibrium. In the long run, the absence of barriers to entry means that firms in monopolistic competition earn zero economic profit.

■ Self Test 16.2

Fill in the blanks

A firm in monopolistic competition produces the quantity where marginal revenue ____ (is greater than; equals; is less than) marginal cost. In the long run, a firm in monopolistic competition ____ (can; cannot) earn an economic profit. A firm in monopolistic competition ____ (does not have; has) excess capacity in the long run. People value product variety and variety is ____ (free; costly) to produce.

True or false

1. A firm in monopolistic competition makes its output decision just like a monopoly and produces the quantity where marginal revenue equals marginal cost.

2. A firm in monopolistic competition can make an economic profit in the short run.

3. A firm in monopolistic competition can never incur an economic loss.

4. A firm in monopolistic competition has a positive markup.

5. In a broader view of efficiency, monopolistic competition brings gains for consumers.

Multiple choice

1. A firm in monopolistic competition maximizes profit by equating
   a. price and marginal revenue.
   b. price and marginal cost.
   c. demand and marginal cost.
   d. marginal revenue and marginal cost.
   e. price and average total cost.

2. Once a firm in monopolistic competition has determined how much to produce, the firm determines its price by referring to its
   a. demand curve.
   b. marginal cost curve.
   c. marginal revenue curve.
   d. average total cost curve.
   e. average variable cost curve.

■ **FIGURE 16.1**
Price and cost (dollars per lunch)

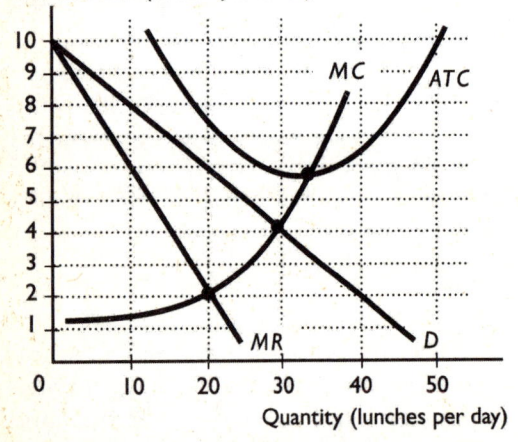

3. Figure 16.1 shows Louie's Lunches, a lunch counter in competition with many other restaurants. To maximize its profit, Louie's produces ____ lunches per day.
   a. 10
   b. 20
   c. 30
   d. between 31 and 40
   e. more than 40

4. Figure 16.1 shows Louie's Lunches, a lunch counter in competition with many other restaurants. To maximize its profit, Louie's sets a price of ____ per lunch.
   a. $2
   b. $4
   c. between $5.00 and $5.99
   d. $6
   e. more than $6.01

5. Figure 16.1 shows Louie's Lunches, a lunch counter in competition with many other restaurants. Louie's is in the ____ and is ____.
   a. short run; earning an economic profit
   b. short run; earning a normal profit
   c. short run; incurring an economic loss
   d. long run; earning an economic profit
   e. long run; earning a normal profit

6. A firm in monopolistic competition definitely incurs an economic loss if
   a. price equals marginal revenue.
   b. price is less than average total cost.
   c. marginal revenue equals marginal cost.
   d. marginal revenue is less than average total cost.
   e. price is greater than marginal cost.

7. In the long run, a firm in monopolistic competition
   a. earns zero economic profit.
   b. produces at a minimum average total cost.
   c. has deficient capacity.
   d. can earn either a normal profit or an economic profit.
   e. produces a quantity where its demand curve is upward sloping.

8. A firm's efficient scale of production is the output at which
   a. marginal cost is at a minimum.
   b. average total cost is at a minimum.
   c. profit is maximized.
   d. marginal revenue is at a maximum.
   e. marginal revenue equals marginal cost.

9. In the long run, a firm in monopolistic competition ____ excess capacity and a firm in perfect competition ____ excess capacity.
   a. has; has
   b. has; does not have
   c. does not have; has
   d. does not have; does not have
   e. might have; might have

10. In the long run, a firm in monopolistic competition ____ a markup of price over marginal cost and a firm in perfect competition ____ a markup of price over marginal cost.
    a. has; has
    b. has; does not have
    c. does not have; has
    d. does not have; does not have
    e. might have; might have

11. Monopolistic competition is efficient when compared to
    a. perfect competition.
    b. complete product uniformity.
    c. the short run.
    d. the long run.
    e. None of the above answers is correct.

Complete the graph

1. Figure 16.2 shows the demand and marginal revenue curves for Seaside Pizza, a firm in monopolistic competition. Draw the average total cost curve and marginal cost curve so that Seaside's output is 40 pizzas a day and its economic profit is $160. Is this a short-run or long-run equilibrium?

2. Figure 16.3 shows the demand and the marginal revenue curves for Surf Pizza, a firm in monopolistic competition. Draw the average total cost curve and marginal cost curve so that Surf's output is 20 pizzas a day and Surf's earns zero economic profit. Is this a short-run or long-run equilibrium?

■ FIGURE 16.2
Price and cost (dollars per pizza)

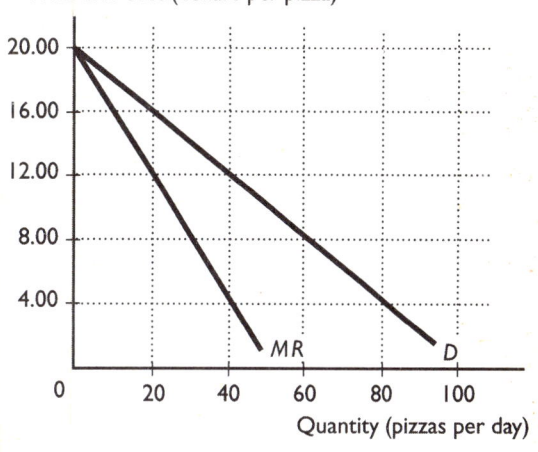

■ FIGURE 16.3
Price and cost (dollars per pizza)

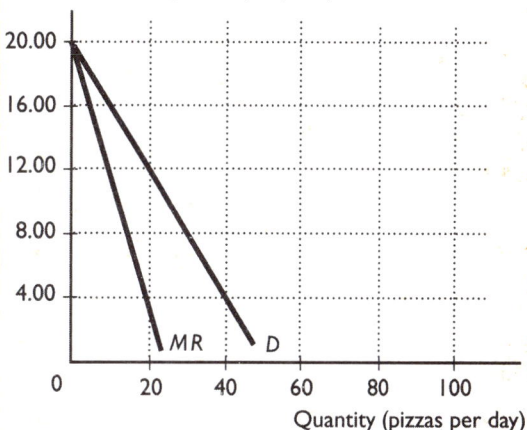

Short answer and numeric questions

1. What rule do firms in monopolistic competition follow to determine their profit-maximizing quantity of output? How does this rule compare to the rule followed by a monopoly?
2. Why do firms in monopolistic competition earn zero economic profit in the long run?
3. Is monopolistic competition efficient?

CHECKPOINT 16.3

■ **Explain why advertising costs are high and why firms use brand names in monopolistic competition.**

Quick Review
- *Selling costs* Selling costs such as advertising expenditures might lower average total cost if they increase the quantity sold by a large enough amount.

Additional Practice Problems 16.3

1. The figure to the right shows a firm in monopolistic competition.
   a. What quantity does the firm produce and what is the price?
   b. How much is the firm's markup?

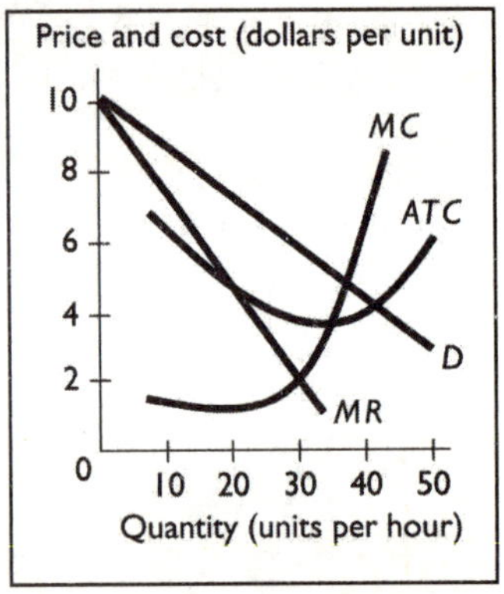

2. Selling costs are high in monopolistic competition. The table gives the costs of producing a pair of Nikes.
   a. The cost of producing the shoe in Asia is $20. The remaining costs are selling costs. What percentage of the retail price is selling costs?
   b. When the shoes reach America, selling costs are the result of activity at Nike Headquarters and local retailing activity. What proportion of the $70 price is attributable to Nike and what proportion to local retailers?

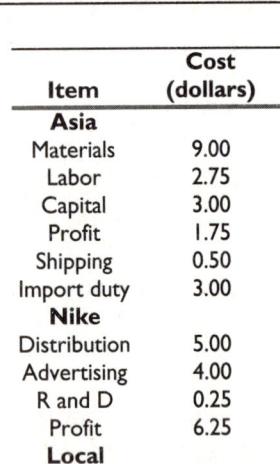

Item	Cost (dollars)
Asia	
Materials	9.00
Labor	2.75
Capital	3.00
Profit	1.75
Shipping	0.50
Import duty	3.00
Nike	
Distribution	5.00
Advertising	4.00
R and D	0.25
Profit	6.25
Local	
Labor	9.50
Shop rent	9.00
Other costs	7.00
Profit	9.00

Solutions to Additional Practice Problems 16.3

1a. As the figure shows, the firm produces 30 units and sets price of $6 per unit.

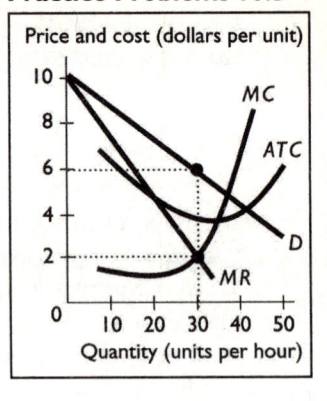

1b. The markup equals the difference between the price and the marginal cost. The price is $6 and the marginal cost is $2, so the markup is $4.

2a. Selling costs account for ($50 ÷ $70) × 100, which is 71.4 percent of the price.

2b. Nike accounts for ($15.50 ÷ $70) × 100, which is 22.1 percent of the price. Local retailers account for ($34.50 ÷ $70) × 100, which is 49.3 percent of the price.

■ Self Test 16.3

Fill in the blanks

Firms in monopolistic competition ____ (are; are not) continuously developing new products. In monopolistic competition, product improvement ____ (does; does not) equal its efficient level. Advertising costs ____ (are; are not) large in monopolistic competition. Advertising costs are a ____ (fixed; variable) cost and shift the average total cost curve ____ (downward; upward). Monopolistic competition ____ (definitely is; might be; definitely is not) efficient.

True or false

1. Firms in monopolistic competition innovate without regard to cost.
2. Firms in monopolistic competition often undertake extensive advertising.
3. Because advertising increases the demand for a firm's product, increasing the amount of advertising shifts the firm's cost curves downward.
4. Brand names give the firm an incentive to achieve a high and consistent standard of quality.

5. Whether monopolistic competition is efficient depends on the value people place on product variety.

Multiple choice
1. Because economic profits are eliminated in the long run in monopolistic competition, to earn an economic profit firms continuously
   a. shut down.
   b. exit the industry.
   c. innovate and develop new products.
   d. declare bankruptcy.
   e. decrease their costs by decreasing their selling costs.

2. A firm in monopolistic competition that introduces a new and differentiated product will temporarily have a ____ demand for its product and is able to charge ____.
   a. less elastic, a lower price than before
   b. less elastic, a higher price than before
   c. more elastic, a lower price than before
   d. more elastic, a higher price than before
   e. less elastic, the same price as before

3. The decision to innovate
   a. depends on the marketing department's needs.
   b. depends on whether the firm wants to benefit its customers.
   c. is based on the marginal cost and the marginal revenue of innovation.
   d. is unnecessary in a monopolistically competitive market.
   e. None of the above answers is correct.

4. Advertising costs and other selling costs are
   a. efficient.
   b. fixed costs.
   c. variable costs.
   d. marginal costs.
   e. considered as part of demand because they affect the demand for the good.

5. For a firm in monopolistic competition, selling costs
   a. increase costs and reduce profits.
   b. always increase demand.
   c. can change the quantity produced and lower the average total cost.
   d. can lower total cost.
   e. has no effect on the quantity sold.

6. If advertising increases the number of firms in an industry, each firm's demand
   a. increases.
   b. does not change.
   c. decreases.
   d. might increase or decrease depending on whether the new firms produce exactly the same product or a product that is slightly differentiated.
   e. None of the above answers is correct.

7. One reason a company advertises is to
   a. signal consumers that its product is high quality.
   b. lower its total cost.
   c. produce more efficiently.
   d. lower its variable costs.
   e. lower its fixed costs.

8. The efficiency of monopolistic competition
   a. is as clear-cut as the efficiency of perfect competition.
   b. depends on whether the gain from extra product variety offsets the selling costs and the extra cost that arises from excess capacity.
   c. comes from its excess capacity.
   d. is eliminated in the long run.
   e. is equal to that of monopoly.

Short answer and numeric questions
1. Why do firms in monopolistic competition engage in innovation and product development?
2. How might advertising lower average total cost?
3. How does advertising act as a signal?
4. Are advertising, brand names, and product differentiation efficient?

SELF TEST ANSWERS

■ CHECKPOINT 16.1

Fill in the blanks

In monopolistic competition there are a <u>large</u> number of firms producing <u>differentiated</u> products. Firms in monopolistic competition <u>do</u> compete on product quality. In monopolistic competition, barriers to entry <u>do not exist</u>. The square of the percentage market share of each firm summed over the 50 largest firms (or summed over all firms if there are fewer than 50) is the <u>Herfindahl-Hirschman Index</u>. Concentration ratios <u>do not</u> measure barriers to entry.

True or false

1. True; page 408
2. False; page 408
3. False; page 409
4. False; page 410
5. True; page 412

Multiple choice

1. a; page 408
2. c; page 408
3. d; page 408
4. a; page 409
5. e; page 409
6. b; page 409
7. d; page 410
8. e; page 411
9. b; page 411
10. d; pages 410-411

Short answer and numeric questions

1. Monopolistic competition occurs when a large number of firms compete; each firm produces a differentiated product, the firms compete on product quality; price, and marketing; and firms are free to enter and exit; page 408.

2. a. The total revenue shares are in the table above. The total revenue within the market is $5,000 million. A firm's total revenue share equals its total revenue divided by $5,000 million and then multiplied by 100.

Firm	Total revenue (millions of dollars)	Percent of total revenue (percent)
Dell	1,000	<u>20</u>
HP	800	<u>16</u>
IBM	500	<u>10</u>
Toshiba	400	<u>8</u>
Other 46 smaller firms	2,300	<u>46</u>

   b. The four-firm concentration ratio is the percentage of the total revenue accounted for by the four largest firms in the industry, which is 20 percent + 16 percent + 10 percent + 8 percent = 54 percent; page 410.

   c. To calculate the Herfindahl-Hirschman Index (HHI), square and then sum the market shares of the firms. The market shares are equal to each firm's percentage of total revenue. Each of the 20 smaller firms has total revenue of $50 million, so each has a 1 percentage point market share. So the HHI = $(20)^2 + (16)^2 + (10)^2 + (8)^2 + (1.0)^2 \times 50 = 400 + 256 + 100 + 64 + 50$, which is 870; page 411.

3. a. The four-firm concentration ratios are the same for both industries, 60 percent; page 410.

   b. The Herfindahl-Hirschman Index is 3,292 for Industry A and 940 for Industry B; page 411.

■ CHECKPOINT 16.2

A firm in monopolistic competition produces the quantity where marginal revenue <u>equals</u> marginal cost. In the long run, a firm in monopolistic competition <u>cannot</u> earn an economic profit. A firm in monopolistic competition <u>has</u> excess capacity in the long run. People value product variety and variety is <u>costly</u> to produce.

True or false

1. True; page 414
2. True; page 414
3. False; page 415
4. True; page 417
5. True; page 418

Multiple choice
1. d; page 414
2. a; page 414
3. b; page 414
4. d; page 414
5. c; page 415
6. b; page 415
7. a; page 416
8. b; page 417
9. b; page 417
10. b; page 417
11. b; page 418

Complete the graph

■ FIGURE 16.4
Price and cost (dollars per pizza)

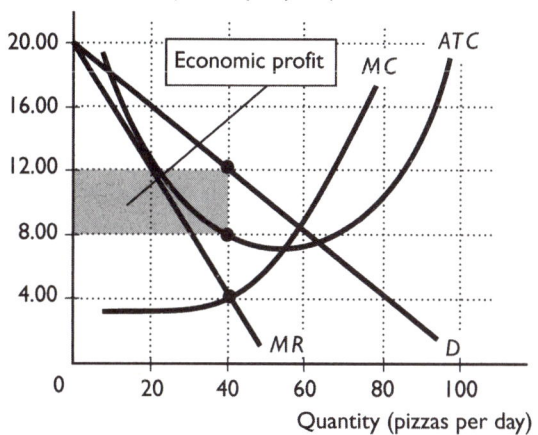

1. Figure 16.4 shows the average total cost curve and marginal cost curve so that Seaside Pizza's output is 40 pizzas a day and economic profit is $160. The figure shows a short-run equilibrium because Seaside is earning an economic profit; page 414.

2. Figure 16.5 shows the average total cost curve and marginal cost curve so that Surf Pizza's output is 20 pizzas a day and it earns zero economic profit. The figure shows a long-run equilibrium because Surf is earning zero economic profit; page 416.

■ FIGURE 16.5
Price and cost (dollars per pizza)

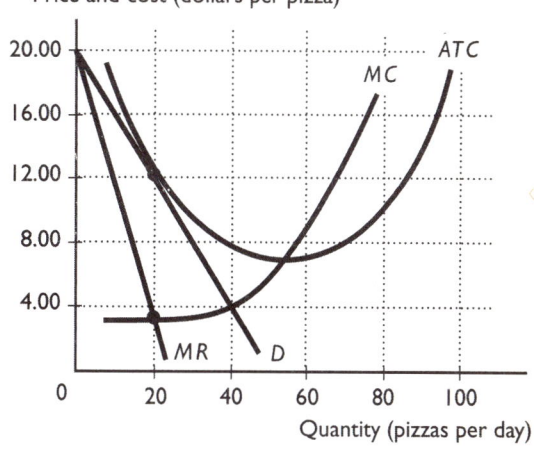

Short answer and numeric questions

1. Firms in monopolistic competition produce the quantity at which marginal revenue equals marginal cost. This rule is the same rule that a monopoly follows; page 414.

2. There is no restriction on entry in monopolistic competition, so if firms in an industry are making an economic profit, other firms have an incentive to enter the industry. The entry of new firms decreases the demand for each firm's product. The demand curve and marginal revenue curve shift leftward. When all firms in the industry are earning zero economic profit, there is no new incentive for new firms to enter and the industry is in long-run equilibrium. Similarly, if firms in an industry are incurring an economic loss, firms have an incentive to exit the industry and in the long run the remaining firms make zero economic profit; page 416.

3. In monopolistic competition, price exceeds marginal revenue and marginal revenue equals marginal cost, so price exceeds marginal cost—a sign of inefficiency. But this inefficiency arises from product differentiation that consumers value and for which they are willing to pay. So the loss that arises because marginal benefit exceeds marginal cost must be weighed against the gain that arises from greater product variety; page 418.

■ CHECKPOINT 16.3

Fill in the blanks
Firms in monopolistic competition <u>are</u> continuously developing new products. In monopolistic competition, product improvement <u>does not</u> equal its efficient level. Advertising costs <u>are</u> large in monopolistic competition. Advertising costs are a <u>fixed</u> cost and shift the average total cost curve <u>upward</u>. Monopolistic competition <u>might be</u> efficient.

True or false
1. False; page 420
2. True; page 421
3. False; page 422
4. True; page 425
5. True; page 425

Multiple choice
1. c; page 420
2. b; page 420
3. c; page 420
4. b; page 422
5. c; page 422
6. c; page 423
7. a; page 424
8. b; page 425

Short answer and numeric questions
1. Firms innovate and develop new products to increase the demand for their product and earn an economic profit; page 420.
2. Although advertising increases a firm's total costs, it also might increase sales. If the quantity sold increases by a large enough amount, it can lower *average* total cost of the quantity produced because the greater fixed cost is spread over an even greater amount of output; page 422.
3. Advertising sends a signal to the consumer that the product being advertised is high quality. Producers are willing to pay for expensive advertising only if they know that their product is of high enough quality that the consumer will buy it repeatedly; pages 424-425.
4. The bottom line on the question of whether advertising, brand names, and product differentiation are efficient is ambiguous. Advertising and product differentiation provide consumers with variety, which is a benefit. Brand names provide a signal to consumers, which also benefits consumers because they know the product's quality. But these benefits need to be weighed against the costs of advertising and product differentiation as well as the possibility that the actual differences between products might be very small; page 425.

Chapter 17
Oligopoly

CHAPTER CHECKLIST

In Chapter 17 we study oligopoly, a market structure that lies between perfect competition and monopoly.

1 Describe and identify oligopoly and explain how it arises.

An oligopoly is a market structure in which a small number of firms compete and natural or legal barriers prevent the entry of new firms. Because there are a small number of firms in the market, the firms are interdependent because each firm's actions affect the other firms. Firms in oligopoly have a temptation to form a cartel and collude to limit output, raise price, and increase economic profit. A duopoly is a market with only two firms. The key feature to identifying an oligopoly is uncovering whether the firms are so few that they recognize the interdependence among them.

2 Explain the dilemma faced by firms in oligopoly.

A cartel is a group of firms acting together to limit output, raise price, and thereby increase economic profit. Firms in oligopoly make the same economic profit as a monopoly if they act together in a cartel to restrict output to the monopoly level. In the cartel, each firm can make a bigger economic profit by increasing production, but this action decreases the economic profit of the other firms. The dilemma faced by a firm in an oligopoly cartel is that if each firm in the cartel increases output to maximize profit, then each firm ends up making a smaller economic profit.

3 Use game theory to explain how price and quantity are determined in oligopoly.

Game theory is the tool economists use to analyze strategic behavior. Games have rules, strategies, and payoffs. The prisoners' dilemma is a game between two prisoners that shows why it is hard to cooperate, even when it would be beneficial to both players to do so. The Nash equilibrium of a game occurs when each player takes the best possible action given the action of the other player. The equilibrium of the prisoners' dilemma game (each confesses) is not the best outcome for the prisoners. The duopolist's dilemma is like the prisoners' dilemma: the firms reach a Nash equilibrium in which they produce more and have lower profit than if they restricted production. In a repeated game, a punishment strategy can produce a monopoly output, a monopoly price, and an economic profit.

4 Describe the antitrust laws that regulate oligopoly.

Antitrust law regulates and prohibits certain kinds of market behavior. The Sherman Act of 1890 was the first federal antitrust law in the United States. Section 1 outlaws "every contract, combination in the form of a trust or otherwise, or conspiracy in restraint of trade." Section 2 declares that "every person who shall monopolize, or attempt to monopolize, ... shall be deemed guilty of a felony." The Clayton, Robinson-Patman, and Celler-Kefauver Acts prohibit practices if they "substantially lessen competition or create monopoly." Price fixing is *always* illegal. But resale price maintenance and tying arrangements are more controversial because they might lead to efficiency or inefficiency.

CHECKPOINT 17.1

■ **Describe and identify oligopoly and explain how it arises.**

Quick Review
- *Oligopoly* An oligopoly is characterized by having a small number of firms competing with natural or legal barriers preventing the entry of new firms.

Additional Practice Problems 17.1
1. What is the key difference between oligopoly and monopolistic competition?
2. What does it mean for firms to be interdependent? Why are firms in oligopoly interdependent?

Solutions to Additional Practice Problems 17.1
1. The key difference between oligopoly and monopolistic competition is that oligopoly is characterized by having only a small number of interdependent firms. Monopolistic competition has a large number of competing firms. Because there are only a few firms in oligopoly and because they are interdependent, the firms in oligopoly face the temptation to collude, which is an incentive missing from monopolistic competition.
2. Firms are interdependent when one firm's actions have an impact on another firm's profit. Firms in oligopoly are interdependent because there are only a few firms. In this case, one firm's actions have a major effect on the profits of its few competitors.

■ **Self Test 17.1**

Fill in the blanks
In oligopoly a ____ (large; small) number of firms compete. A ____ (cartel; duopoly) is a group of firms acting together to limit output, raise price, and increase economic profit. A market with an HHI that ____ (lies between 1,000 and 1,800; is greater than 1,800) is usually an oligopoly.

True or false
1. Oligopoly is a market in which a small number of firms compete.
2. The aim of a cartel is to lower price, increase output, and increase economic profit.
3. Only legal barriers to entry can create oligopoly.
4. Economies of scale can limit the number of firms that are in a market.
5. A market in which the HHI exceeds 1,800 is usually an oligopoly.

Multiple choice
1. Oligopoly is a market structure in which
   a. many firms each produce a slightly differentiated product.
   b. one firm produces a unique product.
   c. a small number of firms compete.
   d. many firms produce an identical product.
   e. the number of firms is so small that they do not compete with each other.

2. The fact that firms in oligopoly are interdependent means that
   a. there are barriers to entry.
   b. one firm's profits are affected by other firms' actions.
   c. they can produce either identical or differentiated goods.
   d. there are too many of them for any one firm to influence price.
   e. they definitely compete with each other so that the price is driven down to the monopoly level.

3. Collusion results when a group of firms
   i. act separately to limit output, lower price, and decrease economic profit.
   ii. act together to limit output, raise price, and increase economic profit.
   iii. in the United States legally fix prices.
   a. i only.
   b. ii only.
   c. iii only.
   d. i and iii.
   e. ii and iii.

4. A cartel is a group of firms
   a. acting separately to limit output, lower price, and decrease economic profit.
   b. acting together to limit output, raise price, and increase economic profit.
   c. legally fixing prices.
   d. acting together to erect barriers to entry.
   e. that compete primarily with each other rather than the other firms in the market.

5. A market with only two firms is called a
   a. duopoly.
   b. two-firm monopolistic competition.
   c. two-firm monopoly.
   d. cartel.
   e. two-firm quasi-monopoly.

6. The efficient scale of one firm is 20 units and the average total cost at the efficient scale is $30. The quantity demanded in the market as a whole at $30 is 40 units. This market is
   a. a natural duopoly.
   b. a legal duopoly.
   c. a natural monopoly.
   d. a legal monopoly.
   e. monopolistically competitive.

7. Even though four firms can profitably sell hotdogs downtown, the government licenses only two firms. This market is a
   a. natural duopoly.
   b. legal duopoly.
   c. natural monopoly.
   d. legal monopoly.
   e. market-limited oligopoly.

8. To determine if a market is an oligopoly, we need to determine if
   a. the market's HHI is less than 900.
   b. there are many firms in the market.
   c. the firms are so few that they recognize their mutual interdependencies.
   d. the firms make identical or differentiated products.
   e. cartels are legal in their market.

Short answer and numeric questions
1. What conditions define oligopoly?
2. Firms in oligopoly are interdependent. Firms in monopolistic competition are not. What accounts for the difference?
3. What is a cartel?
4. How does the HHI for monopolistic competition compare to the HHI for oligopoly?

CHECKPOINT 17.2

■ **Explain the dilemma faced by firms in oligopoly.**

Quick Review
- *Duopoly* A market with only two firms.
- *Range of outcomes* The price and quantity in a duopoly can range from the competitive outcome to the monopoly outcome.

Practice Problem 17.2
1. Just as in the textbook, Isolated Island has two natural gas wells, one owned by Tom and the other owned by Jerry. Each well has a valve that controls the rate of flow of gas, and the marginal cost of producing gas is zero. The table gives the demand schedule for gas on this island. Suppose Tom and Jerry agree to operate as a monopoly. A monopoly produces 6 units and charges $6 a unit. Tom and Jerry agree that each will produce 3 units and charge $6. There are no fixed costs

Price (dollars per unit)	Quantity demanded (units per day)
12	0
11	1
10	2
9	3
8	4
7	5
6	6
5	7
4	8
3	9
2	10
1	11
0	12

   a. If neither Tom nor Jerry cheat on the agreement what is Tom's profit? Jerry's profit? The combined profit?
   b. Suppose Tom decides to cheat on the agreement by producing 4 units. Jerry sticks to the agreement. If 7 units are produced, what is the price? What is Tom's

profit? Jerry's profit? The combined profit?

c. Why would Tom ever consider cheating on the agreement he made with Jerry?

Solution to Additional Practice Problem 17.2

1a. Profit is equal to total revenue because total cost is zero. Tom's profit is $18, Jerry's profit is $18, and the combined profit is $36.

1b. If 7 units are produced, the price is $5 a unit. Tom's profit on his 4 units is $20 and Jerry's profit on his 3 units is $15. Combined profit is $35.

1c. Tom considers cheating because cheating increases his profit. Tom realizes that if he alone cheats, his profit will be more, $20 versus $18. Jerry's profit falls more than Tom's rises but Tom is concerned only about his own profit.

■ Self Test 17.2

Fill in the blanks

When a duopoly charges the perfectly competitive price, each firm receives ____ (no; positive) economic profit. When a duopoly charges the monopoly price, economic profit is ____ (maximized; minimized).

True or false

1. In a duopoly, the highest price that the firms might set is the perfectly competitive price.
2. The only possible outcome for a duopoly is the monopoly outcome.
3. Once a duopoly has achieved the monopoly outcome, neither firm can increase its total profit.
4. A duopoly is currently making, in total, the same economic profit as a monopoly. If one firm increases its output, the economic profit of the other firm increases.
5. A duopoly's total profit is the largest when it produces more than the monopoly level of output.

Multiple choice

■ FIGURE 17.1
Price and cost (dollars per bottle of shampoo)

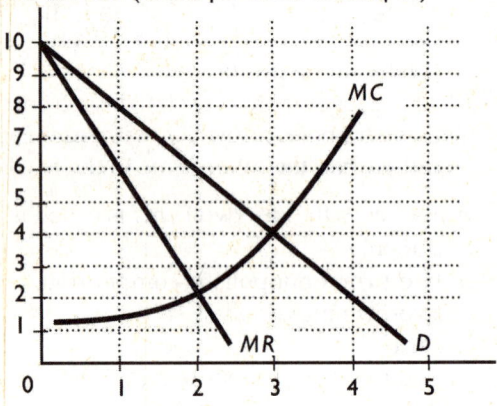

1. Suppose only two companies make shampoo. Figure 17.1 shows the market demand curve and associated marginal revenue curve. It also shows the combined marginal cost curve of the two companies. If these companies formed a cartel that operated as a monopoly, production would be ____ million bottles of shampoo and the price would be ____ per bottle of shampoo.
   a. 5; $4
   b. 2; $6 ✓
   c. 3; $6
   d. 2; $2
   e. 3; $4

2. Suppose the two companies that make shampoo illustrated in Figure 17.1 operate as perfect competitors. In this case, production would be ____ million bottles of shampoo and the price would be ____ per bottle of shampoo.
   a. 5; $4
   b. 2; $6
   c. 3; $6
   d. 2; $2
   e. 3; $4 ✓

3. For a duopoly, the highest price is charged when the duopoly achieves
   a. the competitive outcome.
   b. the monopoly outcome.
   c. an outcome between the competitive outcome and the monopoly outcome.
   d. its noncooperative equilibrium.
   e. Both answers (a) and (d) are correct because both refer to the same price.

4. For a duopoly, the smallest quantity is produced when the duopoly achieves
   a. the competitive outcome.
   b. the monopoly outcome.
   c. an outcome between the competitive outcome and the monopoly outcome.
   d. its noncooperative equilibrium.
   e. Both answers (a) and (d) are correct because both refer to the same quantity.

5. For a duopoly, the maximum total profit is reached when the duopoly produces
   a. the same amount of output as the competitive outcome.
   b. the same amount of output as the monopoly outcome.
   c. an amount of output that lies between the competitive outcome and the monopoly outcome.
   d. more output than the competitive outcome.
   e. less output than the monopoly outcome.

6. If a duopoly has reached the monopoly outcome, a firm can increase its profit if it and it alone ____ its price and ____ its production.
   a. raises; increases
   b. raises; decreases
   c. lowers; increases
   d. lowers; decreases
   e. raises; does not change

7. If a duopoly has reached the monopoly outcome and only one firm increases its production, that firm's profit ____ and the other firm's profit ____.
   a. increases; increases
   b. increases; decreases
   c. decreases; increases
   d. decreases; decreases
   e. increases; does not change

8. Suppose a duopoly had reached the monopoly outcome and then the first firm increased its production. If the second firm next increases its production, the second firm's profit ____ and the first firm's profit ____.
   a. increases; increases
   b. increases; decreases
   c. decreases; increases
   d. decreases; decreases
   e. increases; does not change

9. If both firms in a duopoly increase their production by one unit beyond the monopoly output, each firm's profit ____ and the *total* profit of the duopoly ____.
   a. increases; increases
   b. does not change; does not change
   c. decreases; decreases
   d. does not change; increases
   e. decreases; does not change

10. The very best outcome possible for the firms in a duopoly is to produce the
    a. monopoly level of output.
    b. perfectly competitive level of output.
    c. output level that maximizes total revenue.
    d. output level that minimizes total cost.
    e. equilibrium level of output if the game is not repeated.

Complete the graph

Quantity (thousands of newspapers per day)	Price (cents)	Marginal revenue (cents)
0	60	60
2	50	40
4	40	20
6	30	0
8	20	−20

1. Anytown, USA has two newspapers that have a duopoly in the local market. The table contains information on the market demand and marginal revenue for newspapers. Marginal cost of a newspaper is 20 cents.
   a. Graph the demand curve, marginal revenue curve, and marginal cost curve in Figure 17.2.

■ **FIGURE 17.2**
Price and marginal revenue (cents per newspaper)

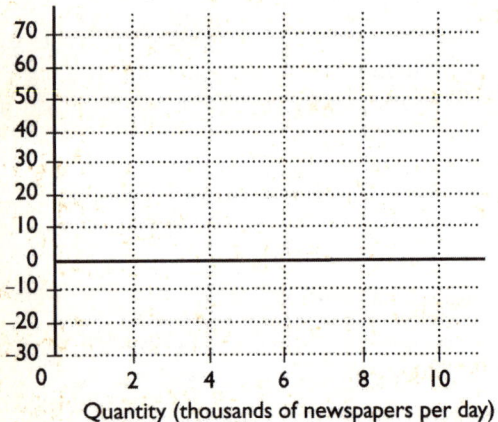

[Graph with y-axis from −30 to 70, x-axis: Quantity (thousands of newspapers per day) from 0 to 10]

   b. What price and quantity represent the competitive outcome?
   c. What price and quantity represent the monopoly outcome?
   d. What range of price and quantity represent the potential duopoly outcomes?

Short answer and numeric questions
1. In oligopoly, one firm's profit-maximizing actions might decrease its competitors' profits. Why is this fact a problem for firms in oligopoly?
2. Why do firms in an oligopoly have an incentive to form a cartel that boosts the price and decreases the output?
3. Why does a firm have the incentive to cheat on a collusive agreement to limit production and raise the price?

CHECKPOINT 17.3

■ **Use game theory to explain how price and quantity are determined in oligopoly.**

Quick Review
- *Game theory* The tool that economists use to analyze strategic behavior—behavior that recognizes mutual interdependence and takes account of the expected behavior of others.
- *Nash equilibrium* An equilibrium in which each player takes the best possible action given the action of the other player.

Additional Practice Problem 17.3
1. Coke and Pepsi are engaged in an advertising game. They each know that if they both limit their advertising, they will make the maximum attainable joint economic profit of $400 million, divided so that each has an economic profit of $200 million. They also know that if either of them advertises while the other does not, the one advertising makes an economic profit of $300 million and the one that does not advertise incurs an economic loss of $100 million dollars. And they also know that if they both advertise, they both earn zero economic profit.
   a. Construct a payoff matrix for the game that Coke and Pepsi must play.
   b. Find the Nash equilibrium. How is this game similar to the prisoners' dilemma?
   c. What is the equilibrium if this game is played repeatedly?
   d. Suppose that Coke and Pepsi are both playing a tit-for-tat strategy and that last time both did not advertise. Today, however, Coke really needs some extra income. So Coke advertises. What takes place today and in the future?

Solution to Additional Practice Problem 17.3

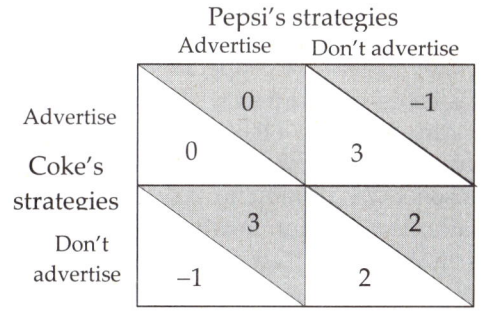

	Pepsi's strategies	
	Advertise	Don't advertise
Coke's strategies Advertise	0 / 0	−1 / 3
Don't advertise	3 / −1	2 / 2

1a. A payoff matrix is a table that shows payoffs for every possible action by each player, Coke and Pepsi, given every possible action by the other player. The payoff matrix is above. The number in each square is the economic profit in millions of dollars.

1b. To find the Nash equilibrium of a game, place yourself in the position of the first player. Ask yourself "what if" your opponent takes one action: What will you do? Then ask "what if" the opponent takes the other action: now what will you do? This analysis allows you to determine the first player's action. Then place yourself in the position of the second player and repeat the "what if" analysis to determine the second player's action. So, to find Coke's strategy, ask what Coke will do for each of Pepsi's choices. If Pepsi advertises (the first column of the payoff matrix), Coke advertises because that gives Coke a larger profit ($0 versus a loss of $1 million). If Pepsi does not advertise (the second column of the payoff matrix), Coke advertises gallons because that gives Coke a larger profit ($3 million versus $2 million). Regardless of Pepsi's action, Coke advertises. Similar reasoning shows that Pepsi also advertises. So the Nash equilibrium is for each to advertise and earn zero economic profit. The game is similar to a prisoners' dilemma game because there is a conflict between each player's incentives to do what is best for the player versus what is best for both of them taken together. In the prisoners' dilemma game, both prisoners confess, leading to the worst joint outcome. In this game, both players advertise, again leading to the worst joint outcome.

1c. In a repeated game, Coke and Pepsi both do not advertise and earn the maximum joint economic profit. This outcome occurs if they use a tit-for-tat strategy.

1d. Today, Coke earns an economic profit of $3 million and Pepsi incurs an economic loss of $1 million. But in the second year, Pepsi will advertise. Coke might go back to not advertising to induce Pepsi to not advertise in the third year. So in the second year, Pepsi earns an economic profit of $3 million and Coke incurs an economic loss of $1 million. Over the two years, Coke earns a total economic profit of $2 million (and Pepsi also earns a total economic profit of $2 million.) But if Coke had not "cheated" on the agreement and advertised in the first year, then over the two years Coke's total economic profit would have been $4 million, not just $2 million. So, by cheating on the agreement Coke earns more profit immediately but over the longer haul earns less profit.

■ Self Test 17.3

Fill in the blanks

Game theory is the main tool that economists use to analyze ____ (irrational; strategic) behavior. Games feature ____, ____, and ____. The Nash equilibrium is ____ (always; not always) the best possible equilibrium for the players. Game theory shows that duopolists ____ (can; cannot) always reach the best possible equilibrium. In a ____ (repeated; single-play) game, a tit-for-tit strategy can be used. The ____ (larger; smaller) the number of firms, the harder it is for an oligopoly to maintain the monopoly output.

True or false

1. Game theory is used to analyze strategic behavior.
2. A prisoners' dilemma has no equilibrium.
3. A Nash equilibrium is the best outcome for all players in a prisoners' dilemma game.

4. The monopoly outcome is more likely in a repeated game than in a one-play game.
5. If firms in oligopoly play a repeated game and end up restricting their output, then oligopoly is efficient.

Multiple choice

1. One of the main tools economists use to analyze strategic behavior is
   a. the Herfindahl-Hirschman Index.
   b. game theory.
   c. cartel theory.
   d. the collusion index.
   e. dual theory, which is used to study duopolies.

2. A Nash equilibrium occurs
   a. when each player acts without considering the actions of the other player.
   b. when each player takes the best possible action given the action of the other player.
   c. only when players use the tit-for-tat strategy.
   d. only if the game is played in Nashville, TN.
   e. when each player takes the action that makes the combined payoff for all players as large as possible.

3. Game theory reveals that
   a. the equilibrium might not be the best solution for the parties involved.
   b. firms in oligopoly are not interdependent.
   c. each player looks after what is best for the industry.
   d. if all firms in an oligopoly take the action that maximizes their profit, then the equilibrium will have the largest possible combined profit of all the firms.
   e. firms in an oligopoly choose their actions without regard for what the other firms might do.

4. The prisoners' dilemma game
   a. shows that prisoners are better off if they cooperate.
   b. shows it is easy to cooperate.
   c. has an equilibrium in which both prisoners are made as well off as possible.
   d. would have the same outcome even if the prisoners can communicate and cooperate.
   e. has an equilibrium in which one prisoner is made as well off as possible and the other prisoner is made as worse off as possible.

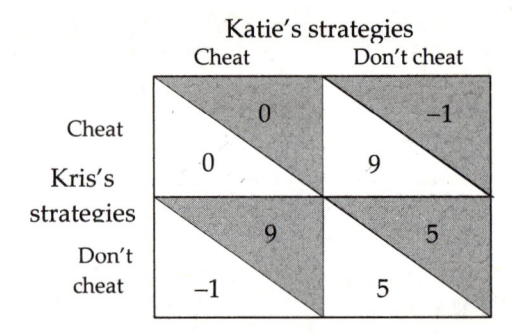

	Katie's strategies	
Kris's strategies	Cheat	Don't cheat
Cheat	0 / 0	−1 / 9
Don't cheat	9 / −1	5 / 5

5. Katie and Kris are duopolists who formed a collusive agreement to boost prices and decrease production. Their payoff matrix is above and the entries are millions of dollars of economic profit. They now have the choice of cheating on the agreement or not cheating. If Kris cheats, then
   a. Kris definitely earns an economic profit of $9 million.
   b. Kris definitely earns $0.
   c. Kris definitely incurs an economic loss of $1 million.
   d. Kris definitely earns an economic profit of $5 million.
   e. Kris might earn an economic profit of $9 million or might earn $0 depending on what Katie does.

6. Based on the payoff matrix above, the Nash equilibrium is for
   a. Kris to cheat and Katie to cheat.
   b. Kris to not cheat and Katie to not cheat.
   c. Kris to cheat and Katie to not cheat.
   d. Kris to not cheat and Katie to cheat.
   e. Kris and Katie to invite a third person to determine what each of them should do.

7. Based on the payoff matrix above, in the Nash equilibrium the total profit that Katie and Kris earn together is ____ million.
   a. $8
   b. $9
   c. $10
   d. $0
   e. −$1

8. A collusive agreement to form a cartel is difficult to maintain because
   a. each firm can increase its own profits by cutting its price and selling more.
   b. forming a cartel is legal but frowned upon throughout the world.
   c. supply will decrease because of the high cartel price.
   d. demanders will rebel once they realize a cartel has been formed.
   e. each firm can increase its profit if it decreases its production even more than the decrease set by the cartel.

9. Firms in oligopoly can achieve an economic profit
   a. always in the long run.
   b. if they cooperate.
   c. only if the demand for their products is inelastic.
   d. only if the demand for their products is elastic.
   e. if they reach the non-cooperative equilibrium.

10. When duopoly games are repeated and a "tit-for-tat" strategy is used,
    a. the competitive outcome is more likely to be reached than when the game is played once.
    b. the monopoly outcome is more likely to be reached than when the game is played once.
    c. both firms begin to incur economic losses.
    d. one firm goes out of business.
    e. because the game is repeated it is impossible to predict whether the competitive or the monopoly outcome is more likely.

11. Oligopoly is
    a. always efficient.
    b. efficient only if the firms cooperate.
    c. efficient only if they play non-repeated games.
    d. generally not efficient.
    e. efficient only if the firms innovate.

Complete the graph

Cameron's strategies

Art's strategies

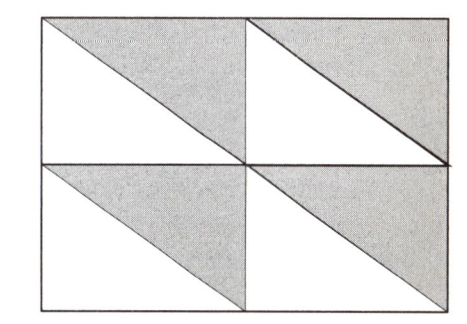

1. Art and Cameron own the only two movie theaters in a small, isolated town. They have recently agreed to an illegal cartel agreement in which they will boost their ticket prices. If they both comply with the agreement, both will make $1 million of economic profit. If one cheats by lowering his price, the cheater will make $1.5 million of economic profit and the other will suffer an economic loss if $0.5 million. If they both cheat by lowering their prices, each makes zero economic profit.
   a. Complete the payoff matrix above.

b. What is the Nash equilibrium of this game?

Intel's strategies

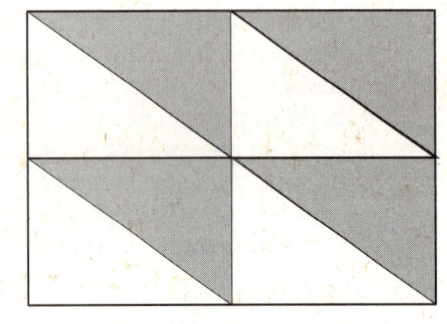

AMD's strategies

2. Intel and AMD are involved in a game to determine the amount they will spend on research and development. If they each spend $2 billion, their economic profit is zero. If they each spend $1 billion, their economic profit is $500 million. And if one spends $2 billion and the other spends $1 billion, the one spending $2 billion has an economic profit of $1,500 million and the other has an economic loss of $100 million.
  a. Complete the payoff matrix above.
  b. What is the Nash equilibrium of this game?

Short answer and numeric questions
1. What are "strategies" in game theory?
2. In a prisoners' dilemma, why don't the players cooperate?
3. In the duopolists' dilemma, why don't the players cooperate?
4. How does the number of players in a game affect its outcome?

CHECKPOINT 17.4

■ Describe the antitrust laws that regulate oligopoly.

Quick Review
- *Sherman Act* The first antitrust law, Section 1 of the Sherman Act prohibits conspiring with others to restrict competition and Section 2 outlaws attempts to monopolize.
- *Clayton Act* The second antitrust law, the Clayton Act prohibits certain business practices if they substantially lessen competition or create monopoly.

Additional Practice Problem 17.4
1. Cooperative agreements among firms such as the New York Yankees and the Chicago White Sox that limit the number of games played and that restrict the number of teams for which an athlete can play show cartel-like behavior. Except for professional sports teams, cartels are generally illegal in the United States. Microsoft and Hewlett Packard do not draft college graduates and so they cannot agree that a particular college graduate will work for Microsoft and not Hewlett Packard. Why do you think the Supreme Court made a decision in the case of professional sporting teams to permit cartel-like behavior?

Solution to Additional Practice Problem 17.4
1. Under competitive conditions, rich teams such as the New York Yankees, with plenty of fans and lucrative media contracts, would be able to purchase all the best players. Putting all the best players on a single team would prevent another team from winning. The teams unable to win would be unable to entice fans to their stadiums. The entire sports industry would die if only one team were profitable and dominant. This situation is unlike the case with Microsoft and Hewlett Packard because if one of these firms becomes dominant, its absolute dominance would not spell the end of the industry. The sports leagues, in an exception to general American policy, are allowed to have league rules that seek to apportion talent equally to preserve the competitive nature of the sport.

■ Self Test 17.4

Fill in the blanks
The first antitrust law in the United States was the ____ (Clayton; Sherman) Act and, in part, it

outlaws ____ (attempts to monopolize; monopolies; oligopolies). The Clayton Act ____ (does not prohibit; prohibits) acquiring a competitor's shares if this act substantially lessens competition or creates monopoly. Resale price maintenance ____ (always leads; does not always lead) to inefficiency. Economists generally believe that predatory pricing is ____ (common; uncommon). The ____ (higher; lower) a market's Herfindahl-Hirschman Index, the more likely the Federal Trade Commission will challenge a merger.

True or false
1. The Sherman Act outlaws contracts and conspiracies in restraint of trade.
2. The Clayton Act outlaws all price discrimination.
3. Price fixing is *always* illegal.
4. Resale price maintenance always leads to efficiency.
5. The Federal Trade Commission uses the four-firm concentration ratio as the guideline to determine which mergers it will examine and possibly block.

Multiple choice
1. The first antitrust act was ____ passed in ____.
   a. the Clayton Act; 1890
   b. the Sherman Act; 1890
   c. the Clinton Act; 1999
   d. the Rockefeller Act; 1890
   e. the Clayton Act; 1914

2. The Clayton Act
   a. replaced the Sherman Act.
   b. along with its amendments, outlawed several business practices if they substantially lessened competition or created monopoly.
   c. along with its amendments, prohibited all business practices that substantially lessen competition or create monopoly.
   d. was the first anti-trust law in the United States.
   e. was repealed in 1985.

3. Which of the following is (are) prohibited if it substantially lessens competition or creates a monopoly?
   i. price discrimination
   ii. tying arrangements
   iii. exclusive dealing
   a. i only.
   b. ii only.
   c. ii and iii.
   d. iii only.
   e. i, ii, and iii.

4. If Polka Cola agrees to sell its cola to a retailer only if the retailer also buys a lemon-lime drink, Polka Up, then Polka Cola is engaged in
   a. a tying arrangement.
   b. a requirement contract.
   c. an exclusive deal.
   d. territorial confinement.
   e. price discrimination.

5. Which of the following is *always* illegal?
   a. possessing a very large market share
   b. selling at a price below other producers because of efficiency
   c. price fixing
   d. attempting to merge with a competitor
   e. price discrimination

6. Resale price maintenance
   a. can lead to efficiency by preventing low-price shops from being free riders.
   b. can lead to inefficiency by preventing low-price shops from being free riders.
   c. is always legal.
   d. is a clear example of predatory pricing.
   e. is an example of a tying arrangement.

7. Predatory pricing occurs when a firm sets a ____ price to drive competitors out of business with the intention of then setting a ____ price.
   a. monopoly; high
   b. monopoly; low
   c. low; monopoly
   d. low; low
   e. high; monopoly

8. In the case against Microsoft, it was claimed that combining Internet Explorer and Windows was
   a. predatory pricing.
   b. an illegal tying agreement.
   c. creating one product that is convenient for the consumers.
   d. illegal territorial confinement.
   e. an inefficient resale maintenance agreement.

9. In a concentrated industry with a Herfindahl-Hirschman Index that exceeds 1,800, the Federal Trade Commission will challenge any merger that increases the Herfindahl-Hirschman index by a minimum of
   a. 50 points.
   b. 100 points.
   c. 1,000 points.
   d. 1,800 points.
   e. 10,000 points.

Short answer and numeric questions

1. General Motors is a huge company, with total revenue exceeding $190 billion a year. Why doesn't the government challenge General Motors and take it to court for antitrust violations?

2. Airlines routinely price discriminate, charging pleasure travelers a significantly lower price than business travelers. The Clayton Act, however, mentioned price discrimination as one of the business practices it covers and prohibits. Why can airlines routinely price discriminate?

3. What is the law about price fixing?

Company	Market share (percent)
Acme	27
ABC	18
Banks	10
Cooper	8
37 individual firms	1 each

4. The table above has a list of companies that make up the market for steel, along with each companies' share of the market.
   a. What is the Herfindahl-Hirschman Index for this market? How would you describe the competitiveness of this market?
   b. If Acme acquires Banks, what is the new Herfindahl-Hirschman Index? Would the Department of Justice challenge this acquisition? Why or why not? How would you describe the competitiveness of this market if the merger occurs?

SELF TEST ANSWERS

■ CHECKPOINT 17.1

Fill in the blanks

In oligopoly a <u>small</u> number of firms compete. A <u>cartel</u> is a group of firms acting together to limit output, raise price, and increase economic profit. A market with an HHI that <u>is greater than 1,800</u> is usually an oligopoly.

True or false

1. True; page 432
2. False; page 432
3. False; page 432
4. True; page 433
5. True; page 434

Multiple choice

1. c; page 432
2. b; page 432
3. b; page 432
4. b; page 432
5. a; page 432
6. a; page 433
7. b; page 434
8. c; page 434

Short answer and numeric questions

1. Oligopoly occurs when a small number of firms compete and natural or legal barriers prevent the entry of new firms; page 432.
2. The difference is because there are only a small number of firms in oligopoly. Because there are only a small number of firms, one firm's actions affect the profits of all its (few) competitors; page 432.
3. A cartel is a group of firms acting together to limit output, raise price, and increase economic profit; page 432.
4. The HHI for monopolistic competition is less than that for oligopoly. For monopolistic competition, the HHI usually lies between 1,000 and 1,800. For oligopoly, the HHI usually lies above 1,800; page 434.

■ CHECKPOINT 17.2

Fill in the blanks

When a duopoly charges the perfectly competitive price, each firm receives <u>no</u> economic profit. When a duopoly charges the monopoly price, economic profit is <u>maximized</u>.

True or false

1. False; page 437
2. False; page 437
3. False; page 437
4. False; page 437
5. False; pages 436-437

Multiple choice

1. b; page 436
2. e; page 436
3. b; page 437
4. b; page 437
5. b; page 437
6. c; page 437
7. b; page 437
8. b; page 438
9. c; page 438
10. a; page 438

Complete the graph

■ **FIGURE 17.3**

Price and marginal revenue (cents per newspaper)

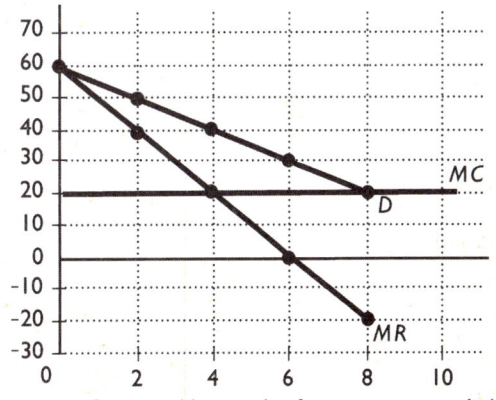

1. a. The curves are graphed in Figure 17.3.

b. The competitive equilibrium is 8,000 newspapers a day and a price of 20¢ a newspaper; page 436.
c. The monopoly equilibrium is 4,000 newspapers a day and a price of 40¢ a newspaper; pages 436-437.
d. The exact price and quantity can't be predicted, but it will be somewhere between the competitive and monopoly outcomes. The price will be between 40¢ and 20¢ a newspaper and the output will be between 4,000 and 8,000 newspapers a day; pages 436-438.

Short answer and numeric questions

1. The point that one firm's actions can decrease another firm's profits is what makes competition difficult in an oligopoly. While the firms might be better off cooperating, each firm trying to increase its profit takes actions that lead the profits of its competitors to decrease, so that all the firms wind up worse off; pages 436-438.
2. If the firms can form and maintain a cartel that boosts the price and decreases the output, all the firms' profits can increase; page 437.
3. Every firm has the incentive to cheat on an output-limiting agreement because if it and it alone cheats by boosting its output and cutting its price, its economic profit will increase; page 437.

■ CHECKPOINT 17.3

Fill in the blanks

Game theory is the main tool that economists use to analyze <u>strategic</u> behavior. Games feature <u>rules</u>, <u>strategies</u>, and <u>payoffs</u>. The Nash equilibrium is <u>not always</u> the best possible equilibrium for the players. Game theory shows that duopolists <u>cannot</u> always reach the best possible equilibrium. In a <u>repeated</u> game, a tit-for-tat strategy can be used. The <u>larger</u> the number of firms, the harder it is for an oligopoly to maintain the monopoly output.

True or false
1. True; page 441
2. False; pages 442-443
3. False; page 443
4. True; page 446
5. False; page 446

Multiple choice
1. b; page 441
2. b; page 442
3. a; page 443
4. a; page 443
5. e; page 442
6. a; page 444
7. d; page 444
8. a; page 444
9. b; page 444
10. b; page 446
11. d; page 446

Complete the graph

Cameron's strategies

	Comply	Cheat
Comply	1 / 1	1.5 / −0.5
Cheat	−0.5 / 1.5	0 / 0

Art's strategies

1. a. The completed payoff matrix is above. The payoffs are in millions of dollars; page 442.
   b. The Nash equilibrium is for both Cameron and Art to cheat on the collusive agreement and each earn zero economic profit; pages 444.

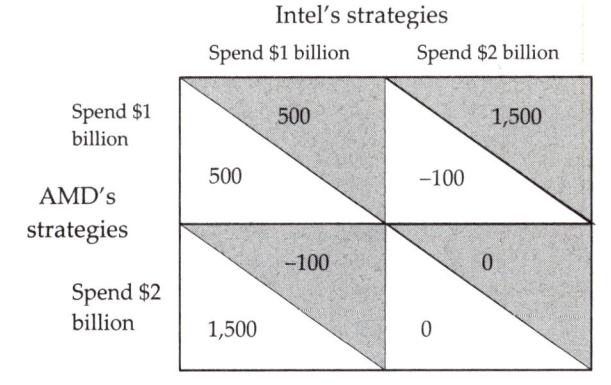

	Intel's strategies	
AMD's strategies	Spend $1 billion	Spend $2 billion
Spend $1 billion	500 / 500	1,500 / −100
Spend $2 billion	−100 / 1,500	0 / 0

1. a. The completed payoff matrix is above. The payoffs are in millions of dollars; page 442.

   b. The Nash equilibrium is for both Intel and AMD to spend $2 billion on research and development and each earn zero economic profit; page 444.

Short answer and numeric questions

1. Strategies are all the possible actions of each player. In the prisoners' dilemma game, strategies are "to confess" or "to deny;" in the Airbus/Boeing duopoly game, strategies are "to produce 4 airplanes a week" or "to produce 3 airplanes a week;" page 442.

2. In the prisoners' dilemma game, the players do not cooperate because they do not see cooperation as being in their best interest. Regardless of what the second player does, the first player is better off confessing. Regardless of what the first player does, the second player is better off confessing. Because it is in each player's separate best interest to confess rather than cooperate by denying, both players confess; pages 441-443.

3. In the duopolists' dilemma game, the players do not cooperate for precisely the same reason they do not cooperate in the prisoners' dilemma game: The players do not see cooperation as being in their best interest. As a result, because each player's profit-maximizing actions harm the other player, the equilibrium can be the worst outcome for both; page 444.

4. The more players in a game, the harder it is to maintain the monopoly outcome; page 444.

■ CHECKPOINT 17.4

Fill in the blanks

The first antitrust law in the United States was the <u>Sherman</u> Act and, in part, it outlaws <u>attempts to monopolize</u>. The Clayton Act <u>prohibits</u> acquiring a competitor's shares if this act substantially lessens competition or creates monopoly. Resale price maintenance <u>does not always lead</u> to inefficiency. Economists generally believe that predatory pricing is <u>uncommon</u>. The <u>higher</u> a market's Herfindahl-Hirschman Index, the more likely the Federal Trade Commission will challenge a merger.

True or false

1. True; page 450
2. False; page 450
3. True; page 449
4. False; pages 449-450
5. False; page 453

Multiple choice

1. b; page 449
2. b; page 450
3. e; page 450
4. a; page 450
5. c; page 449
6. a; pages 449-450
7. c; page 451
8. b; page 452
9. a; page 453

Short answer and numeric questions

1. General Motors is, indeed, a huge company. But it competes with other huge companies in a gigantic market, the new car market. Ford has total revenue over $170 billion a year; Toyota's total revenue is comparable. Antitrust laws deal with markets where there is little competition, not with markets where the many competitors are large; pages 449, 453.

2. The Clayton Act prohibited several businesses practices *only if* they "substantially lessen competition or create monopoly." Price discrimination by the airlines does not substantially lessen competition or create a monopoly. Price discrimination by the airlines is legal; page 450.

3. The law about price fixing is clear: It is *always* illegal. If price fixing can be proven, the firms are automatically guilty because there can be no acceptable excuse; page 449.

4. a. HHI = $27^2 + 18^2 + 10^2 + 8^2 + 37 = 1,254$. Because this falls between 1,000 and 1,800, the market is moderately concentrated; page 453.

b. HHI = $37^2 + 18^2 + 8^2 + 37 = 1,794$. The Federal Trade Commission would challenge this acquisition because it increases the index by more than 100 points. After this merger, the market remains moderately concentrated; page 453.

Chapter 18

Markets for Factors of Production

CHAPTER CHECKLIST

In this we chapter study demand, supply, and equilibrium in factor markets.

1 Explain how the value of marginal product determines the demand for a factor of production.

The four factors of production are labor, capital, land (natural resources), and entrepreneurship. Natural resources are either renewable or nonrenewable. The wage rate is the price of labor services, the (capital) rental rate is the price of capital services, and the (land) rental rent is the price of the services of land. The demand for a factor of production is derived from the demand for the goods and services it is used to produce. The value of the marginal product is the value to a firm of hiring one more unit of a factor of production and equals the price of a unit of output multiplied by the factor's marginal product. To maximize profit, a firm hires labor up to the point at which the value of the marginal product equals the wage rate. A firm's demand for labor curve is its value of the marginal product curve. The demand for labor changes and the demand for labor curve shifts when the price of the firm's output changes, the prices of other factors of production change, or technology change.

2 Explain how wage rates and employment are determined and how labor unions influence labor markets.

An individual's labor supply curve can be backward bending at higher wage rates so that an increase in the wage rate decreases the quantity of labor supplied. The key factors that change the supply of labor are the adult population, preferences, and time spent in school and training. In a competitive labor market, the equilibrium between the demand for labor and the supply of labor determines the wage rate and employment. A labor union is an organized group of workers that aims to increase the wages of its members. Labor unions try to increase the demand for their members' labor (by increasing the value of the marginal product of union members and by supporting minimum wage laws, immigration restrictions, and import restrictions). Unions also try to restrict the supply of non-union labor.

3 Explain how capital and land rental rents and natural resource prices are determined.

The demand for capital is based on the value of the marginal product of capital. Equilibrium in the capital market determines the capital rental rate and quantity of capital. The quantity of land is fixed, so the supply of each particular block of land is perfectly inelastic. Equilibrium in the land market determines the land rental rate. The proven reserves of a nonrenewable resource increase over time because advances in technology enable ever less accessible sources to be discovered. The supply of a nonrenewable resource in any given time period is perfectly elastic at the price that gives the owners the same expected profit as the interest rate. The Hotelling Principle is the proposition that the price of a nonrenewable natural resource is expected to rise at a rate equal to the interest rate.

CHECKPOINT 18.1

■ **Explain how the value of marginal product determines the demand for a factor of production.**

Quick Review

- *Factors of production* The four factors of production are labor, capital, land, and entrepreneurship.
- *Value of marginal product* The value to a firm of hiring one more unit of a factor of production, which equals the price of a unit of output multiplied by the marginal product of the factor of production.

Additional Practice Problems 18.1

1. Tell whether each of the following are land, labor, capital, or entrepreneurship.
   a. oil
   b. an oil worker
   c. an oil platform in the Gulf of Mexico
   d. the Chief Executive Officer of Exxon
   e. a professor
   f. a beach in Florida

2. Casey's lawn service, The Other Side of the Fence, hires workers to mow lawns. The market for lawn mowing is perfectly competitive, and the price of mowing a lawn is $20.00. The labor market is competitive, and the wage rate is $40 a day. The table shows the workers' total product, TP:

Workers	Lawns per day
1	3
2	7
3	14
4	18
5	20
6	21

   a. Calculate the marginal product of hiring the third worker.
   b. Calculate the value of the marginal product of the third worker.
   c. Complete the table to the right showing the value of the marginal product.

Workers	Value of the MP
1	____
2	____
3	____
4	____
5	____
6	____

   d. How many workers will Casey hire to maximize his profit?
   e. How many lawns a day will Casey mow to maximize its profit?
   f. What is Casey's total revenue if he hires 4 workers? What is Casey's total revenue if he hires 5 workers? What is the change in total revenue if Casey hires 5 workers?
   g. How does the increase in Casey's total revenue from hiring the 5th worker compare to the value of the marginal product of the 5th worker?

Solutions to Additional Practice Problems 18.1

1a. Oil is a gift of nature and so it is part of land.

1b. An oil well worker is part of labor.

1c. The oil platform is part of capita.

1d. The Chief Executive Officer is in charge of running Exxon and so is part of entrepreneurship.

1e. The professor is part of labor.

1f. The beach is a gift of nature and so is part of land.

2a. The marginal product of hiring the third worker equals the total product of hiring three workers, which is 14 lawns, minus the total product of hiring two workers, which is 7 lawns. So the marginal product of hiring the third worker is 7 lawns.

2b. To calculate the value of the marginal product, multiply the marginal product of the third worker by the price of mowing a lawn. The value of the marginal product of the third worker is 7 lawns a day × $20.00, which is $140 a day.

2c. The completed table is to the right.

Workers	Value of the MP
1	$60
2	$80
3	$140
4	$80
5	$40
6	$20

2d. To answer this practice problem, recall that to maximize profit, a firm hires labor up to the point at which the value of the marginal product equals the wage rate. So, to maximize his profit, Casey hires up to the point at which the value of the marginal product equals the wage rate. The wage rate is $40 a day and the answer to part

(c) shows that the value of the marginal product of the fifth worker is also $40 a day. So Casey hires 5 workers.

2e. To maximize its profit, Casey hires 5 workers and the 5 workers mow 20 lawns.

2f. When Casey hires 4 workers, Casey's company mows 18 lawns. Total revenue is 18 lawns a day × $20, which is $360 a day. When Casey hires 5 workers, Casey's company mows 20 lawns a day. Total revenue is 20 lawns a day × $20, which is $400 a day. Casey's total revenue increases by $40 when Casey hires the fifth worker.

2g. The change in Casey's total revenue equals the value of the marginal product of the fifth worker.

■ Self Test 18.1

Fill in the blanks

The factors of production are ____, ____, ____, and ____. The value of the marginal product equals the marginal product of the factor of production times the ____ (factor's price; price of a unit of output). The value of the marginal product of labor ____ (decreases; increases) as more workers are hired. The quantity of labor demanded by a firm is the quantity at which the value of the marginal product of labor equals the ____ (wage rate; price of a unit of output). When the price of the firm's output increases, the demand for labor ____ (decreases; increases) and the demand for labor curve shifts ____ (rightward; leftward).

True or false

1. As a factor of production, coal is considered to be land.
2. The demand for labor is derived from the demand for the goods and services that the labor is hired to produce.
3. A firm's demand for labor curve is also its value of marginal product curve.
4. A rise in the wage rate decreases the quantity of labor demanded.

Multiple choice

1. The four factors of production that produce goods and services are
   a. labor, capital, profits, and entrepreneurship.
   b. money, labor, rent, and profit.
   c. labor, capital, land, and entrepreneurship.
   d. wages, interest, rent, and profit.
   e. wages, prices, quantities, and employment.

2. The wage rate paid to labor is
   a. a factor output.
   b. a factor price.
   c. a factor input.
   d. an input of the workforce.
   e. part of the firm's normal profit.

3. The demand for labor is derived from the
   a. supply of labor.
   b. wage rate.
   c. supply of the good the labor is used to produce.
   d. demand for the goods and services the labor helps produce.
   e. supply of all the other factors of production that can be substituted for labor.

4. The value of the marginal product of labor is equal to the marginal product of labor ____ the price of a unit of output.
   a. divided by
   b. multiplied by
   c. minus
   d. plus
   e. squared and then multiplied by

5. The rule for maximizing profit is to hire labor up to the point at which the value of the marginal product
   a. equals the wage rate.
   b. is greater than the wage rate.
   c. is less than the wage rate.
   d. is a mirror image of the wage rate.
   e. equals the price of the product produced.

6. Which of the following is true?
   a. The value to a firm of hiring another worker is the worker's value of the marginal product.
   b. A firm will hire more workers if the wage rate is greater than the value of the marginal product.
   c. The value of the marginal product is the cost of hiring a worker.
   d. The value of marginal product increases as more workers are hired.
   e. The value of the marginal product equals the price of the good produced divided by the marginal product.

7. An increase in the price of a firm's output leads to a
   a. movement up along the demand for labor curve.
   b. movement down along the demand for labor curve.
   c. rightward shift of the demand for labor curve.
   d. leftward shift of the demand for labor curve.
   e. rightward shift of the supply of labor curve.

Complete the graph

Quantity of labor (workers)	Marginal product (lawns per week)	Value of marginal product 1 (dollars)	Value of marginal product 2 (dollars)
1	13	___	___
2	12	___	___
3	11	___	___
4	10	___	___
5	9	___	___

1. Gene's Lawn Service hires workers to mow lawns. The market for lawns is perfectly competitive and Gene charges $25 a lawn. The table above shows the workers' marginal product schedule.
   a. Calculate the value of the marginal product for each quantity of workers and record your answers in the "Value of the marginal product 1" column. In Figure 18.1, plot Gene's demand for labor curve. Label it LD_1.

■ **FIGURE 18.1**
Wage rate (dollars per week)

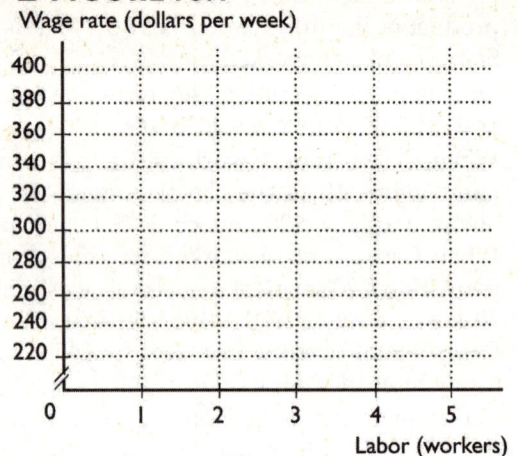

   b. Suppose the price of mowing a lawn rises to $30 per lawn. Calculate the new value of the marginal products and record them in the "Value of the marginal product 2" column. In Figure 18.1, plot Gene's new demand for labor curve and label it LD_2. How did the increase in the price of mowing a lawn change Gene's demand for labor curve?

■ **FIGURE 18.2**
Wage rate (dollars per hour)

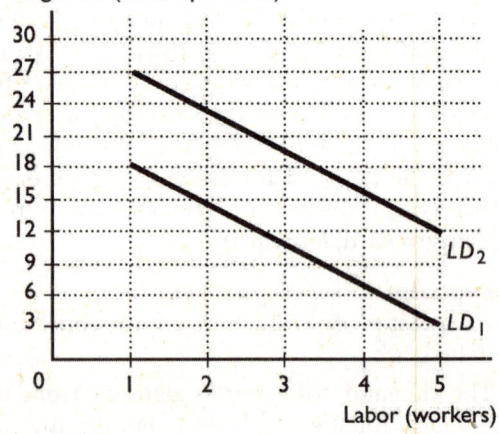

2. Figure 18.2 shows the labor demand curves for two groups of labor.
   a. Which group of labor, group 1 or group 2, has a larger value of its marginal product?
   b. What does the difference in the value of the marginal product between the two groups equal?

Short answer and numeric questions
1. For what are factors of production used?
2. Petroleum is categorized as what type of factor of production?
3. Why does the value of the marginal product decrease as more workers are employed?
4. What is the relationship between the demand for labor curve and the value of the marginal product curve?
5. What factors change the demand for labor and shift the demand for labor curve?

CHECKPOINT 18.2

■ **Explain how wage rates and employment are determined and how labor unions influence labor markets.**

Quick Review
- *Changes in the demand for labor* The demand for labor depends on the price of the firm's output, the prices of other factors of production, and technology.
- *Changes in the supply of labor* The key factors that change the supply of labor are the adult population, preferences, and time spent in school and training.

Additional Practice Problems 18.2
1. Why does an individual labor supply curve bend backward?
2. Tell how each of the events given below affects the labor market. Draw a labor supply and labor demand diagram to determine the effect on the equilibrium wage rate and employment.
   a. More workers reach retirement age and retire.
   b. New technology increases workers' productivity.
   c. Suppose that the price of clothing falls. What is the impact of this change in the labor market for textile workers.

Solutions to Additional Practice Problems 18.2
1. To see how the wage rate influences the quantity of labor supplied, think about Emma's labor supply decision. Emma enjoys leisure time but, if her boss offers her $12 an hour, Emma chooses to work 30 hours a week. This wage rate is high enough to make Emma regard this use of her time as the best available to her. If Emma were offered a higher wage rate, she would want to work even longer hours, but only up to a point. If Emma is offered $25 an hour, she would be willing to work a 40-hour week. But if the wage rate is increased above $25 an hour, Emma would cut back on her work hours and take more leisure. Emma's labor supply curve eventually bends backward.

2a. When more workers reach retirement age and then retire, the supply of labor decreases. The labor supply curve shifts leftward, as shown in the figure by the shift from LS_0 to LS_1. As a result, the equilibrium wage rate rises and the equilibrium quantity of employment decreases.

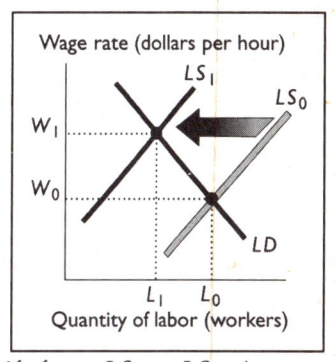

2b. By making workers more productive, the new technology, increases the demand for labor. The labor demand curve shifts rightward, in the figure from LD_0 to LD_1. The equilibrium wage rate rises and the equilibrium amount of employment increases.

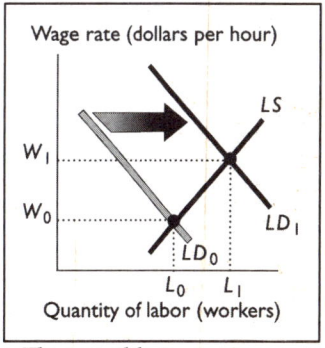

2c. A fall in the price of clothing decreases the value of the marginal product of textile workers. As a result, the demand for labor decreases and the labor demand curve shifts leftward, from LD_0 to LD_1 in the figure. The equilibrium wage rate falls and the equilibrium amount of employment decreases.

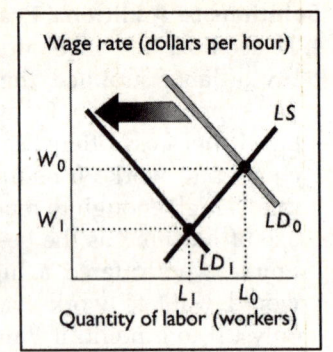

■ Self Test 18.2

Fill in the blanks

An individual's ____ (demand; supply) of labor curve bends backward. An increase in the adult population ____ (decreases; increases) the supply of labor. If the wage rate exceeds the equilibrium wage rate, the quantity of labor supplied is ____ (greater than; less than) the quantity of labor demanded. Unions try to ____ (increase; decrease) the demand for their members' labor and ____ (increase; decrease) the supply of non-union labor.

True or false
1. An individual's supply of labor curve shows that the quantity of labor supplied always increases when the wage rate rises.
2. An increase in college enrollment decreases the supply of low-skilled labor.
3. If the wage rate is less than the equilibrium wage rate, the wage rate will rise to eliminate the surplus of labor.
4. Compared to a competitive labor market, unions boost their members' wages.
5. Unions are likely to support import restrictions.

Multiple choice
1. An individual's labor supply curve eventually bends backward because at a high enough wage rate,
   a. people are willing to work more hours.
   b. employers are willing to hire more workers.
   c. people desire more leisure time.
   d. very few workers are hired.
   e. more people enter the labor market to search for jobs.

2. How does an increase in the adult population affect the labor market?
   a. The demand for labor will become more inelastic.
   b. The supply of labor will decrease.
   c. The supply of labor will increase.
   d. The demand for labor will decrease.
   e. The demand for labor will increase.

3. The supply of labor curve shifts leftward if
   a. the population increases.
   b. the demand for labor curve shifts leftward.
   c. the supply of labor increases.
   d. the wage rate falls.
   e. the supply of labor decreases.

4. If the wage rate is above the equilibrium wage rate, the quantity of labor demanded is ____ the quantity of labor supplied.
   a. greater than
   b. less than
   c. equal to
   d. the negative of
   e. not comparable to

5. The more people who remain in school for full-time education and training, the ____ is the ____ low-skilled labor.
   a. smaller; demand for
   b. smaller; supply of
   c. larger; supply of
   d. larger; demand for
   e. less elastic; demand for

6. If the supply of labor decreases, then the equilibrium wage rate ____ and equilibrium employment ____.
   a. does not change; decreases
   b. rises; increases
   c. rises; decreases
   d. falls; increases
   e. falls; decreases

7. Of the following, a union is *least* likely to support
   a. an increase in the minimum wage rate.
   b. laws that restrict immigration into the country.
   c. on-the-job training that makes their members' more productive.
   d. laws that increase the quantity of the nation's imports.
   e. programs that boost the demand for the goods and services their members produce.

Complete the graph

■ **FIGURE 18.3**
Wage rate (dollars per hour)

1. Figure 18.3 shows Hank's supply of labor curve. At what wage rate does an increase in the wage rate decrease the quantity of labor Hank supplies?

2. Figure 18.4 shows the labor market for Internet security programmers. Suppose that more companies start conducting more of their business on the Internet and so need more Internet security. In Figure 18.4, illus

■ **FIGURE 18.4**
Wage rate (dollars per hour)

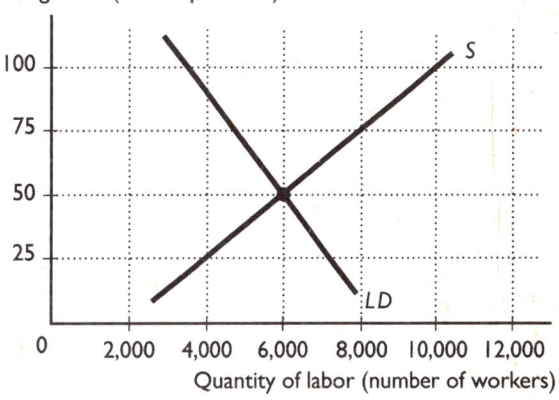

trate the effect in the market for these programmers. What happens to the equilibrium wage rate and number of programmers?

Short answer and numeric questions

1. How does an increase in the adult population change the supply of labor?

2. If more people decide to obtain an advanced education, after they graduate what is the effect on the supply of high-skilled labor? What is the effect on the equilibrium wage rate for high-skilled workers?

3. Why do labor unions support increases in the minimum wage rate even though their members are generally paid more than the minimum wage?

CHECKPOINT 18.3

■ **Explain how rents and natural resource prices are determined.**

Quick Review
- *Renewable natural resources* Natural resources that can be used repeatedly.
- *Nonrenewable natural resources* Natural resources that can be used only once and that cannot be replaced once they have been used.

Additional Practice Problem 18.3
1. Petroleum is a nonrenewable natural resource and is constantly being used. Additionally,

there are new technologies being developed that allow petroleum to be discovered in new locations and also new technologies being developed that make more efficient use of petroleum. What effects do these changes have on the known reserves of petroleum, the demand for petroleum, and the price of petroleum?

Solution to Additional Practice Problem 18.3
1. Using a natural resource such as petroleum decreases its known reserves, which, by itself, raises the price. But new technologies that lead to the discovery of previously unknown reserves increase the known reserves, which, by itself, lowers the price. And the new technologies that enable a more efficient use of a nonrenewable natural resource decrease the demand for the resource, which, by itself, lowers the price. So whether the known reserves increase or decrease and whether the price rises or falls depends on which effect is larger.

■ Self Test 18.3

Fill in the blanks

The higher the rental rate of capital, the ____ (greater; smaller) the quantity of capital demanded. The supply of each particular block of land is perfectly ____ (elastic; inelastic). Over time, advances in technology ____ (increase; decrease) the proven reserves of a nonrenewable natural resource. The Hotelling Principle is the result that as time passes, the price of a nonrenewable natural resource ____ (rises at a random rate; rises at the same rate as the interest rate; does not change).

True or false
1. If the supply of capital increases, the rental rate of capital rises.
2. The demand for land is perfectly elastic, and the supply of land is perfectly inelastic.
3. Because new natural gas deposits are always being discovered, natural gas is a renewable natural resource.
4. The price of a natural resource can only rise over time.

Multiple choice
1. The equilibrium quantity of capital is
   a. determined by only the supply of capital because the supply is perfectly inelastic.
   b. determined by only the supply of capital because the supply is perfectly elastic.
   c. expected to increase at the same rate as the interest rate.
   d. determined by the supply of capital and the demand for capital.
   e. the only factor of production whose quantity is not determined in a market.

2. The supply of each particular block of land is
   a. perfectly elastic.
   b. unit elastic.
   c. elastic.
   d. perfectly inelastic.
   e. inelastic but not perfectly inelastic.

3. A natural resource is nonrenewable if it
   a. never has to rest.
   b. can be used repeatedly.
   c. cannot be replaced once it has been used.
   d. is available at a price of zero.
   e. has a perfectly elastic supply.

4. Oil is an example of
   a. a nonrenewable natural resource.
   b. a renewable natural resource.
   c. physical capital.
   d. a resource for which the true value of the resource cannot be measured.
   e. a resource with a perfectly inelastic demand.

5. The demand for a nonrenewable resource is
   a. determined by the value of its marginal product.
   b. fixed and cannot change.
   c. perfectly inelastic.
   d. perfectly elastic.
   e. not defined because the resource can be used only once.

6. The supply of a nonrenewable natural resource is
   a. always decreasing because the resource is always being used.
   b. perfectly inelastic.
   c. perfectly elastic.
   d. not relevant because nonrenewable resources are used only once.
   e. is determined by the value of the resource's marginal product.

Complete the graph

Rent (dollars per acre per month)	Land (thousands of acres)
400	10
350	20
300	30
250	40
200	50

1. The table above shows the demand for land. The supply of land is fixed at 20,000 square acres.
   a. In Figure 18.5, label the axes and graph the demand curve and the supply curve of land.

■ **FIGURE 18.5**

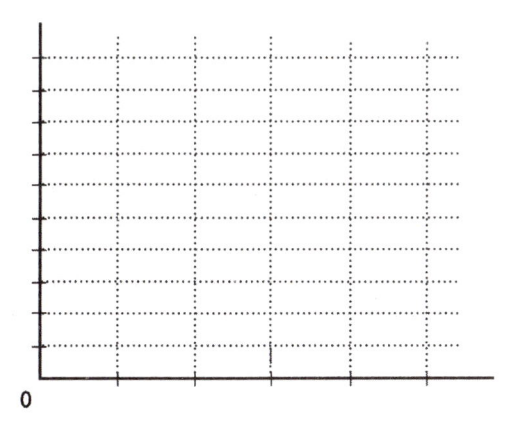

   b. What is the equilibrium rent and quantity?
   c. Suppose the demand decreases so that the quantity of land demanded decreases by 10 thousand acres at each rent. What is the new equilibrium rent and quantity? Comment on the change in the rent and the change in the quantity.

Short answer and numeric questions

Capital rental rate (dollars)	Demand for capital (billions of dollars)	Supply of capital (billions of dollars)
400	150	90
500	130	100
600	110	110
700	90	120
800	70	130

1. The table above gives the demand and supply schedules for capital.
   a. What is the equilibrium rental rate and quantity of capital?
   b. Suppose that population growth increases the quantity of capital demanded by $20 billion at each rental rate and also increases the quantity of capital supplied by $20 billion at each rental rate. Now what is the equilibrium rental rate and quantity of capital?

2. There are billions of barrels of petroleum still in the ground. Why, then, is petroleum considered a nonrenewable natural resource?

3. Explain the role played by the interest rate play in how the price of a nonrenewable natural resource changes over time.

4. The Eye on Your Life discussed salaries of different professions. When you are thinking about a major and a possible career, probably salary implications ought to play some role. And you can use the demand and supply model to help make informal predictions about the future prospects of different career paths. For instance, the U.S. population is aging and older people tend to use more hospital care. How will this fact affect the future job prospects and salary of a person going into nursing?

278 Part 6 · INCOMES, UNCERTAINTY, AND INEQUALITY

SELF TEST ANSWERS

■ CHECKPOINT 18.1

Fill in the blanks

The factors of production are <u>labor</u>, <u>capital</u>, <u>land</u>, and <u>entrepreneurship</u>. The value of the marginal product equals the marginal product of the factor of production times the <u>price of a unit of output</u>. The value of the marginal product of labor <u>decreases</u> as more workers are hired. The quantity of labor demanded by a firm is the quantity at which the value of the marginal product of labor equals the <u>wage rate</u>. When the price of the firm's output increases, the demand for labor <u>increases</u> and the demand for labor curve shifts <u>rightward</u>.

True or false

1. True; page 460
2. True; page 461
3. True; paged 462-463
4. True; pages 462-463

Multiple choice

1. c; page 460
2. b; page 460
3. d; page 461
4. b; page 461
5. a; pages 462-463
6. a; page 462
7. c; page 464

Complete the graph

Quantity of labor (workers)	Marginal product (lawns per week)	Value of marginal product 1 (dollars)	Value of marginal product 2 (dollars)
1	13	325	390
2	12	300	360
3	11	275	330
4	10	250	300
5	9	225	270

1. a. The completed table is above and Figure 18.6 plots the demand for labor curve LD_1; pages 461-363.
   b. The completed table is above and Figure 18.6 plots the demand for labor curve LD_2. The increase in the price of mowing a lawn increases Gene's demand for labor and his demand for labor curve shifts rightward; page 464.

■ FIGURE 18.6
Wage rate (dollars per week)

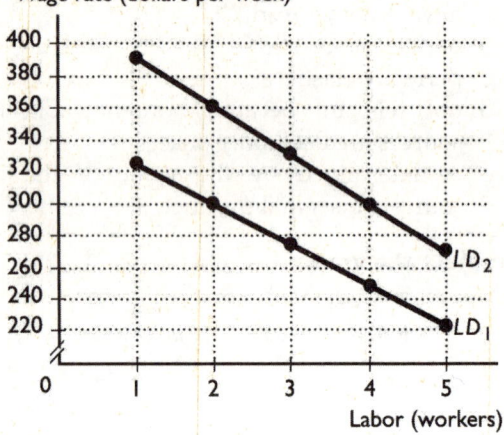

2. a. Group 2 has a higher value of marginal product because its demand curve lies to the right of the demand curve for group 1; page 462.
   b. Because the demand curve is the same as the value of the marginal product curve, the vertical distance between the two demand curves equals the difference in the value of marginal product. So group 2's value of marginal product is $7.50 more per hour than group 1's value of marginal product; pages 462-463

Short answer and numeric questions

1. Factors of production are used to produce goods and services; page 460.
2. Petroleum is one of the gifts of nature, so as a factor of production it is included as land; page 460.
3. The value of the marginal product equals the price of a unit of the output multiplied by the marginal product of the factor of production. As more of the factor of production is employed, marginal product decreases, and as a result, the value of the marginal product also decreases; pages 461-462.
4. The demand for labor curve and the value of

the marginal product curve are the same; pages 462-463.

5. Three factors change the demand for labor and shift the demand for labor curve: changes in the price of the firm's output, changes in the prices of other factors of production, and changes in technology; page 464.

■ CHECKPOINT 18.2
Fill in the blanks
An individual's <u>supply</u> of labor curve bends backward. An increase in the adult population <u>increases</u> the supply of labor. If the wage rate exceeds the equilibrium wage rate, the quantity of labor supplied is <u>greater than</u> the quantity of labor demanded. Unions try to <u>increase</u> the demand for their members' labor and <u>decrease</u> the supply of non-union labor.

True or false
1. False; page 466
2. True; page 468
3. False; pages 468-469
4. True; page 470
5. True; page 471

Multiple choice
1. c; page 466
2. c; page 468
3. e; page 468
4. b; pages 468-469
5. b; page 468
6. c; page 469
7. d; page 471

Complete the graph
1. Figure 18.7 shows that for wage rates exceeding $60 an hour, Hank decreases the quantity of labor he supplies as the wage rate rises; page 466.
2. In Figure 18.8 the demand for Internet security programmers increases. The demand for labor curve shifts rightward from LD_0 to LD_1. The equilibrium wage rate rises and the quantity of these programmers employed increases; pages 468-469.

■ FIGURE 18.7
Wage rate (dollars per hour)

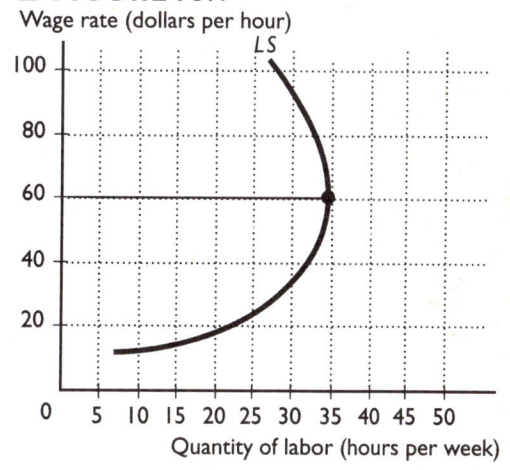

■ FIGURE 18.8
Wage rate (dollars per hour)

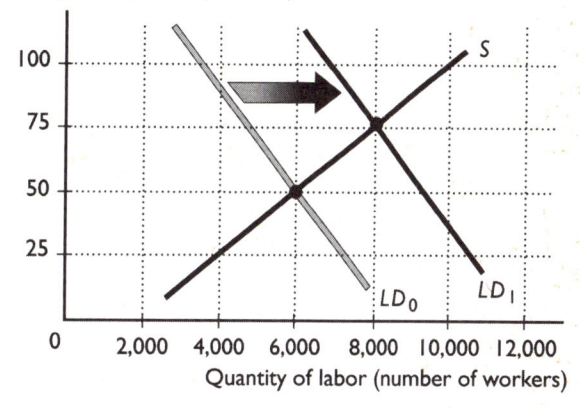

Short answer and numeric questions
1. An increase in the adult population increases the supply of labor; page 468.
2. As more people obtain advanced degrees the supply of high-skilled labor increases. The equilibrium wage rate for high-skilled labor falls; pages 468-469.
3. Unions support hikes in the minimum wage because lower-skilled workers, who are paid the minimum wage, are substitutes for higher-skilled union labor. If the wage rate that must be paid lower skilled workers increases, some firms will hire instead higher-skilled union labor, thereby increasing the demand for union labor; page 471.

Part 6 · INCOMES, UNCERTAINTY, AND INEQUALITY

■ CHECKPOINT 18.3

Fill in the blanks

The higher the rental rate of capital, the <u>smaller</u> the quantity of capital demanded. The supply of each particular block of land is perfectly <u>inelastic</u>. Over time, advances in technology <u>increase</u> the proven reserves of a nonrenewable natural resource. The Hotelling Principle is the result that as time passes, the price of a nonrenewable natural resource <u>rises at the same rate as the interest rate</u>.

True or false
1. False; page 473
2. False; page 474
3. False; page 475
4. False; page 476

Multiple choice
1. d; page 473
2. d; page 474
3. c; page 475
4. a; page 475
5. a; page 475
6. c; page 475

Complete the graph

■ **FIGURE 18.9**

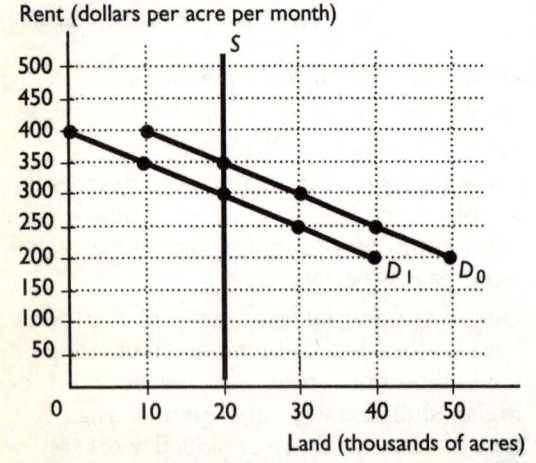

Rent (dollars per acre per month)

[Graph showing S (vertical line at 20), D₁ and D₀ demand curves; y-axis 0–500, x-axis 0–50 thousands of acres]

Land (thousands of acres)

1. a. Figure 18.9, shows the completed figure; page 474.

b. The equilibrium rent is $350 an acre per month and the equilibrium quantity is 20,000 acres; page 474.

c. The decrease in demand lowers the equilibrium rent to $300 per acre and the equilibrium quantity remains 20,000 acres. The change in demand changed *only* the rent; the quantity is unchanged. Because the supply is perfectly inelastic, changes in demand change only the rent and do not affect the quantity; page 474.

Short answer and numeric questions

1. a. The equilibrium rental rate is $600 because this is the rental rate at which the quantity of capital demanded equals the quantity of capital supplied. The equilibrium quantity of capital is $110 billion; page 473.

   b. In this question, both the demand and supply of capital have increased by the same amount. So the equilibrium rental rate remains the same, $600, and the equilibrium quantity of capital increases to $130 billion; page 473.

2. Petroleum is a nonrenewable natural resource because once any particular barrel is used, that barrel cannot be used again; page 475.

3. The Hotelling Principle is the result that the price of a nonrenewable resource is expected to rise at a rate that equals the interest rate. The explanation for this result lies in the behavior of the owners of the resource: They can either sell the resource and invest the proceeds in an interest bearing asset or else hold the resource and sell it next period. If the price is expected to rise at a rate that is less than the interest rate, the owners will increase their supply today in order to use the proceeds to buy an interest bearing account. The supply will continue to increase, which lowers the price, until today's price falls enough so that its rate of increase from today to the next period is equal to the interest rate. At this point, the owners will no longer increase the supply. Similarly, if the price is expected to rise at a rate greater than the in-

terest rate, the owners will decrease their supply in order to hold the resource and enjoy the high return. The supply will continue to decrease, which raises the price, until today's price rises enough so that its rate of increase from today to the next period is equal to the interest rate. At this point, the owners will no longer decrease the supply. So the equilibrium, which occurs when the owners are neither increasing nor decreasing the supply (that is, the supply curve is not shifting) occurs only when the price of the resource is expected to rise at a rate that equals the interest rate; page 477.

4. A large fraction of nurses are hired by hospitals. As the nation ages and more individuals require hospital care, the demand for nurses is likely to increase. The increase in the demand for nurses will raise the salary paid nurses and increase the quantity employed. So by using the supply and demand model, it is possible to make an informed prediction that the career possibilities of nurses are fairly bright; page 475.

Chapter 19
Uncertainty and Information

CHAPTER IN PERSPECTIVE

1. Explain how people make decisions when they are uncertain about the consequences.

In a situation with uncertainty, the outcome, say wealth, is not known. Expected wealth is the money value of what a person expects to own at a given point in time. It equals the weighted average of wealth in all the different outcomes, weighted by the probability of each outcome. Risk aversion is the dislike of risk. Risk aversion can be demonstrated using the utility of wealth, which shows the amount of utility a person has from different amounts of wealth. The marginal utility of wealth decreases as wealth increase the pain from a loss is greater than the pleasure from an equal sized gain. Expected utility is the utility value of what a person expects to own at a given point in time. It equals the weighted average of wealth in all the different outcomes, weighted by the probability of each outcome. In a risky situation, people maximize expected utility. The utility of wealth curve can measure an individual's cost of risk, that is, the amount by which expected wealth must be increased to give the same expected utility as a no-risk situation. This difference in wealth is the cost of the risk.

2. Explain how markets enable people to buy and sell risk.

People buy insurance to reduce risk. Insurance works by pooling a large number of risks so that the total number of adverse outcomes is relatively certain. Insurance is profitable because people are risk averse. A large number of people pay for the insurance, which limits their potential loss and thereby decreases their risk and increases their utility. The company uses these payments to compensate the few that suffer losses.

3. Explain how markets cope when buyers or sellers have private information.

Asymmetric information is a situation in which the person on one side of a transaction has private information about things that are relevant to the transaction. Asymmetric information creates two problems, moral hazard (an incentive after making an agreement to behave in a way that imposes costs on the other party to the agreement) and adverse selection (the tendency for people to enter into agreements in which they can use their private information to their own advantage and to the disadvantage of the uninformed party). A warranty on a used car can help overcome the lemon problem. Without warranties, the outcome will be a pooling equilibrium, when an uninformed person cannot determine quality and the prices of a lemon and a good car are the same; with warranties, the outcome will be a separating equilibrium, when the messages signaled provide full information to a previously uninformed party and the prices of the lemons and good cars differ. In the market for loans, signals such as length of time on the job can overcome asymmetric information problems so that the equilibrium is a separating equilibrium, with the riskier borrower paying a higher interest rate. In the insurance market, a person's past driving record and deductible payments limit adverse selection and moral hazard.

CHECKPOINT 19.1

■ **Explain how people make decisions when they are uncertain about the consequences.**

Quick Review

- *Expected utility* The average value of utility arising from all possible outcomes, weighted by their probability.

Additional Practice Problems 19.1

Occurrence	Utility (units)	Probability of occurrence (percent)
A	200	40
B	190	20
C	160	20
D	120	10
E	60	10

1. The table above shows the probability of five different events and each event's utility.
   a. What is the expected utility?
   b. Does the expected utility equal any of the possible utilities in the table?

2. The figure shows David's utility of wealth curve. David has $2,500 to invest. David can make an investment, which, if successful, will increase his $2,500 of wealth to $5,000. However if it fails, his $2,500 will be reduced to $1,000. David puts the odds of success or failure at 50% each.
   a. What is David's expected wealth if he takes advantage of the opportunity?
   b. Will David make this investment? Explain.

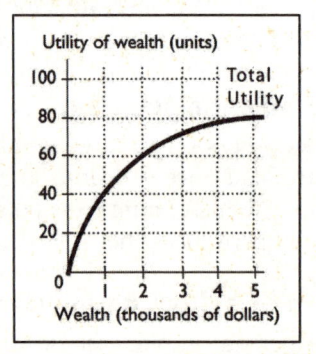

Solutions to Additional Practice Problems 19.1

1a. The expected utility can be calculated as the sum of the utility of each event weighted by the probability of its occurrence. In this case the expected utility is (200 units × 0.40) + (190 units × 0.20) + (160 units × 0.20) + (120 units × 0.10) +(60 units × 0.10), which is 168 units.

1b. The expected utility does not equal any of the possible utilities in the table. Expected utility shows what will happen, on average, if an uncertain situation is repeated a large number of times.

2a. The expected wealth is as the sum of the wealth of each outcome weighted by the probability of its occurrence. David's expected wealth from the investment is ($5,000 × 0.5) + ($1,000 × 0.5), or $3,000.

2b. David will not make the investment. His expected utility from the investment is less than his utility with his $2,500. The figure shows that David's expected utility if he makes the investment is 60 units, which is less than his utility if he doesn't make the investment, 70 units. (David's expected utility if he makes the investment is his utility with the good outcome, 80 units, weighted by the probability of the good outcome, 0.5, plus his utility with the bad outcome, 40 units, weighted by the probability of the bad outcome, 0.50.)

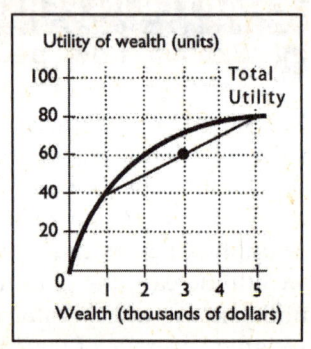

■ **Self Test 19.1**

Fill in the blanks

The utility of wealth curve shows that the marginal utility of additional wealth ____ (increases; decreases) as wealth increases. In an uncertain outcome, people ____ (are; are not) guaranteed to have an actual utility that equals their expected utility. In situations with an uncertain outcome, people make the choice that gives them the largest expected ____ (wealth; utility).

True or false

1. The utility of wealth curve shows that the

marginal utility from additional wealth diminishes as wealth increases.
2. Expected utility always equals the actual utility the person receives.
3. For the same expected wealth, the greater the range of uncertainty, the lower the expected utility.
4. In a risky situation, people maximize their expected wealth.
5. The cost of a risk equals the difference between the expected wealth minus the actual wealth that gives the same utility.

Multiple choice
1. If offered two investments, a risk averse person will accept
   a. the less risky investment always.
   b. the investment which yields the largest expected wealth always.
   c. neither investment due to the risk.
   d. the more risky investment if the expected wealth from it is high enough.
   e. the less risky investment only if its expected wealth is greater than that from the more risky investment.

2. As Al's wealth increases, his total utility of wealth ____ and his marginal utility of wealth ____.
   a. increases; increases
   b. increases; decreases
   c. decreases; increases
   d. decreases; decreases
   e. increases; does not change

3. Julio is offered a job that pays either $40,000 if he is successful or $20,000 if he is unsuccessful. His probability of success is 50 percent. The expected wealth from the job is
   a. $60,000.
   b. $40,000.
   c. $30,000.
   d. $20,000.
   e. impossible to calculate without more information.

4. Julio is offered a job that pays either $40,000 if he is successful or $20,000 if he is unsuccessful. His probability of success is 75 percent. The expected wealth from the job is
   a. $40,000.
   b. $35,000.
   c. $30,000.
   d. $20,000.
   e. impossible to calculate without more information.

5. Job A offers a chance to make $10,000 with a probability of 50 percent and a chance to make $0 with a probability of 50 percent. Job B offers a chance to make $20,000 with a probability of 25 percent and a chance to make $0 with a probability of 75 percent. The expected wealth from Job A is ____ and the expected wealth from Job B is ____.
   a. $5,000; $10,000
   b. $0; $0
   c. $5,000; $5,000
   d. $10,000; $15,000
   e. $10,000; $20,000

6. Job A offers a chance to make $10,000 with a probability of 50 percent and a chance to make $0 with a probability of 50 percent. Job B offers a chance to make $20,000 with a probability of 25 percent and a chance to make $0 with a probability of 75 percent. The expected utility from Job A is ____ the expected utility from Job B.
   a. greater than
   b. less than
   c. equal to
   d. not comparable to
   e. To answer the question, more information is needed.

7. Tim's expected utility from a risky investment with an expected wealth of $1,000 is 80 units and his utility from a no-risk opportunity with wealth of $600 is 80 units. Tim's cost of risk is
   a. 80 units.
   b. $400.
   c. $1,600.
   d. $1,000.
   e. $600.

Complete the graph

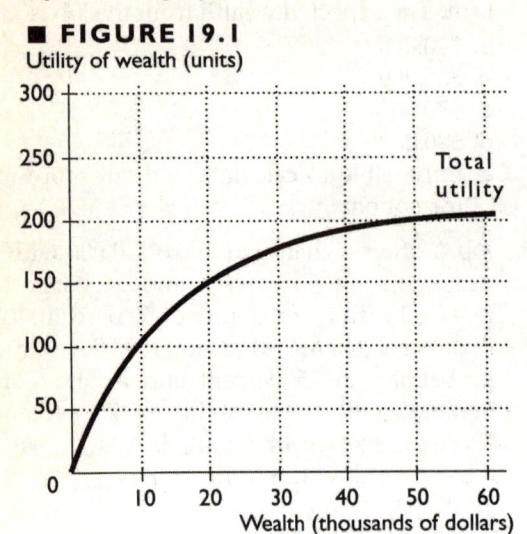

■ FIGURE 19.1
Utility of wealth (units)

[Graph showing total utility curve rising from 0, concave, reaching approximately 210 at wealth = 60 thousand dollars. X-axis: Wealth (thousands of dollars) 0-60.]

1. Figure 19.1 shows Lisa's utility of wealth curve. She is considering an investment that will pay her either $10,000 with a probability of 50 percent or $50,000 with a probability of 50 percent.
   a. What is Lisa's expected wealth?
   b. What is Lisa's utility if she receives $10,000? Her utility if she receives $50,000? Her expected utility?
   c. What is the cost of this risk to Lisa? Show Lisa's cost of risk on the figure and carefully explain what is meant by "the cost of risk."

2. Figure 19.2 shows Ken's utility of wealth curve. He is considering an investment that will pay him either $10,000 with a probability of 50 percent or $50,000 with a probability of 50 percent.
   a. What is Ken's expected wealth?
   b. What is Ken's utility if he receives $10,000? His utility if he receives $50,000? His expected utility?
   c. Show Ken's cost of risk on the figure. How does Ken's cost of risk compare to Lisa's cost of risk in the preceding question?

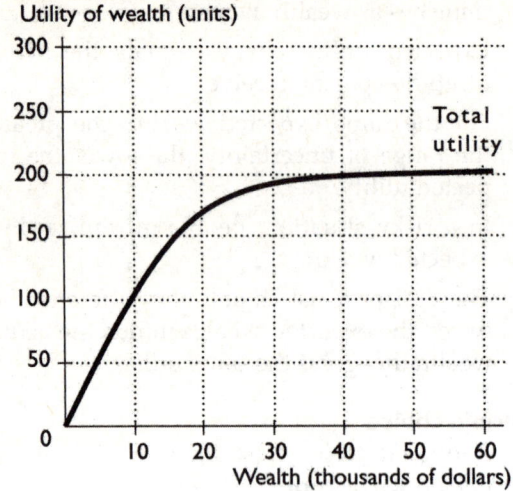

■ FIGURE 19.2
Utility of wealth (units)

[Graph showing total utility curve rising steeply from 0, becoming nearly flat around 200 by wealth = 30 thousand dollars. X-axis: Wealth (thousands of dollars) 0-60.]

Short answer and numeric questions

Wealth (dollars)	Utility (units)
0	0
4,000	52
5,000	60
8,000	79
10,000	87
15,000	98
20,000	104

1. The table presents Leonard's utility of wealth schedule. Leonard is considering an investment that will pay either $0 or $20,000 with equal probability, that is, there is a 50 percent chance of obtaining $0 and a 50 percent chance of gaining $20,000.
   a. What is Leonard's expected wealth from the investment?
   b. What is Leonard's expected utility?
   c. What is Leonard's cost of risk for this investment opportunity?
   d. Is Leonard willing to make the investment if it costs him $5,000?

2. What does risk aversion mean?

3. How does the expected utility from an uncertain investment differ from the actual utility from the investment's outcome?

4. In a risky situation, why do people maximize their expected utility and not their expected wealth?

CHECKPOINT 19.2

■ **Explain how markets enable people to buy and sell risk.**

Quick Review
- *Risk aversion* The dislike of risk.

Additional Practice Problems 19.2
1. Are there situations in which it is rational for a person to *not* buy insurance?
2. How can insurance increase a person's utility?

Solutions to Additional Practice Problems 19.2
1. Yes, there is a situation in which it is not rational to buy insurance. In particular, if the price of the insurance is too high, even a risk averse person will not buy insurance.

2. Insurance decreases the risks that the buyer faces. Take auto insurance. Without insurance, the buyer faces the risk of an accident which would decrease his or her wealth significantly. By purchasing insurance, the buyer eliminates the risk of a large fall in wealth from an accident by replacing it with a small, certain fall in wealth from the insurance premium. This decrease in risk can increase the buyer's utility.

■ **Self Test 19.2**

Fill in the blanks
Insurance reduces the risk that people face by ____ (totally eliminating; pooling) the risks of many individuals. People buy insurance if their utility after paying the insurance premium is ____ (greater; less) than their expected utility if they do not buy insurance. Insurance companies ____ (can always; might be able to) earn an economic profit.

True or false
1. Buying insurance reduces the purchasers' risk.
2. Insurance companies pools risks.
3. If Kevin buys auto insurance, Kevin has decreased the risk that he will have an auto accident.

4. Buying insurance can increase a risk averse person's utility.

Multiple choice
1. Insurance companies
   a. pool risk and thereby lower people's utility.
   b. never can earn a profit.
   c. can increase risk averse people's utility.
   d. pool utility of wealth curves.
   e. always earn an economic profit.

2. In the United States, on all types of insurance, people spend the most on ____ insurance.
   a. auto
   b. property and casualty
   c. life
   d. health
   e. hurricane

■ **FIGURE 19.3**
Utility of wealth (units)

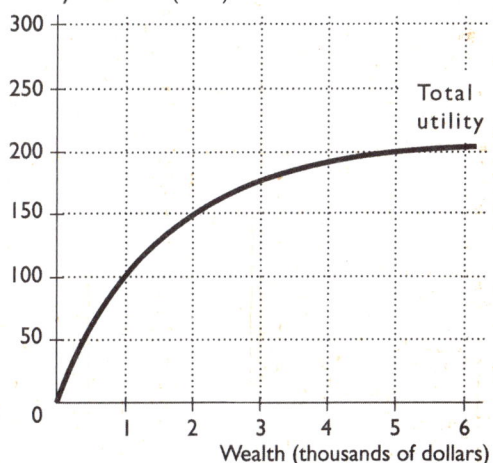

3. Figure 19.3 shows Kris's utility of wealth curve. Kris has a boat worth $5,000. There is a 50 percent probability that she will have an accident, in which case the boat is worth $1,000. Kris's expected wealth is ____ and her expected utility is ____.
   a. $3,000; 300 units
   b. $3,000; 200 units
   c. $4,000; 200 units
   d. $5,000; 200 units
   e. $3,000; 150 units

288 Part 6 · INCOMES, UNCERTAINTY, AND INEQUALITY

4. Figure 19.3 shows Kris's utility of wealth curve. Kris has a boat worth $5,000. There is a 50 percent probability that she will have an accident, in which case the boat is worth $1,000. The value of the boat insurance to Kris is ____.
   a. $5,000
   b. $4,000
   c. $3,000
   d. $2,000
   e. $1,000

5. Which of the following statements is true?
   a. Insurance companies always earn a normal profit.
   b. To stay open, insurance companies must earn an economic profit to compensate them for the risks they accept.
   c. Insurance companies collect premiums from only those who suffer a loss.
   d. Risk averse people can often increase their utility be purchasing insurance.
   e. All risks can be insured.

Complete the graph

Wealth (dollars)	Utility (units)
100	400
80	350
60	280
40	200
20	110
0	0

1. Igor owns a valuable bat worth $100. Unfortunately, this species of bat has a 20 percent annual probability of dying and becoming worthless — even to Igor.
   a. Igor's utility of wealth schedule is given in Table 19.3. What is Igor's utility if his bat lives? If it dies? What is Igor's expected utility?
   b. In Figure 19.4, draw Igor's utility of wealth curve.
   c. It is potentially fortunate for Igor that he is able to purchase bat insurance. Bat Farm Insurance Company is willing to sell him a policy that costs $40 a year and that promises to replace his bat if it dies. Might Igor buy insurance from Bat Farm?
   d. Is Igor willing to pay $20 for bat insurance? Why or why not?
   e. In Figure 19.4, show the value of insurance for Igor.

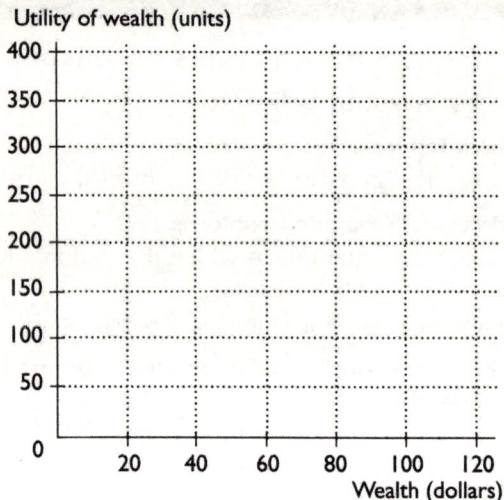

■ **FIGURE 19.4**
Utility of wealth (units)

Short answer and numeric questions

1. The risk of an auto accident is always present, so how does auto insurance increase people's expected utility?
2. Why would it be difficult for an insurance company confined only to south Florida to offer insurance against hurricane damage?
3. How does the value of insurance to Joanna affect Joanna's decision about purchasing the insurance?

CHECKPOINT 19.3

■ **Explain how markets cope when buyers or sellers have private information.**

Quick Review
- *Moral hazard* An incentive after making an agreement to behave in a way that imposes costs on the other party to the agreement.

- *Adverse selection* The tendency for people to enter into agreements in which they can use their own private information to their own advantage and to the disadvantage of the uninformed party.

Additional Practice Problem 19.3

1. Which of the following are examples of adverse selection and which are examples of moral hazard?
   a. A skier takes additional risks once she has health insurance.
   b. A baseball player takes more days off for minor injuries after signing a long-term contract.
   c. A person who is a poor credit risk is more likely to use pay-day advance loans.
   d. A student who is likely to work little in a class signs up for a section that has extensive group work rather than a section that is graded solely on the basis of exams.
   e. A lazy used car salesperson applies for a job with a car dealership where the pay is a fixed amount rather than based on sales.
   f. A realtor shows a house for sale only once a month rather than once a week as was verbally promised before the sales contract was signed.

Solution to Additional Practice Problem 19.3

1a. Moral hazard; the skier is changing behavior after the health insurance was purchased.

1b. Moral hazard, the ball player's behavior is changing after the contract was signed.

1c. Adverse selection, the pay-day loan company is attracting poor credit risks.

1d. Adverse selection, the class section based on group work is attracting lazy students.

1e. Adverse selection, the car dealership is attracting lazy salespeople.

1f. Moral hazard, the realtor's behavior is changing after the contract was signed.

■ Self Test 19.3

Fill in the blanks

The incentive to change behavior to benefit yourself after a contract is signed reflects ____ (moral hazard; adverse selection) and the incentive to enter into an agreement in which you know you will get additional benefits of which the other party is presently unaware reflects ____ (moral hazard; adverse selection). The lemon problem in the used car market primarily reflects the problem of ____ (moral hazard; adverse selection). If there are no signals in the used car market, too ____ (many; few) good used cars are sold. Signals that allow buyers to distinguish between good used cars and lemons result in a ____ (pooling; separating) equilibrium. Banks can use the length of time on the job as a ____ (pooling mechanism; signal; moral hazard) to help determine the risk of loaning to a particular individual. A driver with private information that he or she is a safe driver will want a policy with a ____ (high; low) deductible.

True or false

1. Adverse selection occurs when one party enters into a contract with private information that will enable them to increase their benefits at the cost of decreasing the other party's benefits.
2. In a pooling equilibrium, the price of a good used car is different than the price of a lemon.
3. In the used car market, warranties can lead to an equilibrium in which good cars have higher prices than do lemons.
4. In the market for loans, if everyone pays the same interest rate, the market is efficient.
5. The number of traffic tickets a driver has accumulated is an example of a signal.
6. Risky drivers are likely to prefer auto insurance policies with low deductibles.

Multiple choice

1. When Sam makes an agreement and then behaves after the agreement in a way to increase his benefits and harm the other party to the agreement, Sam is illustrating
   a. signaling.
   b. adverse selection.
   c. moral hazard.
   d. the cost of contracting.
   e. a pooling equilibrium.

2. Ben becomes more likely to play with matches after he has fire insurance. This situation illustrates the idea of
   a. moral hazard.
   b. adverse selection.
   c. the lemon problem.
   d. the "don't play with fire" principle.
   e. a separating equilibrium.

3. JCPenney guarantees to refund a customer's money if the customer returns poorly made clothing. This guarantee is an example of
   a. the adverse selection problem.
   b. the moral hazard problem.
   c. the cost of risk.
   d. signaling.
   e. a lemon problem.

4. If buyers cannot assess the quality of used cars and there are no warranties,
   a. only lemons are sold.
   b. only good used cars are sold.
   c. good cars are sold at a higher price than bad cars.
   d. there is no adverse selection problem.
   e. lemons and good cars sell for the same price.

5. In the used car market, with a pooling equilibrium the price of a lemon is ___ the price of a good used car and with a separating equilibrium the price of a lemon is ___ the price of a good used car.
   a. less than; equal to
   b. equal to; less than
   c. equal to; more than
   d. more than; more than
   e. equal to; equal to

6. When deciding on a loan, banks use screening because
   a. they are not trying to maximize their profit.
   b. there is no asymmetric information in the market for loans.
   c. of moral hazard.
   d. it helps them to distinguish between high-risk and low-risk borrowers.
   e. there are too many signals in the market for loans.

7. If you have private information that you are a riskier driver than your record indicates, you are likely to buy from your insurance company a policy that has a ___ deductible and a ___ premium.
   a. high; high
   b. high; low
   c. low; high
   d. low; low
   e. None of the above answers are correct because private information has no effect in the market for insurance.

Complete the graph

■ FIGURE 19.5
Interest rate (percent per year)

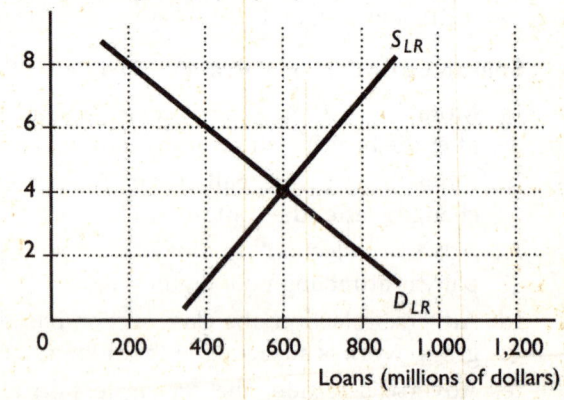

1. Figure 19.5 shows the market for low-risk loans. What is the separating equilibrium interest rate and quantity of low-risk loans? If the pooling equilibrium interest rate is 6 percent and lenders cannot determine who is a low-risk borrower, what is the equilibrium interest rate and what will be the quantity of

low-risk loans? In Figure 19.5 show the deadweight loss from the pooling equilibrium.

Short answer and numeric questions

1. Igor owns a pet bat. Sadly, this species has a 20 percent annual probability of dying Igor eventually buys insurance from the All Bat Insurance Company which will pay Igor in case his bat dies. Suppose that Igor knew his bat was already sickly and had a higher than normal chance of dying, but that All Bat did not know this, and so charged Igor the premium that applies to healthy bats. Who expects to gain more than usual from this policy? What does this situation illustrate?

2. What is the difference between a pooling equilibrium and a separating equilibrium? From society's vantage point, is one more desirable than the other?

3. Why do banks often lend more readily to people who have credit cards and have previously borrowed from the bank than to people who have always paid in cash and have never borrowed?

4. Larry and Harry have private information about their safety as drivers. Larry is a safe driver; he never speeds and comes to a full stop at every stop sign. Harry believes that speed limit signs give the minimum speed and that yellow lights mean "full speed ahead."

   a. If you owned an automobile insurance company and had to charge everyone the same rate, who do you want to insure?

   b. You want to sell insurance to safe drivers, like Larry, for $500 a year and to risky drivers, like Harry, for $1,500 a year. If you cannot determine who is safe and who is risky, you offer both Larry and Harry insurance for $1,000 a year with no deductible. Is Harry likely to buy the insurance? Is Larry? Does Larry's decision depend on whether he can convince another insurance company that he is a safe driver?

   c. Suppose that you decide to sell two types of insurance policies: one costs $1,300 a year and has a $100 deductible (so that the car owner pays the first $100 of any claim) and the other costs $300 a year and has a $1,500 deductible. Which type of insurance is Harry most likely to buy? Larry? Why?

   d. What do your answers to part (c) tell you about the role played by deductibles?

5. The Eye on Your Life discusses the role grades and a college education play in signaling your ability. Signals also play a role in assigning grades. Frequently instructors who assign group projects base some of the grade on grades each group participant assigns to the other participants. Using the concepts discussed in this chapter, explain why instructors use this method rather than assign everyone in the project the same grade.

SELF TEST ANSWERS

■ CHECKPOINT 19.1

Fill in the blanks

The utility of wealth curve shows that the marginal utility of additional wealth <u>decreases</u> as wealth increases. In an uncertain outcome, people <u>are not</u> guaranteed to have an actual utility that equals their expected utility. In situations with an uncertain outcome, people make the choice that gives them the largest expected <u>utility</u>.

True or false
1. True; page 485
2. False; page 486
3. True; page 486
4. False; page 487
5. True; page 487

Multiple choice
1. d; page 484
2. b; page 485
3. c; page 484
4. b; page 484
5. c; page 484
6. a; page 486
7. b; page 487

Complete the graph
1. a. Lisa's expected wealth equals the probability of receiving $10,000 multiplied by $10,000, plus the probability of receiving $50,000 multiplied by $50,000. In this case, each probability is 0.5, so Lisa's expected wealth equals $30,000; page 484.
   b. Figure 19.6 shows that Lisa's utility if she receives $10,000 is 100. The figure also shows that if she receives $50,000, her utility is 200. Lisa's expected utility equals the utility if she receives $10,000 (100) multiplied by the probability of receiving $10,000 (0.50) plus the utility if she receives $50,000 (200) multiplied by the probability of receiving $50,000 (0.50). Lisa's expected utility is 150; pages 485-486.

■ **FIGURE 19.6**
Utility of wealth (units)

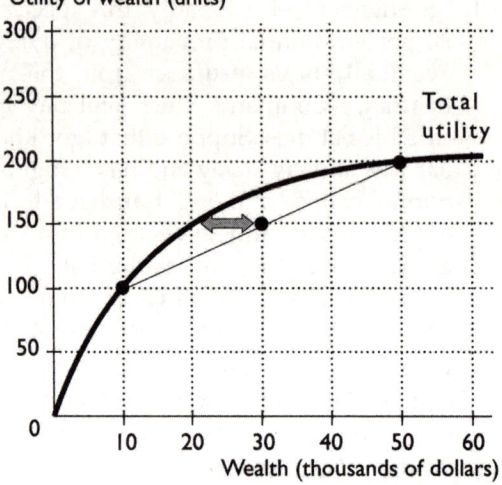

c. Lisa's cost of risk is the difference between Lisa's expected wealth and the certain wealth that gives her the same utility. In the risky situation, Lisa's expected utility is 150. From the utility of wealth curve, if Lisa received certain wealth of $20,000, she would have the utility of 150. The cost of risk to Lisa is $30,000 − $20,000 or $10,000, illustrated by the length of the gray arrow in Figure 19.6. The cost of risk reflects the fact that Lisa dislikes uncertainty. The outcome of Lisa's investment is uncertain; it may pay off in big (wealth of $50,000), or it may pay off little (wealth of $10,000.). Because Lisa dislikes risk, she can achieve the same utility if she receives a certain wealth of only $20,000; page 487.

2. a. Ken's expected wealth is the same as Lisa's in the preceding problem, $30,000; page 484.
   b. Ken's utilities are the same as Lisa's in the preceding problem—100, 200, and 150; pages 485-486.
   c. The length of the gray arrow in Figure 19.7 (on the next page) shows Ken's cost. Ken's cost of risk exceeds Lisa's cost of risk; page 487.

■ FIGURE 19.7
Utility of wealth (units)

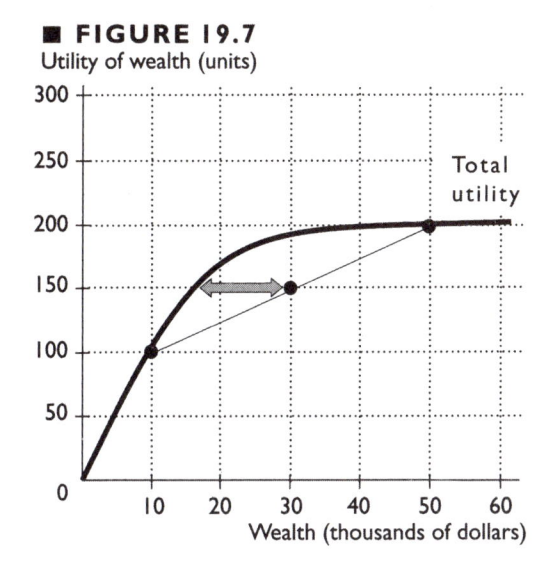

Short answer and numeric questions
1. a. Leonard's expected wealth is ($20,000 × 0.5) + ($0 × 0.5) = $10,000; page 484.
   b. Leonard's expected utility is (104 × 0.5) + (0 × 0.5) = 52; page 486.
   c. The risky situation yields expected wealth of $10,000 and expected utility of 52. The table shows that certain (no-risk) wealth of $4,000 also yields utility of 52. The cost of risk is $6,000 ($10,000 − $4,000), the amount by which (expected) wealth in the risky case must be increased beyond no-risk wealth to give the same utility as the no-risk situation; page 487.
   d. For Leonard, the foregone utility, 60, of the $5,000 cost of the investment is greater than the expected utility of the risky project, 52. Leonard is not willing to make the investment; page 487.
2. Risk aversion means that the person dislikes risk. For instance, the riskier an investment, the less the person likes it; page 484.
3. The expected utility is the weighted average utility a person would obtain if the investment were repeated many times. For any one time the investment is made, the actual utility the person receives from the investment might differ from the expected utility; pages 486-487.
4. People maximize their expected utility because utility measures their satisfaction or well-being. Maximizing expected utility is making the person, on average, as well off as possible. Wealth is related to utility, but the diminishing marginal utility of wealth means that additional wealth increases the person's utility by less and less. So, maximizing expected wealth is *not* the same as maximizing expected utility; pages 485, 487.

■ CHECKPOINT 19.2
Fill in the blanks
Insurance reduces the risk that people face by <u>pooling</u> the risks of many individuals. People buy insurance if their utility after paying the insurance premium is <u>greater</u> than their expected utility if they do not buy insurance. Insurance companies <u>might be able to</u> earn an economic profit.

True or false
1. True; page 489
2. True; page 489
3. False; page 489
4. True; page 492

Multiple choice
1. c; pages 489, 492
2. d; page 490
3. e; pages 484, 486
4. c; page 492
5. d; pages 489, 492

Complete the graph
1. a. If Igor's bat lives, he has utility of 400; if it dies, he has utility of zero. Igor's expected utility equals his utility if the bat lives multiplied by the probability it lives plus his utility if the bat dies multiplied by the probability it dies. The expected utility is (0.8 × 400) + (0.2 × 0) = 320; page 486.
   b. Figure 19.8 (on the next page) shows Igor's utility of wealth curve.

■ FIGURE 19.8

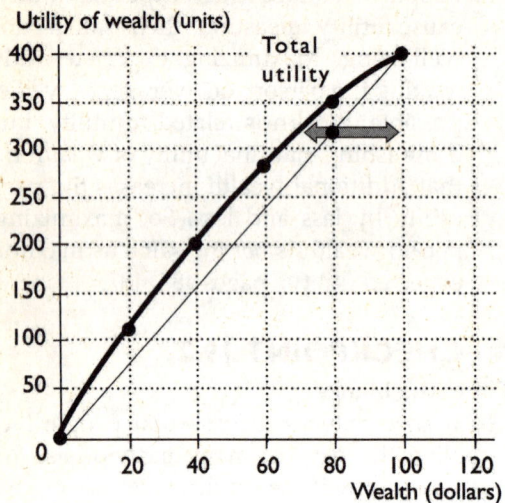

Utility of wealth (units) vs Wealth (dollars) — Total utility curve.

c. If Igor buys insurance from Bat Farm, he is guaranteed wealth of $60 (wealth of $100 minus the insurance payment of $40). Certain wealth of $60 gives Igor utility of 280. That amount of utility is less than the expected utility Igor gets from being uninsured (320), so Igor will not buy insurance from Bat Farm; pages 491-492.

d. Igor is willing to pay $20 for bat insurance. If he pays $20 for insurance, his wealth is $80, which gives utility of 350. This level of utility exceeds the expected utility of 320 when he is uninsured; pages 491-492.

e. The value of insurance is the difference between Igor's wealth if his bat lives and he has no insurance and the certain wealth that gives him the same utility as his expected wealth. Figure 19.8 shows this value as the length of the gray arrow; page 492.

Short answer and numeric questions

1. While the risk of an auto accident is always present, auto insurance removes the financial risk. Auto insurance means that the driver's wealth is known and is not uncertain: If the driver has an accident, the insurance company reimburses the driver and if the driver does not have an accident, the diver pays the insurance company its premium. By reducing the driver's financial risk, the driver's expected utility increases; pages 489, 492.

2. For an insurance company to be viable, it must face independent risks so that it does not need to pay damage claims to all its customers at one time. If a company was restricted to offering hurricane insurance only to residents in south Florida, when a hurricane strikes south Florida, the company would need to pay all its customers. The company could not afford to do so and the company would fail; page 492.

3. Joanna will buy the insurance only if the price of the insurance is less than the value of the insurance. If the value of the insurance to Joanna is less than the price of the insurance, then Joanna will not buy the insurance; pages 491-492.

■ CHECKPOINT 19.3

Fill in the blanks

The incentive to change behavior to benefit yourself after a contract is signed reflects <u>moral hazard</u> and the incentive to enter into an agreement in which you know you will get additional benefits of which the other party is presently unaware reflects <u>adverse selection</u>. The lemon problem in the used car market primarily reflects the problem of <u>adverse selection</u>. If there are no signals in the used car market, too <u>few</u> good used cars are sold. Signals that allow buyers to distinguish between good used cars and lemons result in a <u>separating</u> equilibrium. Banks can use the length of time on the job as a <u>signal</u> to help determine the risk of loaning to a particular individual. A driver with private information that he or she is a safe driver will want a policy with a <u>low</u> deductible.

True or false

1. False; page 494
2. False; page 496
3. True; page 497
4. False; page 500
5. True; page 501
6. True; page 501

Multiple choice
1. c; page 494
2. a; page 494
3. d; page 497
4. e; pages 495-496
5. b; page 496
6. d; page 499
7. c; page 501

Complete the graph
■ **FIGURE 19.9**
Interest rate (percent per year)

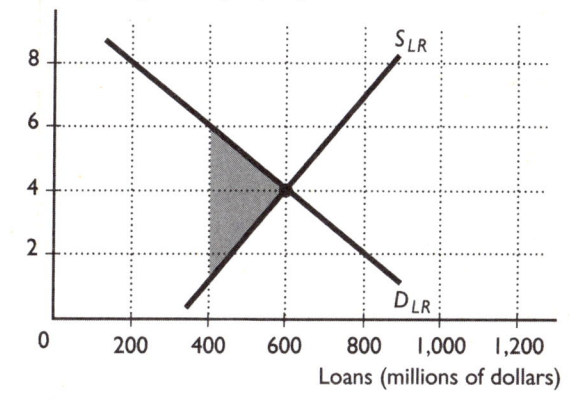

1. The separating equilibrium, when lenders can separate low-risk borrowers from high-risk borrowers, has an interest rate of 4 percent and $600 million of low-risk loans made. If lenders cannot make this separation, the pooling equilibrium interest rate of 6 percent is charged and $400 million of low-risk loans are made, less than the case with the separating equilibrium. Figure 19.9 shows the deadweight loss as the area of the gray triangle; page 500.

Short answer and numeric questions
1. Igor expects to gain more from the policy because the probability of his bat dying exceeds the normal probability. Thus the probability that All Bat will need to pay off on the policy exceeds normal. This situation illustrates the adverse selection problem: The people who most want to buy bat insurance are those who have sickly bats; pages 494, 501.

2. In a pooling equilibrium, only one message is sent so that an uninformed person cannot determine the quality of the good under consideration. In a separating equilibrium, more than one message is sent that provide full information to a previously uninformed person about the quality of the good. From the social perspective, the separating equilibrium is more desirable because then the appropriate amounts of the high and low quality goods are sold; pages 496-497, 500.

3. Banks have more information about the ability and willingness to pay of people who have previously borrowed from them or from other financial institutions. These screens include a good loan repayment record because this record is evidence (a signal) that the customer is a low-risk borrower. If a customer has never borrowed before, the bank must find other ways to assess whether the customer is a high-risk or a low-risk borrower; page 499.

4. a. You most want to sell insurance to Larry because you expect that his policy will be more profitable than Harry's policy; page 501.

   b. Harry is likely to buy the policy. If Harry does not buy the policy, he expects to pay $1,500 a year for his accidents. If he buys the policy, he pays only $1,000, a saving to Harry of $500. Larry may or may not buy a policy. If he is very risk averse and cannot obtain a lower price from another company, he will buy your insurance. But, if he is only a little risk averse, he may decide to do without insurance. If another company can recognize him as a safe driver, it will therefore offer him a less expensive policy. Larry then will buy from your competitor; page 501.

   c. Harry probably will buy the first policy; Larry likely will buy the second. From Harry's standpoint, the second policy is more expensive than the first. Harry, the risky driver, is likely to have an accident and thereby incur the $1,500 deductible. Larry realizes that he is unlikely to have an accident and is not likely to have to pay the deductible. Larry is more likely to opt for the second policy because, if he has no accident, he pays only $300 rather than $1,300 for his insurance; page 501.

d. Insurance companies use deductibles to separate risky and safe drivers. Safe drivers prefer a low premium and high deductible because they realize that they are not likely to have an accident and be forced to pay the deductible. Risky drivers prefer a high premium and low deductible because they know that an accident is probable and they do not want to be hit with a high deductible payment. High-risk drivers know that they are accident prone and they are willing to pay higher premiums for nearly full coverage, but low-risk drivers know that they seldom have accidents and they will choose lower premiums with lower coverage; page 501.

5. The group members have private information about each member's contribution, that is, who worked hard and who shirked. The instructor would like to know this private information, so the instructor allows the group members to signal this information by the grades they assign the other members. By acquiring this information, the instructor helps overcome the moral hazard created by the group members' incentives to not work and count on the other members to carry the load.

Chapter 20

Inequality and Poverty

CHAPTER IN PERSPECTIVE

In chapter 20 we conclude our study of income determination by looking at the extent and sources of economic inequality and examining how taxes and government programs redistribute income.

■ **Describe the economic inequality and poverty in the United States.**

Market income is a household's income earned from the markets for factors of production before paying taxes. Income and wealth are distributed unequally. The extent of inequality is measured using a Lorenz curve. A Lorenz curve graphs the cumulative percentage of income (or wealth) against the cumulative percentage of households. The farther the Lorenz curve is from the 45° line of equality, the more unequally income (or wealth) is distributed. In the United States, inequality has increased over the past few decades and economic mobility, moving up or down 1 quintile in the distribution of income, has decreased. Education, household size, and martial status are important factors affecting a household's income. Poverty is a state in which a household's income is too low to buy the quantities of food, shelter, and clothing that are deemed necessary. Poverty rates for blacks and Hispanics fell during the 1990s but still exceed those for white households. The longer poverty lasts, the larger the problem for the household. For 30 percent of poor households poverty lasts for more than 9 months.

■ **Explain how economic inequality and poverty arise.**

Human capital is people's accumulated skill and knowledge. Differences in skills lead to large differences in earnings. High-skilled labor has a greater value of marginal product of skill than low-skilled labor, so at a given wage rate, the quantity of high-skilled labor demanded exceeds that of low-skilled labor. Skills are costly to acquire, so at a given wage rate, the quantity of high-skilled labor supplied is less than that of low-skilled labor. The equilibrium wage rate of high-skilled labor is higher than that of low-skilled labor. Discrimination according to race and/or sex is another possible source of inequality. High income people typically own large amounts of physical and financial capital. Some have great entrepreneurial ability. Personal and family characteristics also affect an individual's income.

■ **Explain why governments redistribute income and describe the effects of redistribution on economic inequality and poverty.**

The government redistributes income using income taxes, income maintenance programs, and subsidized services. Income maintenance programs include Social Security, unemployment compensation, and welfare programs. The distribution of income after taxes and benefits is more equal than the market distribution. Utilitarianism suggest that more equality is fairer. But government redistribution weakens work incentives both for the recipient and the wage earner and creates the big tradeoff between equity and efficiency. A major challenge is to insure that welfare programs do not weaken the incentive to acquire human capital; the current approach attempts to avoid weakening these incentives. The negative income tax is a redistribution scheme that provides every household with a guaranteed minimum annual income and taxes all earned income above the minimum at a fixed rate.

CHECKPOINT 20.1

■ **Describe the economic inequality and poverty in the United States.**

Quick Review

- *Lorenz curve* A curve that graphs the cumulative percentage of income (or wealth) against the cumulative percentage of households. The farther the Lorenz curve is from the line of equality, the greater is the inequality.

Additional Practice Problems 20.1

1978

Households	Income (percentage)
Lowest 20 percent	4.3
Second 20 percent	10.3
Third 20 percent	16.9
Fourth 20 percent	24.7
Highest 20 percent	43.8

1. The table above shows the distribution of income in the United States in 1978:
   a. Draw the Lorenz curve for the United States in 1978.
   b. Was the distribution of income in the United States more or less equal than in recent years?

2. The figure shows the Lorenz curves for three nations, A, B, and C. In which nation is income distributed the most unequally? The most equally? In which nation is average income the highest?

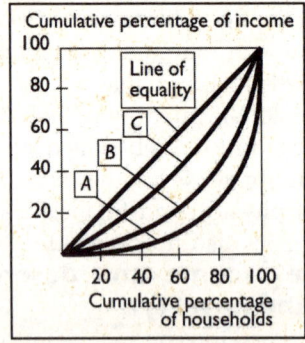

Solutions to Additional Practice Problems 20.1

1a. When drawing a Lorenz curve, the key is that it plots the *cumulative* percentage of income against the *cumulative* percentage of households. To create a Lorenz curve calculate cumulative percentages, which is done by adding the income owned by *all* the people who fall in the income group in and below the percentage being considered. So, to draw the Lorenz curve, we first need to calculate the cumulative percentage of households and the cumulative percentage of income. The table above has these percentages. The Lorenz curve in the figure plots the cumulative percentage of income and cumulative percentage of households from the above table.

1978

Households (cumulative percent)	Income (cumulative percent)
20 percent of households	4.3
40 percent of households	14.6
60 percent of households	31.5
80 percent of households	56.2
100 percent of households	100.0

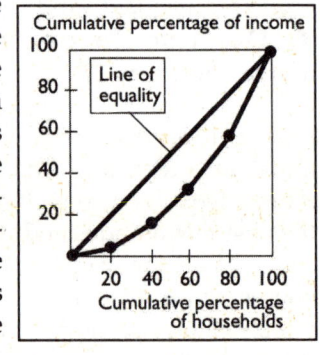

1b. The distribution of income in the United States in recent years is less equal that what it was in 1978.

2. Income is distributed the most unequally in nation A because its Lorenz curve is farthest from the line of equality. Income is distributed the most equally in nation C because its Lorenz curve is the closest to the line of equality. Based on the Lorenz curves it is impossible to determine in which nation average income is the highest. Lorenz curves give information about the distribution of income, *not* about its amount.

■ **Self Test 20.1**

Fill in the blanks

In the United States, the poorest 20 percent of households receive less than ____ (4; 12) percent of total income and the richest 20 percent receive about ____ (25; 50) percent of total income. A Lorenz curve for income plots the ____ (percentage; cumulative percentage) of income against the cumulative percentage of households. Since 1967, the distribution of income and wealth has become ____ (less; more) unequal in the United States. Education has a ____ (small; large) role in influencing a household's income. The poverty level of income in the United States for a family of four is approximately ____ ($19,800; $28,600; $35,600). About ____ (30; 50; 75) percent of households that live in poverty do so for more than 9 months.

True or false
1. The Lorenz curve always lies above the line of equality.
2. Since 1967, the percentage of the total income received by the richest 20 percent of households decreased.
3. Inequality of annual income overstates the degree of lifetime inequality.
4. When it comes to determining household income, education is a more important characteristic than is race.
5. In the United States, poverty is distributed equally across the races, with approximately 15 percent of households of each race living in poverty.

Multiple choice
1. Which of the following is correct about the United States?
   a. Income is equally distributed.
   b. Wealth is equally distributed.
   c. Income is equally distributed but wealth is unequally distributed because of inheritances.
   d. Both wealth and income are unequally distributed.
   e. Both wealth and income are equally distributed.

■ **FIGURE 20.1**
Cumulative percentage of income

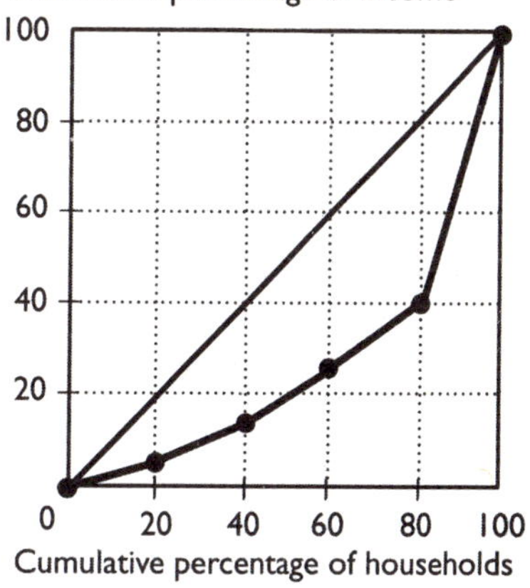

2. In Figure 20.1, the richest 20 percent of households receive ____ percent of total income.
   a. 20
   b. 100
   c. 80
   d. 40
   e. 60

3. If the income distribution is more unequal than the wealth distribution, then the
   a. Lorenz curve for income will be farther away from the line of equality than the Lorenz curve for wealth.
   b. government has imposed a higher tax rate on income.
   c. Lorenz curve for wealth will be farther away from the line of equality than the Lorenz curve for income.
   d. Lorenz curve for wealth will lie above the Lorenz curve for income.
   e. It is not possible to draw the Lorenz curve for wealth on the same figure with the Lorenz curve for income.

4. In the United States in 1998, the wealthiest 1 percent of households held approximately ____ percent of all wealth.
   a. 1
   b. 13
   c. 27
   d. 38
   e. 88

5. In the United States since the late 1960s, the share of total income received by the richest 20 percent of households has ____ and the share of income received by the lowest 20 percent of households has ____.
   a. increased; not changed
   b. not changed; increased
   c. not changed; decreased
   d. decreased; increased
   e. increased; decreased

6. The inequality of annual income
   a. overstates the degree of lifetime inequality.
   b. understates the degree of lifetime inequality.
   c. cannot change from one year to the next.
   d. is about the same as the amount of lifetime inequality.
   e. cannot be compared to the amount of lifetime inequality.

7. Of all the characteristics that lead to income inequality, the factor with the largest impact is
   a. race.
   b. sex.
   c. age.
   d. education.
   e. location.

8. Which of the following statements about poverty is (are) correct?
   i. Blacks and Hispanics have higher poverty rates than whites.
   ii. Over the last 40 years, poverty rates for all groups have generally increased.
   iii. Most household spells of poverty last well beyond 9 months.
   a. i only.
   b. ii only.
   c. iii only.
   d. ii and iii.
   e. i, ii, and iii.

Complete the graph

Household percentage	Percentage of income	Cumulative percentage of income
Lowest 20 percent	5.0	____
Second 20 percent	9.0	____
Third 20 percent	20.0	____
Fourth 20 percent	26.0	____
Highest 20 percent	40.0	____

■ FIGURE 20.2

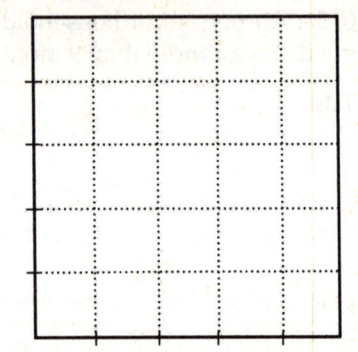

1. The table above has data for the nation of Beta. Complete the table by calculating the cumulative percentages for the last column. In Figure 20.2, plot the Lorenz curve for Beta.

Short answer and numeric questions

1. Can a Lorenz curve ever lie above the line of equality? Why or why not?

2. What does the distance between a Lorenz curve for income and the line of equality tell about the distribution of income?

3. How has the distribution of income and the amount of economic mobility changed in the United States over the past few decades?

4. Is the distribution of annual or lifetime income more equal? Why?

5. What is poverty? How many Americans live in poverty? How have poverty rates changed over the last few decades?

CHECKPOINT 20.2

■ **Explain how economic inequality and poverty arise.**

Quick Review

- *Demand for high-skilled labor and low-skilled labor* The vertical distance between the demand curve for low-skilled labor and the demand curve for high-skilled labor is equal to the value of marginal product of skill.
- *Supply of high-skilled labor and low-skilled labor* The vertical distance between the supply curve of low-skilled labor and the supply curve of high-skilled labor is equal to the compensation that high-skilled workers require for the cost of acquiring the skill.

Additional Practice Problems 20.2

1. What is the opportunity cost of acquiring a skill?

2. The figure shows the demand and supply curves for high-skilled and low-skilled labor at the beginning of the 1990s. Since then, new technology has increased the value of the marginal product of skill. In the figure, show the effect of this change. Is the income difference between high-skilled labor and low-skilled labor greater now or in 1990?

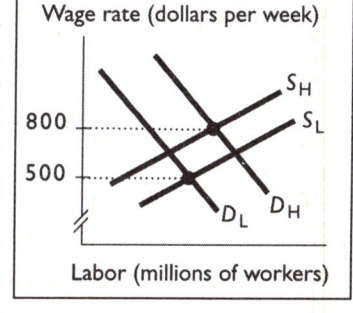

Solutions to Additional Practice Problems 20.2

1. The opportunity cost of acquiring a skill includes actual expenditures on tuition and books, as well as costs in the form of lost or reduced earnings while the skill is being acquired. When a person goes to school full time, that cost is the total earnings forgone. When a person receives on-the-job training, he or she is paid a lower wage than one who is doing a comparable job but not undergoing training. In this case, the cost of acquiring the skill is equal to the wage paid to a person not being trained minus the wage paid to a person being trained.

2. This practice problem studies the relationship between skill differentials and the wage rate. Remember that high-skilled labor has a higher value of marginal product than low-skilled labor and the technology changes increased the value of the marginal product even more. As a result, the demand for high-skilled labor increased and the demand curve shifted rightward. As the figure shows, the wage rate paid high skilled-workers increased. So the income difference between high-skilled labor and low-skilled labor is greater now than in 1990.

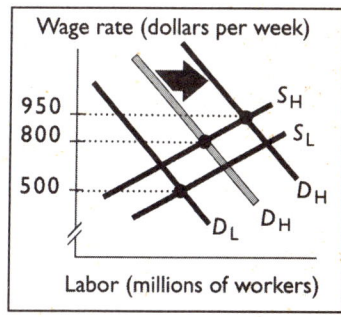

■ **Self Test 20.2**

Fill in the blanks

The demand curve for high-skilled workers lies ____ (above; below) the demand curve for low-skilled workers and the supply curve of high-skilled workers lies ____ (above; below) the supply curve for low-skilled workers. The wage rate paid high-skilled workers is ____ (greater; less) than the wage rate paid low-skilled workers. On the average, men earn ____ (more; less) than women. Entrepreneurial ability ____ (can; cannot) account for why some people become very wealthy.

True or false

1. At a given wage rate, the quantity of high-skilled labor demanded exceeds the quantity of low-skilled labor demanded.

2. The horizontal distance between the demand curve for high-skilled labor and the

demand curve for low-skilled labor measures the value of marginal product of skill.
3. The greater the cost of acquiring a skill, the greater is the vertical distance between the supply curve of high-skilled labor and the supply curve of low-skilled labor.
4. The equilibrium wage rate paid high-skilled workers exceeds that paid low-skilled workers.
5. Discriminating against some group of workers has no cost to a prejudiced employer.

Multiple choice
1. Differences in skills
    i. can arise partly from differences in education and/or partly from differences in on-the-job training.
    ii. can lead to large differences in earnings.
    iii. result in different demand curves for high-skilled and low-skilled labor.
    a. i only.
    b. ii only.
    c. ii and iii.
    d. i and iii.
    e. i, ii, and iii.

2. Other things being equal, the demand curve for low-skilled workers ____ the demand curve for high-skilled workers.
    a. lies below
    b. lies above
    c. is the same as
    d. is not comparable to
    e. at high wages lies below and at low wages lies above

3. The cost of acquiring a skill accounts for why the
    a. demand for high-skilled workers is different than the demand for low-skilled workers.
    b. supply of high-skilled workers is different than the supply of low-skilled workers.
    c. demand for high-skilled workers is different from the supply of high-skilled workers.
    d. demand for high-skilled workers is different from the supply of low-skilled workers.
    e. supply curves of high-skilled and low-skilled workers cross.

4. The vertical distance between the supply curves for neurosurgeons and for fast-food servers
    a. represents the difference in the demand for these two occupations.
    b. is the compensation that neurosurgeons require for the cost of acquiring this skill.
    c. is the difference in the value of the marginal product of the two professions.
    d. is the difference in on-the-job training.
    e. equals the difference in the equilibrium wages paid these two professions..

5. The wage rate that high-skilled workers receive is ____ the wage rate that low-skilled workers receive.
    a. greater than or equal to
    b. equal to
    c. less than or equal to
    d. greater than
    e. less than

6. If discrimination against women decreases their value of marginal product, then you would expect women to have ____ wage rate than men and there will be ____ high-paying jobs for women.
    a. a lower; more
    b. a higher; fewer
    c. a lower; fewer
    d. a higher; more
    e. the same; fewer

■ FIGURE 20.3
Wage rate (dollars per hour)

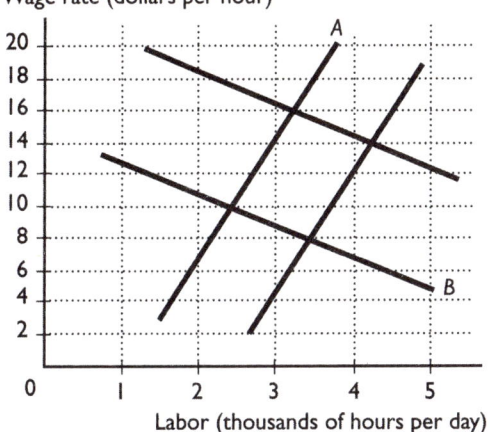

7. Figure 20.3 shows supply and demand curves for high-skilled and low-skilled labor. The curve labeled A is the supply curve for ____ workers and the curve labeled B is the demand curve for ____ workers.
   a. both high-skilled and low-skilled; both high-skilled and low-skilled
   b. high-skilled; high-skilled
   c. high-skilled; low-skilled
   d. low-skilled; high-skilled
   e. low-skilled; low-skilled

8. Figure 20.3 shows supply and demand curves for high-skilled and low-skilled labor. The wage rate paid high-skilled workers is ____ per hour and the wage rate paid low-skilled workers is ____ per hour.
   a. $14; $10
   b. $16; $14
   c. $14; $10
   d. $16; 10
   e. $16; $8

9. Inequality in the distribution of income and wealth is increased by
   a. the point that the children of the poorest find it difficult to get into college.
   b. saving to redistribute an uneven income over the life cycle.
   c. marrying outside one's own socioeconomic class.
   d. donating money to charities.
   e. the U.S. income tax.

Complete the graph

■ FIGURE 20.4
Wage rate (dollars per hour)

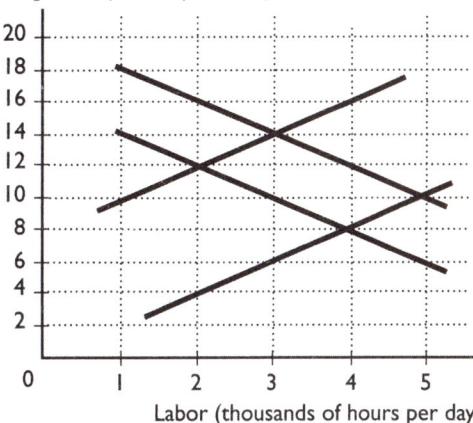

1. Figure 20.4 shows demand and supply curves for high-skilled and low-skilled workers.
   a. Label the demand curve for the high-skilled workers D_H and the demand curve for low-skilled workers D_L. Label the supply curves similarly, using S_H and S_L.
   b. What is the value of marginal product of skill?
   c. What is the compensation required for the cost of acquiring the skill?
   d. What is the equilibrium wage rate for high-skilled workers and low-skilled workers?

■ FIGURE 20.5
Wage rate (dollars per hour)

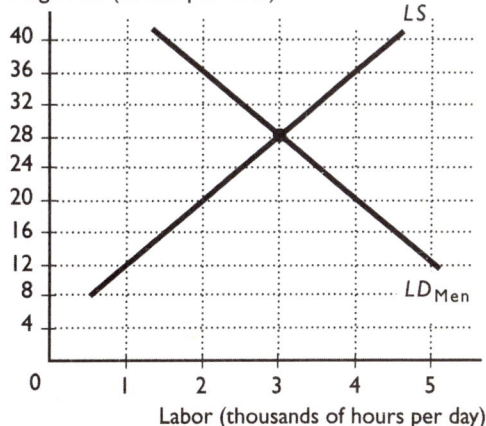

2. Suppose that the supply of labor for men and

women is identical and Figure 20.5 shows this supply curve, labeled LS. It also shows the demand curve for men, labeled LD_{Men}.

a. Suppose that men and women have equal values of marginal products but employers are prejudiced against women. As a result, at any wage rate employers demand 2,000 fewer hours of female labor. Draw the demand curve for women in Figure 20.5.

b. What is the wage rate paid men? Paid women?

c. How do these wage rates make it costly for employers to discriminate against women?

Short answer and numeric questions

1. a. How does the demand for high-skilled workers compare to the demand for low-skilled workers? How does the supply of high-skilled workers compare to the supply of low-skilled workers?

   b. How does the wage rate of high-skilled workers compare to the wage rate of low-skilled workers?

   c. How does the quantity of high-skilled workers employed compare to the quantity of low-skilled workers employed?

2. Why is discrimination costly for a prejudiced employer?

CHECKPOINT 20.3

■ Explain why governments redistribute income and describe the effects of redistribution on economic inequality and poverty.

Quick Review

- *Market income* Market income equals income earned from factors of production with no government redistribution.
- *Money income* Money income equals market income plus money benefits paid by the government.

Additional Practice Problem 20.3

Households	Income (millions of dollars per year)	Income (percentage of total income)
Lowest 20 percent	5	2.5
Second 20 percent	15	7.5
Third 20 percent	35	17.5
Fourth 20 percent	55	27.5
Highest 20 percent	90	45.0

1. The table above shows the distribution of market income in an economy.

   a. Suppose the government imposes a proportional income tax of 10 percent upon everyone. It then distributes the funds it collects by paying benefits to the bottom two percentile income groups. The lowest 20 percent group receives one half of the funds collected and the second lowest receives the other half. Calculate the income shares of each 20 percent of households after tax and redistribution

   b. Draw the Lorenz curves for this economy before and after taxes and benefits. Have the government's taxes and benefits made the distribution more or less equal?

Solution to Additional Practice Problem 20.3

Household percentage	Tax paid (millions of dollars)	Income after tax and benefits (millions of dollars)	Income (percentage of total income)
Lowest 20 percent	0.5	14.5	7.25
Second 20 percent	1.5	23.5	11.75
Third 20 percent	3.5	31.5	15.75
Fourth 20 percent	5.5	49.5	24.75
Highest 20 percent	9.0	81.0	40.50

1a. To solve this practice problem, subtract the amount paid as income tax and add the income received as benefits to obtain the new amount of income of each group. Then construct the Lorenz curve for the new income shares. In the above table, the second column shows the tax paid by each group. Total taxes collected are $20 million. The lowest and second lowest 20 percentile groups each receive half of this amount, so each receives $10 million in benefits. The third column adds benefits to the market income and subtracts the tax. The last column has the income shares. To find a group's income share divide income after tax and benefits by total income, which is $200 million, and multiply by 100.

Household percentage	Cumulative percentage (before)	Cumulative percentage (after)
Lowest 20 percent	2.50	7.25
Second 20 percent	10.00	19.00
Third 20 percent	27.50	34.75
Fourth 20 percent	55.00	59.50
Highest 20 percent	100.00	100.00

1b. The above table has the cumulative percentage of income before tax and benefits and after tax and benefits. These cumulative percentages are plotted in the Lorenz curve in the figure. The Lorenz curve after the taxes and benefits is closer to the line of equality so the government's taxes and benefits have made the distribution of income more equal.

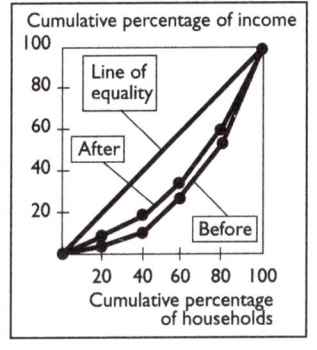

■ Self Test 20.3

Fill in the blanks

Governments redistribute income using ____ taxes, ____ maintenance programs, and ____ services. Education is an example of a ____. A household's ____ (market; money) income is the income it earns in factor markets before taxes and excluding government redistribution. A household's ____ (market; money) income is its market income plus money benefits paid by the government. The distribution of income after taxes and benefits is ____ (more; less) equal than the distribution of market income. Redistribution of income creates the big tradeoff between ____ (equity; tax revenue) and ____ (efficiency; redistribution). The ____ (median voter theory; utilitarianism voter theory) says that programs, such as redistribution programs, and also taxes are such that they make the median voter as ____ (poor; well) off as possible. A tax and redistribution plan that provides every household with a guaranteed minimum annual income and taxes all market income at a fixed rate is called a ____ (negative; fair; constant) income tax.

True or false

1. In general, U.S. federal and state taxes are progressive.
2. Subsidized services from the government go to only households with below-average incomes.
3. The distribution of income after taxes and benefits is more equal than the market distribution of income.
4. The redistribution of income creates the big tradeoff between earning an income and losing welfare benefits.
5. Under a negative income tax, some households would receive more money from the government than they would pay in taxes.

Multiple choice

1. Which of the following is a way income is redistributed in the United States?
   i. subsidizing services
   ii. income taxes
   iii. income maintenance programs
   a. i only.
   b. ii only.
   c. ii and iii.
   d. ii and iii.
   e. i, ii, and iii.

2. A ____ tax is one that taxes income at an average rate that increases with the level of income.
   a. regressive
   b. progressive
   c. flat
   d. consumption
   e. proportional

3. Of the following types of income tax systems, the one that provides the greatest amount of redistribution from the rich to the poor is a
   a. progressive income tax.
   b. proportional income tax.
   c. regressive income tax.
   d. flat-rate income tax.
   e. money-income tax.

4. The three major types of income maintenance programs are
   a. Social Security programs, unemployment compensation, and welfare programs.
   b. food stamps, unemployment compensation, and agricultural price supports.
   c. student loans, rent control, and welfare programs.
   d. corporate welfare, minimum wages, and affirmative action laws.
   e. minimum wages, food stamps, and student loans.

5. A household's income earned from the markets for factors of production and with no government redistribution is
   a. money income.
   b. welfare.
   c. market income.
   d. exploitative income.
   e. factored income.

6. Which of the following measures shows the most equality?
   a. money income
   b. market income
   c. income after taxes and before benefits
   d. wealth
   e. money wealth

7. When government redistributes income, one dollar collected from a rich person translates into ____ received by a poor person.
   a. one dollar
   b. less than one dollar
   c. more than one dollar
   d. zero dollars
   e. either exactly one dollar or, with some programs, more than one dollar

8. With a negative income tax that has a $10,000 guaranteed minimum income and a 25 percent tax rate, a household that has earned income of $16,000 has a total income of
   a. $16,000.
   b. $22,000.
   c. $26,000.
   d. $24,000.
   e. $10,000.

Short answer and numeric questions

1. Would progressive or regressive income taxes redistribute more money from the rich to the poor? Why?

2. What are the nation's three main types of income maintenance programs?

3. Currently the government more heavily taxes high-income households and transfers money to low-income households. What are the likely reactions of the recipients of the money? Of the taxpayers? How do these reactions reflect the big tradeoff?

4. Suppose a negative income tax plan is passed so that a household is guaranteed an income of $20,000 and market income is taxed at a rate of 25 percent.
   a. What is the total income of a household that has a market income of $20,000?
   b. What is the total income of a household that has a market income of $60,000?

SELF TEST ANSWERS

■ CHECKPOINT 20.1

Fill in the blanks

In the United States, the poorest 20 percent of households receive less than <u>4</u> percent of total income and the richest 20 percent receive about <u>50</u> percent of total income. A Lorenz curve for income plots the <u>cumulative percentage</u> of income against the cumulative percentage of households. Since 1967, the distribution of income and wealth has become <u>less</u>; unequal in the United States. Education has a <u>large</u> role in influencing a household's income. The poverty level of income in the United States for a family of four is approximately <u>$19,800</u>. About <u>30</u> percent of households that live in poverty do so for more than 9 months.

True or false

1. False; page 509
2. False; page 510
3. True; page 511
4. True; page 512
5. False; page 513

Multiple choice

1. d; page 508
2. e; page 509
3. a; page 509
4. d; page 508
5. e; page 510
6. a; page 511
7. d; page 512
8. a; page 513

Complete the graph

1. The table and Lorenz curve (in Figure 20.6) are in the next column. In the table, the cumulative percentage of income for any income group equals its percentage of income plus the percentages of income of all groups lower than it. The Lorenz curve plots these cumulative percentages of income against the cumulative percentage of households; pages 508-509.

Household percentage	Percentage of income	Cumulative percentage of income
Lowest 20 percent	5.0	<u>5.0</u>
Second 20 percent	9.0	<u>14.0</u>
Third 20 percent	20.0	<u>34.0</u>
Fourth 20 percent	26.0	<u>60.0</u>
Highest 20 percent	40.0	<u>100.0</u>

■ **FIGURE 20.6**

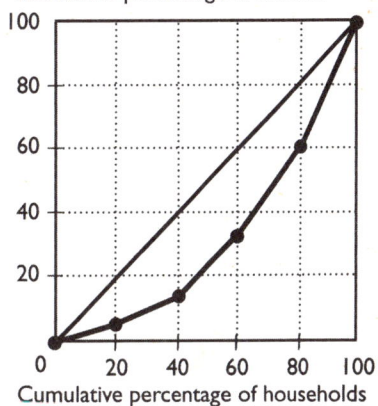

Short answer and numeric questions

1. A Lorenz curve can never lie above the line of equality. The Lorenz curve plots the cumulative percentage of income against the cumulative percentage of households. Because the households are arranged by order of income, the cumulative percentage of income must always be less (except at 0 percent and 100 percent) than the cumulative percentage of households; pages 508-509.

2. The farther away the Lorenz curve is from the line of equality, the less equal is the distribution of income; page 509.

3. The distribution of income has become less equal in the United States over the last few decades. The distribution of income changed because higher income groups have gained more income than the lower income groups. Economic mobility has decreased over the same years. Fewer families are now moving up or down 1 or more quintile in the distri-

bution of income and more families are remaining in the same quintile; pages 510-511.

4. The distribution of lifetime income is more equal than the distribution of annual income because in any given year, different households are at different stages in their life cycle; page 511.

5. Poverty is a state in which a household's income is too low to buy the quantities of food, shelter, and clothing that are deemed necessary. Approximately 36 million Americans lived in poverty in 2006. Over the last several decades, poverty rates for whites and blacks have generally decreased, while poverty rates for Hispanics at first rose and then decreased, strikingly, during the 1990s; pages 513-514.

■ CHECKPOINT 20.2

Fill in the blanks

The demand curve for high-skilled workers lies <u>above</u> the demand curve for low-skilled workers and the supply curve of high-skilled workers lies <u>above</u> the supply curve for low-skilled workers. The wage rate paid high-skilled workers is <u>greater</u> than the wage rate paid low-skilled workers. On the average, men earn <u>more</u> than women. Entrepreneurial ability <u>can</u> account for why some people become very wealthy.

True or false

1. True; pages 516-517
2. False; page 517
3. True; pages 516-517
4. True; pages 517-518
5. False; page 519

Multiple choice

1. e; pages 516-518
2. a; page 517
3. b; pages 516-517
4. b; page 517
5. d; pages 517-518
6. c; page 519
7. c; page 517
8. e; page 517
9. a; page 520

Complete the graph

■ FIGURE 20.7

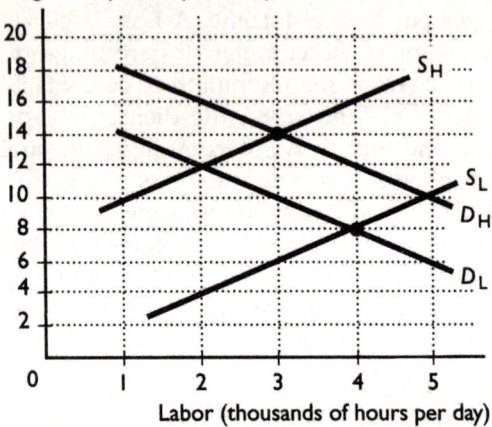

1. a. Figure 20.7 labels the curves.
   b. The value of marginal product of skill is $4 an hour because that is the vertical distance between the demand curve for high-skilled workers and the demand curve for low-skilled workers; page 517.
   c. The compensation required for the cost of acquiring the skill is $8 an hour because that is the vertical distance between the supply curve for high-skilled workers and the supply curve for low-skilled workers; page 517.
   d. The equilibrium wage rate for high-skilled workers is $14 an hour and the equilibrium wage rate for low-skilled workers is $8 an hour; page 517.

2. a. Figure 20.8 (on the next page) has the demand curve for women. It lies to the left of the demand curve by men by 2,000 hours of labor at every wage rate; page 519.
   b. Men are paid a wage of $28 an hour and women are paid a wage of $20 an hour; page 519.

■ **FIGURE 20.8**

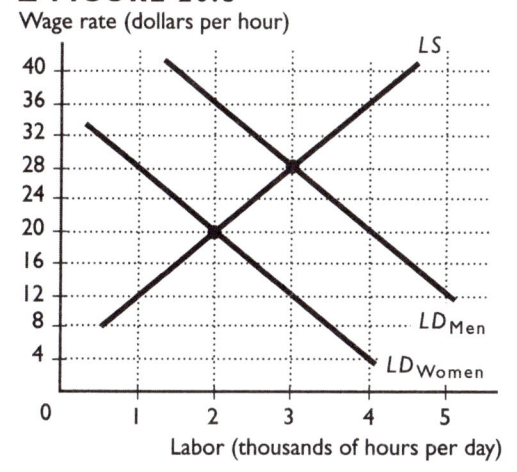

Wage rate (dollars per hour)

[Figure 20.8: Graph showing wage rate versus labor (thousands of hours per day). LS curve (labor supply) slopes upward. LD_Men demand curve intersects LS at wage $28 and 3 thousand hours. LD_Women demand curve intersects LS at wage $20 and 2 thousand hours.]

c. If a firm discriminates against women, it costs the firm $28 an hour to hire a man when it could get the same output if it hired a woman for $20. A discriminating firm's costs are higher as a result of its discrimination; page 519.

Short answer and numeric questions

1. a. Because the value of the marginal product of high-skilled workers exceeds that of low-skilled workers, the demand for high-skilled workers exceeds the demand for low-skilled workers. Because skills are costly to attain, the supply of high-skilled workers is less than the supply of low-skilled workers; pages 516-517.

   b. The demand for high-skilled workers exceeds the demand for low-skilled workers and the supply of high-skilled workers is less than the supply of low-skilled workers. So the wage rate received by high-skilled workers exceeds the wage rate received by low-skilled workers; page 518.

   c. The quantity of high-skilled workers employed compared to the quantity of low-skilled workers employed depends on the positions of the demand and supply curves of both types of labor. The demand curve for high-skilled labor lies to the right of the demand curve for low-skilled labor. The supply curve of high-skilled labor lies to the left of the supply curve of low-skilled labor. Because the positions of these curves determine the quantity of labor employed, we cannot say with certainty how the quantity of high-skilled workers employed compares that the quantity of low-skilled workers employed; page 517.

2. Discrimination is costly for employers because it means that they hire the higher-priced favored group of workers rather than the lower-priced unfavored group of workers. As a result, the firm's costs are higher than necessary and so its profit is less than it could. The shortfall in the profit is the opportunity cost a prejudiced employer must pay; page 519.

■ **CHECKPOINT 20.3**

Fill in the blanks

Governments redistribute income using <u>income</u> taxes, <u>income</u> maintenance programs, and <u>subsidized</u> services. Education is an example of a <u>subsidized service</u>. A household's <u>market</u> income is the income it earns in factor markets before taxes and excluding government redistribution. A household's <u>money</u> income is its market income plus money benefits paid by the government. The distribution of income after taxes and benefits is <u>more</u> equal than the distribution of market income. Redistribution of income creates the big tradeoff between <u>equity</u> and <u>efficiency</u>. The <u>median voter theory</u> says that programs, such as redistribution programs, and also taxes are such that they make the median voter as <u>well</u> off as possible. A tax and redistribution plan that provides every household with a guaranteed minimum annual income and taxes all market income at a fixed rate is called a <u>negative</u> income tax.

True or false

1. True; page 522
2. False; page 523
3. True; page 524
4. True; page 525
5. True; page 527

Multiple choice
1. e; page 522
2. b; page 522
3. a; page 522
4. a; page 522
5. c; pages 523-524
6. a; page 524
7. b; page 525
8. b; page 527

Short answer and numeric questions
1. A progressive income tax will redistribute more income away from the rich to the poor. A progressive income tax has a higher average tax rate as income rises. As a result, the rich pay a greater amount of taxes than do the poor because the rich have more income and because the average tax rate on that income is higher; page 522.

2. The three types of income maintenance programs are Social Security programs, unemployment compensation, and welfare programs; page 522.

3. The recipients of the money payments likely will work less. If they were to work more, they might earn enough to move into a higher tax bracket and lose the money the government is giving to them. The taxpayers also will tend to work less. On both counts, people work less and so the nation's total income decreases. These effects illustrate the force of the big tradeoff: By making incomes more equal, the government program has blunted people's incentives to work, lessened economic efficiency, and decreased the overall size of the nation's income; page 525.

4. a. The household receives its $20,000 guaranteed income. Then, on its market income of $20,000, it pays ($20,000 × 25 percent) = $5,000 in taxes, leaving $15,000 in income after taxes. Its total income is $20,000 + $15,000 = $35,000. This household receives a "negative income tax" payment of $15,000; page 527.

  b. The household receives its $20,000 guaranteed income. Then, on its market income of $60,000, it pays ($60,000 × 25 percent) = $15,000 in taxes, leaving $45,000 in income after taxes. Its total income is $20,000 + $45,000 = $65,000. This household receives a "negative income tax" payment of $5,000; page 527.